ROYAL LONDON – THE FIRST 150 YEARS

ROYAL LONDON
THE FIRST 150 YEARS

The story of The Royal London Mutual Insurance Society Limited

MURRAY ROSS

SilverWood

Published in hardback by SilverWood Books 2011
www.silverwoodbooks.co.uk

Text copyright © The Royal London Group 2011

The right of The Royal London Group to be identified as the author
of this work has been asserted by them in accordance
with the Copyright, Designs and Patents Act 1988.

ISBN 978-1-906236-52-6

British Library Cataloguing in Publication Data
A CIP catalogue record for this book is available from the British Library

Set in Sabon by SilverWood Books
Printed in the UK by The Short Run Press on paper certified as being from responsible sources

Contents

Appendices

Tables

Foreword

There are many impressions that stay with you after reading this history of Royal London. I was struck by the vision and ability of the founders, the courage of Benjamin Braham and the forcefulness of Ernest Haynes. Then there are the great changes of recent years.

In their early 20s, the founders left secure jobs with Royal Liver to set up a new business that they nursed through its early days and saw grow. All three died in harness. William Hambridge lived the longest and when he died in 1899, Royal London was a thriving, well-respected organisation with, by modern standards, an annual income of £41 million and assets of £61 million.

Benjamin Braham, a director before and during World War I, found himself a minority of one, believing that the course being followed by his colleagues was fundamentally wrong. He could have resigned and walked away, although that would have done nothing for the members. Instead he continued the fight in a way that must have been extraordinarily difficult for him, especially while he remained a member of the Board.

Ernest Haynes, the chairman at the time of the centenary, could see that the cherished right of agents to sell their collecting books was an obstacle to an effective and efficient service and that the Board needed a wider range of skills and experience, and full time directors, free from direct responsibility for business in parts of the country. These were major issues and ones that he could have easily left in the 'too difficult' file. Instead he confronted them and was able to drive through both reforms.

I can speak with first-hand knowledge of the last 11 years, having been a Board member throughout the period during which, Murray Ross suggests, a metamorphosis has taken place. There will, of course, be those who say that there must have been other such periods in Royal London's long history, especially against the background of the huge changes of the last 150 years. But the last decade has indeed seen a metamorphosis in financial markets, in public expectations and in regulation, and Royal London has succeeded in successfully adapting to these. I would simply like to add that I think it is a remarkable achievement by Mike Yardley, who has been chief executive since 1998, his senior team and all who work for Royal London that we approach our 150th anniversary having achieved a significant presence in our chosen markets, with a strong reputation and balance sheet, and a total commitment to applying the financial sense that you would expect from an organisation that aspires to be a leading customer-owned financial institution.

Events do not happen in real life for the convenience of authors of history books, and there are a number of unfinished stories as Murray brings his account to an end, with the 150th anniversary just a few weeks away. Joseph Degge, Henry Ridge and William Hambridge gave up good jobs at Royal Liver to form Royal London. The boards of the two organisations have just agreed terms by which Royal London will acquire Royal Liver – the deal is currently subject to the approval of the Royal Liver delegates at a meeting in the first half of 2011, and of the Financial Services Authority. What perfect symmetry it will be if, a century and a half later, the company that they left becomes part of the one that they founded.

In November, the Board decided to mark the 150th anniversary by setting up a trust that, operating as a registered charity, will make grants for specific purposes to local community causes nominated by members. It will come into being during 2011 when all the formalities have been addressed and trustees appointed. The process is also under way to appoint a new chief executive following Mike Yardley's decision that this was the appropriate time for the search to begin for the person to lead the company in its next phase of development – it is anticipated that Mike's successor will be appointed in 2011. It will fall to a subsequent Royal London historian to report on the outcomes of these various initiatives.

This book is an extraordinarily well researched and well written exploration of the development of an institution that represents an important thread running through the commercial and social life of the last century and a half. I would like to congratulate and thank Murray Ross on this considerable achievement. The result will appeal greatly to those with an interest in economics, the financial sector, mutuality and the still sometimes imperfectly understood world of insurance. It is also a human story of some elegance, and for all those reasons I hope very much that it will reach a wide readership.

Tim Melville-Ross
Chairman, Royal London Group
December 2010

Introduction

When I retired from Royal London in July 2007, I was asked to write a history of the last 50 years of the company, to be ready for the 150th anniversary in 2011. It was suggested that I might find this an interesting little project for the early part of my retirement.

I soon had to decide how to deal with the previous hundred years. A history of the Royal London entitled *We the Undersigned...* by W Gore Allen, an experienced biographer and corporate historian, had been published in 1961 to mark the centenary. So it seemed that I could either write what amounted to the second volume of Gore Allen's work, or briefly summarise his account of the pre-1961 history in my opening chapter. Neither option, however, would have provided an entirely satisfactory solution. The second volume approach requires readers to have read, or at least have access to, the first volume which would rarely be the case, and while *We the Undersigned...* is an attractively presented book, written in an engaging style, it comes over as a history of Britain into which some Royal London events had been skilfully slotted. In fairness, I did not know what Gore Allen's brief had been, what archives had been made available to him, nor how fit he was to examine them. He died in April 1960, aged 49, before the book was published.

Now an altogether more daunting third option was emerging – that I write a history of Royal London from the beginning. At the point that I agreed to take this on, the 'interesting little project' escalated into a way of life. My decision was influenced in part by my confidence that the Royal London archives would provide a wealth of valuable material. Stored at the Wilmslow office are, for example, the minutes of board and committee of management meetings and the annual reports and accounts back to 1861. For many years the reports and accounts contained only the barest minimum required by law, but from 1936 they were augmented by the publication of the speech delivered by the chairman or managing director at the annual general meeting. These booklets, running to several thousand words, are an invaluable source of information, but I have much sympathy for those who had to read them aloud, and even more for the audiences who had to listen to them. They would not rate highly today in terms of corporate communications. It was not until 1983 that the two were combined and a modern-looking report and accounts produced. The back numbers of the various incarnations of the staff journal make rather easier reading.

Also within the archives are papers considered at the time too important, or too confidential, to be included in the day-to-day filing system. These include the original documents of the Auxiliary Company litigation, including Benjamin Braham's momentous letter quoted in Chapter 7 and transcripts of all the hearings, and many files dealing with extinguishing the right of agents to sell their collecting books. Several documents have been presented to the Society as contributions to its history, including the recollections of two post-war chairmen and the results of extensive research undertaken by a former official on Royal Londoners killed during World War I. There is no shortage of what might be termed memorabilia – *In Memoriam* booklets produced after the founders' deaths, photographs, publications to mark great events and menus of innumerable lunches and dinners.

So far so good, but what surprised me, and first alerted me to the extent of the task that I had agreed to undertake, was the amount of material available elsewhere. All the annual reports from the chief registrar of friendly societies and the industrial assurance commissioner are within the parliamentary papers that were available to me in the reading room of the National Library of Scotland. The industry had been much investigated – royal commissions and government committees came and went, leaving their reports (and often the evidence they took and papers they considered) bound in these large, dusty volumes. The National Archives at Kew contained material on the conversion from friendly society to company in 1908, and the threats that emerged two years later, including the record of a meeting at which a deputation from Royal London, headed by the then chairman, persuaded two Government ministers to help Royal London out of a little local difficulty by passing new legislation.

The back numbers of the two journals that provide a continuous commentary on the insurance industry were made available to me at the library of the Chartered Insurance Institute in the City of London. *Post Magazine* first appeared in July 1840, just seven months after the introduction of the penny post, and was apparently the first publication anywhere in the world to be distributed by post. It appeared every week since then. *The Policy-Holder: an Insurance Journal* was published in Manchester from 1883 until 1981. After several reformulations, it was acquired by and merged into *Post Magazine*.

Books played a big part in the project and I was soon building up something of a library. Royal London was formed as a friendly society. Two studies of friendly societies have been written – by Professors P H J H Gosden

(University of Leeds) in 1961 and Simon Cordery (Monmouth College, Illinois) in 2003. Royal London and its competitors became known as 'collecting societies': Gosden refers to them only briefly, and although Cordery gives a little more detail, both authors are primarily concerned with the more traditional societies. A comprehensive history of industrial assurance was written by Dermot Morrah in 1955, the preface suggesting that the Prudential may have assisted him with his task. Morrah, according to his obituary in *The Times* (1 October, 1974) was "a journalist and writer of exceptional intellectual range, a polymath, gifted with an exceptional memory and a passionate curiosity that led him into many fields of knowledge". He was a civil servant, a leader writer on *The Times* for 30 years, a royalist and a herald.

Family histories by Dudley Ridge and Peter Sanders and an autobiography found their way onto the shelf. Dr Ridge was the grandson of one of the founders and Dr Sanders' father had been a Royal London agent before and after World War II and was later an official of the in-house trade union. His mother took over the agency during the war when her husband was away on war service. Sir Norman Wooding was a non-executive director and deputy chairman of Royal London whose autobiography was published posthumously in 2005. The company receives only passing references in these books but the very different human insights that they provide have greatly added to the story. The published histories of other organisations helped in plotting the progress of competitors and companies that are now part of the Royal London Group.

As I would have anticipated, *The Times*, the *Dictionary of National Biography* and *Who was Who* were much consulted and the internet has, of course, revolutionised this type of research. Anyone who has explored the history of their family will know what can be pieced together from certificates of births, deaths and marriages, from census returns and from the probate registries. There is much that we will never know about the founders and what prompted them to embark on their great venture, but it has been rewarding to be able to sketch in some details of their lives.

Finally, a few words by way of assistance to anyone about to turn to the chapters that follow. Some readers might find themselves asking "How much would that be today?" This is a complex area but to give some guidance I have included comparisons based on the calculations of American economics professors Lawrence H Officer and Samuel H Williamson (Lawrence H Officer, *Purchasing Power of British Pounds from 1264 to Present*, MeasuringWorth, 2009) explained in their website www.measuringworth.com. The comparisons appear as '(today: £2 million)' and are between the year in question and 2008. Until decimalisation on 15 February 1971, there were 12 pennies in a shilling and 20 shillings in a pound. This was written as £10 9s 8d.

Three terms warrant clarification at this preliminary stage. 'Industrial assurance' involved life policies for small sums where the premiums were paid to an agent, who called regularly, often weekly, at the policyholder's home and who was remunerated on a commission basis. The rationale for the service was that, if the policies were to be maintained, premiums had to be related to the pay packet and collected before the money was used in other, less laudable, ways. I have referred to the person who did the calling as an 'agent'. Sometimes 'collector' was used, and it appears in some of the quotations, but this term can be misleading because collectors were generally responsible for selling new policies as well as collecting the premiums on existing ones. Industrial assurance was undertaken by friendly societies (particularly the 'collecting societies') and companies, and the terms 'office' or 'industrial assurance office' were coined to cover an industrial assurance provider, regardless of corporate status. The confusion arises because the term applies to the organisation and not the premises from which it operated. So Royal London, Royal Liver, the Prudential and Pearl were all 'offices'.

Gore Allen concluded *We the Undersigned...* with these noble words:

> We have now traced – we believe with simplicity and fidelity to truth – the history of Royal London, from its quiet and practically unremarked beginning to a time when its name and work are known and praised throughout the world. Inevitably, from the restricted compass of this book, some notable incidents have been discarded and more than one honourable name has had to be left out. Such omissions are regretted by the author; but he would be still more disturbed were he not conscious that the story, as it stands, is sufficiently vital and moving to command attention.
>
> The author, in concluding what he set out to write, does not only greet the immediate friends whom he hopes that this book may win. He sees also with his mind's eye a man, as yet unborn, who, at a date far distant in the future, will take up the tale where he himself was forced to break it off. As he acknowledges his debt to vanished letter-writers and compilers of documents whose ink is already faded, so too perhaps this author of the future will be glad to scan the present record, regarding its last page as properly the page before his first one.
>
> As to what he will see during the hundred years on from 1961 – none would dare to forecast. Only the most limited prophecy lies within our power to make. So long as civilization has been preserved, in the year two thousand and sixty-one, the Royal London will still be transacting its business, going about its tasks, and will still be able, at any hour, to give account of all it is and does – to embark on such a rendering with pleasure and pride.

I have done my best to take up the tale, and to expand upon the pre-1961 history, benefiting from access to material not available to Gore Allen. While gently dissenting on the extent of the worldwide reputation, and regretting the notion that any future author has to be male, I adopt his sentiments and admire the eloquence with which they were expressed. Many will no doubt feel aggrieved that they have not been mentioned in the pages that follow, especially those towards the end of the story, while former colleagues may believe that they had much to tell me, and complain that I failed to make contact with them. I would just say in my defence that I have talked and corresponded with many people but, if I explored in depth every avenue that may have been relevant, and talked to everyone who could have valuable recollections, the publication of the book would have missed the 150th anniversary by several years, instead of making it with a few days to spare.

Gore Allen's confidence in Royal London's survival has proved entirely justified and I hope that one day a man or woman, now unborn or very young, will read what he and I have written, and then turn to whatever by then has replaced the desktop and laptop and begin:

In 2011, the Royal London Group…

Murray Ross
December 2010

Preface – Royal London Today

Royal London is the largest mutual life and pensions company in the United Kingdom. It is owned by, and run for, the benefit of its members, has no shareholders and employs nearly 2,800 people.

Royal London today is a group of specialist businesses:

- **RLAM** (Royal London Asset Management) is the dedicated fund management arm providing investment solutions for the Group and a wide range of external clients including pension funds for FTSE companies, local authorities, wealth managers, universities and charities, as well as individuals.

- **Royal London Cash Management** and **Royal London Asset Management Channel Islands** provide cash management services for a wide range of clients including charities, insurance companies, universities and plcs.

- **Scottish Life** is a pension specialist with a proud history of innovation and the objective of helping its customers enjoy financial freedom in their later years.

- **Bright Grey** is a modern, forward-thinking protection specialist that offers flexible protection solutions and has acquired a significant market share since its launch in 2003.

- **Scottish Provident** has in-depth understanding of what is needed when it comes to personal, mortgage and business protection.

- **Royal London Plus** provides a quality administration service for over two million customers, including the majority of Royal London members and offers new products to existing customers on a non-advised basis via a sales contact centre.

- **Royal London 360°** is building an international reputation founded on trust and personal service. It offers investment, savings and protection products, as well as providing bespoke trust and tax planning solutions.

- **Ascentric** provides investment administration and consolidation services to financial advisers, large distributors and product providers.

In 2009 the Group's profit after tax was £404 million. Performance during 2010 was impressive – by December, the forecast for the full year suggested that all parts of the Group will have performed well. In 2009 the Group's embedded value increased 28 per cent to £1.84 billion – it is predicted to have increased to more than £2 billion during 2010.

In the 2009 report and accounts, the group chief executive wrote:

> *Our guiding principle was established over coffee 150 years ago. It still holds good today. Tradition has it that in 1861 Henry Ridge and Joseph Degge were sitting in a London coffee shop when they came up with the idea of launching what was to become the Royal London Group. Maybe it was the stimulus of the caffeine they consumed, but their idea for a company dedicated to helping people provide for the future fulfilled a vital need. What's more, it made sound financial sense.*

What do we know today about these two men and the organisation that they created?

CHAPTER 1

The Beginning

Oh! where are the mourners? alas, there are none,
He has left not a gap in the world, now he's gone,
Not a tear in the eye of child, woman, or man,
To the grave with his carcass as fast as you can.

Rattle his bones, his bones, his bones,
Over the stones, the stones, the stones,
He's only a pauper who nobody owns,
Nobody owns, nobody owns.

The Pauper's Drive (1845)[1]

Up and down the City Road,
In and out the Eagle,
That's the way the money goes,
Pop goes the weasel.

Pop Goes the Weasel (1853)[2]

On 2 February 1861 two young men met in London, tradition has it in a coffee shop in City Road.[3] Joseph Degge, born in Staffordshire, the son of a farm labourer, was 24 and had worked in Liverpool in the pub trade and as a clerk. Henry Ridge, a Londoner, was two years younger and a carpenter. His father was a cheesemonger. Both men were married, Degge had a young daughter, and they were now working for an organisation, founded a decade earlier, that provided insurance against funeral expenses. By the end of the meeting, Degge and Ridge had decided to set up a business in competition with their employer, to be called the Royal London Life Insurance and Benefit Society. Before they parted, they took time to set down in writing what they had agreed. Both men signed the document.

In the early 1860s many working-class people were paying a few pence a week to ensure that every member of the family could have a decent funeral and avoid the risk of being buried by the parish – the dreaded pauper's funeral, the horrors of which were captured by Charles Dickens in *Oliver Twist*. The body in a rudimentary coffin of pine or elm, with the deceased's name scrawled on it in chalk, was often carried through the busy streets on the shoulders of pallbearers provided by the workhouse. No consideration was given to the feelings of the mourners:

> *… when they reached the obscure corner of the churchyard in which the nettles grew, and where the parish graves were made, the clergyman had not arrived; and the clerk, who was sitting by the vestry-room fire, seemed to think it by no means improbable that it might be an hour or so, before he came. So, they put the bier on the brink of the grave; and the two mourners waited patiently in the damp clay, with a cold rain drizzling down, while the ragged boys whom the spectacle had attracted into the churchyard played a noisy game at hide-and-seek among the tombstones, or varied their amusements by jumping backwards and forwards over the coffin.[4]*

The committal was cursory: "The reverend gentleman, having read as much of the burial service as could be compressed into four minutes, gave his surplice to the clerk, and walked away again".[5] The burial was in a common grave that was already "so full, that the uppermost coffin was within a few feet of the surface. The grave-digger shovelled in the earth; stamped it loosely down with his feet: shouldered his spade; and walked off, followed by the boys, who murmured very loud complaints at the fun being over so soon".[6] It could have been even worse – it was routine in London and other big cities for several pauper funerals to take place at the same time. There was no headstone and so no site to which the bereaved could return for the remembrance of their loved one.

Dreadful as these experiences must have been for those involved, they would probably not, of themselves, have inspired so many to take steps to avoid them. What brought this about was a change of attitude, referred to by Thomas Laqueur, a distinguished American academic,[7] in a paper on death and pauper funerals:

> *The poor, of course, had always been buried with less splendor than the rich, and the very poor had, since the sixteenth century if not before, been buried at the expense of the parish. Yet no special meaning seems to have been attached to these burials until the middle of the eighteenth century. Then, however, the funerals of the poor became pauper funerals and pauper funerals became occasions both terrifying to contemplate oneself and profoundly degrading to one's survivors.*[8]

A pauper funeral had become the ultimate disgrace for a Victorian family, stigmatising both the deceased and the bereaved. It was seen as the final stamp of failure representing, in addition to abject poverty, "social worthlessness, earthly failure, and profound anonymity" and proclaimed "the failure to create bond's with one's fellow men".[9] 'Respectability' was becoming one of the most pervasive of mid-Victorian social concepts and the one condition to which a respectable man or woman could not descend was that of dependence. "At its most basic level, this meant dependence on the poor law and charity".[10] A decent funeral that would preserve the family's standing in the community had become a measure of basic respectability.[11]

It had to be admitted that the desire to demonstrate respectability did sometimes prompt expenditure that might be regarded as excessive, not only on the coffin, funeral and interment but also on mourning clothes for the family and a feast for all those who attended. Funerals were often events on a scale never enjoyed by the deceased during his or her lifetime. Charles Dickens suggested that the "tendency of the populace to equate extravagant funerals with respectable status did little more... than render such spectacles absurd"[12] while a Royal Commission in the 1870s was told that "the excess [of the] insurance money received, over and above the cost of burial, is too often squandered upon the funeral feast. A sort of natural instinct which has no doubt a healthy origin seems almost to preclude a parent from putting the money so acquired to any profitable use".[13] Subsequent commentators have tended to be more sympathetic.[14]

Whether motivated by the need to demonstrate respectability, or a desire to show respect to the dead and to create a place to mourn them, the fear of the pauper funeral had a profound impact on the Victorian working class: "Nothing tended to keep up in the imaginations of the poorer sort of people a generous horror of the workhouse more than the manner in which pauper funerals are conducted".[15] If they saved for anything, they saved for death. Friendly societies, or in most cases burial clubs that were on the fringe of the friendly society movement, provided a means by which they could save.[16] Friendly societies grew out of mutual benefit societies brought from France in the 1680s by Huguenot refugees, and by the end of the eighteenth century there was a friendly society in nearly every British town and village. The purpose of these local benefit or box clubs, often based at a public house, was to enable the "industrious classes, by means of surplus of their earnings to provide themselves a maintenance during sickness, infirmity and old age".[17] There was a significant social element, with induction ceremonies, regular meetings, annual club days and excursions. It was estimated that in 1803 there were nearly ten thousand societies, with over seven hundred thousand members, and that by 1872 this had grown to over thirty thousand societies with perhaps four million members.[18] Between 35 and 40 per cent of the adult male population were members of friendly societies.

It is a myth that financial services regulation is a creature of the late twentieth century. Between 1793 and 1896 Parliament passed more than 20 Acts that regulated friendly societies, several of which followed reports by parliamentary committees, and appointed a Royal Commission to investigate them. The 1793 Act[19] recognised friendly societies as legal entities capable of suing and being sued. Regulation, or at least the approval of the rules and subsequently the tables of contributions and benefits, was initially the responsibility of the local magistrates. Later the magistrates had to obtain prior approval from at least two actuaries or "persons skilled in calculation"[20] and then they were required to act on the advice of a government-appointed barrister. In 1834 the magistrates ceased to have any role and it was the barrister,[21] soon to be given the title Registrar of Friendly Societies, who gave the approval and collected the five-yearly returns of sickness and mortality.[22]

The financial stability of friendly societies was, however, a matter of public concern with societies often going out of business so that members who had contributed, perhaps for many years, received no benefits. Between 1793 and 1867, out of a total of 38,315 friendly societies in England and Wales, no fewer than 13,935 collapsed. Sometimes too much had been spent on socialising, or benefits, set to attract new members, were too generous; for example, sick pay continued to be paid at the full rate instead of being reduced after a short initial period. In fairness to those running these societies, it was difficult to determine the right level of contributions and benefits in the absence of any reliable information on sickness and mortality. The societies themselves possessed the data from which conclusions could be drawn, and from 1829[23] they were required to provide returns every five years of the rates of sickness and mortality that they had experienced. The first reliable tables were based on returns for the period 1836–40 and, although it took a little time to realise that occupations impacted upon mortality, it was at last becoming possible to determine a proper balance between contributions, which in due course were graduated according to age, and benefits.[24]

Many traditional local friendly societies still existed in the mid-nineteenth century, but they were suffering from the fluidity of labour brought about by the industrial revolution:

> *A man who had been paying his penny a week into the funds of the Scissorsmiths Benefit Society at Sheffield or the Shipwrights Benefit Club at Liverpool, or perhaps some much humbler brotherhood of ploughboys meeting at the village inn, was likely to lose the benefit of his subscriptions if he went to seek his fortune at the new ironworks in Lincolnshire.[25]*

What was required was an organisation that covered the whole country, or a large part of it, so that a member who travelled in search of work might be passed on from branch to branch.

This demand was met at first by the affiliated orders, notably the Manchester Unity of Oddfellows (founded in 1810) and the Ancient Order of Foresters (1834), formed in the areas where the earliest impact of the industrial revolution had been felt but that spread quickly both geographically and socially. Initially they were a federation of local offices, each with control over its own funds, but in due course central funds were established. Gradually societies began to be formed that were not confined to a locality or trade and where there was no socialising or personal link between the members. These were the general societies such as the Royal Standard (founded in 1828) and Hearts of Oak (1841), which did business over the counter.[26]

A traditional society required contributions of a shilling a month, for which members would be entitled to sick pay that generally reduced after six months and a £10 payment on death.[27] Low-paid workers could not afford to belong to a true friendly society and the prospect of a pauper funeral persuaded many to contribute a halfpenny or penny a week (and sometimes a small entrance fee) to a local burial club that paid only a death benefit.[28] Burial clubs were particularly susceptible to poor financial management: "The burial club which survives a generation is an exception", it was suggested in evidence to a Royal Commission.[29] The new friendly societies with no link to an area or trade did nothing for those who could only afford to pay a penny a week to a burial club and who prayed that it would still be in existence at the time of their deaths. But help was on hand. By the middle of the nineteenth century two concepts were being developed in parallel that would provide a means by which a low-paid worker could insure to avoid a pauper funeral for himself and his family. One involved the creation of a new type of friendly society, and the other a novel form of business for assurance companies. What both provided came to be known as industrial assurance – life policies for small sums where the premiums were paid to a collector who called regularly at the policyholder's home and who was remunerated on a commission basis.

It was realised in Liverpool that organisations providing the same service as the burial clubs but run on commercial lines could be registered under the friendly societies legislation. Liverpool Victoria was one of the first of what came to be known as 'collecting societies'.[30] The Liverpool Independent Legal Victoria Society was formed in 1843 by a group of local citizens presided over by William Fenton, a customs officer, who became the first president, with the object of affording "the poorer classes of the community the means of providing for themselves and their children a decent interment at the trifling expense of a halfpenny, a penny or three pence per week, according to the age of the member".[31] Royal Liver began life in July 1850 when a small group of working men met in the Lyver Inn on St Anne Street, Liverpool.[32] The Liverpool Liver Burial Society was registered three weeks later. The driving force behind its formation was John Lawrence, a former mariner and estate agent, and a collector for the Loyal Philanthropic Society. The object of the society was "to provide for the decent interment of deceased members". Other collecting societies formed at the time included Scottish Legal in Glasgow, St Patrick's and Royal Oak in Liverpool and Integrity Life in London. These new collecting societies were fundamentally different from the traditional friendly society that operated over a limited area, was run by the members, generally on a voluntary basis apart perhaps from a secretary who was paid a modest stipend, and that often provided the members with socialising as well as welfare.

Collecting societies were not welcomed by everybody. The Reverend J Frome Wilkinson, a country cleric, writer and supporter of traditional societies, spoke for many when he complained that a collecting society "is not the invention of the working classes themselves. Collecting Societies are in reality 'trading bodies', 'projected and worked' in the first instance by a few individuals who make their profession and their living out of the business that they have created".[33] To Wilkinson, the voluntary, self-governing and social elements were vital. He saw the fact that the agents and other employees did their work not out of love but for financial gain, earning not personal satisfaction but an income, as creating a vacuum where comradeship and fellowship should have existed. If profit were to prevail, voluntarism would collapse.[34] This somewhat idealistic view overlooks the parlous financial state of many traditional societies, often due to an excess of comradeship and fellowship.

The corporate approach to a more commercial burial club was born in London. The Joint Stock Companies Act 1844 had made it easier to form a company (before then a Royal Charter, private act of Parliament or letters patent were required) although limited liability was not introduced until 1855 or, in the case of an insurance company, 1862. The 1844 Act introduced a two-stage registration process and between 1844 and 1853, 311 assurance companies were provisionally registered and 140 were completely registered, of which only 96 were still in existence by 1853. In June 1852 a deputation of working men called at the offices of a company that had been formed four years earlier to provide life assurance and loans to the middle classes. The company had survived but hardly flourished, selling only 62 policies in its first year, 194 in the second and 139 in the third, with many of the sales being made to personal contacts of the directors. The suggestion put forward was taken sufficiently seriously for it to be recorded in the minutes of the next board meeting of the company:

> *A deputation of operatives had visited the office to find out if it were disposed to grant them small policies varying from £20 upwards premiums to be paid weekly or in monthly instalments as adopted by Friendly Societies, promising to introduce a very large amount of such business.*[35]

The board was interested in the proposal, produced tables of premiums and benefits, but took no further action at the time. Their interest was rekindled the following year by a report from a House of Commons Select Committee on Assurance Associations that referred to "a sort of intermediate business, something between the great majority of life assurance offices and the friendly societies" that were supplying assurance for small sums. The Committee had been impressed with the idea of extending assurance to "the humbler classes to whom it has been recently considerably applied" and was anxious that "no check or impediment should be placed in the way of further extension of this enterprise [that is] not absolutely necessary for the security of the public".[36] By September 1854 the company had paid its first dividend and the board was satisfied that it was strong enough to embark upon this new venture. Collecting agents were appointed and, after some early difficulties, the business flourished. The name of the company was The Prudential Mutual Assurance, Investment and Loan Association. The Select Committee may well have been referring to the activities of the British Industry Life Assurance Company, incorporated in 1852, that was solely devoted to life assurance for small sums, and probably the source of the term 'industrial assurance'.[37] In its first six months it sold 12,837 policies and by the late 1850s was issuing more than 20,000 policies a year. It offered six tables of policies. Table II provided, for example, that for a weekly payment of a penny, a 20-year-old would have cover of £8, a 30-year-old would be covered for £6 7s 6d and a 40-year-old covered for £5.

When, in 1860, the Prudential acquired British Industry Life, the two companies had a combined premium income of £43,000. By then, the Royal Liver had 139,000 members and an annual income of £45,000. Two of its district managers in London were Joseph Degge and Henry Ridge. Although holding responsible positions with Royal Liver, they had not worked for the society for long and neither of them had any previous experience of industrial assurance.

Joseph Degge was born near Rugeley in Staffordshire in what, according to a local inhabitant, was one of the prettiest places in Europe, where there was "nothing else but noblemen's mansions and grounds".[38] The Marquis of Anglesey, Lord Hatherton, Lord Bagot and Earl Talbot all had estates there. Rugeley itself was rather less attractive. Situated to the east of Cannock Chase and with a population of around 3,500, it appeared a straggling, overgrown village, rather than a town that had enlarged itself without any apparent design beyond the whim of the bricklayer and the varying price of building sites.[39] Noted for the manufacture of hats, it also had iron foundries and agricultural machinery manufacturers, a brass foundry, a sheet iron and tin plate mill, corn mills, a tannery and a brewery. Just outside the town but within the parish were extensive collieries.[40]

Joseph Degge's grandparents, William Degge and Mary Barnes were married at Leigh in Staffordshire on 30 April 1812. They had six children: John (1812), Mary (1814), Samson (1816), William (1818), Joseph Barnes (1820) and Robert (1823).[41] They were all baptised at Blithfield in Staffordshire, just to the north of Blithfield Hall, home to the Bagot family for many centuries, and were probably all born at Newton, a hamlet within the Blithfield parish.[42] Samson appears to have died in childhood. By the mid-1830s John, the eldest son, had married Sarah and they were living a few miles away at Abbots Bromley, described in 1851 as "a decayed market town, consisting of one long street of irregularly built houses" with a population of 1,508.[43] John was working as a farm labourer on the Earl of Dartmouth's 1,000-acre Bromley Park estate, a little to the south of the 'town'. John and Sarah's first child was born in the summer of 1836 and was baptised Joseph at St Nicholas, the parish church of Abbots Bromley, on 26 June 1836.[44] His date and place of birth is unknown – in later life, Joseph Degge could never decide if he had been born in Newton or Abbots Bromley.[45] They were only three miles apart, separated by fields and small areas of woodland.[46] Mary, Joseph's grandmother, was probably living in Newton, and perhaps his mother was staying with her at the time of her confinement, so Joseph may have been born at Newton, although his parents lived at Abbots Bromley.[47]

Joseph Degge would have remembered little of the Bromley Park estate because his father soon acquired the tenancy of a farm of his own. By 1841 John was a farmer living at Bromley Hurst, Abbots Bromley, with his wife, the five-year-old Joseph, two daughters (Harriet, aged two, and Sarah, born earlier in the year) and a servant. Joseph presumably attended the local school in Abbots Bromley and his subsequent success suggests that he received a good, albeit brief, education there.[48] In 1842 an event occurred that was to have a profound effect on the Degge family. On 6 November Mary Degge (sister of John, William and Joseph Barnes and Joseph's aunt) married another Joseph – Joseph Bishop, a Londoner ten years her senior – at Abbots Bromley. By the time William, their first child, was born in September 1843 they were living in Liverpool where Bishop was in business as a spirit dealer.[49] The reports that they sent back must have been positive because this marked the beginning of the exodus of the Degge family from Newton and its surrounds to Liverpool. Within a few years, Mary had been joined in Liverpool by her mother and two of her brothers. They were living in Toxteth, on both sides of Park Street. Mary's brothers had been servants (farm labourers may have been a more accurate description) at a farm at Hartley Green, Gayton, not far from Newton, but were now both Liverpool publicans: Joseph Barnes at 17 Hughes Street and William on the corner of Longville Street and Park Street. Mary and Joseph Bishop lived a short walk away at 225 Bedford Street (later renamed Beaufort Street) with three servants and Mary's mother, who was now also in the pub trade, as a licensee in Hughes Street, probably of the pub run by her son, Joseph Barnes.[50]

Back in Staffordshire, John Degge's farming of Bromley Hurst had not been a success and the family was in much reduced circumstances. By 1851 Sarah was living in a cottage at Abbots Bromley with their children – Joseph and his sisters now had three brothers (Edwin, aged eight, Arthur, five, and John, one).[51] Their father was away from home, living and working as a labourer on a 184-acre farm at Colton, a few miles to the south-west of Abbots Bromley, towards Rugeley. We can only surmise what discussions went on within the family as the time approached for Joseph to leave school. Sarah may have been keen to keep her eldest son with her, encouraging him to look for work on the land, perhaps hoping that his modest wages would augment their limited income. Was seeking a job in Rugeley contemplated? Were his uncles suggesting that he be allowed to join them in Liverpool where there were plenty of openings for a bright young lad? Did John and Sarah worry about their son completing his education in a pub? All that we know for certain is that by 1851 the 15-year-old Joseph Degge had left rural Staffordshire for ever and was living with Uncle William at 1 Longville Street, Liverpool and working as a barman (presumably) in his uncle's pub.[52] Many of the customers would have worked in the docks and shipbuilding yards, or at the massive Mersey Forge in Sefton Street where they were building the largest gun in the world, although the employment provided by the forge came at an environmental cost. The noise was mind-bending – a 15-ton steam-hammer there could be heard across the Mersey in the Wirral.[53]

A previous historian wrote in these terms about Joseph Degge's early years in Liverpool:

> *He was, however, destined to fill a more responsible position in society than that of agriculturist, and it soon became apparent that his forte in life would be that of the desk, and an intimate acquaintance with the rules of arithmetic. At the age of 16 he made his debut to the commercial world by entering the well known firm of Messrs Hughes and Bishop, Brewers of Liverpool, as a Junior Clerk. In this capacity he was painstaking and assiduous in the discharge of his duties; and by attention to the interests of his employers he soon won their regard and esteem. But a temperament such as that possessed by Mr Joseph Degge could not rest satisfied with a monotonous come-and-go sort of life. He felt he could make himself more useful in other ways both for himself and the community at large. He therefore determined to change the scene of action, and undertook the management of the Aigberth Hotel, at Aigberth near Liverpool. He had not then seen twenty summers; and this fact clearly shows the indomitable energy which regulated his after life.[54]*

Degge's first encounters were, in fact, with a bar counter rather than a desk, and knowledge of the rules of arithmetic was required so as not to short-change his uncle's customers. What of the well-known firm of brewers? There was a family connection with Messrs Hughes and Bishop – the partners were John Hughes and Joseph Bishop, Aunt Mary's husband. They operated the Alton Brewery at 74 Stanhope Street, a little to the north of where the Degge families were living. Searches have failed to find any references to Hughes and Bishop in local newspapers or trades directories earlier than 1852[55] and the firm ceased trading in April 1856 when the partnership was dissolved by mutual consent[56] although there is nothing to suggest that it was insolvent or that the split was acrimonious. Hughes and Bishop seem to have been entrepreneurs in the pub trade who moved from venture to venture.

Hughes and Bishop was not well known, in the sense of being long-established, but there is no reason to doubt that Joseph joined the firm at the age of 16, probably in 1852. The fact that he was living nearby in 1851, and that one of the partners was his uncle by marriage, provides some corroboration, although 'junior clerk' may have been an exaggeration – he might perhaps have had a rather more 'hands-on' role, utilising the experience gained in his uncle's pub. Whatever its nature, the job would have come to an end with the dissolution of the partnership in 1856. Joseph was then only 19 and would not have been permitted to be the licensee of a hotel. As such, it comes as no surprise that the trades journals of the period contain no reference to him in relation to the Aigburth Hotel.[57] No journals were published or have survived for 1856 or 1858, but an 1857 journal shows "John Hughes" as the landlord of the Aigburth Hotel. This was almost certainly the Hughes of Hughes and Bishop, his previous employer, and it seems quite possible that Degge was helping Hughes in running the Aigburth Hotel. The earlier account continues: "In the year 1856, when just 20 years of age, he received the appointment of corresponding Clerk to the Royal Liver Friendly Society, at their Chief Offices at Liverpool". Again this is probably accurate – if it is, Degge's time at the hotel must have been brief unless perhaps he had left Hughes and Bishop before the partnership was dissolved.

On 1 February 1859 Degge married Elizabeth McGinn from County Down at St Bride's Church, Liverpool. He was now living in West Derby, a part of Liverpool some way away from Toxteth Park, and was described as a 'clerk in office'. He would have had less than three years' service with Royal Liver, but the timing of his wedding may have been prompted by the fact that he had been appointed to manage its London office – Elizabeth would only be able to move to London with him if they were married. They must have headed south soon afterwards because a notice in *Lloyd's Weekly Newspaper* of 10 April 1859 shows Degge as the London manager of the Royal Liver[58] and by 30 May he was advertising for local canvassers and collectors and for agents for all towns near to London. He and Elizabeth were installed in the manager's accommodation over the office at 77 Bridge Road, Lambeth, close to Westminster Bridge.[59] A daughter, Harriet, was born in 1860 and Joseph's brother Arthur, now aged 14, came to lodge with them. His education complete, he too had decided that a big city offered more than rural Staffordshire. The 1861 census return shows his profession as "office boy" – it is possible that his elder brother had found him a job as well as somewhere to live.

We know something of the family of Henry Ridge, Degge's companion in the coffee shop, because of a book published in 1975 by Dr Dudley Ridge, his grandson. In *A Sussex Family*[60] he traced the Ridge family back to John Ridge of Ovingdean near Brighton, a husbandman,[61] who was born in or about 1506 and died in 1558. William Ridge, Henry's great-grandfather, had died in 1802 a wealthy man having devoted his life to managing and enhancing a large estate near Lewes he had inherited in 1755. Henry's father, George Henry Ridge, the middle child of 11, was born in 1814 but left Sussex as a young man to join his eldest brother, Luke, who was a cheesemonger at 32 Lower Sloane Street, Chelsea. George probably worked as an apprentice there until he was 21 when, with the help of a legacy under his grandfather's will, he set up his own cheesemongering business at 12 Grosvenor Row, Pimlico in 1835.[62] These premises were less than ten minutes' walk from his brother's – the family history says nothing about any concerns that Luke may have had about his former apprentice setting up nearby in competition. The following year, George married Martha Jessop at St George's, Hanover Square and on 18 April 1838 their only son Henry was born at 12 Grosvenor Row. In July Henry was baptised at St George's.

Pimlico lies between Westminster and Chelsea and is bounded today by Vauxhall Bridge Road to the east, Chelsea Bridge Road to the west and to the north by a line that runs along Pimlico Road and Ebury Street and then loops round below Victoria Station. The Pimlico that the Ridge family knew was very different. There was no Chelsea Bridge, and so no Chelsea Bridge Road, just gardens and osier beds. There was no Victoria Station, and so no Grosvenor Railway Bridge nor swathe of railway tracks heading north from the river – just the Grosvenor Canal flowing to a basin that was later to become the site of the station. There was no road along the northern bank of the Thames (nor indeed on the southern) and most of the area between the Grosvenor Canal and Vauxhall Bridge Road was still market gardens serving, as they had done for centuries, two vital needs of the London population: fresh vegetables and a place to dispose of the dung from the streets and stables by way of manure. But change was underway as the Marquess of Westminster, whose family owned much of the land, had contracted with Thomas Cubitt[63] to develop the area and, when Henry was born, work was just beginning on the creation of the stuccoed streets and squares of Pimlico.[64]

By 1841 George and Martha, still in their mid-20s, were living in some style at 12 Grosvenor Row with young Henry and three servants. The cheesemongering business was either flourishing or they were living beyond their means, perhaps with the balance of grandfather's legacy being used to augment their income from the business. All we know of them in the next decade is that they moved from Pimlico to Shoreditch in north-east London – if the directories are to be relied upon – during 1847 or 1848.[65] In 1851 the family was living at Weymouth Terrace West, Shoreditch: George was still a cheesemonger, Henry was a scholar and there were no servants.

Henry Ridge would have been about ten years old at the time of the family move from Pimlico to Shoreditch. It seems reasonable to conclude that his education started in the Pimlico/Chelsea area and continued in north-east London. At some point during the early 1850s, he was apprenticed to a carpenter but nothing of him is known for certain until 1860 when he was living at 27 York Street, Haggerston, home of Paradine Hodgkins. On 30 August 1860 he married Hodgkins' daughter Ann at the local parish church – the groom was 22 and the bride 16. Both Ridge and his father-in-law were described on the marriage certificate as carpenters. Haggerston and Shoreditch are adjoining districts of north-east London.

To whom and where was Ridge apprenticed? An *In Memoriam* booklet produced after his death suggests that, at the age of 14, Ridge "was apprenticed to Mr. Maddox, Builder, Bristol, having served his time he came to London and was employed at Messrs Cubitt and Co".[66] Although the booklet states that Ridge was born in Bristol, that was certainly not the case, and so its reliability is questionable, but the reference to Cubitt and Co. could be credible. Thomas Cubitt's firm was engaged in the development of Pimlico, and had a massive builders' yard on the Grosvenor Canal, a short walk from where Henry had spent the first ten years of his life. But Bristol? There is no suggestion in the Ridge family history of any connection with the Bristol area and recent searches in trades directories have failed to identify a builder there called Maddox or any similar name. The obvious alternative is that he was apprenticed to Paradine Hodgkins, for whom he continued to work after his apprenticeship was over. The geography certainly makes more sense as the Ridges and the Hodgkins were living in almost adjoining streets.[67]

Soon after his marriage, Henry Ridge must have turned to industrial assurance because, by early the following year, he was manager of Royal Liver's office in Hammersmith and living with Ann, probably over the office, at 2 Bridge Road.[68] From carpenter in Haggerston to industrial assurance district manager in Hammersmith seems a big jump for him to have made in one leap. Was there perhaps an intervening role as an agent? Did Ridge respond to an advertisement placed by the new London manager of Royal Liver? Is that when they first met? Was Degge so impressed that he recommended him for the manager's job in Hammersmith… and talked to him later about his plans for a new venture?

We can never know for certain what brought Joseph Degge and Henry Ridge together on 2 February 1861, or what they discussed over their coffee.[69] City Road had been built a hundred years earlier to extend London's first ring road – the New Road between Paddington and Islington – to the City. Near to the coffee shop was the Artillery Ground, the scene of many great cricket matches in the eighteenth century, Wesley's Chapel, the 'cathedral of Methodism', and Bunhill Fields, a dissenters' burial ground and the last resting place of William Blake, John Bunyan and Daniel Defoe. Close by too, was a workhouse and a lunatic asylum. As they waited for their coffee, did they perhaps speak of any of the local landmarks that they had just passed? Another talking point would have been the improvement in the weather. For much of December 1860 and January 1861 London had been bitterly cold – on Christmas Day the temperature had dropped to an alarming 9°F (–12°C) and a few days later the launching of a new warship at Millwall was disrupted when the ship refused to move because the grease on the slipways had frozen. On

1 February, however, the temperature had reached a surprising 52°F (11°C) and 2 February was a clear, pleasant day with temperatures in the early 40s°F.[70] It seems probable that this meeting which was to have such consequences began, following that great British tradition, by discussing the weather. Who set up the meeting? Degge had the longer service with Royal Liver, and was known in Liverpool, and so, unless they had become very close friends it seems unlikely that the initial suggestion would have come from Ridge – talking to a senior work colleague about setting up in competition with their employer can be a dangerous course. Perhaps they were simply discussing their frustrations with the job over a cup of coffee and the idea emerged.

What prompted them to think of setting up a new collecting society? They may have been unhappy with some of Royal Liver's rules. An article appeared in *Post Magazine* on 9 April 1887,[71] the main purpose of which was to describe Royal London's new office although by way of background it dealt with the formation of the Society. It referred to Degge and Ridge (and William Hambridge who will shortly be introduced into the story) working for Royal Liver in London and suggested that they "unitedly endeavoured to prevail on the committee of that society to abolish a very arbitrary rule then recognised by all Collecting Friendly Societies, and known as the suspension clause, whereby 'any member being six weeks in arrear would be out of benefit for four weeks after paying up such arrears'". So it seems that the two men had strong objections to a rule that provided that a defaulting policyholder would only be covered four weeks after paying-up the arrears. The committee of management of Royal Liver "declined to initiate this measure of reform and the result of that refusal in the end was that Messrs Degge, Ridge and Hambridge founded the Society now known as the Royal London Friendly Society". When the article appeared Ridge and Hambridge were still active in the management of the Society and they must have provided this information to the reporter from *Post Magazine*. It seems reasonable to assume that this was a reason for deciding to form a new society, but it may or may not have been the only one.

The minutes of the meetings of the committee of management of Royal Liver say nothing about the suspension clause but suggest another reason why Degge may have decided to leave. He was mentioned at the meeting on 1 January 1861 when a resolution was passed:

> ... *that a letter be written to William & George Sinclair of Glasgow, R M Robertson of Glasgow and Joseph Degge of London explaining that this Committee will have nothing whatever to do with the proposition of the Secretary to change this Society from a Friendly Society into an Assurance Company, and any agent either directly or indirectly giving their influence to*

forward such a change or in any way interfere [sic] *in the matter will be dealt with accordingly.*[72]

Shortly afterwards, John Bates Lawrence, the secretary, was removed from office for secretly planning to convert Royal Liver into a limited company. Lawrence was rather more than secretary and one of the trustees – he had been the leading force behind the formation of the society – and each of its four offices had been Lawrence's home. The fact that within a few weeks of the resolution Degge decided to leave may not have been a coincidence. If Degge had an objection to friendly societies, he would hardly promote a new one and devote his life to getting it established. Lawrence must have made, or at least been involved in, the decision to send the young Joseph Degge to London and Degge may have regarded Lawrence as his patron and felt that his future career at Royal Liver would suffer as a result of his departure, or from 'backing the wrong horse' in the conversion debate. Alternatively he may have been aggrieved by the way in which he was treated over the incident.

Whatever the reasons, it was clear that they were contemplating a commercial venture and not a charity, although they clearly believed in the service that the new society would provide. Degge would have seen pauper funerals in Staffordshire and in Liverpool and, although the Ridge family were never at risk themselves of burials by the parish, the degradation to which the poor were subjected at times of bereavement cannot have escaped the attention of anyone in London and the other great cities. The pauper funeral had become "a symbol of great power even to those in no danger of ever being subject to it"[73] and, of all the horrors that the Earl of Shaftesbury,[74] a great Victorian philanthropist and social reformer, saw as a boy in London, it was the sight of drunken pall-bearers unsteadily conveying a pauper to his grave that converted him to a life of reform.[75] There can be little doubt that Degge and Ridge regarded providing a means by which working-class people could achieve respectable funerals for their loved ones as an honourable employment. We can never know from the very limited material available to what extent they approached the reforming zeal of the Earl of Shaftesbury and others – was it a worthwhile job or a crusade? They can hardly be criticised for the fact that their venture was a commercial one. At a banquet a hundred years to the day after the meeting in the coffee shop, Ernest Haynes, who was then chairman and joint managing director of Royal London, mused over what had prompted the formation of the Society:

I have often wondered what the motives of our two founders were. I imagine that personal gain played a great part, and I cannot see anything wrong in that. I think it is only right and proper that a man should want to improve himself in life. It may be that, as they were insurance men already before coming to us, they had seen the need for insurance; but I should like to think that they started this great venture because they felt impelled to get out and to do something, because they felt the need to make a change and to get out of the rut, and the need to go into uncharted seas.[76]

Degge and Ridge would have realised that London was a huge market for industrial assurance and probably felt that a society located there with a local name would have an appeal over one based elsewhere. They would have chosen 'Royal' as a mark of respect for their sovereign. It did not occur to either of them at the time that this might suggest some active royal sponsorship or that any approval needed to be sought. Over and above their concern with the suspension clause, they may have been frustrated working for bosses in Liverpool who they felt did not understand the problems confronting them in London. The prospect of working for themselves would have been appealing – few ambitious managers have never felt that they could do a better job if only they were not shackled by the constraints of the organisation. They would have hoped that their local contacts would enable them to recruit good people who would also be attracted by the prospect of working for local management.

These were able young men discussing their future at a time when there was a general air of confidence in Britain. They had little except their own ability to put into the venture, but no capital was required to form a collecting society over and above the cost of renting and equipping a modest office, since the agents would be remunerated entirely out of the premiums of policies that they sold. They would have been reassured and perhaps even inspired by the precedents of Royal Liver, Liverpool Victoria and others that proved it was possible for working men to set up collecting societies. If the secretary of Royal Liver had formed a high opinion of Degge while he was working in the office in Liverpool, Lawrence may even have talked to him (or in his hearing) about the founding of Royal Liver and its early days. Degge and Ridge would have seen the potential for greater rewards in working for themselves, or at least for an organisation that they were running.

It is rare to find that both people in these situations have the same level of enthusiasm. One is generally more doubting and needs convincing. Let us assume that the idea to create a new society having emerged from their discussions, it was the youthful Ridge who adopted it, and enthusiastically presented the reasons for going ahead. "That's all fine and good," Degge may have replied, "but why would anybody, let alone somebody with a steady job, come and work in a new business being set up by us? And I doubt if the two of us can carry this through on our own. My experience is all about how things work in the office[77] – you're the only one with any collecting experience and

34

neither of us has been in the business for long. And how will we pay the claims when they start coming in – we'll not have collected enough in premiums and we've nothing of our own that we could put in to tide things over? We'll be on the edge of going bust and if this happens we'll have lost everything including our reputations and the policyholders will have paid their premiums for nothing. We'll have been responsible for the collapse of yet another insurance company."

Perhaps at this stage they ordered more coffee. Fortunately they kept talking. They decided that it would make sense to try to persuade another person to be involved in the venture and the name of William Hambridge, a colleague from Royal Liver, was mentioned. They knew he shared their views on the unfairness of the suspension clause. They agreed that they would take great care in selecting the people for whom cover was provided so as to avoid bad risks, and accepted that, at first, yesterday's premiums would have to be used to pay today's claims and that sometimes they might even have to look to their own wallets to address short term deficiencies. They might optimistically have believed that their families would help them if they were in difficulties. Ridge had ten aunts and uncles but there was no reason to believe that they would be attracted to industrial assurance, while Degge's family was in Liverpool and hardly in a position to meet an urgent need. Of course it would be tough going and success could not be guaranteed, and if they failed then the great and the good would be quick to point out how irresponsible they had been in setting up what amounted to an industrial assurance company with no capital and thus no substance to back the promises contained in the early policies.

They probably went back over all the positive points. After much discussion, the decision to go for it was made. A pen, ink and paper were provided by the owner of the coffee shop and Ridge wrote:

2/2/61
We the undersigned hereby mutually agree to form and promote
the Royal London Life Insurance and Benefit Society to devote
the whole of our time and Interest to its welfare and to receive
an equal remuneration for our Services from the time of its open
appearance before the public.[78]

Both men signed the paper. If they celebrated their decision with something stronger than coffee, they may have done so at the nearby Eagle Tavern. There remains uncertainty as to what some of the customers had to pawn ('pop') in order to afford the pleasures of the Eagle. Was the weasel in 'Pop Goes the Weasel' their best clothes – in cockney rhyming slang, a coat is a 'weasel and stoat' – or perhaps a tool used by carpenters and hatters, or a tailor's flat iron? Subsequent generations would have been better informed if only Degge and Ridge had recorded two things: what was being pawned by the regulars who were "Up and down the City Road/ In and out the Eagle" and what prompted them to set up a new friendly society.

CHAPTER 2

Early Years

1861–1874

The collector must go into all kinds of neighbourhoods, he must visit fever-infested districts, and go into houses which, in some towns, are hardly fit to venture in. He has to solicit from door to door, and ask persons to become members. The collector must work very hard to earn in the first instance 2s. in a week... He must be a very industrious man if he can obtain at the end of two years business which will bring him in 18s. a week, for the people we have to deal with are very improvident and hence there is great difficulty in collecting the money... No man can imagine what a collector has to put up with or what he has to do to get that commission.

Evidence of Henry Liversage,
one of the joint-secretaries of the Royal Liver Friendly Society,
to the Royal Commission (1872)[1]

The reason why they continue their subscriptions is on account of being spurred up from week to week by the agents who call upon them, in the same way as, if a man is collecting rents, or tally-money, or anything else, if the parties know that he will come for the money weekly they provide for it; but if he omits calling the money is used for other purposes.

Evidence of Joseph Degge,
secretary of the Royal London Friendly Society,
to the Royal Commission (1872)[2]

The news that two of their district managers were leaving to set up a new society was not well received in Liverpool and both the president and secretary of Royal Liver sought to persuade Ridge and Degge to stay. They were no doubt flattered by the attention but their minds were made up. Breakaways were not uncommon in the friendly society movement. Liverpool Victoria was founded by agents from the Liverpool Independent Burial Society and Royal Liver itself was a breakaway from the Loyal Philanthropic Society. Ridge and Degge approached William Hambridge who had been a successful agent with Royal Liver for several years. He was a Londoner, born on 24 September 1838 at Old Jewry in the City, the son of a tailor, and educated privately in Southborough, near Tonbridge in Kent, at a school founded by the Reverend Edward Holme in 1781. He had briefly followed his father and worked as a tailor before joining Royal Liver as an agent. He agreed to join the new venture and this caused the management of Royal Liver further irritation.

Before their new society could open for business, rules had to be drafted for the approval of the Registrar of Friendly Societies. By 1861 the draftsman would have had a number of precedents available to assist him in his task and whoever drafted the rules did a good job, generally adopting straightforward language and avoiding legalese. There may only have been 44 rules but this was a comprehensive document with Rule 2 running to more than 800 words. Rule 1 dealt with the objects of the Society:

> *The objects of the Society, which is to be called the ROYAL LONDON FRIENDLY SOCIETY, and the business whereof is to be carried on at the PHOENIX HOUSE, SHEPHERD'S BUSH, LONDON, in the County of Middlesex, are to raise from time to time, by regular and special subscriptions from the several Members thereof, a stock or fund, for any of the following purposes, viz:-*
>
> *First. – For insuring a sum of money not exceeding £200, to be paid on the death of a Member, to the widower or widow of a Member, as the case may be, or to the child, or to the executors, administrators or assigns of such member, for defraying the expense of the burial of a Member, or of the husband, wife or child of a Member.*
>
> *Secondly. – For the relief, maintenance or endowment of the Members, their husbands, wives, children or kindred, in infancy and sickness.*

The rule showed a change of name from "Royal London Life Insurance and Benefit Society" envisaged in the 2 February agreement and indicated that the founders were contemplating more than a burial society. Other rules dealt with the appointment and duties of the committee of management (who were to "remain in office so long as their conduct shall be satisfactory to the members of the society… "), the trustees, secretary, treasurer and auditor, the requirements for general meetings (who could call them, who could attend, periods of notice that had to be given) the need to keep proper books of account, various issues relating to the policies and many formalities of the type generally found in the articles of association of a company.

The 1887 article in *Post Magazine* referred to in the previous chapter[3] suggested that "the rules were framed in a just and liberal spirit and avoided all the arbitrary regulations which were then so common in Collecting Friendly Societies". That seems broadly correct, and there was certainly no suspension clause, although a potential policyholder who was provided with a copy of the rules and who was capable of reading them may well not have regarded Rule 17 as particularly liberal, providing as it did for the forfeiture of any policy that was 13 weeks in arrears, with all premiums that had been paid being "absolutely forfeited for the use of the said society". In practice the Society allowed members three months' arrears and then to give them written notice before forfeiting their policies. Every member was issued with a policy document on the back of which was printed the rules, a practice not followed by every competitor.[4]

Attached to the rules were three simple tables. They were not the work of an actuary but had been prepared after a careful study of the tables of other offices doing similar business.[5] Table I set out the weekly contributions required "to insure the following Sums at Death". The sum payable on death depended upon the age of the assured on the next birthday after the policy was taken out – 1d a week (today: 29p) and an entrance fee (that included the first premium) of 4d would provide a payment on death of £6 (today: £419) for a person who would be between 10 and 35, and £2 for those between 50 and 55. Members would be entitled to "full benefit in Twelve Calendar Months", although, at the first revision of this table, provision was made for half benefit after six months. Table II dealt with the Sick Department – a 30-year-old who paid an entrance fee of 1s (today: £3.49) and a premium of 4d a week would receive, while the sickness continued, 4s a week for 13 weeks, 2s a week for the next 13 weeks and 1d a week for the next 6 months. Table III dealing with the Endowment Department was soon replaced because initially the premiums were not age-related. An entrance fee of 1s and a premium of 2d week would provide a payout of £5 1s 4d (today: £353) after ten years or £11 16s 4d after 20 years. The modern endowment policy pays out on a defined date or (if earlier) on the death of the assured but in these early days the latter was not the case. A Note to Table III stated that: "The money paid in to be returned if death takes place before the time of the Endowment becoming due".

Within ten weeks of the coffee shop meeting the rules had been approved. A certificate dated 10 April 1861 and signed by the Registrar of Friendly Societies, John Tidd Pratt,[6] had been endorsed on them that read:

> *I hereby certify, that the foregoing Rules of the ROYAL LONDON FRIENDLY SOCIETY, at the Phoenix House, Shepherd's Bush, London, W., in the County of Middlesex, are in conformity with law, and that the Society is duly established from the present date, and is subject to the provisions and entitled to the privileges of the Acts relating to Friendly Societies.*

'Phoenix House, Shepherd's Bush' has proved something of a mystery. The 1887 article in *Post Magazine* suggests that the first chief office was a small room at 51 Moorgate (then Moorgate Street) in the City of London and the Society's first general meeting was certainly held there on 17 October 1861. The first accounts were prepared for the period beginning on 11 May 1861. So we can assume that the Royal London Friendly Society opened for business in early May. The reference in the rules suggests that Phoenix House was used by the founders while the Society was being formed.[7] But where was its first trading address? There are indications that it was in Hammersmith, perhaps in Bridge Road and possibly over a coffee shop, although it seems likely that the transfer to the top floor of 51 Moorgate Street took place fairly soon after the formation.[8]

The first policy was apparently sold by William Hambridge to his father-in-law James Hepden of Dry Hills, Tonbridge, Kent – the sum assured was £6 and the premium 4d a week. It was 'entered' on 10 June 1861.[9] Ridge and Hambridge would have been active as agents from the beginning but apart from them we know neither the names nor number of the first agents, nor from where they were recruited. We can, however, have our suspicions. A booklet produced at the Jubilee of Royal London in 1911 to record the progress in Birmingham stated: "The Royal London Friendly Society was founded early in the year 1861 by a few practical men, workers from the Royal Liver Friendly Society". 'A few' suggests that there were more than the three of whom we are aware. It may well have been that many of the early agents were former colleagues at Royal Liver who decided to throw in their lot with Degge, Ridge and Hambridge.

Did they seek to persuade their existing contacts to abandon their policies with Royal Liver and to take a similar policy out with their new society – 'transferring', as it was known at the time? There probably were some cases of this but it is significant that Royal London was not among the examples included in a Royal Commission report in 1874 of societies that were set up on the basis of large-scale transfers from their founders' former employers.[10] Later, a number of societies including Royal London entered into an agreement restricting transfers.[11] New agents were recruited by means of advertisements placed in the *Clerkenwell News* and in the prospectus. One was addressed to "tradesmen and others having spare time upon their hands" while another, under the heading "Agents wanted everywhere", invited "respectable and energetic persons desirous of increasing their incomes" to reply without delay to the secretary at the chief office. Many agents were only part-time, combining assurance work with their day-job – "an actual working man, who undertakes the office as a mere supplement to his usual source of income, and collects in his evenings, his Saturday afternoons or Sundays, or at most during certain days in the week".[12]

The London into which the Royal London Friendly Society was born was the biggest city in Europe, the world's largest port, the centre of international finance and the heart of the expanding British Empire. Just a decade before, more than a third of the population had visited the Great Exhibition celebrating the position of the United Kingdom in the world market-place and housed in the Crystal Palace in Hyde Park. Queen Victoria had been overwhelmed – the opening on 1 May 1851 had been "the greatest day in our history", "the most beautiful and imposing and touching spectacle ever seen", and "the happiest, proudest day in my life".[13]

There was, however, another side to London and it was here that the industrial assurance agents operated. London was grossly overcrowded. Its population had trebled between 1801 and 1861. The overcrowding led to appalling living conditions and misery for many – the failure to address the problems of the poor, in particular their need for adequate housing, was the great failure of the Victorian era. The lack of a sewage system, the reliance on the horse and donkey for transport, the driving of animals to market through the streets and the presence of tanneries, breweries and other polluting industries, not to mention the consequences of the "unwashed, soddened, unkempt, reckless humanity",[14] gave London (and many other cities) a smell that would be unbearable by modern standards. Millions of gallons of untreated sewage were discharged every day into the Thames. The river, which was also a major source of drinking water, had virtually become an open sewer. There were frequent cholera epidemics and the link between the disease and contaminated drinking water was only just being recognised.

In the hot summer of 1858, in what came to be called the Great Stink, the smell was so rank that nobody went near the Thames unless they had to and the business of Parliament and the law courts (then in Westminster Hall) were interrupted, with consideration being given to relocating them to temporary sites out of London. Heavy rain and the end of the hot summer brought some relief. In the debate in the House of Commons on the need to take action to address the problem, Benjamin Disraeli referred to the Thames as a noble river that had "become a Stygian pool reeking with ineffable and intolerable horrors. The public health is at stake; almost all living things that existed in the water of the Thames have disappeared or been destroyed; a very natural fear has arisen that the living beings upon its banks may share the same fate".[15]

London had for many years been a series of massive construction sites with all the noise, dust and disruption that went with them. The railways had been a major contributor. It was not until 1825 that the first passenger line was opened between Stockton and Darlington and the railway did not come to London until 1836 when a commuter line was opened between Greenwich and London Bridge. By 1861 much of the national rail network was in place and many of the great London stations had been opened – Euston in 1837, Fenchurch Street in 1841, Waterloo in 1848, King's Cross in 1852, Paddington in 1854 (replacing a wooden structure opened in 1838) and Victoria in 1860. The railways sliced through neighbourhoods, truncated streets, swept away buildings, cut tunnels and demanded not only stations but bridges and other structures. They did nothing to improve traffic congestion and in fact made it worse with rail travellers completing their journeys by road. In 1861 work was underway on Joseph Bazalgette's ambitious scheme to provide London with an extensive underground sewerage system and, now that the finances had at last been organised, construction had begun on the Metropolitan Railway between Paddington and Farringdon Street via King's Cross that was to be the first part of the London Underground. In the short term, these massive projects caused only greater congestion as yet more streets had to be dug up.

The noise in the busy and often narrow streets was such that it was impossible to hold a conversation amongst the flow of carriages, carts and wagons with bands of iron or steel holding the wooden wheels together being pulled by horses and donkeys over the cobbled streets. Examples of what we would term 'road rage' were a constant feature, although in the absence of any rules of the road or highway code it is easy to see how misunderstandings could arise. Street traders, beggars and street performers were commonplace. There was no compulsory free education, sick-leave, affordable medical care, paid holidays, unemployment benefit or old-age pensions, and laws relating to employment, discrimination, health and safety and the family either did not exist or were in their infancy. Without any of these safeguards, brutality and desperation were everywhere.[16]

In a letter written in 1924,[17] Charles, Henry Ridge's son, indicates how near the Society came to collapsing:

> *The early days of the Royal London were anxious times – there was difficulty in paying claims, the expenses were heavy in proportion to the income, our families underwent great privations in meeting*

them. In addition to the sacrifices made by my parents, the various members of the Degge family gave great financial help. We all had very frugal fare in those days. At one time the affairs of the Royal London were so gloomy, that several of the workers left the Royal London and resumed their former occupations. Mr Hambridge was one and when success returned Mr Hambridge came back, but Mr Ridge and Mr Degge stuck to the Royal London throughout and lived to see their action amply justified.

Charles omits to mention a further stress suffered by the Ridges during this difficult time. On 30 October 1861 Ann gave birth prematurely to twins of whom only Charles survived. The reference to Hambridge is interesting, although there is nothing by way of corroboration in the archives or minute books.[18] In due course, Henry Ridge took out a policy on Charles' life – the weekly premium was one penny and the sum assured £3. It remained in force until Charles' death in 1948.

The early directors were not slow to remind later generations how often the pockets of those in the chief office had to be turned out to meet claims. These financial difficulties may explain the high turnover on the Committee of Management. Between April and October 1861 the Society was apparently run by Degge, Ridge and Hambridge. At the first annual general meeting of the Society, held on 17 October 1861 at 51 Moorgate Street, Joseph Degge's two younger brothers were much in evidence: Arthur, aged 15, who had been lodging with Joseph and Elizabeth, proposed the resolution to appoint the trustees and Edwin, who was three years older, proposed the appointment of the Committee of Management. Their presence was probably essential, not only because they would have done what they were told, but also because it is unlikely that the notice of the meeting would have attracted many members. The first three pages of *The Times* were given over to classified advertisements – a "Notice to members of the Royal London Friendly Society" appeared on page three on 11 October, less than a week before the meeting. It was signed by "Joseph Degge, Secretary *pro tem*", ran to a mere eight lines, occupied less than 2 cm of a single column and was positioned between appeals by the Royal National Lifeboat Institution and the Wanstead Orphan Asylum. The minutes are silent on the number of members who attended.

At the meeting Ridge and Degge were elected president (although the title seems to have lapsed almost at once) and secretary respectively, and seven gentlemen including William Hambridge were appointed to the Committee. The involvement of some of them, however, was to prove transient. William Head soon resigned and, by the following spring, Thomas Bowen had attended only one meeting and Edgar Cheesman only three, and neither had been to a meeting for months. Henry Green, who had been elected chairman of the

Committee, Robert Drewitt Hilton, John Head and William Hambridge were the regular attenders.

The minutes of the meetings held between 23 April and 17 September 1862 have not survived. By the autumn, Henry Green, who was also an agent, was in arrears – his last meeting was on 17 September and he resigned on 29 October – and the names of Hilton and Head were no longer appearing in the minutes. We know not whether they resigned or if, like their former colleagues, just faded away. Charles Sheffield had briefly been a trustee but then he too resigned. By now, however, many of the directors (as the members of the Committee tended to be called) who were to preside over the successful establishment and early expansion of Royal London, were in place. During the summer of 1862 Hambridge had been joined on the Committee by Henry Ridge together with Laurence Francis Barrett, Benjamin Bexfield, James Birnie and Thomas Robinson. Thomas Forster was appointed on 29 October and, they were all re-elected the following day at the second annual general meeting held at the Hall of Science, 58 City Road. Hambridge was the only survivor from the Committee appointed the previous year. Barrett and Forster were appointed trustees.

The fact that a hall had been booked for the annual meeting suggests that an attendance of Royal London members was expected, but again the minutes are silent on the number who gave up some of their time on an October morning to participate in the management of the newly created oganisation that they owned and with which they were insured. This time the notice of the meeting made it onto the front page of *The Times* (of 16 October), and was rather more conspicuous than the previous one, although it still did not appear amongst the corporate notices. Observant members who were readers of *The Times* would have found it between appeals that illustrate the environment into which the Royal London was born. The Ragged Schools in Whitechapel could provide accommodation for more than 500 children but only if a further £150 was raised to complete the building. The Refuge for Homeless and Destitute Boys at 4 Mansell Street, also in Whitechapel, provided a home and work for 120 poor boys, but the latest half-year accounts showed a deficit of £175. Unless this was made-up, numbers would have to be reduced "during the ensuing winter months". The institution was "situated in the east of London, where vice and misery greatly abound, but where a visit from the wealthy is rarely known". Although not every member of the new Committee was to remain in post for long, an element of continuity had now been introduced into the management of the Society. There was a range of skills around the table – Barrett was a carpenter from Deptford who initially was also an agent employing a clerk to make his Royal London collections, Birnie was a printer from Gravesend and Forster a doctor practising in Stepney. There was no permanent chairman, the Committee electing one of its members on a quarterly basis to take the chair.

The lack of any documentary evidence of the events of 1862 is frustrating – how was the replacement of six members of the Committee accomplished? The Committee was permitted to appoint another member of the Society in place of a committee member who had resigned, subject to confirmation at the next general meeting. So the position was straightforward where there was a formal resignation. The problem was where there was not, because the Committee had very limited powers of removal.[19] If Bowen and Cheesman, for example, could not be persuaded to resign, the only safe course would have been to propose a resolution for their removal at a general meeting and this does not seem to have been done. However they went about it, the founders succeeded at the second attempt to put in place a group of men who, with one exception, proved themselves competent to lead this embryonic organisation. If they did, perhaps, have to adopt robust methods to accomplish the changes, they would argue that the subsequent history of the Society justified them and that, in any case, the resolution at the second general meeting validated the appointments.

The other business of the meeting was to lay before the members the first annual report and accounts. The trading period was 11 May 1861 to 20 September 1862 during which premiums of £624 16s 0½d (today: £43,850) were collected. When all the expenses had been paid the profits ('Cash in Treasurer's Hands' as it was called) was £109 19s 5d (today: £7,720). The report, signed by Degge by order of the Committee of Management, was upbeat. The results were "highly gratifying" and "a good augury of future prosperity". These were bold words considering that the reserves of the Society were less than a fifth of its income. A run of unexpected claims would very quickly have used up £109 and, no doubt, the limited assistance that could be provided by the Ridge and Degge families.

This was a time when insolvency of assurance companies was commonplace. The Friend-in-need, for example, had been established as a friendly society in 1853 and at the time of Degge's first report was converting into a company. In 1867 it sold its business to the Empire Insurance Company which had already absorbed the Scottish Industrial Friendly Society but in 1869 the Empire was wound up. Some Friend-in-need policyholders had already transferred to the Provincial Union Assurance Company but that too was wound up in 1868 with its secretary receiving a sentence of five years' penal servitude after being convicted at the Old Bailey of obtaining money by false pretences with intent to defraud.

At the end of the report, Degge touched upon what was to become one of the great concerns of industrial assurance:

In conclusion, your Committee beg to say that they avoid all unnecessary expenses, as they well know, by a course of long experience, that industrial business will not afford an extravagant

45

*outlay, therefore, it has been, and will be their greatest aim, to
keep the expenditure as low as possible, which will enable them,
at all times, to meet the honest and just claims of the members,
and thus promote not only the interest of the members, but confer
a lasting honour to themselves and the Society.*

Benjamin Bexfield was soon to provide a salutary example of the speed
with which one can fall from grace. On 9 September 1863 he chaired a meeting
of the Committee but at a special meeting on 11 September it was resolved
to suspend him from the Committee, as a collector and from all other offices
"until the whole of the business in the Poplar district has been investigated".
Bexfield was invited to select any two members of the Committee to carry out
the investigation. Ridge and Hambridge were appointed and their investigation
revealed that Bexfield had withheld some £6 (today: £440) from the Society.[20]
On 23 September he was expelled from the Committee, discharged from all
offices in the Society and required to pay all sums owing at once. When he
did not do so, the secretary was instructed to commence proceedings in the
Guildhall Police Court to recover the sum owed. The minutes say nothing
about the outcome of the litigation but at a special meeting of the Committee
on 7 October, chaired by Ridge, it was resolved to elect "Mr Joseph Degge
Senior" to fill the vacancy on the Committee created by Bexfield's departure.
This was none other than Joseph Barnes Degge, the secretary's uncle and
former Liverpool publican and, more recently, dock labourer, who had moved
to London with his wife and three children and become an industrial assurance
agent in the organisation formed by his nephew.

Bexfield was not the only agent who failed to account to the Society
with sums they had collected and sometimes a severe approach was adopted.
In August 1865 a clerk appointed by his employer, a Royal London agent,
to collect on his behalf, was charged at the Old Bailey with embezzling and
stealing 16s 5d (today: £60). No serious defence was advanced but his aunt
had already paid Degge all the money that was due. The jury convicted but
recommended mercy. The sentence of six weeks' imprisonment seems severe
although, by the harsh standards of the day, the judge would have been
reflecting the jury's recommendation.

There was rather more than friendly rivalry between agents of competing
companies. Frequent accusations often backed up by handbills and other
printed material abounded. Degge complained that in a large town:

*... the agents of the different institutions are very numerous, and
perhaps there is ill-feeling between the officers of two particular
institutions, and they give their agents instructions to vilify each
other as much as they possibly can, or the institutions which they*

represent, and to secure all the subscribers that they possibly can; and they fortify them with all sorts of publications which are detrimental to each other, and it is a regular fight to destroy the business of each other.[21]

The accusations about a rival's financial stability were often totally unjustified. In February 1864 solicitors had to be instructed in relation to the activities of the Royal Liver's agent in Norwich – a full and ample apology was to be sought for the false statement he had made. Was he perhaps a former colleague of the triumvirate heading up Royal London? Unfortunately the archives do not reveal how the matter was resolved.

It might have been felt that London provided a large enough market but as early as July 1864 a decision was taken "to open provincial districts". Laurence Barrett spent from November 1864 until the following March establishing the Society in Birmingham and in 1868 a branch office was opened there – one room in Colonial Buildings, Essex Row (later renamed Horse Fair) to be replaced in 1869 by a larger office at 78 Hurst Street. The first agent in Manchester was appointed in 1865 and by the end of 1866 he had been joined by four more agents and two canvassers.[22] The expansion involved members of the Committee being away for long periods and in December 1864 it was resolved that "Mesdames Hambridge, Ridge, Barrett and Robinson be allowed third-class railway fares from town to town if they feel desirous of accompanying their husbands during the time that they are opening up districts for the Society". History does not tell us by which class their husband's travelled, or whether they desired their wives to accompany them.

Royal London made its first acquisition in December 1864 when, at a meeting in the Horse and Groom in Curtain Road, Shoreditch, the members of the Prince of Wales Friendly Sick and Assurance Society resolved to amalgamate with the Royal London Friendly Society. John Monk, the leading light of the Prince of Wales, was appointed a director of Royal London. In fact, he was appointed twice because in December the seven directors permitted by the rules were already in place and no one would resign to accommodate Monk. The appointment was a term of the acquisition and so the Committee resolved to make an additional appointment in view of the great increase in the Society's business and the delicate state of Thomas Robinson's health. Shortly afterwards Robinson died and this enabled the Committee to replace the invalid appointment of Monk with a valid one.

By early 1866 "the two small rooms on the top floor of a very lofty building in Moorgate Street" (as they were described by Thomas Byrne, a director, at the 1902 annual general meeting[23]) were no longer adequate for the chief office and the Society took a 21-year lease of the ground floor at 5 Aldermanbury Postern at a rent of £150 (today: £10,200) per year. As a result of enemy action in December 1940, Aldermanbury Postern no longer exists. It was a continuation of Aldermanbury north of London Wall to Fore Street and was named after a postern gate in the city wall that had been located there. This was a bold move as the annual rent at Moorgate had been only £30 and one made at a time of uncertainty in the City in the light of the failure of Overend, Gurney & Company, known as the 'bankers bank' that went into liquidation owing £11 million (today: £752 million).[24] As is inevitable with any move there were other expenses – the fitting-out of the new office cost £65 (today: £4,300), the lawyers charged £8 7s 2d (today: £570) and later in the year £25 10s 0d (today: £1,750) was spent on a board table and chairs. To complete the effect, and to provide the Committee with a suitable environment for its deliberations, the boardroom was carpeted at a cost of 4s 4d (£15) per square yard.

Expansion was rapid. In the first quarter of 1867, for example, no less than 60 new agents were appointed – not only in Barnsley, Birmingham, Bradford, Bristol, Leeds, Liverpool, Manchester, Sheffield and Wednesbury but also in Bournemouth, Bury St Edmunds, Godalming, Ipswich, Peterborough, Tonbridge, Weston-super-Mare, and Worthing. The Society's activities were extended into Wales during the quarter – with agents appointed in Abertillery, Abergavenny, Cardiff and Merthyr Tydfil – and later in the year into Scotland, with appointments being made in Glasgow in July and Edinburgh in August. Royal London adopted the practice common at the time – and indeed for generations to come – of allowing agents to sell their collecting books to a successor who they nominated, subject to the successor being approved by the Society.[25] Much later, the right of agents to nominate their successor would cause great difficulties and, from the beginning, Degge was uncomfortable with the concept of agents 'owning' their books. His point was that the business belonged to the Society[26] although this was a matter of semantics rather than substance because it was a fact that agents could pass their books on to their successor and receive payment from the transferee for so doing. Agents had to account to the chief office on a weekly basis and were not allowed to retain any balances.[27] Canvassers backed up the efforts of the agents – these were specialist salesmen who had no collecting responsibility and who operated alongside agents, earning 30s a week (today: £115).[28]

Many of the early policies were on the lives of children and it was the aim of collectors to get all the family signed-up. The Royal Commission investigating friendly societies regarded this as so significant that it quoted in full in its final report in 1874 the relevant extract of the assistant commissioner's report:

> *Perhaps the most important fact to be borne in mind in characterising the collecting Burial Societies is, that they differ from the local burial clubs, and from the district funeral funds*

of the affiliated orders, in subsisting primarily upon insurance of the lives, not of the working men themselves who pay the contributions, but of the women, and especially the children in working men's families. It is true that in most Friendly Societies of the usual types there is a funeral benefit on death of a member's wife, amounting generally to one half that is payable on the death of the member; but hardly any, even of the so-called 'death clubs', will insure the lives of children, and 'baby clubs' are not frequent. Agents of the large collecting societies have told me, and I have tested the fact by examination of their books, that a great majority of the names on their lists are those of children and women. One gentleman informed me, and the same thing has been confirmed by others, that he never rested satisfied after he had insured one life in a household until he had got the whole household in his book; and that in most cases he would have two, three, or more subscriptions to collect in the same house when he called. In fact it would by no means pay to go through the drudgery of an agent's profession, if each penny or twopence required that a separate house should be visited to obtain it.[29]

The records do not tell us how the deal with the Prince of Wales Friendly Sick and Assurance Society turned out but we know that Royal London's second acquisition was not a success.[30] The Victoria Legal Provident Association, known locally as 'the Victoria', also had an office in Colonial Buildings, Birmingham. It had been formed by two agents from the Liverpool Victoria who seemed to have transferred a number of their previous employer's policyholders to the new society without telling either the employer or the policyholders. It was felt that acquiring the Victoria would speed up Royal London's expansion into Birmingham and the Midlands, and Degge was soon talking to William Davies, the Victoria's secretary. A deal was struck in 1868 that involved Royal London taking on all the Victoria's members, on the same terms that they were enjoying with the Victoria, and all its assets and liabilities, although doubts were later expressed as to whether Davies (who by now was a director of Royal London) was empowered to enter into the transaction. It had been represented that the Victoria had an income of over £100 a week but no actuarial advice was sought and limited due diligence undertaken. In fact the administration of the Victoria was "in a deplorable state of confusion"[31] and there were no assets, just liabilities. As Degge admitted:

We imagined that we were making a good bargain at the time when we concluded it [but we] *have always regretted it ever since.*

We found a great many accounts owing, such as printing and
medical officers' accounts, and different other things, which we
were not aware of, and had no idea at the time were owing.[32]

Significant changes had to be made to both products and the procedure. In May 1870 Royal London followed Royal Liver's example and stopped offering sickness and endowment policies.[33] Many friendly societies of all types were experiencing problems with the former because, with people living longer, it was becoming difficult to determine when a sickness benefit became an old age pension. As is inevitable in the case of any sickness benefit there were enforcement problems – there were several cases where a member receiving sickness benefit was expelled after being found not to be at home, "such absence having a tendency to retard his recovery". Degge and his colleagues realised that charging premiums at the rates offered by competitors would not enable Royal London to make a profit on sickness and endowment policies having regard to the level of expenses. The lower volume sold may have been due, in part, to the fact that agents received only 12.5 per cent of the premium by way of collecting commission, rather than the 25 per cent for life policies.

The original rules of the Society required a medical before a life policy could be issued.[34] This proved to be impossible – potential policyholders were not prepared to undergo one while the cost could not be justified given the size of the premiums. So the rule was changed requiring the proposer to complete a declaration about his or her health and giving the Committee of Management the right to require a medical where they felt that one was necessary.

Members were supplied with magnificent policy documents. They were printed on massive sheets of blue paper, 21 x 17 inches, more than a quarter of which was taken up by the heading that included the Society's name in letters of nearly an inch deep, a large coat of arms with two terrifying animals supporting the shield (one apparently a cross between a dragon and an eagle; the other that, rather strangely, is looking away from the shield, is part dragon and part lion). The date on which the Society was established was set out in Roman numerals – how many members, one wonders would have realised that MDCCCLXI was 1861? The legislation under which the Society had been formed was set out in full "18 and 19 Vic. cap. 68; 21 and 22 Vic. cap. 101; 23 and 24 Vic. cap. 58". The purpose of all of this was more to impress than to communicate, a sentiment that applies equally to the wording of the policy, which adopted that strange language, never spoken even by lawyers, but beloved by some who drafted legal documents. For all the legalese, however, the document was commendably brief.[35] Originally cards were issued annually to policyholders on which the agent acknowledged receipt of the premiums. In time, the cards were replaced by the premium receipt book that was to become an integral part of industrial assurance.

The Victoria debacle was not significant enough to do any real harm and at the end of its first decade the Royal London Friendly Society appeared to be flourishing. The premium income for the year ended 30 September 1871 was £16,659 (today: £1.1 million). The reserves stood at £4,964 (today: £344,000) – not a large sum (in fact less than a third of the annual premium income) but at least some protection against an unexpected run of claims. The Society had sold 75,000 policies and employed nearly 200 people. There were 150 agents and 20 canvassers out and about collecting premiums and seeking new business with Degge, the secretary, and the seven members of the Committee of Management, including Ridge and Hambridge, presiding over the business. A superintendent of agents was employed to monitor the performance of the agents and five clerks dealt with the administration. There was no middle management – it was the directors who went out to open up new districts and to investigate problems with the existing ones. Two meetings of the Committee in early 1874 could not take place because its members were "absent on the Society's business, examining agents' books and accounts". The Committee did not lack practical experience as three of its members were also agents.

The problems were beneath the surface. High lapse rates and expense ratios – the two issues that would haunt industrial assurance[36] – were present in Royal London from the beginning. By the end of September 1872, two-thirds of the policies had already lapsed because the policyholder had stopped paying the premiums.[37] As Degge pointed out there were many reasons why policies lapsed:

> *In the first place the people, whom we insure, as a rule, are of very migratory habits; in the second place sometimes want of employment causes them to lapse their policies, people move away to different colonies, and do all sorts of things, which cause them to lapse their policies.*[38]

It was the Royal Commission on Friendly and Benefit Building Societies, set up late in 1870 under the chairmanship Sir Stafford Northcote,[39] that focused attention on collecting societies for the first, but certainly not the last, time. As industrial assurance expanded, it was inevitable that it attracted close public scrutiny especially as "almost all of it is contributed by the industrial classes and must represent a very considerable part of whatever provision these classes have been able to make for the contingencies of the future".[40] Governments were regularly to invite learned people to review industrial assurance, some of whom were more successful than others in understanding the social environment in which it operated.

Questionnaires were sent by the Royal Commission to societies, assistant commissioners went up and down the country hearing evidence and 277 witnesses appeared before the commissioners in London. Hambridge, Davies and Degge had been appointed to work with delegates from other societies in responding to the Commission but it was Degge alone who, on 24 April 1872, made himself available for questioning by the commissioners. Joseph Degge comes over as a phlegmatic, competent individual but he must have been mildly apprehensive as he took his seat before the commissioners who, by now, were well informed. His inquisitors were Sir Stafford Northcote (the chairman), and Sir Michael Hicks-Beach,[41] able Conservative politicians with impeccable backgrounds (titled family, Eton and Oxford) both of whom would become Chancellor of the Exchequer, Sir Sydney Waterlow,[42] the next Lord Mayor of London, and William Pattison, the actuary to the Commercial Union. Their questions were wide-ranging and probing and if there were any pleasantries they do not appear in the transcript. Degge was well down the batting order of witnesses, and the commissioners had apparently already asked nearly 25,000 questions.[43]

Degge was successful in putting over a number of positive points about Royal London and industrial assurance generally. The Society had never refused a claim, on the basis that the loss of business that this might prompt would almost certainly exceed the loss of paying a bad claim, and no summons or writ had been issued against the Society, neither had it been taken to arbitration.[44] The Society took great care in selecting lives,[45] agents were not allowed to retain any money that they had collected but had to send it all to head office[46] and a letter was sent to every policyholder who was in arrears before any policy was forfeited for failure to pay the premiums.[47] Industrial assurance was in the public interest because without it, many would be unable to pay for the interment of their dead.[48] Those who kept up their payments received the benefit for which they had paid but collecting from policyholders' homes inevitably involved a cost.[49] He may have failed to emphasise a point that was in Royal London's favour. The Commission was to complain that the management of societies was generally in the hands of current or former collectors. In reply to questions, Degge confirmed but did not stress that neither he nor four of the members of the Committee of Management had ever been a collector.[50]

Degge was disarmingly honest about the practice in the accounts of bracketing together a number of items so that it was impossible to see the amount spent on commission and management expenses: "If they were all put in separate items in the balance sheet, the agents of other institutions doing a similar description of business would make an invidious use of it".[51] Keeping down the expense of running the Society, an issue that Degge had flagged in the first annual report, was proving difficult. Edward Lyulph Stanley,[52] one of the assistant commissioners, recast the Society's expenditure for the year ended

30 September 1871 in a way that provided rather more information than was contained in the published accounts.[53]

Table No. 1

Expenditure of the Royal London Friendly Society: for the year ended 30 September 1871

	Actual: £	Today: £
Agents' Commission (150)	3,600	250,000
Agents' rent (90 offices)	925	64,200
Canvassers' salaries (20)	633	43,900
Committee of Management salaries (7)	967	67,100
Secretary's salary	380	26,400
Clerks' salaries (5)	260	18,000
Rent of London and Birmingham offices	195	13,500
Superintendent of agents' salary[54]	200	13,900
Travelling expenses	325	22,500
Printing	477	33,100
Money orders, postage etc.	225	15,600
Miscellaneous[55]	460	31,800
	8,647	600,000

Premium income during the year was £16,775 (today: £1,160,000). Stanley's breakdown graphically illustrates the dilemma that was to confront industrial assurance offices throughout their history. Home collection and canvassing were expensive and, although none of the items of expenditure of themselves appear excessive, more than half of the premiums collected were spent on remunerating the agents and paying all the other expenses involved in running the business. So less than half the money contributed by policyholders was there to be invested in readiness to meet the claims that would in due course be made under the policies.

Degge's view was that, although the agents were well remunerated, they were paid no more than the market demanded and if they were offered less they would go to a competitor and no doubt take their clients with them.[56] On the sale of a life policy, the agent received the entrance fee (4d on a-penny-a-week policy that included the first premium) and the next five weeks' premiums. He was also able to collect 6d from the policyholder for a policy document that incorporated the Society's rules, of which he could retain 4d.

After that he received 25 per cent of the premiums collected. Many agents received 'office rents' of between 2s 6d and 10s a week for the use of a room in their homes as an office.[57]

Degge had to concede that few members attended the general meetings or had any means of knowing when they were being held as the press advertisements appeared only in London[58] and that, as only 5,000 copies of the balance sheet were printed for distribution by the agents, there would be many of the 25,000 members who would be ignorant of the finances of the Society.[59] He suggested that few out-of-town members would go to the expense of attending even if they did know when and where the meetings were being held.[60] Transparency and accountability were concepts of a later century.[61] He acknowledged that there had been no actuarial valuation during the ten years of the Society's life, neither had the officers attempted any valuation.[62]

In some of the sensitive areas, Degge comes over as a blunt man telling the facts of industrial assurance life with little effort to present them in a favourable light. The modern reader looks in vain for passages regretting the number of lapsed policies and outlining the action being taken within the Society to reduce them. In reply to a provocative question from Sir Stafford about the number of persons who have "withdrawn from the society, or thrown themselves out of benefit", Degge replied that he always calculated "that at least two-thirds of the people who become insured in our office, and in similar institutions, allow their policies to lapse, and consequently deprive themselves of benefit".[63] Later, when being questioned about the limited reserves, he volunteered that he regarded it as "possible for a life office not doing any sick or endowment business to pay its way without any accumulated fund, considering the lapses".[64] In other words, as the Commission was to put it in the final report, this type of society lives by its lapses "that are a great source of profit".[65]

This somewhat robust approach was displayed by other witnesses. The secretary of the Royal Liver was dismissive of education:

> The fact of intelligence and education has no bearing whatever as to the character or ability of a collector in making a book; it has nothing to say to it; in fact, we find that the more refined and educated a man is, the less hope we have that he will succeed amongst the working classes. We find that a man who is educated only to a certain point, just to the standard of the poor people, and who is able to meet them from time to time, is just that character of man who will get the business in a society like ours.[66]

This sentiment was, no doubt, correct but expressing it this way was inviting the commissioners to conclude, as in due course they did, that because they were uneducated, many collectors must inevitably be unscrupulous.[67]

The opinion of the Royal Commission was "on the whole... decidedly adverse" to collecting societies.[68] Legislation introduced in the light of its recommendations would have posed difficulties for the Society if it had been in place any earlier because, as Degge had testified, several members of the Committee of Management were also collectors. The Friendly Societies Act of 1875 provided that a collector, even if he was a member could neither vote at nor take part in, general meetings, nor could he be a member of the committee of management or hold any other office other than superintending collectors in a specific area. The days of combining the roles of director and collector were over but by now the size of the Society was such that it could accommodate the new law without too many problems. The 1875 Act also provided that:

- every society had to be audited annually and its funds valued every five years
- the role of the Registrar of Friendly Societies would be widened
- the sum assured on lives of children under ten years was limited to £10 and under five to £6
- before a policy could be forfeited, notice had to be given to the policyholder specifying the amount of the arrears and where payment could be made and giving him or her at least 14 days in which to clear the arrears
- no transfer of a policy from one office to another could be made without the policyholder's written consent and that within seven days of receiving an application for transfer, the potential transferee had to give notice to the potential transferor.

Degge's health was deteriorating at the time he gave evidence and within two years he was dead. December 1874 was a hectic month. There were four meetings of the Committee and he had travelled with Henry Ridge to Liverpool for a meeting of the delegates of friendly societies. Degge may well have met some former colleagues from Royal Liver and perhaps even some old friends who knew him from his days in his uncle's pub. It was on this trip that Ridge and Degge would have spent their last time together. On the train back to London, did they perhaps talk of all that had happened since their conversation on 2 February 1861? If they complimented each other on a job well done, the praise was thoroughly deserved.

The trip must have been difficult for Degge. It is hard to reconcile what we know of him a decade earlier with the description of his attendance at the office on Christmas Eve 1874 that appeared in the *In Memoriam* booklet produced by the Society:

Of late years, Mr. Joseph Degge became very stout, and he endeavoured to prevent so far as he could, any increase in that

direction, but without avail. He avoided as much as possible
everything that would have a tendency to increase his bulk; he
was very abstemious; nevertheless he continued to increase in
weight and suffered much from any extra exertion.

Any sudden exertion brought on excitement of the
circulation and a rush of blood to the head. It will then be at once
understood that this must have given the deceased Gentleman
some additional anxiety irrespective of his business transactions.
But, with all his carefulness, he was doomed to become a martyr
to his daily increasing corpulence.

On 24th December, 1874, he arrived at the Office early in
the morning as was his wont; but it soon became self-evident to
the Clerks and Officials that he was suffering acutely; he was
seized with a fit and at once conveyed in a cab to his residence at
De Beauvoir Town.[69]

He remained barely conscious at 29 Enfield Road throughout Christmas
Day, sank into a coma and died on Boxing Day, aged only 38. The cause of death
was "sanguineous apoplexy" (cerebral haemorrhage) although the symptoms
displayed in the last years of his life suggest that he was also suffering from cardiac
failure. He was buried at St Patrick's Catholic Cemetery at Langthorne Road,
Leytonstone, where an obelisk of polished red granite from Aberdeenshire, paid
for by staff subscription, was later erected in his memory.

The practice of recording in the minutes only decisions was maintained,
with no exception being made for the death of one of the founders. At a
special meeting on 28 December, Henry Ridge was appointed secretary "in
consequence of the death of Mr Joseph Degge" and at the meeting on 30
December it was resolved "that a letter of condolence be sent to the widow of
the late Mr Joseph Degge". And that was that – the minute book was clearly
not felt to be the proper place for tributes.

During Degge's short life, industrial assurance had developed from
nothing to a huge business. The first collecting societies had been formed in
the 1840s but by the early 1870s perhaps a million people were paying a
penny or two a week to one of them so that they and their families would
have a decent burial.[70]

CHAPTER 3

Expansion

1875–1899

Steady and repeated advances in the accretion of business, coupled with excellent management, have brought the Royal London to the very front of Collecting Friendly Societies. No Committee of Management better deserves the confidence of the members than that of the Royal London for no Committee has a better account of stewardship to render.

Post Magazine, 27 February (1897)[1]

In the course of a third of a century, the premium income of Royal London Friendly Society has multiplied nearly seventy times. That is, the modest income of £6,870 (five years after the inauguration of the Society) had grown to the dimensions of £472,263 for the year 1899. In some years, during the interval, the rate of advancement has been more marked than others, but there has always been progression: there has been no turning back. While other years, however, have been able to boast an increase of from £30,000 to £40,000 each [year] the distinction which attaches to 1899 is that it has augmented the premium income by £62,000 – record figures for the Royal London.

Post Magazine, 3 March (1900)[2]

Although missing the wisdom and companionship of Joseph Degge, Henry Ridge and William Hambridge must have been well satisfied with progress by the mid-1870s. The difficult times were behind them and the Royal London Friendly Society was becoming known and respected. *The Sunday Times* of 31 October 1875 reported that the Society:

> ... *has progressed in a most remarkable manner during its fourteen years' operations, and considering the large amount of new business it transacts, it is evidently gaining day by day the confidence of the public, thereby bidding fair to attain a rank of no mean importance in the commercial world.*

A week later the *Birmingham Daily Gazette* commented on the "tact and foresight of the secretary and managers of the society, which has now attained a healthy and prosperous condition".

Those to whom claims had been paid were expressing their satisfaction. Mrs Jones from Bermondsey wrote to the Secretary on 21 January 1876:

> *Dear Sir,*
> *Will you kindly return my sincere thanks to the Board of Management for the straightforward and liberal manner in which my claim of £30 on the death of my dear Husband, John Jones, which was settled immediately it was applied for; and believe me, I shall always do my utmost in recommending such a good Society, which I have spread to the public.*
> *Yours truly,*
> *Margaret Jones.*

Naomi Lovett, writing from Mile End later in the same month, appreciated the straightforward manner in which the claim on the death of her husband had been paid. She was sure that the way in which Royal London had met the claim would "be appreciated by all provident wives and mothers". "Whenever opportunity affords", she too would "not fail to persuade people to join your valuable Society without delay". It seems that Mrs Lovett could neither read nor write because she made her mark by putting a cross at the foot of the letter. One cannot help wondering who wrote the letter for her. By now, Royal London had agencies in all the principal towns throughout the Kingdom. With fine disregard to customer confidentiality, the Society published in its promotional material all claims paid in London in 1876. The £84 (today: £5,500) paid to Naomi was by far the largest – there was one of £48 (today: £3,200) and two of £30 (today: £2,000), but most were below £10 (today: £675).[3]

Immediately after Degge's death, Ridge was appointed secretary. The rules required the secretary to give daily attendance at the office and the Committee was no doubt concerned that the Society would be in breach of this if there was no secretary in place. In January 1875 the Committee, having now had time to consider the question of a long-term successor, appointed William Hambridge. It was probably always intended that Hambridge would take over from Degge, and the interim appointment of Ridge was to allow Hambridge time to move back to London from Newcastle. Hambridge resigned from the Committee and took up the role that he was to retain until his death. In 1875 the premium income was £33,992 15s 7½d and the reserves £14,163 3s 2d.

It was in the final quarter of the nineteenth century that the practice of the working man (or often his wife, on his behalf) taking out policies to provide for funeral expenses, and having the premiums collected on a weekly basis, became truly embedded. The desire to avoid the pauper's grave remained as strong as ever but there were two other factors that contributed to the success of industrial assurance. Real wages of the labouring population doubled between 1860 and 1914, increasing by as much as 45 per cent between 1880 and 1896, and now there were more families with a few pence over to insure against the ultimate humiliation. Not that this was a time of economic growth – during the depression from the mid-1870s to the mid-1890s industry stagnated while industrialisation in Germany, France and Belgium accelerated, and agriculture continued to suffer irreversible damage from cheap grain imported from the New World at prices with which the British farmer could not compete. Henry Ridge, chairing the 1885 annual general meeting, referred to the depressed trade and the unsettled state of affairs at home and abroad.[4] There was uncertainty in the City where Barings, the oldest merchant bank, failed in 1890 following some unwise lending in South America and had to be rescued by the Bank of England and other London banks under a plan developed by the Governor of the Bank of England and the Chancellor of the Exchequer.[5]

The other contributor to the success of industrial assurance was the urbanisation of the population. Until the middle of the nineteenth century, more people lived in the country than in towns and collecting premiums of a few pence from policyholders dispersed over a wide rural area would not have been cost-effective, even by the standards of industrial assurance. When Queen Victoria came to the throne, less than a third of the population lived in towns with a population of more than a hundred thousand. But the move from country to town in search of employment was such that when she died, 77 per cent of the population was living in the principal towns.[6] Between 1841 and 1901 the population of London increased from 1,949,277 to 4,536,267, of the area that was to become Greater Manchester from 860,413 to 2,357,150 and of Liverpool from 286,487 to 684,947. The collecting societies gained from these demographic trends at the expense of the traditional friendly societies. In 1876, returns were received by 58 friendly societies that had been in existence for more than a hundred years, but only 17 of them had more than 100, and only one had more than 500, members.[7]

In 1876 the 27 collecting societies had over 1,725,000 members (every policyholder was a member), 64 per cent of whom belonged to Royal Liver (682,371), Liverpool Victoria (319,747) and Royal London (109,918).[8] By 1899, there were 47 collecting societies. The total membership had tripled to more than 5,094,000, 88 per cent of whom now belonged to Royal Liver (1,686,949), Liverpool Victoria (1,566,604) and Royal London (1,248,178).[9] The funds of the leading three collecting societies had increased six-fold – from £650,000 in 1876 to more than £4 million by 1899.[10] And yet, the collecting societies represented only a part of industrial assurance. In 1900 the Prudential Assurance Company, a proprietary company with shareholders, had 16,000 agents, 14 million in-force industrial assurance policies and assets of close to £40 million.[11] Half a century earlier, Liverpool Victoria's total annual premium income was some £2,500, earnest discussions were going on in the Lyver Inn about forming a burial society, the Prudential was struggling to sell life assurance to the middle classes, the Degge family was contemplating the Liverpool pub trade for young Joseph, and Henry Ridge and William Hambridge had yet to celebrate their 12th birthdays.

Royal London was an active participator in the great expansion.

Table No. 2

Performance of the Royal London Friendly Society: 1876–1899

	Premium Income £	Investment Income £	Claims £	Expenses £	Expenses to Premiums %
1876	40,180	457	25,591	12,032	29.9[12]
1899 (Today)	472,263 (£39.6m)	21,619 (£1.8m)	198,565 (£16.4m)	210,802 (£17.4m)	44.6

In these 23 years of negative inflation, the Society's premium income increased nearly 12-fold. The continued rise in premium income is particularly impressive – as a relatively new business, a five-fold increase during the 1870s may be put down to a low starting point, but the Society succeeded in doubling its premium income during the 1880s and then nearly trebling it in the 1890s:

1870	£ 15,575
1880	£ 82,108
1890	£189,951
1900	£545,545.

In 1876 fewer than 70,000 policies had been issued. No less than half a million policies were issued last year, the members attending the 1900 annual general meeting were told, "representing a weekly premium of £4,493, or an annual premium of £233,636".[13] Unfortunately the number of policies being forfeited because policyholders stopped paying the premium was still an issue, although the Society had no worse a record than the other collecting societies.[14]

The surplus and reserves also greatly improved during the period, albeit (by modern standards) from a low base. A typical example of its statements about the reserves is contained in the 1879 annual report, which, having referred to the income and expenditure, states:

The cash saved for the year 1879 [the difference between the two] amounted to £10,629 9s 0d, being the largest saving ever effected in any one year during the 18 years of the Society's existence, and when added to the previous balance, brought the total reserve funds of the Society up to £46,323 11s 2d.

Some members may have been reassured by this information, although this annual trading account approach said little about the financial strength of the Society. What was required was an actuarial valuation of the assets, including the reserves and the value of future premiums from current policies, and the liabilities represented by the commitments contained in the current policies. Only when this had been carried out, and the extent of any surplus or deficit determined, could members (or indeed the Committee of Management) make a true assessment of the Society's financial position. The law required such a valuation every five years and a detailed return to be submitted to the Chief Registrar of Friendly Societies.

The Society's valuations, undertaken by F G P Neison, its external actuary, demonstrated an ever-increasing surplus from a mere £3,501 in 1879 to £90,279 in 1899. The Society's surplus compared well with its competitors, and by the early 1890s Royal London had "surplus funds which in relation to actuarial liabilities are of about four times greater proportion than the surplus of the next best [collecting society]".[15] Of the valuation as at December 1899, *Post Magazine* commented that:

... the actuary reports a marked abatement, due to careful

selection of lives, in the rate or mortality experienced; together with a decreasing ration of withdrawals, no doubt, in great measure, attributable to the constantly improving financial status of the Society, and evidencing its steady growth in the confidence and estimation of the public, a confidence amply justified by the judicious conduct of its affairs.[16]

The reserves and investment income increased during the same period from £46,324 to £730,417. In 1875, when Hambridge was appointed secretary, most of the £21,000 reserves were in the Post Office Savings Bank. The investment income was minimal. The balance sheet as at 31 December 1898 (the last one that he would have signed-off) showed secured loans of £448,258 made by the Society to public bodies and local authorities at good rates of interest; £86,181 invested in freehold ground rents, property and mortgages; and £21,832 on deposit with the National Debt Commissioners. In 1898 the income from these investments exceeded £18,500.

The perception of collecting societies was gradually improving. Edward Lyulph Stanley, the assistant commissioner who had re-cast the Society's income and expenditure account for the benefit of the Royal Commission in 1874, had not been one of their admirers. So far as he was concerned, although "working under the Friendly Societies' Act, [they] are really insurances offices, started without any capital and under the control of no shareholders, and conducted principally for the benefit of the office-holders, and only incidentally for that of the assured".[17] Fifteen years later, it was acknowledged at least by some that improvements had been achieved. In his evidence in 1889 to a Treasury committee, William Sutton, the actuary to the Registry of Friendly Societies, disagreed with the opinion of the chief registrar that "ordinary friendly societies are maintained for the good of the members, and collecting societies for the good of the officials". Sutton felt that there were "collecting societies and collecting societies. As to the big collecting societies, I do not think it is at all fair to say that they exist for the benefit of the officials any more than you would if you were speaking of a well organised and well conducted life office. With regard to the smaller fry, it is no doubt true, speaking generally, that in their early life they certainly do exist for the benefit of the officials".[18]

The committee was anxious in its report to endorse the evidence supportive of the collecting societies:

Before proceeding to suggest amendments of the law, your Committee desire to express their opinion of the general value of the system of assurance by companies and societies dependent on collecting.

It must be regarded as a means, for which at present there is no effective substitute, of inducing very large numbers of the working classes to make some provision for burial or for benefit to survivors at death, who would otherwise make none; and so far these societies and companies may be regarded, when well-managed, as commendable institutions, always subject to the consideration that, owing to the commission charged by collectors (from 20 to 25 per cent) added to the ordinary cost of management, it often happens that nearly half the premium income never goes to the benefit fund.[19]

The future would have been so much easier for the offices if only they had found it in themselves to do more to reduce their expenses. Scrutiny of industrial assurance was never far away. Select Committees of the House of Commons and the House of Lords appointed in 1890 and 1891 reviewed the assurance of children and the operation of certain aspects of the 1875 Act. William Hambridge gave evidence. The committees had been asked to consider the £10 and £6 limitations in the 1875 Act but after a careful review decided to leave them unchanged.[20]

This was also the period when the collecting societies began to experience situations that would be repeated with greater severity during the twentieth century – an increase in the death rate, or inability to pay premiums, for local or specific reasons. The influenza epidemic in the early 1890s produced a significant increase in claims. Then there were the difficulties experienced by members in maintaining their premiums in areas of high unemployment. The policy of the Society's Committee of Management, explained at the 1894 annual general meeting, was to be as sympathetic as they could:

As a result of the disputes in the coal trade, many of the members had been out of work, and the reports which had been received of distress in various parts of the country had given the Committee an experience which they hoped might never be repeated. It was very gratifying that the rules permitted them to deal with policy-holders in such a manner that, where there was dire necessity, the insurances might be maintained though the payment of premiums was suspended. And in the great industrial districts, there were today many thousands of books which showed that the Society did all it could to prevent its members from losing any of the rights of membership.[21]

The products offered by the Society during this period were few and straightforward. The 1887 prospectus, for example, was a simple four-page document. The first page stressed the Society's financial strength ("Amount of Cash Saved (Reserve Funds): £167,000") and listed the officers, bankers, actuary, solicitors and auditors. The middle two pages provided potential members with the details of the three products that the Society had on offer. The description of a product always required a table and, within the offices, products came to be known as 'tables'. So the Society's Table 1 was a simple life policy, the amount payable on death depending upon the weekly premium and age of the policyholder. Anybody between the age of 1 day and 79 years could be insured. A note indicated that where the assured was a child, half benefit would be payable after 13 weeks but for adults half benefits were payable where death occurred between 6 and 12 months. By inference, no benefit was payable if death took place earlier than this.

Table 2 was an endowment policy and showed "the Weekly Premiums to secure the undermentioned sums at death, or on attaining the respective ages of 50, 55 or 60 years". This was an endowment policy in the modern meaning of the term.[22] Traditionally the name had been applied to policies where the full benefit was payable only on attaining the age in question, with the premiums paid (or a specified proportion of them) being returned if death occurred first. These came to be called 'pure endowment policies'. The Royal London's endowment policy referred to in the original set of rules, the sale of which had soon been suspended, had been a pure endowment. There followed in the prospectus an unnumbered table headed *Special Middle Class Table*. This showed the weekly premium that would be required "to secure the sum of £100 at Death" (today: £8,300). At the age of 20, 11d a week would provide this benefit but at 40, 1s 7d was required (today: £3.80, £6.60). Set out on the back page of the prospectus were some of the "Leading Features" – these included the fact that no medical examination was required unless the sum assured exceeded £20; collectors called at the member's house to collect the premiums; members were "allowed to run 13 weeks in arrears and to receive 14 days' notice before the policy could be forfeited for non-payment"; and forfeited policies could be revived within 12 months "upon satisfactory proof of health, and the payment of the whole of the arrears".

This was the simple product portfolio on which the huge expansion of Royal London was based, and by the end of the nineteenth century, the prospectus was only slightly more complicated. In the light of the success being achieved, it is hardly surprising that the Committee had made no radical changes. Table 1 was now split into two parts – the Infantile Section (age last birthday 0 to 9) and the Adult Section although both the latter and Table 2 were unchanged. Table 3 introduced a life policy with what was, for Royal London, a novel concept – the premiums were to be paid every fourth week rather than weekly.[23] There were no Tables 4 or 7 – policies might have been introduced and quickly withdrawn or blanks were left to accommodate new policies. Table 5 was a pure endowment policy for people under 25 years of age with payment only being made on the expiry of the term. If death occurred first, three-quarters of the premiums were returned under Table 5, and all the premiums were returned under Table 5a, providing the policy had been in force for six months. Table 6 provided another important introduction – a joint life policy with payment being made on the first death. So where two 20-year-olds took out a policy for 2d a week (today: 70p), the survivor would receive £10 9s 0d (today: £877). Table 8 was a life policy that provided £100 at death and Table 9 a modern-style endowment policy to secure £100 "the sum of £100 in the event of Death, or at the end of the fixed Term of Years". Both had surrender values after five years of at least 25 per cent of the premiums paid.

Within the Royal London archives are some account books that provide an insight into the role of the agents who promoted these products and then collected the premiums. In 1899 the Society's office in Mexborough, Yorkshire, was in Wath Road, the main road that runs through the town and heads westwards towards Wombwell and Barnsley. This was a mining area, with Doncaster to the east and Rotherham and Sheffield (where there were five Royal London district offices) to the south-west. The number of agents attached to a district office depended upon the amount of business to be serviced within an accessible radius. Offices were under the control of a superintendent who, in larger offices, would have an assistant and there was generally a clerk to deal with the administration. Once a week, every agent came into the office to hand over all the cash that he had collected. He had to account for every penny and provide the superintendent with a reconciliation with his collecting book. He would also hand in completed proposal forms for new policies, the documents relating to any claims that he had received, and report on policies that were in arrears. The exact amount of the arrears was required if a notice before forfeiture was to be served. Every week, the superintendent, assisted by the clerk, would transfer the figures for each agent into the district account book and send an account and the cash balance to the chief office. The process was repeated week by week, office by office.

The week ending 2 December 1899 was a typical week for the eight agents attached to the Mexborough office. They and their superintendent collected £45 19s 7½d (today: £3,857), almost half of which was contributed by the two most successful agents. Nearly all the premiums related to basic Table 1 policies. The agents were due £11 0s 0½d commission on their collections and £1 10s 0d procurement fees for selling new policies. The superintendent received £2 10s by way of salary although he or she[24] may have had to pay the wages of the clerk out of this, and claims of £8 17s were paid to the families of policyholders who had died. There had been some business travelling during the week (rail fares of 1s 7d were claimed) and pen nibs, ink and postage stamps had been bought (1s 8½d). All these deductions had to be made from the sum collected and this meant that only £21 19s 3½d (today: £1,840) was left to be remitted to the chief office.[25] There were some weeks when an office made a trading loss – in the last week of 1899, for example, there was a shortfall of nearly £9 at Mexborough as a result of claims of £44 having to be paid during the week. Where this occurred, the account was sent off in the usual way and a couple of days later the superintendent received reimbursement from chief office. The requirement for weekly accounting was absolute – there could be no setting off one week's loss against next week's profit.

The increasing status of the Society was reflected by the attention that it was beginning to receive in the trade press. A brief report of the 1875 annual general meeting received less than 7 cms of column space in *Post Magazine* and twice referred to the secretary as 'Mr Hembridge'.[26] By the mid-1880s the annual report and accounts were appearing in full, together with a transcript of the meeting and, on a different page, an editorial comment on the performance of the Society during the preceding year.

The editor was generally supportive of the Royal London executive, although he did not hold back when he felt that criticism was due. In 1885, for example, he suggested that the "attention of the Committee of Management should be given to the question of expenditure, with the view of effecting any economy that is possible".[27] In 1886 he pointed out that in spite of "a slight improvement last year, the proportion of the funds to premium receipts still remains small and we should be glad to see a further increase in this direction" and commented that the accounts did "not speak very favourably" on "the all-important question of expenditure".[28] When Hambridge and Ridge complained that the editor had misunderstood the accounts, a somewhat disingenuous retraction was printed, in which the magazine acknowledged:

> ... the error to which we gave currency in our last issue [but did] not hesitate to lay the blame... upon the executive of the Royal London whose improper combination of items [in the accounts] that should be kept separate was the real cause.[29]

By 1887 a truce seemed to have been called on expenses, the editor finding "reason to be satisfied with the results for 1886", reminding his readers that industrial assurance inevitably entails heavy expenses and concluding that "we see nothing but favourable features in the accounts for 1886".[30]

In 1889 the editor was completely won over:

> Simultaneously with the great development of its business, the rate of expenditure of the Royal London Friendly Society steadily

diminishes. These two circumstances, taken together, point to good management and satisfactory progress. The Royal London Friendly Society is now one of the leading Industrial Offices of the Kingdom.[31]

In 1890 all criticisms of the accounts had been forgotten – they were "rendered in a form which is at once comprehensive and understandable by the members" at a time when the "accounts of some societies are presented in such a form that nobody but accountants can understand them". The editor concluded that the "managers appear to be actuated by high and honourable motives in the conduct of the Society's affairs. They continue to manifest the same caution and prudence which have characterised their past conduct of the Society's business and we have no reason to doubt the continued prosperity of the Royal London Friendly Society under its existing regime".[32]

The positive view was maintained through the 1890s. There was some mild criticism of the presentation in 1893[33] when the editor would have preferred the account to describe an item as "Funds in Hand" rather than "Balance of Income over Expenditure" but, this detail apart, the praise was generous. "Integrity of purpose and a faithful regard for the general good of the members" continued to be the characteristics of the managers of Royal London in 1894[34] while by 1897 "no committee of management better deserves the confidence of members than that of Royal London".[35]

The Society's expansion was such that the chief office had to move twice during the period to accommodate the increasing staff needed to support and manage the business: 5 Aldermanbury Postern into which the Society had so proudly moved in 1866 proved to be too small within ten years and in October 1876 a move was made to 28 Finsbury Place, later renamed 70 Finsbury Pavement. It was, according to the Society's promotional material: "six doors from the terminus of the Metropolitan Tramway Co., and within three minutes' walk from Broad Street and Moorgate Street Railway stations". Now it is the site of a Marks & Spencer store. In another decade Finsbury Pavement had become inadequate and the chief office relocated early in 1886 to 108 Paul Street, on which the Society took a lease from the Church Commissioners for 32½ years from 24 June 1885 at an annual rent of £100 (today £7,740) with no rent review. The numbering was to change in 1897, when the building became 6 Paul Street. Paul Street runs from just north of Finsbury Square towards Old Street and Shoreditch. Beside the new office, on the east side of the junction of Paul Street and Worship Street, was a Home and Colonial store. Six Paul Street has not survived but the building next door (at the time of writing, the former store is a bar and restaurant with offices on the upper floors) remains, and illustrations suggest that it resembles the Society's office.

The importance of Royal London was such that a full description of the new office appeared in *Post Magazine*:

The frontage of the building is 75 feet, and the elevation of a plain and solid character of the utmost utility. The ground floor is fitted up as a public or general office and is divided by a glass screen, so that the portion nearest the street is available for members who call to pay premiums or receive claims, and for the superintendents, collectors and canvassers who have business to transact at the Office, while the rear is occupied by a large staff of clerks busy with such routine work as writing policies, checking collectors' accounts and books, sending notices to members in arrears, registering removals and claims. A numerous staff is also permanently engaged in the valuation department where there is kept a record of the admission, deaths, and secession of members, the rates of mortality, and the whole experience of the Society.

The first floor contains board room, also offices for the use of secretary, treasurer, trustees, accountants, auditors, corresponding clerks, policy examiners and others. These are furnished in a manner which is at once useful, durable and inexpensive. In the board room a quorum of the Committee meet every day, whilst full meetings are held every Tuesday and Thursday, the members of the Committee being engaged exclusively in the work and interests of the Society. In the basement there is a large fire-proof room where the deeds and other muniments of title belonging to the Society are safely deposited. In another part are two of Perkin's hot water apparatus which supply the necessary warmth throughout the building. The stock of stationery also occupies a very great proportion of this floor, and gives some idea of the great detail of work necessary to conduct an Industrial insurance office.

The sanitary arrangements for ensuring the health and comfort of the large staff of clerks employed in the office have not been overlooked and are all that are necessary.[36]

Nothing is said about how the building was lit. The clerks in the earlier offices would probably have had to rely upon candles and oil – probably paraffin – lamps. Although most streets in London were lit by gas, there had been a reluctance to use it for interior lighting, and this only changed when gas fittings were introduced into the new Houses of Parliament in 1859. The Paul Street office was probably built after this and a photograph suggests gas lighting. A clerk recalled being shown on his first morning "into a glass roofed room about 30 feet square".[37] The photograph is of this room – no doubt the architect had been keen that the occupiers of the building would benefit as much as possible from natural light. It shows rows of clerks sitting at long, sloping desks and, in the background, a flight of stairs leading upwards, suggesting that this may have been the office at the rear of the ground floor that, presumably, formed an extension at the back of the building, rather than the first floor office.

As the report indicates, the role of the Committee of Management was to do just that – to manage the business as a committee. There was little or no delegation and decisions that would be made today by line managers or within the customer services were all referred to the Committee. The description of the Paul Street office and the minute books suggest that the Committee was in almost constant session. The report indicates two levels of meetings – full meetings on Tuesdays and Thursdays and quorum meetings on every other day of the week. The rules provided that any three members of the Committee formed a quorum.[38] The 1887 minute book does not quite confirm this – the Tuesday and Thursday meetings are recorded but any intervening ones are not. This, however, may have been due to an approach to minuting rather than the lack of the meetings – perhaps the 'quorum meetings' were not regarded as meetings of the Committee. By the early 1890s, however, the approach envisaged in the report was in place. For example, in the nine weeks beginning on Monday 2 May 1892, which seems to have been a typical period, the Committee met on no less than 31 occasions. Two of the directors were district managers, located away from London – William Bowrey in Manchester and John Price in Sheffield. They travelled south to attend meetings at the beginning of each month – a week in London often enabled them to attend four meetings – and usually more frequently.

The punishing routine of meetings must have meant that the directors came unprepared to each matter. There cannot have been time between meetings to circulate, let alone read, papers and the time for informal discussions outside the meetings must have been severely limited. Sometimes important topics were deferred from meeting-to-meeting because there was no time to consider them. The minutes contain no references to budgets or business plans, and the Committee seems to have been provided with little management information, over and above the weekly 'Secretary's Statement of Income and Expenditure'.

It is difficult to believe, however, that the Society could have achieved the success that it did without the directors thinking carefully about the strategy and performance of the business. They must have had discussions about the vital issues of the day, and the actions that had to be taken to address them, but either these did not take place at the meetings of the Committee, or they were not minuted. The record suffers from the absence of any of the documents referred to in the minutes, and the prevailing view that minutes were only for recording decisions and not for setting-out the discussions that preceded them. Strategic decisions were certainly made. In 1893, for example, when two-thirds of the Society's premium income was coming from outside Greater London,[39] a programme designed to acquire more business in London was put in place. By the end of 1893 six new London offices had been opened and more followed in 1894. At the 1895 annual general meeting the Committee was pleased to report that the increase of business in London in 1894 was greater than the increase made throughout the Society in 1893.[40]

The lack of a chairman appears strange to modern eyes. It may have been the unfortunate precedent of Henry Green, the first chairman who resigned owing the Society money, which prompted subsequent Committees to decline to make a permanent appointment. Instead, the directors elected one of their number to chair meetings for the following month or quarter. This, and the fact that the secretary was not a member of the Committee, served to reiterate the collective responsibility of the Committee, and a reluctance to confer the mantle of leadership on individuals. Human resource issues occupied a large part of most meetings. Initially all appointments and promotions and the remuneration that these would attract were made by the Committee. There was a hint of 'Scrooge and Marley' in December 1888 when a petition from the clerks at the chief office asking for a holiday on Christmas Eve was considered – it was granted except the front counter had to be kept open for the payment of claims. There was still a lack of middle management and the secretary and directors carried out the investigative work themselves when concerns reached them about the workings of a district. They set themselves punishing schedules. For example, the minutes of the meeting of 17 July 1888 considered reports from two directors and the secretary of visits that they had made in the preceding two weeks to the Manchester office and the Oldham, St Helens, Wigan, Bath, Bristol, Cardiff, Pontypridd, Merthyr Tydfil, Tredegar and Pontypool districts. There then followed six resolutions implementing the recommendations made in the reports that included accepting the resignations of two of the superintendents. In 1889 there are early signs of management information when *Synopsis of the Workings* for the year 1888 in various districts were discussed. The secretary was instructed to see the superintendents of three of these districts "in reference to their non-progress".

There was little delegation on facilities issues – approval of the Committee was given in October 1885 for the purchase of an umbrella stand for the Leeds office and three months later for the purchase of a gas stove at Oldham. Ridge and Hambridge may have founded the Society but this gave them no special status – matters concerning their offices still had to be referred to the Committee, that decided in July 1886 that Ridge could have a new desk, providing it did not cost more than £14, and that both he and Hambridge could have new revolving chairs.

Women rarely featured in the Committee's discussions, but there were occasional references to "Mrs Davies". She was, for example, allowed "a signboard duly written and fixed" on 8 October 1886. William Davies had been the secretary of the Victoria Legal Provident Association on the acquisition of which in 1868 he had been appointed a director of Royal London. He was not, however, asked to assume responsibility for the Birmingham area where the Victoria Legal had been based but was appointed to manage the busy Stepney District and he and his family moved to London. His wife Mary Ann had been a part-time agent of the Liverpool Victoria but gave that up to help her husband with the Victoria. At the time of the Royal Commission into friendly societies, and the debates in Parliament, husband and wife worked, wrote and spoke in defence of the principles of industrial assurance.[41] Mr Davies was in poor health and his wife assisted him with his work at Stepney. When he died in 1874 she replaced him as superintendent. She was an energetic lady with a strong character who quickly won the respect of her staff. In October 1875 a document was prepared and signed by her team that included both a future secretary and future joint managing director of the Society. It read:

> *To Mrs Davies, Manager of the Stepney District of the Royal London Friendly Society.*
>
> *Dear Madam,*
> *We, the undersigned, Agents, Collectors, and Canvassers of the above district, under your superintendence, beg to offer you a small tribute, as a mark of esteem and respect with which you are held by us; at the same time hopeing [sic] that the business which has been transacted in this District during the past year has met with your approval, and that you may receive that praise which we all consider is due to you. Also, that it may act as a stimulant for those that may be employed by you hereafter with a still greater success than that which we have experienced. In conclusion, we hope you may be long spared, with God's blessing, to carry out your duties with health, happiness and prosperity.*

It is not clear what prompted this noble document, nor is the small tribute identifiable, although perhaps the letter itself was the tribute. Mary Davies was to be one of the Society's most effective superintendents. She was held in high esteem by both her staff and the directors. She was ahead of her time in motivating staff. In May 1882 she wrote to the Committee, explained that she was entertaining her team of collectors to dinner at Southend-on-Sea and invited the directors "to assist her in her endeavours to increase the popularity of the Society". The Committee resolved that as many as possible would attend and that second-class fares to Southend would be allowed. The next year she wrote again, this time about two collectors "who had gained experience under her employ [and] were desirous of being promoted". Her judgment was respected and both were promoted to supervisory roles in other districts.

Agents continued to be dismissed and sometimes prosecuted for failing to account to the Society or for writing business that did not exist. Thomas Storer's defence in May 1888 was that one dark night in Spitalfields he had been set upon and robbed of the money due to the Society. The learned stipendiary magistrate considered it an improbable story, fined him £5 and ordered him to pay back the money or suffer a month's imprisonment.[42] At the Old Bailey in May 1895 Thomas Hayes received a sentence of nine months' hard labour from Sir Forrest[43] Fulton, the Common Sergeant, for unlawfully obtaining 15s commission from the Royal London Friendly Society on proposals that were fictitious.[44] The role of the agent was unclear in the case of John Fitzsimmonds of Whitehaven who completed five Royal London proposal forms in the names of people who did not exist. He paid the premiums for a while and then forged evidence of the deaths. Three claims were paid before the fraud was discovered. When the case came on at the Cumberland Assizes in October 1884 Fitzsimmonds pleaded guilty and was sentenced to five years' penal servitude.[45] He was unlucky with his judge – Mr Justice Day's sentences were severe even by Victorian standards. It was said of him that when "administering the criminal law, especially on circuit, he showed a sternness and upheld a standard of conduct that belonged to another age".[46]

There were times when the misconduct was nearer home. In 1887 "the discharge of Mrs Burnham (cleaner) and Mr Gillett (porter) for riotous conduct in the Chief Office" was confirmed, and at the meeting of the Committee on 10 September 1891:

> J. Huggins, later porter, was brought before the Board when he confessed to having stolen £20 in Bank Notes from Mr Hunter's desk in No 4 Room, the property of the Society. When it was resolved to prosecute him for the same he was taken to Worship Street police station and sentenced to six weeks' imprisonment with hard labour.

The sentence would have been imposed at the Worship Street Police Court rather than the station. Police Courts were the ultimate tribunals of summary jurisdiction – a magistrate who sat at Worship Street a few years later was proud of dealing with 128 cases in less than a morning.[47] Hambridge, in his capacity as secretary, was summonsed for failing to allow a member to inspect the Society's books. The hearing was brief, Hambridge's counsel pointing out that the section of the Act that gave members the right of inspection was not yet in force. The summons was dismissed with costs of £2 2s being awarded to the defendant.[48]

The fear of the pauper's funeral remained. A resident of the East End looking back on his childhood in the 1890s remembered that the premiums for funeral policies on all the children came second only to the rent:

> That was the first and last duty of everyone, to pay the rent 'cos you knew how damned hard it was to find another room. So the rent came first. What came next was insurance, a penny a week for each of us. For funerals. One thing they dreaded was that the parish would take them. So they paid. Every child was paid for. Eventually there were four of us so it was fourpence a week. The funeral of my little brother – the one I never saw – cost thirty shillings. Thirty shillings. Thirty shillings was like a million pounds to them.[49]

Insuring the lives of the children continued to be a significant part of the business of collecting societies. As at 31 December 1889, more than 220,000 of the Society's policies were on the lives of children under the age of ten – 124,678 insured the lives of children under five years and 102,086 were on children aged between five and ten. The average sums assured were £3 1s 7d and £4 16s 8d respectively with premiums ranging between a halfpenny to two pence per child per week. Mortality was far worse for the younger children – during 1889, 4,997 claims were paid in relation to children under five and 408 claims paid for children between five and ten.[50] The terms of the Society's child policies had been varied towards the end of the period with the separate 'Infantile Section' being included in the prospectus. This may well have been added to focus minds on the legislation that limited the amount for which the life of a child could be assured to £6 for a child under five years and £10 for one between five and ten, but it also recognised the increasing number of children being assured by the Society at a time of high infant mortality. The new table introduced a sliding scale of benefits, depending upon when the death of the child occurred. Parents paying a penny a week would receive nothing if their five-year-old child died within 13 weeks and would only receive the full benefit of £10 10s if the child survived for more than four years.

Early in 1890 Henry Ridge suffered a stroke at a meeting of the Committee at 108 Paul Street and died later in the day. The *In Memoriam* booklet describes the scene in the language of the day:

> In the vigour of health and strength our friend Mr Henry Ridge was suddenly and unexpectedly summoned to pay the debt of

nature, on the 9th January, 1890. While sitting at the Board room table assisting to transact the ordinary business of the Society he was seized with a fit, two medical men were soon in attendance but their skill was unavailing and without recovering consciousness he died within 3 hours of the first attack. The feelings of his colleagues may be more easily imagined than described. His family who had been summoned arrived just too late. In this situation neither the Committee nor friends were capable of affording much solace to the disconsolate widow.

The minutes of the meeting read:

The Clerks' Salaries in Chief Office were being discussed when Mr Henry Ridge was seized with an attack of apoplexy to which he succumbed in a short time when the meeting was adjourned to the next day.[51]

Once again, it was business as usual, the death of the founder warranting a reference only to explain why it was necessary to appoint a temporary treasurer. Ridge was only 51. The comment about the family arriving too late may not be entirely accurate because Henry's eldest son, Charles, was present at his father's death. He had been a clerk at the chief office since 1878 and would probably have been summoned to the boardroom when his father was taken ill. All three founders died in harness but Ridge's death caused the greatest shock. Degge, although much younger, had not been a well man for some time and Hambridge was to suffer years of ill health. Ridge, however, hardly seems to have had a day's illness.

The lack of a permanent chairman meant that the task of chairing the annual general meeting was shared by the members of the Committee. Here Ridge was greatly missed. He had frequently been in the chair and the members seem to have shown him the respect due to one of the founders of the Society. There were, however, some contentious meetings after his death. In 1894 word must have reached the directors that trouble could be expected because the services of a sergeant and eight constables were retained for the purposes of retaining order at the meeting. Less trouble must have been expected in 1896 when only four constables were required to support the sergeant. Twice, the directors' nomination to fill a vacancy on the Committee was voted down and an alternative proposed by members was elected – and on both occasions the unfortunate Thomas Fyans, the superintendent from Wigan, was the unlucky nominee, the meetings preferring a London man. It seemed that Fyans was unpopular in Lancashire too, although this may only have been amongst the local agents who did not welcome his attempts to introduce efficiencies.[52]

The 1891 meeting was closed in a state of disorder. A former employee of the Society made various statements when the report and accounts were being discussed but received little support and the resolution was passed. That was the only item on the agenda but a gentleman who identified himself as an agent of the Pearl then tried to propose a resolution directing the Committee to make certain changes to collectors' remuneration. The intervention was well handled by William Bowrey in the chair. He pointed out that the rules of the Society gave the Committee sole control of collectors' remuneration, that the Committee was always ready to hear from its collectors upon this or any other matter at a proper time and place but he could not permit a discussion at the general meeting. The gentleman from the Pearl and his colleagues would not give up and when they refused to come to order, the chairman declared the meeting closed and left the platform with his colleagues. The view was that the meeting had been packed by representatives of the National Union of Life Assurance Agents. A year later, Royal London's rules were changed to prevent visiting collectors from attending general meetings and in due course this was reflected in legislation.

Ridge was also missed in dealing with Joseph Barnes Degge, the founder's uncle, one of the early agents and a member of the Committee since 1863. He had chaired many a meeting and played an active part in establishing the Society. One of his daughters was married to Charles, Henry Ridge's son. Now ill-health was making his attendance at chief office, at best, spasmodic. Ridge, one senses, would have had a gentle word with him and persuaded him, perhaps over time, to leave with honour. Instead the Committee purported to dismiss Degge in April 1893 but, as it was far from certain that they had power to do so, they can hardly have been surprised to hear a few days later from his solicitors.

The matter was to feature at the next three annual general meetings. In 1893 Degge was voted a pension of £5 a week, Frederick de la Bertauche, his longstanding colleague making an impassioned speech about the contribution in those early years of the Committee members who were also collectors. Degge's chronic rheumatism was said to have been caused by a soaking he suffered while out collecting. After the meeting Degge declined to accept the pension, presumably on the basis that he was not prepared to concede that he had been properly dismissed. It was then suggested that, in any case, the resolution was invalid because the payment of a pension was not covered by the rules of the Society. The pension was revoked and at the 1894 meeting a new rule was inserted that empowered the Committee to pay a weekly amount not exceeding two-thirds of his weekly salary as pension to any salaried officer on him becoming incapacitated after continuous service of 25 years. Somebody then suggested that, as drafted, the rule was not retrospective and did not cover a pension already granted. Leading counsel agreed with the criticism and so it was not until the 1895 meeting that the wording could be adjusted. In December 1895 the Committee finally agreed to pay a gratuity of £100 and a pension of £2 2s per week, back-dated. Degge was not happy with this but apparently accepted it. He died in November 1898. By now, the directors seemed to have realised that almost daily meetings were not the most efficient way to run a business and the Committee was meeting only once or twice a week. In May and June 1897, for example, there were 12 meetings.

Mary Davies died in 1897. Her funeral, the *Assurance Agents Chronicle* of 30 October 1897 reported, was attended in addition to members of the family:

> ... *by the directors, secretary and treasurer of the Society which she had so long and faithfully served. There were also present from the chief office the heads of various departments and the whole staff of the Stepney (H) District, together with many other Royal London servants (some of whom had travelled long distances), and not a few representatives of other kindred societies and private friends.*

This was at a time when there were few women in business and the "upper levels of nursing and running hotels seemed... the nearest most women could get to a professional career".[53] Mary Davies would not have been able to vote, would have had difficulty in finding a woman doctor and would not have been able to consult a woman solicitor.[54] Her daughter married William Crabtree Martin, who worked for Royal London for 42 years and was a director from 1909 to 1920. Their son, Roly Martin, was a director from 1963 until his death in 1967.

In July 1898 a young man, not yet 15, left Alleyn's School in Dulwich[55] at the end of the summer term and joined the Society as a clerk in the Agency Department at the chief office. Bertram Fitzgerald Simpson made an immediate impression – his first appraisal read: "In Dept. 3 mths, work and conduct excellent; will become acquisition; salary small for duties performed; would recommend substantial Increase. Typist". His performance was maintained after moving into Investment and Audit: "The transfer of this clerk into the department has proved an acquisition and his undoubted ability has enabled me to place him in a position of trust and importance". Here was somebody with great potential. Now in New Business, he was regarded in the reports for 1901 as an excellent clerk and first-rate correspondent. By the end of 1902, however, he had clearly decided to move on – although he remained "a most capable clerk" his manager was not prepared to recommend any special treatment as he was "not likely to remain in the Office". Simpson was destined for the Church – he left the Society to take up a theological scholarship at Durham University but was to retain contact with Royal London and reappears from time to time in the story of the Society.

Soon after Ridge's death, Hambridge's health began to deteriorate. The annual general meeting is the big day of the year for the secretary of any organisation – Hambridge missed the 1891, 1894 and 1896 meetings through ill health. In 1891[56] he had influenza and in 1894 was "suffering from nervous debility and required rest and change of air at a seaside place".[57] An assistant secretary was appointed in 1895. This was no senior clerk there to help Hambridge with the paper-work, but William Bowrey, a member of the Committee who had joined the Society in 1873 as an agent and had been district manager at Newcastle and then Manchester. Later in the year, Bowrey had to be recalled from his summer holiday because of the severe illness of the secretary. There were references to "congestion of the kidneys", "bronchitis" and "serious illness", and for periods Hambridge was unable to perform his duties. He was present at the 1899 annual general meeting on 28 February but died aged 60 after a "short and painful illness"[58] on 10 April 1899 at his home, Bridge House, Forty Hill, Enfield. It was said that he had often expressed a desire to die in harness.[59] The cause of death was cerebral apoplexy (a stroke), *Post Magazine* reporting that he had been failing in health for some time past although death occurred somewhat suddenly".[60] Hambridge's poor health in the years before his death suggests that he may have been suffering from an underlying illness although no secondary cause was shown on the death certificate.

The precedent set on the death of Degge was followed and memorial funds for Ridge and later for Hambridge were opened to which staff were invited to contribute. They must have felt under considerable pressure to do so, because the practice was to publish in an *In Memoriam* booklet the amount donated against each subscriber's name. Handsome monuments of red granite from Aberdeenshire were erected at Abney Park, Stoke Newington, and New Southgate cemeteries.

At the time of Hambridge's death, the impact of war was being seen for the first time. In 1899 a note was sent out from the chief office indicating that favorable consideration would be given for an extension of time to pay premiums and arrears where the collector could vouch for the fact that the policyholder had "rejoined the Colours". Chairing the 1900 annual general meeting, Edward Smith reported that:

The lamentable war in South Africa... had caused not a few claims, but it had been a pleasure (perhaps a painful pleasure) to our representatives to be able to pay to the widow or other relatives immediately upon proof from the War Office, the full sum assured, and thus help to mitigate the suffering and appease

the grief of the bereaved. At Glencoe, Dundee, Belmont Graspan,
Elands Laagte, Moder River, Tugela River, Spion Kop and on
to our last engagement there had fallen fighting for Queen and
country members of the Society and the Board had taken every
means to secure to those left behind due and prompt recognition.[61]

Ridge's death and Hambridge's failing health had provided openings
during the 1890s for the next generation of directors who were to lead the
Society into the twentieth century – ambitious men like Edward Smith, John
Price and Horace Duffell. All were former agents who had been effective
superintendents – Price in Sheffield and Duffell in Woolwich. Smith, who had
joined as an agent in Finsbury in 1877, apparently taking over his father's
collecting book, and was later the superintendent there, seemed to relish the
additional responsibilities and challenges that came with membership of the
Committee. Shrewd observers may have identified him as a potential leader
who, in time, would be uncomfortable with the constraints inherent in the
Society's approach of management by a group of equals.

CHAPTER 4

The Founders

[Joseph Degge] *did not, however, relinquish his post of Manager* [of Royal Liver's London office] *with the intention of secluding himself from the world, on the contrary he was gifted with the qualification of looking some distance in advance, and he believed – and with good truth – that he could see his way clear to render himself still more active than he had hitherto been, and right well did he prove by his subsequent actions, how correct he was in his judgment... He had seen sufficient of the world to feel satisfied that the working population of the Country would be prudent if they were only shown the way and it was with that conviction predominant in his mind that he did in conjunction with the present Secretary and Mr Henry Ridge, establish the Royal London Friendly Society.*

In Memoriam booklet for Joseph Degge (1875)

It was one of his striking characteristics that [Henry Ridge] *mastered every detail of the matter under his consideration. As he filled the dual position of treasurer and director, the demands upon his energies were both great and constant. Almost a slave to method and order, his counsels in the management of the business of the Royal London were of great value to his co-directors.*

Post Magazine (18 January 1880)[1]

Mr W H Hambridge... was one of the Founders of the Society, and for the first 14 years of its existence acted as a member of the Board of Management, and for the last 24 years discharged the duties of Secretary in a manner which has deservedly won the highest esteem and respect of all with whom he has come into contact.

Committee of Management (12 April 1899)

What sort of men were Joseph Degge, Henry Ridge and William Hambridge? What were their strengths and weaknesses? What role did each of them play in the early years of Royal London? Not surprisingly, a century and a half later, it is impossible to answer these questions with certainty. No personal papers have survived and indeed most of their communications with each other and their colleagues would have been spoken rather than written, in view of the time spent in each other's company at the innumerable meetings of the Committee of Management. It was the practice at the time to record only decisions, and the lack of any report of the discussions means that the minutes tell us little about the personalities and attitudes of those attending. Nevertheless, material accessible today enables tentative replies to be suggested to at least some of these questions.

At the beginning, their attitude to their own remuneration must have been vital. They clearly accepted that the considerable efforts required of the founders in the early days of any business would not be well rewarded. They recognised too that they might have to seek help from within the family and were apparently successful in doing so. Charles Ridge, Henry's son, wrote of the sacrifices made by his parents and the financial help given by various members of the Degge family, although the records say nothing about the extent of that help.[2] Contribute they may have done, but it is difficult to believe that any of the Degge family would have been able to do very much for the Royal London Friendly Society if it had experienced any serious cash-flow problems.[3] Charles made no reference to assistance from the Ridge family, apart from the sacrifices made by his parents. The financial state of Henry Ridge's parents is far from clear from the scraps of information that are available today although these suggest that they would have been unable to provide short term finance for the business that their son had founded.[4]

There can be no doubt of the collective competence of Degge, Ridge and Hambridge – the Society's progress is evidence of that. William Hambridge was the longest surviving founder. He died on 10 April 1899, the 38th anniversary of the date on which the Registrar of Friendly Societies certified that the Royal London Friendly Society was duly established. By then it had not only survived the initial period, when funds were short and meeting claims was a challenge, but was on the way to catching up Royal Liver and Liverpool Victoria, at least in terms of annual premium income. The Royal London of 1899 was a thriving, well-respected organisation with, by modern standards, an income of £41.6 million and assets of £61.3 million. It is true that the cost of running the business was high, and that many members stopped paying the premiums soon after taking out the policies, but these cannot be classed as failures because this was the case in every industrial assurance office.[5]

While the founders were involved, Royal London avoided the type of problems that beset other collecting societies. These proved to be major distractions for their managements and agents, and often were symptoms of significant underlying unrest.[6] In 1868, for example, the majority of the management sub-committee of Liverpool Victoria accused the founder and treasurer of misuse of funds. The president and secretary refused to take any further part in the meeting, whereupon they were replaced by the majority who proceeded to pass a series of motions by which they seized control of the society. At a meeting of the general committee a week later, the majority was dismissed from the sub-committee and peace restored. In 1884 the view that the chief office of Liverpool Victoria should be moved to London was causing huge unrest in Liverpool. A general meeting was held to be null and void and had to be reconvened, then a rift in the boardroom enabled a group of London agents to take control of the committee of management. In September the following year all the chief office staff were dismissed and later reinstated. In 1885 concern was expressed at the remuneration being paid to joint secretaries of Royal Liver coupled with allegations of misconduct. Chief office staff were dismissed. An enquiry was carried out by an inspector appointed by the Registrar of Friendly Societies following a petition of more than five hundred members. Before the inspector's report was published, the joint secretaries and three members of the committee of management resigned. The inspector made a number of recommendations and his report prompted the creation of a delegate system still in force within Royal Liver today.[7]

Many of these governance issues seem to reflect a difficulty on the part of those managing collecting societies to accommodate the changes that were taking place in their organisations as a result of the huge expansion of industrial assurance during the final third of the nineteenth century. Rapid change has the potential to cause unrest or worse and it is safe to conclude that the prudence, competence and integrity of Degge, Ridge and Hambridge played a large part in Royal London avoiding trauma of this type, which can be so damaging to an organisation. There was some minor skirmishing at annual general meetings, but no signs of any widespread dissatisfaction amongst staff or members that could disrupt the steady progress of Royal London. It was in the years following the death of the last surviving founder that Royal London was to experience its own upheaval. If only Hambridge had been in better health, and survived into the twentieth century, perhaps that too would have been avoided.

Joseph Degge was to live only for the first 13 years of the Society's life. He was its first secretary, a role in friendly societies at the time that was somewhere between that of company secretary and managing director, although the secretary was not a member of the Committee of Management. In early 1861 Degge was living with his wife Elizabeth and daughter Harriet in Lambeth. Four more children were born to them between 1863 and 1868, another daughter and three sons. They had moved to Islington when Elizabeth became ill, and died in December 1869. She was only 34 and was probably suffering from tuberculosis.[8] She was buried at St Patrick's Catholic Cemetery in Leytonstone.

'Stress' was not a word that entered the Victorian vocabulary but Degge now had to cope with his grief, his role as a single parent to five children aged between one and nine and the demands of his job with Royal London, still very much at the start-up stage. The family and two servants, one employed primarily for domestic duties and the other to look after the children, moved to 29 Enfield Road, only a couple of miles away from the office and within the attractive area of De Beauvoir Town, near Hackney.[9] Degge must have been able to create some time for himself because he was successful in courting and winning the hand of Eleanor Watson, nearly ten years his junior, the daughter of a local builder. They were married at the church of Our Lady and Saint Joseph in Hackney on 25 May 1871.

His first wife appears to have been Catholic and, although Degge was a "sincere Christian"[10], they had been married in the Church of England and there was no suggestion that he shared Elizabeth's religion. It seems that Eleanor too, was Catholic. Father William Lockhart, the parish priest at Hackney, was a converted Anglican and a friend of John Henry (later Cardinal) Newman. Perhaps he and Degge met and, as a result of their discussions and the encouragement of Eleanor and her family, Degge converted to Catholicism. A son, Alfred, was born in 1873. Degge died on Boxing Day 1874 and was buried beside Elizabeth at St Patrick's.

At the time of Joseph Degge's death, Eleanor was pregnant. She moved to South Shields soon after the funeral and a son, christened Bernard Aloysius, was born the following year. Sadly, the relationship between the Degge family and Royal London ended on a sour note. The collecting societies were operating in a cash environment and it was apparently customary for the secretary to have a significant float. There may additionally have been technical problems in operating a bank account because the legislation provided that a society's assets vested in the trustees, and not in the society itself. On Hambridge's appointment in 1875, for example, it was resolved that he "be allowed a balance of two hundred pounds on hand to meet current claims and expenses". There was a dispute between Degge's widow and the Committee over how much of the cash in Joseph's possession when he died was the Royal London float. After the Society's trustees commenced proceedings against Eleanor, a sum was agreed and she paid up. Whatever the rights and wrongs of the claim, and acknowledging that the Committee had a duty to protect the Society's funds, litigation against his widow was hardly a fitting end to Joseph Degge's relationship with the organisation that he helped to found.

Eleanor remained in South Shields, and in the early 1880s was living there with her mother, two of the children of Joseph's first marriage to Elizabeth (Mary and Lucian), her two sons (Alfred and Bernard) and six lodgers (four lady schoolteachers and two brothers in business together as grocers). She no doubt welcomed the income that the lodgers would have provided – Joseph had died intestate with an estate of less than £600 (today: £42,000).

The immediate reaction to Degge's life is one of profound sadness that he did not live to enjoy his second marriage and his children ("… as a Husband he possessed those sterling qualities which endeared him to the beloved partner of his joys and sorrows; as a father he was not only a good parent, but his affection for his children seemed even to approach the species of idolatry"[11]) nor to see the success of the friendly society that he had helped to found. At least he would have known that Royal London had become sufficiently established to ensure its survival.

Degge would have received a limited and brief education. He must have learnt a great deal about life working in the pub trade in Liverpool but by the age of 20 had realised that this was not to be his life's work. Royal Liver was a substantial organisation – it had over 100,000 members, had just opened its first London office and had an office in most major towns and cities. London, if only for the size of its population, would have been seen as a major market and the manager of the district there was an important post. To appoint a clerk from chief office with only three years' service, to manage the London office says much for the ability and potential that Degge displayed.

Degge was shrewd and hard-working with plenty of common sense and a natural aptitude for figures. The *In Memoriam* booklet referred to him as a man who "never for a moment hesitated to give utterance to his thoughts in a gentlemanly straightforward and honest manner" and mentions later his "urbanity and amiable disposition." There are some examples of the former in his evidence to the Royal Commission where he was almost too straightforward.[12] A differently expressed reply to several of the questions might have encouraged the commissioners to look more favourably on collecting societies, although their view had probably been formed by the time he gave evidence. As to the amiable disposition, the founders persuaded people to join this embryonic business. Those early agents would not have joined if they had not enjoyed the company of, and been excited by the prospect of working with and for, these three young men. Degge was certainly much more than 'a safe pair of hands' back at the office and must have possessed a genuine entrepreneurial spirit. Many in his position would have been content with the progress made within Royal Liver, and decide to make their career with this established and expanding society. It is impossible to tell for how long and to what extent his performance was impaired by failing health. Towards the end the dynamic young man who so impressed the hierarchy of Royal Liver must have been replaced by a more sedentary and prematurely aged administrator but one still possessing all his commercial acumen and commitment to the venture that he helped to found.

Henry Ridge was made president of the Society in 1861 but the office lapsed almost at once. He was appointed to the Committee in 1862 and remained a member until his death in 1890. He took his turn chairing meetings of the Committee and annual general meetings. He was treasurer from 1877 to his death. Charles, the first of his eight children, was born in October 1861. After Hammersmith, the Ridge family lived at Stoke Newington and Hackney. Ridge was clearly proud of the trade he had acquired before turning to life assurance – in the 1871 census return he described himself as a 'Master Carpenter'. In the previous return he was an 'Insurance Agent' and in the subsequent one an 'Insurance Director'. Perhaps when he was asked to complete the 1871 return he was having a bad day at the office. Dudley Ridge wrote of his grandfather:

> *Building up the Royal London was an exacting task but Henry Ridge found time for some relaxation. His individualism manifested itself in mild eccentricities. He would return home from a tiring and worrying day at the office, shut himself in his study and play the concertina for an hour or more. Again, he would suddenly say to his wife, 'Ann, I shall be away for the next week', to which the reply would be 'Very well, Henry'. In a few days postcards would begin to arrive from Boulogne, Rouen, Paris, Brussels, indicating that he was off on one of his solitary continental journeys.*[13]

Ridge had taught himself French from two school textbooks and the trips would have given him the opportunity to improve his pronunciation. It may very well be that Ridge took his holidays on his own but the statement is misleading to the extent that it suggests that he was frequently away from the office at short notice. Members of the Committee had to seek permission from their colleagues to miss meetings and the attendance record of all the directors including Ridge was excellent.

Henry Ridge must not be dismissed as an amiable eccentric. He had interests that went beyond industrial assurance and would, no doubt, have been an agreeable companion over a meal, drink or cup of coffee. Both his father and uncle had set up businesses and he could well have been the visionary at the meeting in the coffee shop who persuaded the more prudent Degge that it could be done. Ridge was sufficiently practical to keep things together in the early years. In the years after Degge's death, the minutes give the impression that Ridge as treasurer (and often as chairman of the Committee and annual general meetings) and Hambridge as secretary, were the two executives running the Society, albeit with active involvement and support from the other members of the Committee. Ridge was commercial and hard-working:

> *A lengthened practical experience in all departments of the work, combined with great natural shrewdness, enabled him to do much in moulding the unchequered, and successful career of the society. In business and in private life he was somewhat reserved, whilst an amiability of temper and a candour which at all times was patent, won for him the confidence and esteem of all with whom he came into contact, and enabled him to make many lasting friends, at the same time preserving him from giving cause to any man to become his enemy.*[14]

It was suggested that there was "much reason for the belief that his death was hastened, if not actually caused, through his thorough devotion to the well-being of the society". Ridge's reserve may have been the key to his good relationship with Hambridge – two outgoing extroverts may not have got on so well together. Ridge left £5,216 11s 3d (today: £428,000). In a simple will, he had appointed his wife sole executrix and sole beneficiary.

In 1894, Henry's eldest son Charles (Charlie to his friends) left the chief office for Colchester to develop the Society's business there. Two years later, he moved to Brighton and was an agent there for the rest of his working life, operating over a wide area between Worthing and Eastbourne. He had married Emily, the daughter of Joseph Barnes Degge in 1886. Charlie, according to his son, was a kindly and tolerant man who "inherited the mildly eccentric nature of his father and to an even greater degree his love of the French language".[15] Charlie had three brothers and four sisters. Two brothers emigrated (John to New Zealand and Harold to Canada), and Charlie was in Brighton, but Henry and Ann's other children all remained in the suburbs of London. Apparently only Charlie worked for Royal London. Ann died in 1929, and was buried beside Henry at Abney Park, and Charlie in 1948.[16]

William Hambridge's Royal London career, throughout which "he rendered efficient, devoted and whole-hearted service to the Institution he had helped to found",[17] divides into four. Initially he combined his role on the Committee with that of an agent operating over a large part of south London. As "a pioneer superintendent [he] was eminently successful in opening up many of the most flourishing districts throughout the Country".[18] Then he was responsible for the Society's business in the north of England, moving to Newcastle in 1871 and travelling down to London infrequently to attend meetings of the Committee. He returned to London in 1875 to become secretary and retained the role until his death in 1899. An elderly pensioner speaking in the 1950s remembered Hambridge as a heavily built man, not very tall, who was austere and strict.[19] Staff, he recalled, held him in awe but recognised that he was a good businessman.

It was Hambridge who, above anybody else, went out and got the business of the Society. He possessed huge energy and drive and was totally dedicated to the expansion of the Society. His philosophy was that, just as a cell multiplies to produce new and ultimately countless fresh cells surrounding it, so a business, provided its centre was sound, could throw out from that centre reproductions of itself and they in turn reproduce on the same pattern.[20] Birmingham provided a good example of the organic cell approach. In the mid-1860s, Laurence Barrett, a director and experienced agent, had been sent there to take charge of the branch and to develop the surrounding area. Within a few years not only was Birmingham thriving but agencies in Coventry, Gloucester, Walsall, Warwick, Wolverhampton and Worcester had been opened. This pattern was repeated all over the country.

Hambridge was successful in putting in place a network of Royal London agents that operated across the country and sold an ever-increasing number of policies. His effectiveness is illustrated by the fact that by 1893 two-thirds of the Society's premium income was collected from outside Greater London. He seems to have been the archetypal sales director to whom sales – or in this case premium income – was the crucial indicator. It is probably fair to say that he tended to be more interested in quantity than quality but that was a factor of the industry of the time and to criticise involves an element of hindsight. As the Society grew and the legislation impacting on friendly societies increased, the role of secretary became more onerous but Hambridge was well able to cope. He was as comfortable dealing with the Society's actuary on a complicated valuation point, or discussing (what we would term) a compliance issue with an official from the Registry of Friendly Societies, or giving evidence to a Select Committee of the House of Lords,[21] as he was in 'encouraging' a superintendent to increase sales in his district. He would, of necessity, have acquired considerable knowledge of the legislation that regulated the Society's business – no easy task given Parliament's interest in the topic. Royal London had been formed under the Friendly Societies Act 1855. This was amended by the Acts of 1875, 1887, 1889, 1893 and 1895. In 1896 the law was consolidated into two Acts – the Friendly Societies Act and the Collecting Societies and Industrial Assurance Companies Act, the latter recognising that both the companies and friendly societies were providing the same industrial assurance.

The 1887 article in *Post Magazine*, already quoted in relation to what prompted the founders to create a new collecting society and the Paul Street office, concludes with a tribute:

> *Mr Hambridge's long experience in every department of the work*
> *of such an Institution has given him the power to deal with an*

*enormous amount of work in the least possible space of time, but
we question if many of the members who form the Society have
any adequate idea of the task that he has to accomplish daily.
Every penny they pay ultimately passes through his hands; under
his supervision a weekly statement detailing each item of income
and expenditure is prepared and laid before the Committee, whose
duty it is to check the items by vouchers referring thereto every
week. He also has the sole control of the correspondence, and
much of his time is taken up with the new business department.
It is not too much to say that Mr Hambridge is the right man in
the right place, and we hope he may live long to fill the position
he now holds so creditably.*[22]

Hambridge is the most difficult of the founders to assess but he must
have been a dynamic natural leader, capable of motivating the superintendents
and agents who reported to him. On his death, it was said of him that the
"effect of his genial disposition and tender sympathy was such that the large
staff under his control looked up to him as a friend and guide, as well as
a Master".[23] Frederick de la Bertauche, who joined the Society as an agent
in 1866 and had been on the Committee since 1875, knew Hambridge as
well as anybody. He spoke of his large-heartedness, consistency and thorough
devotion to duty:

*... he was ever ready to give a willing ear to the troubles of the
workers, and his best thoughts and energies, and every moment
of his time, to the building up of the institution that he had so
much at heart.*[24]

There were two women in Hambridge's life. He married Jane Hepden
in Tonbridge on 7 February 1857. He was 19 and she was 21, the daughter
of a gardener. A son, Thomas, was born the following year. At the time Royal
London was founded in 1861, Hambridge and Jane were living in Greenwich
with Thomas and Edward Hambridge, William's six-year-old brother,[25] who
was to work as an agent for Royal London for many years and become a
director on the death of William. In July 1863 during that difficult period
when the survival of the Society was far from certain, Hambridge married
Selina Jane Wade at the parish church, Kennington. Selina, who was only
17, was pregnant and a daughter, Martha Jane, was born later in the year.
She was to be the first of 11 children born to Selina and William Hambridge
between 1863 and 1879. In 1881, after their time in Newcastle, they were
back in London living near Finsbury Park with their children, aged 2, 4, 7, 8,
9, 10, 13, 14, 16 and 17 – a son had died, aged 2, in 1871.[26] On 22 June 1881

Selina died, aged only 36. The cause of her death was given as rheumatism and congestion of the brain and the informant was Hambridge who was described as "widower of deceased, present at the death".

Selina, however, had never been legally married to Hambridge because, at the time they went through the ceremony in Kennington in 1863, his wife Jane was alive. Jane appears in census returns between 1871 and 1891 where she is referred to as 'married' although no husband is shown as living with her. In the first return she described herself as a 'Traveller's wife'. In his will made in 1895 Hambridge left £200 (today £16,800) to "Jane Hambridge formerly known as Jane Hepden of Tonbridge Kent and in the event of her predeceasing me then the said amount to be paid to her Children in equal portions". In the census return following his death, Jane is referred to as a 'widow'.[27] She died in Tooting in 1908 and is described on her death certificate as the widow of William Henry Hambridge.[28]

That, however, is only part of the story. Jane gave birth three times after William's bigamous union with Selina in 1863 – daughters were born in 1866 and 1867 and a son in 1869 – and the birth certificates of all three children show Hambridge as the father.[29] There can only be two explanations: Hambridge was maintaining two homes, or at least living with Selina and visiting Jane, or there was fraud in the registration of these three births. A conspiracy theorist might suggest that, as an act of nobility, Hambridge lent his name to another man's children, so that they and their mother would not suffer from the stigma of illegitimacy, or perhaps Jane simply stated that the father was her husband, knowing this to be untrue. If the latter, Jane would have required somebody to impersonate her husband because the middle birth was registered by "Wm Hy Hambridge Father". Anything is possible, but anyone carrying out such a fraud would have been running the risk of prosecution if detected, and people generally seem to have been honest when it came to registering births.

The formalities of Hambridge's will suggest that the existence of two Mrs Hambridges may have been no great secret. He appointed as one of his executors William Bowrey, the Society's assistant secretary and a member of the Committee, and asked Alfred Skeggs, the chief clerk and Bowrey's successor, to witness his signature. It is unlikely that you would ask work colleagues to be involved if your will revealed something that you had been trying to hide, although it is possible – after all, the witness need never read the will (but may get a furtive look at it) and the executor need only see the will after the testator's death.

The complexities of Hambridge's personal life are reflected in the will. After the £200 legacy to Jane, his household furniture was left to his daughters "known as Isabella Kate Hambridge (Wade) and Gertrude Hambridge (Wade)" and the balance of his estate was to be "divided between my Children by the late Selina Jane Wade (daughter of Edward and Jane Wade formerly of Camberwell Surrey)" – seven of the children received 5 per cent shares, Isabella and Gertrude each received 20 percent and Dunstan Edgar, 25 per cent. Each child is listed in the will and referred to as "Hambridge (Wade)". Neither Selina nor Jane is referred to as 'wife'. Hambridge left £1455 4s 9d (today: £122,000) and so the legacy to Jane represented nearly 14 per cent of his estate.

Hambridge's conduct must be viewed in the context of the nineteenth century, throughout which many couples, particularly from the working class, entered bigamous marriages. The Matrimonial Causes Act 1857 introduced the first formulation of divorce law as we know it today, but the expense of litigation and the absence of legal aid meant that in the 1860s divorce was still available only to the few who could afford it. For those who could not, many preferred a bigamous marriage to living together – they saw the wedding ceremony as somehow validating a sinful union. Sometimes a prosecution followed these bigamous marriages: between January 1860 and December 1869, for example, 180 bigamy cases were tried at the Old Bailey.

On the basis of a study of 221 cases of bigamy in England between 1830 and 1900, Ginger Frost, Professor of History at Samford University in Birmingham, Alabama, concluded that bigamous unions tended to be accepted, at least by the court of public opinion, where three conditions were met – the bigamist had good reason for leaving his or her spouse, had been honest with the second 'spouse' and (where male) was supporting the multiple families.

> *Within these parameters, neighbors and friends accepted illegal marriages, following in a long tradition of self-marriage and self-divorce. In fact, by the end of the century, judges followed community standards in their sentencing and often gave nominal punishment to both male and female bigamists.*[30]

Every prosecution required somebody to bring the matter to the authorities – usually the first or second spouse, or a family member – and Dr Frost's research indicated that few outside the families instigated bigamy cases. This suggests that, providing Jane and Selina and their families made no complaint and Hambridge was making proper provisions for Jane and her children, he was unlikely to be prosecuted.[31] If, however, the fraudulent registration theory is rejected, and the birth certificates are taken as evidence of a continuing relationship with Jane, Hambridge might have found it difficult to demonstrate that he had a good reason for leaving her. It would also be interesting to know what knowledge Jane and Selina had of each other, and when that knowledge was acquired. The answer to these questions would have influenced the views of contemporaries to Hambridge's conduct, Dr Frost suggesting that many "people did not see any harm in bigamy, as long as all the parties were satisfied with (and aware of) their relationships".[32]

Stories were handed down about Hambridge. It was said that his children were sent out from an early age as canvassers and that, when one of his sons working at the chief office threw his sandwich papers out of the window, he was summarily dismissed, taken home, flogged and banished to Australia where it was believed he flourished, becoming a substantial farmer.[33] Hambridge's response would have been that a warning had been issued that the next offender would be dismissed and that his son should have realised that his father was not one to display favouritism. There is some slight corroboration for this incident because searches of census returns and indices of marriages and deaths have failed to find any mention of Thomas Hambridge, his eldest son, after 1861.

The ill health that dogged Hambridge's final years must have reduced his effectiveness, but one senses that by the early 1890s 'the Royal London machine' was in place and that it was Hambridge's wise input that was most needed. Energetically rushing around the country could be left to younger men. Obituaries in trade journals may not be renowned for perception, let alone criticism, but *Post Magazine* was unequivocal in its praise of Hambridge:

> *It might truly be said that he was not only the loyal and faithful servant of the Royal London, but was ever the devoted, kind and gentle servant of all connected with the Institution. He enjoyed the esteem of both the indoor and outdoor staff, who felt confidence in his sound judgment and in his unfailing sense of fairness and justice.*[34]

There was to be at least one Hambridge (and often several of them) employed by Royal London for more than a hundred years. William's brother Edward, who had been an agent and superintendent in east London, was appointed a director shortly after William's death in 1899. He resigned in 1920. Another Edward Hambridge, born in 1868, was the fourth child of William and Selina. He worked for the Society for 48 years, many of them as superintendent at Bournemouth. Benjamin, William and Selina's seventh child, worked briefly for the Society. His son Norman, born in 1908, joined the Society in 1924 and retired as manager of the valuation department in January 1973. Norman was actively involved in the early computerisation of the Society – it is fitting that there should have been a Hambridge on hand to help usher Royal London into the modern era. In his speech at the banquet in 1961 to mark the Society's centenary, Ernest Haynes, the chairman, reported that "Young Hambridge has in recent months been preparing the way for the installation of an electronic computer at head office, so we have the ancient and the modern linked together in what I think is a very striking way".[35]

A booklet was produced in 1911 to mark the jubilee of Royal London with particular emphasis on the business in Birmingham. It contains what is probably the best description of Royal London's founders:

> [They] *had no fame nor wealth, but they possessed what proved to be equal, if not superior in their case, viz., stout hearts, plenty of pluck, faith in themselves and in each other. They did not sit still and wait for something to turn up, but set out to sow the seeds of thrift and provident habits amongst the workers of England in the face of prejudice and misunderstanding, never dreaming of the mighty harvests that the year of Jubilee would reveal.*

The 1900 annual general meeting, the first after the death of William Hambridge, was chaired by Edward Smith. He reported that, although they would shortly be unveiling a marble monument at Southgate Cemetery, the Committee felt that Hambridge's "true and lasting memorial was, and would ever be, found in the abiding prosperity of the Royal London".[36] There can be no doubt that, had the occasion demanded it, Smith would have extended his statement to include Joseph Degge and Henry Ridge.

CHAPTER 5

Conversion

1900–1908

After having had an opportunity of perusing the present Rules of the Society and the proposed memorandum for the new Society, it seems to us that [the proposed articles] *are so drawn up as fully to safeguard the members and to give full power to transact all kinds of assurance business, by which the Institution should benefit immensely. If the present safeguards contained in the new constitution are retained, which we presume they will be, the members will remain where they are now – owners and sole recipients of the profits of the Society. Our correspondents have, however, for the most part written from the point of view of the collector, and not from that of the member. In our judgment, if the Management has erred at all, it is in being too liberal to the collector. It is the first time on record, we should think, that any Society or Company has been formed, having as one of its fundamental objects the profit from various rates of commission for its staff, with the right to sell the business of the Institution. The suggested new constitution appears to us to be of the most helpful character, especially to the collectors. Altogether the new scheme appears to us to be a good one from the point of view of both members and workers.*

Reynolds Weekly (24 May 1908)

A young man began work in the chief office of Royal London at 6 Paul Street on Monday 5 April 1904. More than 50 years later Steve Else described the recruitment process:

> *I had reached the age of fourteen when I noticed in the press that an 'Old Established Insurance Society' required Junior Clerks providing they were of 'good appearance' and offered in exchange for services 'excellent opportunities for promising lads' and eight shillings a week. I accepted without question the age of the Society, was somewhat dubious as to my good appearance and doubted whether I was in a position to promise much.*
>
> *Hoping for the best but fearing the worst I presented myself at 6 Paul Street at 9 o'clock on Monday and was somewhat reassured to find myself in the company of several other lads of no better appearance and all in the same predicament. We were told that we should have to pass an educational test for at that time employers were able to choose from numerous applicants. We were asked to name the County Town of several counties, do six sums, some spelling, and last but not least to declare in writing 'our ambition in life'. Sinking for the occasion preconceived visions of becoming an engine driver in favour of the more immediate possibility of becoming a clerk 'with excellent opportunities,' I settled for the latter and, like all the other applicants, sold my cherished dreams for eight shillings per week. At that early age I could place no value on excellent opportunities even assuming that I was a promising lad.*[1]

Steve was successful and he started work the following Monday. His job was "to write three hundred policies a day and to expect a reprimand for doing less" in a large glass-roofed room that was home to the agency, valuation and policy departments, the post room and the office of Alfred Skeggs, of whom we shall hear more later. Nobody could live on eight shillings a week and the junior clerks continued to need support from their parents.

Steve may have noticed that the heading of his new employer's notepaper included the line 'Telephone P.O. 12170 (Central)' although this would have had no impact on the working life of the junior clerks. The Central Exchange, the first Post Office telephone exchange in London, had been opened in 1902 with a capacity for 14,000 subscribers and the Royal London Friendly Society soon embraced the technology and became one of them. The City, Mayfair, West End, Western and Victoria exchanges soon followed.[2]

Not long after he joined, Steve received a beautifully printed invitation to attend the Society's annual outing to Henley-on-Thames:

Needless to say, I accepted with alacrity and, apart from the fact that I lost my straw hat through sticking my head out of the train window on the way to Henley and a brief interlude of violent sickness through overeating a magnificent lunch, the day was an unparalleled success. We were taken up the river on a steam launch, and, there being no gramophone or wireless in those days, we had to provide our own musical entertainment. This we did by thumping an ancient honkey tonk piano and, no doubt, destroyed the peace of all other occupants of that part of the river by our amateur vocal efforts.

The next major event in Steve's career was the relocation to the magnificent new building at the corner of Finsbury Square. For some time, the directors had been looking for a site on which they could build a chief office that was appropriate to an organisation of its size and status, and that would provide ample scope for expansion. They finally focused on the northern side of Finsbury Square and by 1900 were acquiring leases there as they became available. These were then surrendered to the Church Commissioners, who owned the freehold, in return for building leases. By late 1901 a site on the corner of Finsbury Square and City Road had been assembled. An 'advising architect' was retained and a brief sent to a number of architects inviting them to submit designs. Seven responses were submitted to the Committee, each one being referred to merely by number. The directors, with the assistance of the advising architect, were unanimous in their choice and it was only after the decision was made that the envelopes were opened and the identities of the architects revealed. The winner was John Belcher, a Londoner born in Southwark who was about to be President of the Royal Institute of British Architects.[3] His work included the Royal Insurance and the Mappin & Webb buildings in the City (both now demolished, the latter to be replaced by No. 1 Poultry), the hall of the Institute of Chartered Accountants, and Colchester Town Hall. He was to design the Ashton Memorial, the green dome of which is visible today to the west of the M6 Motorway near Lancaster.[4] By the end of 1902 Walter Lawrence and Son had been appointed to build a new chief office, the Committee selecting their quote of £60,860 (today: £4.5 million) on the basis that it was the lowest of the seven that they had received. The building, faced with Cornish granite up to the first floor and with Portland stone above, was completed late in 1904, the Committee holding its first meeting in the new boardroom on 20 December.

The directors were delighted with the ornate baroque building with its corner turret. Horace Duffell had referred at the 1904 annual general meeting to the magnificent building "with its handsome elevation, its beautiful architecture, and its towering erection of massive stone and granite" that when finished would "not only be worthy of its name as head offices of a great and prosperous Institution, but will be a credit and improvement to the City of London". The junior clerks had a rather more down-to-earth approach, Steve Else reporting that "this startling uplift in the social status of the Society, giving enormous pride to the Management, was viewed with restrained enthusiasm by the majority of the Staff when it became known that a corresponding uplift in salaries was unlikely". The industrial assurance offices' major contribution to the urban landscape was still a few years away – in 1911, the Royal Liver Building on the Pier Head at Liverpool was opened by Lord Sheffield, one of Royal Liver's trustees, who, as Edward Lyulph Stanley, had re-cast Royal London's expenditure in the early 1870s for the benefit of the Royal Commission.[5] It was to be the tallest building in Liverpool for more than 50 years.

Looking beyond Royal London in the early years of the twentieth century, the directors would probably have shared the view that things were not quite the same as they had been when Queen Victoria was on the throne. The Boer War had lasted for three years rather than the anticipated few months, was hugely expensive and caused considerable unease. A scorched-earth policy and concentration camps were regarded by many as 'un-British' and concerns about the effectiveness of the Army, first raised at the time of the Crimean War, began to resurface. There were fears that Britain's economy had deteriorated against the USA, Germany, France and Russia. The Empire was seen as over-extended, uncoordinated and difficult to govern. A belief was emerging that the level of poverty at home was simply not acceptable and that Government had to take action, prompting doubts as to whether the 'laissez faire' approach adopted by both political parties when in government during the nineteenth century would still be appropriate in the twentieth century. But none of this seemed to be having an impact on the Royal London Friendly Society whose period of great expansion continued into the new century. By 1904 it had 4,500 agents operating out of more than 300 district offices, an annual premium income of almost £800,000 and assets of nearly £1.5 million (today: £64.2 million and £120 million).

The question exercising the directors was whether a change of status was required for this rapidly growing business. A friendly society could only provide life policies up to a maximum sum assured of £200, the modern equivalent of which would be around £15,000.[6] This was expressed as a maximum per person so that anyone who had policies with one or more friendly societies could not take out further policies if this would take the total sum assured with them to over £200.[7] It was felt by some that the £200 ceiling, and the inability to provide other types of insurance such as property and contents cover, would put the Society at a disadvantage in the better-off households on which the agents were now calling.

The friendly societies legislation allowed societies to convert themselves into companies and in mid-1905 rumours were rife that Royal London was about to convert.[8] The directors felt that they could not ignore this, although conversion was not what they had in mind. The Royal London Staff Association, founded in 1900, was to become the trade union for Royal London staff.[9] In August 1905 the directors were due to attend a meeting of the association at the Midland Hotel, Manchester. On the following day they would be participating in the annual outing to Southport of the Manchester branch of the association that would include a dinner at the Scarisbrook Hotel. They felt that these events would provide them with ideal opportunities to share their plan with the staff.[10] The trip to Lancashire was not a success in terms of staff communications, however, and a meeting had to be arranged at the chief office on 12 October with the executive council of the association so that the directors could try to address the uncertainty that they had created.

The directors expressed the view that Royal London would be damaged if it continued to be shackled by the friendly societies legislation. They were contemplating, not a conversion, but rather the creation of a new company, able to undertake all insurance outside the powers of a friendly society that would sit alongside and work in conjunction with the Royal London Friendly Society. It would be a proprietary company, the staff getting the first offer of shares. Assurances were given that the new company would not compete with the Society, although the directors suggested that for various ill-defined reasons the company would not be able to commit not to do so. The directors were asked if it was legal for the machinery of the Society, built up and paid for over the years by the members, and the services of its salaried officials, to be used for the benefit of a private company. Their reply was that it would be in order provided a fair and reasonable allocation of expenses was made and the company reimbursed the Society for all expenditure attributable to the company. The executive sought the views of the directors on converting the Society itself into a company, thereby freeing itself from the restrictions of the friendly societies legislation and removing the need for the new company. The reply was that, although the directors were unanimous in their support for the new company, they were divided on the conversion option although, if the staff preferred a conversion, this would be considered.[11]

The executive of the association reported back to its members. There remained little enthusiasm – the further clarification had made the plan no more palatable. Royal London was a mutual society; it had been so for 45 years and few were attracted by the involvement of a proprietary company especially as the reason given for the change was of little concern to most of the agents who never sold a policy for anywhere near £200. In early January 1906, the officers of the association were summoned back to the boardroom at Finsbury Square. An angry Edward Smith complained bitterly about the way in which the views of the Committee had been misrepresented, misunderstood and misused. By now Smith seems to have assumed the role of chairman of the Committee. The directors, he reiterated, were convinced of the case for setting up the company but accepted that, in order to succeed, the company would need to have the near unanimous support of the staff. As this would clearly not be the case, the Committee had decided to take the matter no further. The deputation, shocked by the outburst, expressed their regret that the directors believed that it had misrepresented their views and stressed that this had certainly not been their intention.[12]

In fact most of the opposition was directed, not at conversion itself, but at the concept of the proprietary company. Shortly before the executive had been summoned to the chief office, Laurence McAra, a superintendent in Sheffield, had proposed a resolution at a meeting of the local district of the staff association requiring the association's executive to appoint a committee to explore if the Society could convert to a company without the proprietary element, thereby achieving the advantages of conversion without losing the spirit of the friendly society. The majority of those attending the meeting must have been attracted by (or at least interested in) this idea because the resolution was passed. No decision had yet been made by the executive but the deputation made an instant decision to share the outcome of the Sheffield meeting with the directors. When they were told that, at its next meeting, the executive intended to appoint a committee to look at the whole question of conversion, harmony was restored and the proceedings concluded on an amicable note, with the directors indicating that they would be pleased to receive a report from that committee in due course.[13]

The Committee of Fifteen, as it soon became known, was formed by the executive council of the Royal London Staff Association in February 1906 "to consider whether or not it would be advantageous to the workers, and conducive to the welfare of the Royal London Friendly Society, that some change should be made in the constitution of the Society with the view of overcoming the restrictions imposed by the Friendly Societies Act". While the committee was sparing "neither time nor pains to ascertain exactly what a change in the Society's constitution would involve" another collecting society was involved in a very public debate on conversion. The board of Liverpool Victoria supported conversion, but rather distanced itself from a campaign that had prompted huge opposition. The anger and frustration vented at the special general meeting in September 1906 was such that the chairman could not make himself heard and it was only by exhibiting a placard saying "A vote will now be taken" that he was able to put the resolution for converting Liverpool Victoria into a proprietary company with 300,000 shares of which 20,000 were to be allotted to the committee of management, 100,000 to the field staff and 30,000 to the chief office staff, with 150,000 shares for the three million members. In due course the chairman declared that the resolution had been passed by the required majority. The meeting in early October to confirm the resolution was even more rowdy and placards were again needed to put the resolution that was declared carried. The dispute moved to the High Court and after a nine-day hearing an injunction was granted restraining the Liverpool Victoria from implementing the conversion.[14]

These external events reminded the Committee of Fifteen of the difficulty of its task but in February 1907 it submitted a lucid and concise report to the executive council of the staff association. It found that it would be possible to convert Royal London to a mutual company "based largely upon the present Rules and giving to all members the same absolute control over the affairs of the Institution which is now their right". In other words, there was an alternative to the proprietary company of the type suggested by the directors, and contemplated for Liverpool Victoria. A converted society would be able "to issue policies up to any amount in all clauses of life assurance". The committee stopped short of making a final recommendation seeing its role as clearly setting out the points at issue. An advantage of conversion to a mutual company, to which the committee did not feel able to refer, was that it would remove the need for the type of proprietary company envisaged by the Board two years earlier... or at least that was what everybody thought at the time.

The impression given subsequently by the directors was that the conversion debate had been instigated by the Royal London Staff Association. There was reference in circulars to "a deputation from the Staff Association who explained that they had taken steps to ascertain the feeling of the workers as to a change in the constitution of the Society, and, as a result of that enquiry, they reported that there was quite a considerable majority in favour of further enquiry being made".[15] Later the point was made even more forcefully – some time since "the Board of Management of the Society was approached by a Union of its workers, viz., the Royal London Staff Association, numbering thousands, who called attention to the serious disabilities under which they laboured by reason of the restrictions of the Friendly Societies' Act, pointing out among other things the limitation of the sums assured, which must not exceed in the aggregate £200 insured in any Friendly or Collecting Society, also the need for profit sharing Tables, etc., etc., which we, as a Friendly Society could not offer. The staff were told that the matter could not be favourably considered by the Board unless it was proved that there was a considerable majority in favour of a change".[16] This view was repeated much later when, in a memorandum submitted to the Government in 1910,[17] the directors wrote that a "large Trade Union of the employees of the Society called 'The Staff Association' eventually waited on the Directors of the Friendly Society, on or about January, 1908, with a request that the Board should favourably take into consideration the desirability of the conversion of the Society into a Mutual Company".[18]

These statements were at best disingenuous – it was true that the proposal to convert to a mutual company had come from the staff association but only as a result of the directors' comments in 1905 that the restrictions of the friendly societies legislation were holding back Royal London, and the staff's rejection of the proprietary company that the directors had put forward as their preferred way of dealing with the restrictions.

The Committee of Fifteen recognised that support for the proposal to convert would not be unanimous. It commented that "there was also in the minds of many a fear that the privileges and emoluments now enjoyed might be jeopardised as a result of a change". This proved to be a massive understatement. The question of whether or not to convert generated a great deal of heat. Groups formed – the Royal London Collectors' League was anti-conversion and in October 1907 launched its own journal, *The Anti-Conversionist*. The Royal London Collectors' Watch Committee was pro-conversion and by February 1908 felt that they needed to respond with their own publication.[19] In the first edition of *The Sentinel*, the editor explained that its purpose was "to guard the great Royal London camp against the intrusion of insidious enemies, and to give warning of any surprise attack attempted under the leadership of that band of deserters whose defection has spread for the moment to some of the rank and file". This was typical of the language of the debate. Booklets were issued by the opposing factions and sometimes by the Committee of Management and numerous meetings were held, called by one side or the other or by branches of the staff association. Poets were brought into play – 'The Anti' by Autolycus appeared in *The Sentinel* of 8 April 1908:

> *There's a man you sometimes meet,*
> *Brimming o'er with self conceit,*
> *And an egoist complete,*
> *He's an Anti.*
>
> *He has grievances galore,*
> *Entre nous, he'd wish for more;*
> *Summarised, a perfect bore,*
> *Is the Anti.*
>
> *Let him spout for all he's worth,*
> *He just rouses us to mirth;*
> *There's no room in heaven or earth*
> *For the Anti.*

There were many agents who were passionately opposed to the conversion. They were aware – any agents who were ignorant of them were soon briefed by their better informed colleagues – that there were certain advantages enjoyed by a friendly society in relation to taxation, stamp duty and fees payable for death certificates that would be lost on conversion. The directors were prepared to give all these up to be freed of the restrictions of the friendly societies legislation. Many agents genuinely did not believe that the reason they were being given for converting was valid – they had never sold a life policy for anything near £200 (nor had anybody they knew) and their inability to offer fire and other general insurance did not seem to be holding them back as they went about their business selling life policies and collecting the premiums. The anti-conversionists believed that there had to be other reasons for the conversion and that these could only be bad news for them. The battle between the rival factions went on unabated during the winter of 1907/08.

The glaring omission from the debate was highlighted by the *Bristol Mercury* in its 1907 Christmas Eve edition:

> *This great friendly society, which has an annual income of a million pounds, numbers its members in Bristol in thousands. From those Bristol members are collected contributions to the amount of over £15,000 per annum. They have, therefore, a large interest in any scheme which affects the constitution of their society. Up to the present they have not been consulted.*

The objection was not, of course, limited to Bristol but applied throughout the country. Consulting the members was not seen as part of the process. Meanwhile, the acrimonious conversion debate was continuing at Liverpool Victoria. After the court had prevented the conversion from going ahead, the whole question was referred to arbitrators. They agreed with the court, but intimated that a subsidiary could be formed to promote the interests of the Society. The Liverpool Victoria Insurance Corporation Limited came into being in late 1907 with the 350,000 shares allotted mainly to staff. The board comprised directors of Liverpool Victoria and several outsiders.[20]

It was clear that the annual general meeting of Royal London to be held at the Royal Albert Hall on 25 February 1908 would provide an indicator of the likely support for conversion. The much-respected William Bowrey, who had succeeded Hambridge as secretary of the Society, had died in January. The directors' nomination to succeed him was Alfred Skeggs, the president of the staff association, who had 30 years' service in the chief office, nine of them as chief clerk, and who, as a member of the Committee of Fifteen, was a supporter of conversion. Standing against him was Edward Wright, the president of the Collectors' League and a collector for 30 years with (it was claimed) one of the largest collecting books in London who was an opponent of conversion. Technology was in evidence at the meeting:

> *There was a very large attendance, and to ensure that every person should thoroughly understand the purport of the resolutions to be placed before them, a large sheet had been fixed up, and on this intimation of the nature of the next business was made by means of an oxy-hydrogen lantern.*[21]

Skeggs' appointment was confirmed by an overwhelming majority although harmony had not prevailed throughout. Edward Smith, who chaired the meeting, refused to put the resolution proposing Wright as secretary on the basis that the first duty of the meeting was to confirm, or otherwise, the present incumbent. Presumably he would have allowed the resolution to be put if Skeggs' appointment had not been confirmed. Three notices of motion had been received but, to the disappointment of those who supported them, Smith declined to put them to the meeting on the basis that "they had been advised by eminent counsel that such notices were out of order". According to *The Anti-Conversionist*, one resolution was "calling on the Committee to immediately put a stop to the Conversion, another instructing the Committee to introduce the Cash Bonus System, and another instructing them to provide a Delegate System". [22]

So Alfred Skeggs had been confirmed as secretary of the Royal London Friendly Society as successor to Bowrey and successor-but-one to William Hambridge. Skeggs was not popular among at least some of the junior clerks from whose ranks he had been promoted, Steve Else recollecting that:

> *So much concerned were the Management that the glamorous appearance of the new office should not be defiled that Mr Skeggs who had then advanced from the position of Chief Clerk to that of Secretary, would, at lunchtime, and again at five o'clock, emerge from his room on the third floor and watch the clerks descending the stairway to reprimand those who dared to lay a finger on the pillars on each landing.*

When he at last achieved the office to which he had, no doubt, long aspired, the role was not quite what Skeggs would have wished. His predecessors – particularly Degge and Hambridge – seem to have been managing directors in all but name, albeit working closely with Ridge. Now, Edward Smith, James Price and Horace Duffell were increasingly being seen as the triumvirate who ran the Society and the new secretary would be unlikely to change that. Worse still, if the conversion went ahead, his status would reduce even more because, unless and until he was appointed a director, he would just be the company secretary.

Soon after the annual general meeting, the directors circulated to staff model memorandum and articles of association. The memorandum provided that the scale of remuneration to be paid to all the office staff from the directors downwards, and the rates of commission to be paid to the agents, would not be less than that being paid at the time of the conversion. The latter was to apply to future agents and to any new policies that might be introduced. An agent could only be dismissed for wilful dishonesty or such neglect or conduct as would be calculated, in the opinion of the directors, to be injurious to the interests of the Society. Any agent who had acquired his agency by nomination could not be deprived of his right to dispose of it by nomination. The Committee of Fifteen reviewed the documents and concluded (not altogether surprisingly) that a more liberal and democratic constitution could not be framed and gave its support to the proposal to convert. Whether they were expressing their satisfaction on behalf of the members, as the owners of the business, or the staff of the Society, was not entirely clear.

The anti-conversion agents and their trade union had friends in high places. In the House of Commons on 6 April, James O'Grady, a former president of the Trades Union Congress and the Labour MP for Leeds East,[23] asked the Secretary to the Treasury if he was:

> ... aware of the attempt now being made by the committee of management of the Royal London Friendly Society to convert the society into a mutual insurance society under the Companies Acts; and, having regard to the methods recently employed by the committee... in the conduct of the annual meeting... on 25 February of this year, he will instruct the Registrar General [sic] to take action as provided in Section 76 of the Friendly Societies Act 1896 in the event of the committee... deciding to call further conversion meetings.

Under section 76 the chief registrar had power to appoint an inspector or convene a special meeting of a society where an application was made to him by a specified number of members. The terse reply was that the chief registrar had no information on the subjects raised in the question and that no application had been made under section 76. O'Grady then asked a more general question – was the secretary aware of the tendency of committees of management to seek to convert collecting societies to companies and "the injury such conversions would cause to the interests of the members as well as being subversive of their rights?" The minister replied that he was not aware of any such trend but, even if there was one, it did not follow that any such injury would follow.[24]

A poll of all staff organised by external accountants had revealed an overwhelming majority in favour of converting to a mutual company and the directors decided that the time had come to put the matter to the members. The Royal Albert Hall was booked for 24 June 1908 and notice of the special general meeting was given to members. On 18 June an application under section 76 to appoint an inspector to investigate Royal London was received by the chief registrar of friendly societies and this was followed up on 23 June by another question in the House, this time from William Clough, the Liberal member for Skipton. Charles Hobhouse, the newly appointed Financial Secretary to the Treasury, confirmed that he was aware that the application had been made, that the registrar was considering it and that the registrar had neither power to take any action in relation to the forthcoming meetings nor to intervene on any policy to convert.[25]

At last the special general meeting took place. It was to begin at 6pm but members started arriving during the afternoon. They were entertained while they waited by concert artists and an organist booked by the secretary. The stage was decorated with banners and balloons. More than 5,000 members were present when the platform party took their seats. Alfred Skeggs read the notice of the meeting. The one resolution to be considered was straightforward and, as it was a special resolution, it would have to be passed by a majority of at least three-quarters of those present at the meeting:

> That the ROYAL LONDON FRIENDLY SOCIETY, established in the year 1861, and registered under the Friendly Societies Act, 1896 (hereinafter called 'the Society'), be converted in pursuance of Section 71 of the Friendly Societies Act, 1896, into a Company limited by guarantee and not having a capital divided into shares under the Companies Acts, 1862 to 1900, by the name of THE ROYAL LONDON MUTUAL INSURANCE SOCIETY, LIMITED, and that the following be the Memorandum of Association of the Company and that the Articles of Association now before the meeting (which for the purpose of identification, are endorsed with the signature of the Chairman) be adopted as the Articles of Association of the Company.

So what were the issues of the conversion debate? In the booklet published with the notice of the meeting, the Committee of Management set out a list of "Seven Reasons why we should Change", although the first two amount in practice to the same reason. Two other factors were suggested at various times but were not included in the list. The Committee of Fifteen had, very fairly, identified four reasons for not converting – advantages of being a friendly society that would be lost on conversion. The anti-conversion agents added several more.

Table No. 3

Conversion from friendly society to company in 1908: the cases For and Against

For Conversion:

	Reasons in the Board's SGM booklet	Comments of the author
1 2	The Government are enforcing the law relating to Friendly Societies which means that, as we are now confined to section 8 of the Friendly Societies Act ('FSA'), a member will not be allowed in future to insure his Father, Mother, Sister, Brother, or remoter relative under any circumstance. In future (if the resolution is carried) you will be able to insure anybody whether related or not, if you have an insurable interest.	Funeral expenses were generally insured by life-of-another policies by which the proposer insured the life of the life assured: the proposer paid the premiums and received the benefit on the death of the life assured. The law severely restricted the circumstances in which one could insure the life of another (see Appendix 2). Different regimes applied to friendly societies and companies, although the basic principle was the same, and conversion would involve moving Royal London from one regime to the other. It was debatable whether conversion would improve the position.
3	The Society may then issue policies for any amount, not being limited as at present to £200.	This was undoubtedly true but the Committee of Fifteen had been realistic as to the immediate impact that it would have, pointing out that the average sum assured by friendly societies did not exceed £100 and suggesting that in "our own Society the average is probably below £50".
4	We shall be able to issue tables with profits.	The fact that it was not until 1925 that the Society paid bonuses to industrial assurance policyholders (and then on a non-contractual basis) suggests that there was no pressing need for this change. Furthermore nobody was ever able to come up with any provision that prevented a friendly society from issuing with-profits tables and indeed some friendly societies were already providing such policies. [26]

5	Members will be enabled to raise loans upon their Policies without personal guarantee.	In fact, lenders were very reluctant to lend on the basis of an industrial assurance policy, whether issued by a collecting society or a company.
6	We shall then have the power to extend the operations of the Society by transacting such profitable business as Fire, Accident, Guarantee, Workmen's Compensation, etc, etc.	It was true that a company could and a friendly society could not transact this business but it did not necessarily follow that it would be profitable and thus in the interests of the members. It was also possible that a friendly society could lose business that it could transact where customers went to competitors who could provide all their insurance requirements, although there does not seem to have been anything preventing the Society from selling a third party's general policies and receiving commission from the third party for so long.
7	The great majority of your Collectors want to convert.	This point may have been persuasive for members but it is hardly a reason for change of itself. Whether or not to convert was an issue for the members not the collectors. The conversion debate tended to focus on agents and to overlook what was in the interests of the members as owners of the Friendly Society, although as no change of proprietorship was contemplated, the same members would own the mutual company after conversion.
	Additional reasons advanced but not included in the SGM booklet	
8	A company would have wider investment powers than a friendly society.	When Edward Smith was challenged on this claim after having repeated it in his evidence to the Parmoor Committee in 1919 (see Chapter 8 and Appendix 1) he could only respond "I think you got a little wider under the Companies Act". The Committee did not press him further.[27]

| 9 | The Society had outgrown the scope of the Friendly Societies Legislation ('FSL') and the Registrar etc. would welcome the conversion. | The Registrar had been complaining for over 30 years that the FSL was not designed for collecting societies but his point was not that they should convert to companies but rather that specific legislation was required for collecting societies. In fact, FSL coped, and continued to do so for those collecting societies that never converted and now legislation was being passed that applied to collecting societies (Collecting Societies and Industrial Assurance Companies Act 1896). There was no evidence that any official had encouraged the conversion. |

Against Conversion:

	Reasons identified by the Committee of 15	Comments of the author
1	The exemptions from stamp duty on policies and other documents would be lost at an estimated initial cost of £7,000 a year.	The directors believed that "as there will not be any shareholders to pay... such charges will be covered many times over by the profit derived from the business obtained from sources now closed to us".
2	Friendly societies were exempt from income tax. Tax would be payable on the investment income after conversion. This, it was estimated, would cost the life funds £2,000 a year.	The directors' view in 1 above applied here too – the Committee of Fifteen believed somewhat optimistically that this cost would be more than compensated by the additional returns earned by virtue of the slightly wider investment powers.
3	The fee for obtaining a death certificate of a friendly society member was one shilling – on conversion the normal fees would be payable that were then two shillings and seven pence for the certificate and an extra shilling if a search was required.	This was undeniably true although Edward Smith seemed to be suggesting in his speech at the special general meeting ('SGM') that in future the Society would pay for the death certificate so the cost would be irrelevant to the policyholder. There is no evidence that this happened.[28]
4	Policyholders would lose the friendly society members' statutory right to nominate a person to whom the benefit of a policy should be paid. It was also suggested that a fee would be charged on an assignment whereas a nomination was free.	As the Committee of Fifteen pointed out, the same effect could be achieved by assignment, although a nomination, unlike an assignment, could be revoked. Smith confirmed at the SGM that no fee would be charged on an assignment.

	Additional reasons put forward by the anti-conversioners amongst the agents	
5	Companies tend to pay lower rates of commission so the agents' income may be threatened.	Proprietary companies did tend to pay less commission, no doubt because tighter financial control was required in order to provide a return to shareholders on their investment. But (a) Royal London was to remain a mutual and (b) the directors owe their duty to the members, not the agents.
6	It is rare for companies to allow agents to sell their collecting books to a nominated successor so this right that agents enjoy may be threatened too.	The previous response applies. There was, in fact, no 'hidden agenda' on commission or nominating rights – it would be another 50 years before steps were taken to abolish the latter.
7	The Board of a company has more power to make changes (that may not be in our interest) than the committee of management of a friendly society ('CoM') which will be constrained by the legislation. Even the objects of a company can be changed.	Major changes that the Board of a company wished to make would require a special resolution to be passed at a members' meeting and sometimes the approval of the court. But there is some validity in the argument that a board would have more power than a CoM that would always be constrained by the friendly societies legislation.
8	Friendly societies are better than companies: "I take it that a Friendly Society is on an entirely different basis to an Industrial Company [I.C.], and, that its mission is to provide cheap insurance for its members and the best conditions for its servants. The basic principle of an I.C. is big dividends, dear assurance (comparatively speaking) and the worse possible conditions for its servants". Cave Canem, _The Anti-Conversionist_[29]	In terms of corporate structure, there was very little difference between a friendly society and a mutual company incorporated under the Companies Acts. The latter had no shareholders and so no dividends were paid. Sweeping generalisations such as these cannot have helped the anti-conversion movement but they serve to indicate the strength, at least in some quarters, of the anti-company feeling.

Any members who were genuinely opposed to the conversion (as distinct from those whose opposition was inspired by the views of their local agent) were saying that the case to convert had been made out to their satisfaction. Accordingly the advantages of being a friendly society should be retained and the expense of converting (that was to exceed £9,000) was not justified.

A member who turned to the trade journals for inspiration would have found that _The Policy-Holder_ supported conversion – it regarded the conversion "as another case of a big concern absurdly hampered by the limitations of the Friendly Societies Act which it has long ago outgrown"[30] and described some of the speeches of the opponents as "dumb crambo".[31]

The Insurance Mail was rather more articulate:

> *If the Royal London should be permitted by its members to transfer their society into a mutual company at the forthcoming meetings – as we trust they will – there can be no doubt whatever that the premium income will grow rapidly, as is the case with the Liverpool Victoria Assurance Company to-day. There cannot be much doubt in this respect because so many other ordinary life offices, and fire and accident offices, draw large amounts of business now from Royal London men.*[32]

Not surprisingly the Committee of Management had appointed Edward Smith, now a member of the London County Council and a justice of the peace, to chair the special general meeting. He was a practised orator remembered by Steve Else as "a bachelor of substantial proportions and vocal volume". Smith was mindful of the difficulties that might lie ahead and after welcoming the large number of members for attending, he warned them to be on their best behaviour:

> *Your interest and your confidence embolden me to appeal to you to grant to me your kind indulgence and generous assistance in carrying through this great meeting to a satisfactory issue. I shall need your good temper, your best judgment, and your hearty co-operation. I am sure that I shall not appeal in vain.*

He reiterated the reasons for converting: "We cannot allow [the Society's] onward career to be checked, or its safety to be menaced, or its workers' interests to be placed in jeopardy without serious alarm and an urgent appeal to you, its proprietors, to assist us in re-adapting our machinery to ensure continuous success". Later he stressed that in "this proposed change we have incorporated practically all the old rules of the Society, so conserving all the privileges of its members. There are no shareholders seeking dividends, nor stockholders, nor financial magnates, but it becomes in reality a vast co-operative institution, managed in the interests of and for the benefit of its members who alone are the proprietors, and the sole inheritors of its great future".[33]

There were some heated exchanges but under Smith's firm chairmanship the meeting never degenerated to the chaos experienced by Liverpool Victoria, although "the hall was crowded and the proceedings were of a somewhat noisy character, several of the speakers being quite inaudible to any but those immediately surrounding them".[34] The chairman ultimately put the resolution to the meeting and after the voting declared that it had been passed by the required majority. A poll was demanded and granted and in due course two of the partners of the Society's auditors who had been acting as scrutineers certified that the resolution had been passed by the required majority with 8,817 voting for and 1,014 against.

The opponents had not, however, given up the fight. On 10 July, James O'Grady asked in the House about the Treasury's awareness of the methods adopted by the Committee of Management to secure conversion. Charles Hobhouse, while answering his specific questions in the negative, indicated that the whole matter was receiving the most careful consideration and he gave an assurance that no action would be taken by the chief registrar without all due weight being given to any representations he may receive from the various parties.[35]

On 15 July the confirmatory meeting required under the Friendly Societies Act was held at the Queen's Hall, Langham Place at which 2,256 voted for and 111 against. The restrictions of the friendly societies legislation had been swept away – the memorandum of association permitted The Royal London Mutual Insurance Society, Limited:

> ... *to carry on the business of life assurance in all its branches, and to carry on the business of accident, employers' liability, third party, burglary and theft, fire, marine, storm, vehicular, plate glass, and transit insurance* [and]... *all kinds of guarantee and indemnity business* [and]... *generally to undertake and carry on all kinds of insurance business whatsoever, including re-insurance business.*

The new Society did not have a share capital or shareholders but was limited by guarantee – every member of the former friendly society was a member, every person who effected insurance on his or her own life became a member and the memorandum of association provided that, in the unlikely event of a winding-up, each member undertook to contribute to the debts and liabilities of the Society up to a maximum per member of one penny. So the mutual status was retained.

The articles of association provided that the first directors would be the former Committee of Management of the Royal London Friendly Society with the addition of William Coombes, the treasurer. The jobs-for-life concept in the friendly society's rules was retained – the new directors were excluded from the requirement to retire every few years and seek re-election. A major difference between companies and friendly societies was identified in the articles – Edward Smith was appointed chairman (at the first Board meeting, he was additionally appointed financial director) and John Price and Horace Duffell were appointed joint managing directors. All three were to hold office for so long as they were directors. Royal London had moved away from the collective management by equals concept of a friendly society. Alfred Skeggs was to be the first secretary of the company but was not appointed a director.

On 15 July (the day of the confirmatory meeting) William Clough was once again questioning Charles Hobhouse in the House of Commons, this time about the legality of the poll taken at the 24 June meeting. The reply indicated that neither the Treasury nor the registrar had power to test the legality of the poll – this was a matter for the courts – although the registrar did have to be satisfied that the resolutions were passed in accordance with the Friendly Societies Act. The other accusation being made was that the Committee had 'packed' the meeting. In fact both the pro and anti-factions, as would be expected, had taken steps to ensure that members sympathetic to their views attended the meeting and either there were many more in favour than against, or those in favour were better organised.[36]

By now one senses that Charles Hobhouse and J D Stuart Sim, the chief registrar, were looking for a way of bringing this irritating matter to a conclusion. The questions in the House and the application under section 76 appeared to be part of the campaign mounted by a group of anti-conversion agents. The role of the chief registrar was to protect members of friendly societies and there was no evidence that any of them had suffered or would suffer from the conversion, given the continued mutual status of the Society. No credible evidence had been advanced of any procedural irregularity. Nevertheless both men could see that the dispute was gathering a momentum of its own. The directors too would have been concerned by the prospect of the opposition continuing.

On 22 July Sim called a meeting that was attended by Kingsley Wood, the Society's solicitor, James Whitehead, an officer of the National Union of Life Assurance Agents, and Thomas Weldon, the solicitor representing a number of the opposing agents. Howard Kingsley Wood had been admitted as a solicitor as recently as 1903 at the age of 22 and almost immediately set up his own practice in the City. By 1907 he was acting for both Royal London and Liverpool Victoria in relation to their conversions.[37] The chief registrar, no doubt backed by the Treasury, was anxious to explore if there was some concession that the Society could give that would persuade the agents to withdraw their opposition. On 30 July Clough asked Hobhouse if the chief registrar was aware that agreement had been reached. The minister was aware that the company had offered terms "favourable to the dissentient collectors" that had been accepted – "the main point conceded was that collectors should be guaranteed the market price for their books if they received notice to leave for any cause except 'wilful dishonesty'".[38] Clough wondered if the idea of testing the poll at the conversion meeting had been abandoned but the minister reiterated that this was a matter for the courts, not the Treasury. Arnold Lupton (the Liberal MP for Sleaford in Lincolnshire) asked if those who voted for the conversion had their fares paid by the Society but the minister was able to confirm that the Society's funds were not used for that purpose.[39]

James O'Grady, the first MP to raise the matter of the Royal London conversion in the House of Commons, followed Lupton and put what proved to be the last questions on the topic. He asked:

> ... whether having regard to the recent conversion of the Royal London Friendly Society, he will consider the possibility of presenting a Bill amending the Friendly Societies Act, 1896, section 54 of which confers the absolute right upon wealthier societies to convert themselves into companies and so destroy the benefits in the Act specially designed for the use of the industrial community?

The Secretary to the Treasury confirmed that the Government had no such intention. O'Grady's was a strangely worded question – section 54 said nothing about conversions and having to persuade three-quarters of the members who attend a meeting to vote for a conversion resolution is hardly an absolute right. O'Grady may have been badly briefed, or deliberately exaggerated the concern, but what is beyond doubt is that he and his trade union colleagues were not in favour of friendly societies converting to companies.

The application under section 76 was refused by the registrar on the grounds that it did not show sufficient grounds for an inspection and the formalities of the conversion were implemented at the friendly societies and companies registries. On 31 July 1908 the certificate of incorporation of The Royal London Mutual Insurance Society, Limited was issued by the registrar of joint stock companies. *The Assurance Agents Chronicle* greeted the news enthusiastically:

> This marks an important stage in the history of industrial assurance. For the first time a large collecting society has successfully obtained re-registration under the Board of Trade. It is a sign of the times that the new constitution is a mutual one, for under [section 71 of the Friendly Societies Act 1896] which authorises [transfers] no stipulation is made as to the form of the constitution. Another matter for observation particularly interesting to the readers of this journal is that special and numerous provisions have been made for the workers of this institution. The whole scheme of arrangement [sic], settled as it has been by the most eminent insurance lawyers of the day, and assisted by insurance experts of varied and considerable experience, will doubtless provide a model for others.[40]

The article concluded:

> *It is anticipated that this new yet old venture will be a highly successful one. It is useless to deny the fact that Royal London men, equipped as they will be in all departments of insurance, will have an advantage in the battle and struggle of insurance business which develops more keenly every day. To the men who have opposed this change and their reasons we have naturally every sympathy, and can congratulate them on a fight fought courageously and unceasingly. We have every reason to believe that they will be treated as honourable opponents opposed to a majority to which everyone at some stage had to bow their head.*

"What would the founders have thought of this conversion if they were still alive?" somebody probably asked at the time. If the questioner was an opponent of the conversion who was anticipating a "they would have been horrified" response, he may have been disappointed. While employed by them, Joseph Degge had, of course, been reprimanded for supporting a proposal to convert Royal Liver[41] and Charlie Ridge later wrote that his father "wanted to turn the Royal London into a Company but he was overruled by his colleagues".[42] That would leave Hambridge as the only opponent.

The business immediately after conversion provided limited support for the view that the friendly society restrictions were damaging Royal London.[43] During the next two years, the Society issued about a million industrial branch policies with a total sum insured of £10 million and 10,000 ordinary branch policies with a total sum insured of just over £1 million. So the average sum insured by industrial branch policies was £10 and by ordinary branch was £100. There could have been the occasional policy for more than £200, and sometimes a small policy might have taken the policyholder over the £200 aggregate limit but the figures suggest that these would have been isolated cases. History also proved that there was nothing in the argument that conversion to the status of a company would improve the situation in relation to funeral expense policies where the relationship between proposer and life assured was too remote because legislation passed in 1909 applied the same set of rules to both friendly societies and companies.[44] On the other hand, forty one thousand fire policies had been sold with annual premiums of £9,000 – this was business that was available to a company but not to a friendly society. The directors were later to claim that "a gigantic general insurance business had been transacted"[45] although this rather over-states the position – during the two years, it represented less than 4 per cent of the total policies sold and 2 per cent of the annual premiums. The business had been built up from nothing, however, and early sales of this magnitude would have confirmed the directors' view that general insurance would prove a worthwhile addition to the Society's portfolio.

In August 1908 the directors would have looked back on a difficult job well done and expected calmer days ahead. They were in for a shock. The members too were about to suffer. The booklets prepared for the special general meeting at the Royal Albert Hall and the confirmatory meeting at the Queen's Hall set out in bold and simple language under the heading *Remember* some points designed to encourage members to support the conversion. Among these were:

> *3. Profits on past and future business will belong to the Members.*
> *4. There is no Share Capital in any shape or form: the Members are the **only** proprietors.*[46]

It would take 12 years for these simple objectives to be achieved.

CHAPTER 6

Threats to Conversion

1910

It is the duty of the Court, and it is the habit of the Court, to control and confine bodies of this nature, whether companies or quasi-corporations, strictly within the objects prescribed for them by statute, and I cannot bring myself to doubt that what has been attempted here is unauthorised by the Act, is plainly contrary to the scheme and policy of the Act, and must be restrained by injunction.

Sir Herbert Hardy Cozens-Hardy, Master of the Rolls, *Blythe v Birtley* (1910)[1]

On those words [section 71(2) of the Friendly Societies Act 1896], it was quite a reasonable thing to assume that if you did what was done in this case, passed your special resolution... you had complied properly with sub-section 2; and that the resolution with the attached documents could be registered at the Head Office, as was done in this case; and then the memorandum would have the same effect as a Memorandum of Association duly signed and attested under the Act. But, Sir, if I may say so with all respect to the Judges of the Court of Appeal, that would have been the ordinary meaning which a person who read as he ran would give to the words; and that meaning was undoubtedly given to the words generally by those who were concerned in such matters. I think all my learned friends will agree in saying that the decision in Blythe v Birtley came as a surprise.

Sir Malcolm Macnaghten KC, Arbitration, *Lovett v Smith* (1920)[2]

The directors would have hoped that the conversion would herald a period of peace and prosperity for Royal London, now free from the restrictions of the friendly societies legislation. In fact, there were to be developments so serious that, 12 years later, eight directors had to resign.

In 1909, The Royal Co-operative Collecting Society was in the process of converting from a friendly society to a company. The Royal London precedent had been followed – the objects of the converted company were to include all types of life assurance and all kinds of insurance. But that was the extent of the similarity with Royal London. The Royal Co-operative Life and General Insurance Company Limited was to be a proprietary company with a capital of £100,000, divided into £1 shares, but the shareholders were to be distinct from the members of the society who were to be special members with very limited rights. The assets of the society were to become the property of the new company. Despite this, the special resolution to convert was passed and confirmed at meetings on 28 October and 8 November 1909. Then there was a startling development. A Mr Blythe, who had taken out a policy on his own life with Royal Co-operative, as recently as the previous June, at a premium of 8d per month and who (it was said) had previously been an agent with another insurance institution, began proceedings in the High Court. He sued the trustees, the secretary and the committee of management of Royal Co-operative and applied for an injunction restraining Royal Co-operative from implementing the resolution. He sued, as Mr Justice Joyce put it "as the practice of the Court allows, on behalf of himself and all [the other] members of the friendly society, except the defendants in this action. They are very numerous, and for the most part they are very poor people".[3] There were several thousand members scattered all over the country, but chiefly in the north. Mr Justice Joyce granted the injunction and Royal Co-operative appealed at once. The outcome of the appeal was eagerly, if nervously, awaited because it was recognised that a finding against Royal Co-operative would cast doubt on the validity of the Royal London conversion.

The point at issue was easily defined – Royal Co-operative (and Royal London two years before) had resolved to do two things at the same time: to convert the friendly society to a company and to alter their objects by increasing significantly the range of insurance business that could be undertaken. These wider powers were included in the memorandum of association of the company. There was no difficulty with the former as section 71(1) of the Friendly Societies Act 1896 allowed a friendly society, by special resolution, to convert itself into a company incorporated under the Companies Acts. The problem was changing the objects. The wider powers were not permitted under the Friendly Societies Act. They could have been permitted under the Companies Act but only with the approval of the court, and no such approval had been sought. Royal Co-operative argued that, as the main reason for friendly societies converting to companies was to enable them to broaden their business beyond the restrictions imposed by the Friendly Societies Act, authorisation should be implied – there was little point in converting if the friendly society restrictions had to remain unless and until a court agreed otherwise. No court approval was required for the memorandum of association of a new company and they suggested that the wording of section 71(2) indicated that a memorandum of association of a company created by a conversion resolution was comparable with the memorandum for a newly formed company. Certainly nowhere in the Act was there any statement that the objects could not be widened on a conversion.

Mr Justice Joyce, and on 11 January 1910 the Court of Appeal, found in favour of Mr Blythe (the case appears in the law reports as *Blythe v Birtley*) holding that conversion required a two-stage process. First the friendly society converts to a company but with substantially the same objects as the friendly society. Then the company passes a resolution to change its objects and seeks the approval of the court to do so. Royal Co-operative's case that the two steps could be combined into one was dismissed in withering terms by Lord Justice Buckley[4] in the Court of Appeal:

> *Counsel* [for the Royal Co-operative] *agree, indeed they could not dispute, that the society could not so enlarge its objects under the Friendly Societies Act of 1896. It is quite beyond anything in that Act. They also have to confess that they cannot do it under the Companies Acts for two reasons. In the first place, they are not under the Companies Acts yet until they are registered under them, and, secondly, if they were, they could not do it without the sanction of the Court. But they seek to say that at some moment of time – I cannot myself grasp when it is – they are governed neither by the one Act nor by the other, but are free to do just what they please by way of alteration of their objects. To my mind, that is entirely wrong.*[5]

There was no doubt that the decision in *Blythe v Birtley* came as a surprise although it is difficult to criticise the judges' interpretation of the legislation – there is a compelling logic in Lord Justice Buckley's analysis – and if anybody was at fault it was the parliamentary draftsman. If it was Parliament's intention that the objects could be extended on conversion, then the Act should have said so. If it was not, and the approval of the court had to be obtained under the Companies Act, then this should have been specified. Much was made of the fact that the point in *Blythe v Birtley* had never been taken before. Since 1879, 25 conversions had been made, of which more than half involved an extension of the objects, and no objection had been raised in any of them.[6] The procedural formalities of section 71 had been complied with and the newly converted company had operated as though its powers were those contained in the new memorandum of association. Many societies which had converted were, however, small local organisations where the decisions probably had the support of most of the membership and where any members who were aggrieved would have lacked the resources (or the means of acquiring them) to take the matter any further.[7]

The opposition to the Royal London conversion had been such that, if the opponents had been advised of a potential legal remedy, they may well have gone to the High Court in 1908 to try to prevent the conversion. In fact, they probably never investigated the point – the directors, they knew, had retained high-powered lawyers and the possibility of a major flaw being overlooked seemed remote. Those leading the opposition to the Royal Co-operative plan, however, sought advice from Carruthers & Gedye, a firm of Liverpool solicitors. Robert Carruthers or counsel instructed by him[8] must have taken a close look at section 71 and come up with what they felt was 'an arguable point'. It would be interesting to know how confident they were of the success of their argument.

Whatever litigants may think, judges tend not to be pure lawyers but are sensitive to the wider merits of the case. The several thousand very poor members of Royal Co-operative to whom Mr Justice Joyce referred would have been worse off if the conversion had gone ahead. They would no longer have been the proprietors of the business and the assets of the society would have been transferred to the new company. The judges would inevitably have begun their analysis of the law with those thoughts in their minds. The Royal London members were, for all practical purposes, unaffected by the conversion – Royal London was a mutual organisation owned by its members both before and after the conversion and so its members did not need the protection of the court in the same way. We will never know if the interpretation of the legislation would have been different if the Royal London conversion had been the first one to get to court.

The question exercising the minds of many at Finsbury Square was where did the decision in *Blythe v Birtley* leave Royal London, already converted by the single-stage approach that had been rejected by the judges? This was made all the more pressing in February 1910 when Michael McGlade, a labourer whose two Royal London policies involved premiums of 3d a week, sought an injunction in the High Court restraining Royal London from exercising any of the additional powers conferred by the conversion resolution. Carruthers & Gedye were acting for Mr McGlade. The similarity between the essential facts of the two conversions was such that Mr McGlade and his legal team would have been confident of a successful outcome of the case. Courts, however, consider form as well as substance. Mr McGlade had brought his action against the post-conversion limited company in his capacity as a member of that company. Mr Justice Eve, in March 1910 and in the Court of Appeal two months later, held that, as a general legal principle, a member of a company is not entitled to an order restraining the company from performing part of the objects set out in its memorandum of association.[9]

The decision provided little comfort to Royal London who had succeeded only on a legal technicality. Sir Herbert Hardy Cozens-Hardy, the Master of the Rolls, who had presided in the Court of Appeal in both cases, stressed that he did not qualify or retract a single word that he had said in *Blythe v Birtley* and suggested that Mr McGlade could well have been successful if he had sued as a member of the friendly society. Lord Justice Buckley in the course of his judgment went to some lengths to advise Mr McGlade how to bring a successful action against Royal London. The view of the judges that there were means by which a policyholder could attack the conversion horrified the Royal London Board. They had been reassured by advice received immediately after the decision in *Blythe v Birtley* that had anticipated the decision in the *McGlade* case, that a member of a company could not restrain the company from performing its objects. The counsel they consulted, however, had lacked the legal ingenuity of the judges and had failed to see that there were other ways in which an objection to the Royal London conversion could be brought to court.

Almost immediately two writs were issued against Royal London in the form suggested by the judges. In one of them, a policyholder who had sued the trustees of the Royal London Friendly Society, the directors of the Society and the Society applied at once for an interlocutory injunction that, if granted, would immediately have restrained the Society from acting under the conversion resolution pending the full hearing of the case. Undaunted, or perhaps inspired, by their failure on behalf of Mr McGlade and an award of costs against their client, Carruthers & Gedye were now acting for Mr McCormick, the policyholder. On 11 June 1910 Mr Justice Joyce declined to grant the interlocutory injunction on the basis that two years had passed since the conversion.[10] That was, however, only a procedural success for Royal London and did no more than defer the time when Mr Justice Joyce, who had been the judge at first instance in *Blythe v Birtley*, would consider the substantive issues of the case. Kingsley Wood, the Society's solicitor, had instructed an impressive array of counsel to represent the Society in the policyholders' actions including Edward Carson, one the greatest advocates of that or indeed any other age, and P O Lawrence, who the directors would come across again after his promotion to the bench.

On 15 June 1910 *Blythe v Birtley* was applied in Scotland when Lord Skerrington granted an interdict (injunction) preventing the City of Glasgow Friendly Society from implementing a resolution to convert the friendly society into a company.[11] The City of Glasgow had been founded a year after Royal London and was also a break-away from Royal Liver – some of the members and collectors felt that they were too far away from Liverpool and that, as Glasgow was a bigger city than Liverpool, why should orders be transmitted from a lesser place?[12] Now conversion to a company was being proposed. The memorandum of association made no substantial changes to the objects of the society but permitted the distribution of surplus assets amongst shareholders rather than members, and provided for a distribution from the capital of the company to officials, employees and delegates of the society. This, the judge held, was not permitted under the principle established in *Blythe v Birtley*. The vigorous debate in Glasgow presented this as a local issue – should a much-respected local institution be allowed to convert? It must have come as a surprise, even to those who opposed the conversion, when William Thomas Wilkinson, a policyholder from Accrington, brought the action in the Court of Session in Edinburgh.[13] Close observers would have noted that the firm of Edinburgh solicitors representing Mr Wilkinson was acting as agent for Carruthers & Gedye, and had been instructed by them purely for the purpose of bringing proceedings in Scotland.[14]

These were tense times for the directors of Royal London and their advisers. The principle that had emerged from *Blythe v Birtley* had quickly become established. It was unthinkable that a differently constituted Court of Appeal or the House of Lords would come to a different view of the law and there seemed no prospect of being able to put forward a successful defence in the cases that were pending. The Board had good grounds for believing that it was only a matter of time before a court would declare the Royal London conversion invalid. The consequences of that were unthinkable – policies taken out since July 1908 might be void, premiums would have to be returned, the policyholders would not be covered and perhaps there could be claims for damages, possibly even against the directors personally. New legislation seemed to be the only solution to the dilemma but time was short as it would have to be on the statute book before any of the pending cases came to trial. The onus was very much on the directors to take the initiative because the Society was the only friendly society of any substance that had recently converted and extended its objects.

The directors are to be congratulated for the speed with which they moved. With the help of Edwin Cornwall, the MP for Bethnal Green and one of the Society's trustees, a meeting was set up at the House of Commons on 29 June with Sydney Buxton, the President of the Board of Trade, and Charles Hobhouse, the First Secretary to the Treasury, who was already familiar with Royal London, having fielded the questions in the House of Commons at the time of the conversion.[15] The arguments advanced by the Royal London deputation, headed by Edward Smith, with Kingsley Wood at his side, were not without merit.[16] The membership had voted to convert with wider objects and the conversion and extension of objects had been effected in good faith. There was no suggestion that any policyholders, least of all Messrs McGlade and McCormick had suffered any loss. Uncertainty was not in the public interest and it was important to bring it to an end as soon as possible.

To that extent, Royal London received a sympathetic hearing and the ministers intimated a willingness to legislate. The difficulty was the extent of the legislation. The Society's Board wanted it to put Royal London in the position that they thought had been achieved by the conversion resolution and for the wide insurance powers to be retained. This, however, went too far for the ministers. It was more than Royal London needed to protect the policies issued since the conversion and they were not prepared to put forward legislation that appeared to be critical of the Court of Appeal or to make what would, on the basis of the Court's interpretation of the Act, have been substantive change to the law applicable to future friendly society conversions.

When the Bill was published, Carruthers & Gedye lost no time in writing to the President of the Board of Trade and "protesting most strongly against the action of the promoters of the Bill" in blocking the inquiry into the conversion that would take place if the case in which they were acting went to trial. They suggested that it was unconstitutional to rush a Bill through Parliament to change the law on a point that was directly relevant to a pending case. They complained, with some justification, about the provision in Royal London's articles by which the existing directors were appointed for life and made various general complaints about the voting at the special general meeting, but failed to provide any evidence or to demonstrate how the policyholders or members had suffered.

The ministers were not persuaded by the solicitors' protest and the Companies (Converted Societies) Act 1910 received the Royal Assent on 3 August. It provided that the validity of the resolution to convert a friendly society into a company could not be questioned on the ground that the objects of the company set out in the resolution extended beyond those authorised by the rules of the society. So far so good for the Board, but this was subject to a proviso that:

> ... as from the passing of this Act, the objects of the company shall not extend beyond those authorised by the rules of the society at the date of the passing of the special resolution, except so far as may be necessary for giving effect to, and for carrying out any assurances, contracts or policies, made, entered into, or issued before the passing of this Act.

It followed that the Royal London conversion could not now be challenged and the Society was deemed to have been empowered to carry out the wider insurance business, but only for the period from the date of conversion up to 3 August 1910. From that date, its powers reverted to those of a friendly society. An 'avoidance of doubt' provision confirmed "that nothing in this Act shall be construed as prejudicing the right of any such company to alter its memorandum of association with respect to its objects in accordance with the provisions of the Companies [Acts]". This seemed to be a clear indication by the Government that seeking approval from the court for the wider powers was the step that a recently converted friendly society should take to recover the wider powers now denied to it.

The effect of the Act was that from 3 August, the £200 ceiling for life policies and the exclusion of all other types of business had been re-imposed. The former was of little immediate concern to the Society because the sum assured in its new policies was rarely anywhere near £200. Since the conversion, it had issued a million industrial branch policies with an average sum assured of only £10 and 10,000 ordinary branch policies with an average sum assured of £100. More than 40,000 fire policies had been sold, however, with annual premiums of £9,000 and this business was now denied to the Society.

The Board had a strategic decision to make. Essentially it had two options. The first was to take, as quickly as possible, the minimum action necessary to put the Society in a position to carry on the business that it was conducting as at 3 August 1910. In practice this would have involved applying to the court for authority to undertake fire insurance, or perhaps entering into an agreement with another insurance company to sell its fire policies and to share the profits of so doing. As and when the pre-August business had been restored, the Board could then have reviewed the wider issues at its leisure. The second option was to seek a comprehensive solution that, at a single stroke, would enable all classes of insurance business to be carried out and so put Royal London in the position that it would have been in following the conversion, had it not been for the unwelcome intervention of Mr Blythe and Carruthers & Gedye.

The law reports of the cases in 1910 leave unanswered a fascinating question. Litigation is not cheap. Even if you are successful, and the other party is ordered to pay your costs, you will still be out of pocket because not every payment will be recoverable in full. The real expense is if you lose and find yourself having to pay the costs of the other party or parties as well as your own. So who was funding all these lawsuits? We can be certain that it was not Messrs Blythe, Wilkinson, McGlade or McCormick – they were merely lending their names to enable an action to be brought. They had neither suffered from the conduct complained of in their claims nor would they receive any benefit if the cases were determined in their favour. In fact the question is not so much who was funding the cases but who was bringing them – who were the ultimate clients of Carruthers & Gedye?[17] Who felt so strongly that they were prepared to spend good money to prevent further conversions and to 'de-convert' a society that had already converted?

The strength of feeling amongst the opponents of these conversions is clear, a century later, from reading the documents. If the anti-conversion groups at Royal Co-operative and the City of Glasgow had been advised that there could be a way of preventing the conversions, they may well have set about collecting funds so that the cases could be brought to court. It is possible too that in 1910 the Royal London Collectors League was reconstituted and began fund-raising, inspired by the thought that if the conversion was held to have been ineffective, the Royal London Friendly Society would be reborn and their campaign would belatedly have achieved its objective.

There is, however, no evidence of any such revival. Supporting a lawsuit against your employer is unlikely to be a career-enhancing move and, after two years, during which none of the terrible things that were predicted had occurred and Royal London had continued to make steady progress, many would have been reassured while other opponents, although still unconvinced, would no longer have felt strongly enough to take militant action. So who was it to whom McGlade, McCormick and others were lending their names?

The interventions of James O'Grady and others in the House of Commons at the time of the Royal London conversion revealed a general concern within Labour and the trade union movement about friendly society conversions. Two letters sent to journals in June 1910 highlight the political interest. "Justice", writing to the *Evening Citizen*, felt that the decision restraining the City of Glasgow's conversion:

> ... *will assuredly strengthen the hands of the Trades' Councils, who are about to start an agitation against the manipulation of this and similar societies in the interests of certain classes and encourage to action the members of Parliament who are watching developments on behalf of the working classes, whose weekly privations have created the great funds of these societies, and which should be secured to them for all times.*[18]

In a letter to the *Labour Leader* "A Socialist Member" issued a call to arms. The City of Glasgow Friendly Society:

> ... *was started 50 years ago by working men through delegates whom they elect. If the management carry the new scheme and*

form a company it will be managed by a board of directors, elected by shareholders… If these working class societies are allowed to become private companies they will become close vested interests. It is surely within the province of the [Independent Labour Party] and other Socialist bodies throughout the country to take action at once to make their influence felt in these institutions which belong to the people. Otherwise, depend upon it, they will be spirited away by legal chicanery into the hands of the moneyed classes, who are just out for what they can get by way of inflated value when the State assumes control, as it surely will, in the near future. Trusting officials in the Movement will realise their duty in this matter, and the immense organised effort it will take to save the societies from the dividend hunters.[19]

Perhaps, unknown to the correspondents, action was already being taken and members of the movement were amongst those instructing Carruthers & Gedye in the cases. A tantalising cryptic clue as to others who may have been involved is provided in the transcript of the meeting that the Royal London deputation had with the ministers on 29 June 1910 to explore the possibility of legislation being passed to address the Society's difficulty. Although the ministers indicated at the outset that the Government was prepared to legislate, Edward Smith seemed determined to deliver the opening statement that he had prepared, during the course of which he referred to the remarks of the judges "giving rise to a band of blackmailers in the north". Warming to his theme, he complained that:

… there is in the North of England and elsewhere a gang that is becoming notorious; they are well known as men who pool together the results of whatever may be gained and therefore there is a great difficulty threatening the constitution of every organisation if they once prey upon them… [These] people are on the backs of several other Friendly Societies endeavouring to find some flaw in their constitution. We are not able to get at them and every time we issue a writ the thing becomes public, and the whole of the staff working the country, the agents, I mean the competing staff, say there is some doubt about the position in which they are, and these contracts may be determined to be null and void. It may be said: "Well, you have no verdict against yourselves". No, but by implication the same principle governs our case as the others.[20]

This is not an example of Smith at his most articulate but he seems to be suggesting that this mysterious group were doing two things – threatening to proceed against organisations alleging flaws in their constitutions unless a payment was made to them, and taking action so that doubt was cast on the standing of the defendant company in the minds of potential customers to the benefit of the defendant's competitors. Sir Henry Dalziel, another member of the Royal London deputation, was rather more concise when he returned to the point later in the meeting:

> I should like to say a word or two on the blackmail point of view. There is not a policyholder who has a complaint: there is not a genuine policyholder who is under any complaint at all. As the Chairman of the Society has said, there is a gang of people going about who pool the results that are obtained from going against any company whom they happen to come across: our solicitor is here and he can give you the amount that they have divided between them. It will all come out some day in the Police Court but I need not take up your time about that.[21]

The ministers did not seem particularly interested in the group from the north but were content to steer the Bill through Parliament. When it became law, the potential to challenge the Royal London conversion was at an end, as was any interest in the notorious gang. What was of interest to many observers, however, not to mention the staff and perhaps even some members and policyholders, was the action that Royal London would be taking, now that the Companies (Converted Societies) Act 1910 was in force.

CHAPTER 7

The Royal London Auxiliary Insurance Company, Limited

1910–1921

I was only expressing my astonishment that a company should have been formed under those circumstances to compete with the parent Company. But still there it is. It may be that that is the position, but of course it puts the Directors in an impossible position.

Mr Justice P O Lawrence, High Court of Justice (Chancery Division),
The Royal London Auxiliary Insurance Company, Limited v Lovett (February 1921)[1]

Our members will remember that the [Braham Benevolent] *Fund was inaugurated to perpetuate and honour the name of Mr Benjamin Braham for his untiring efforts on behalf of Royal London Workers, both as a member of this Association and a Director of the 'Royal London'... Undoubtedly he was as staunch as any man could be to what he considered true and correct procedure, and his name, aided by the Braham Benevolent Fund, will stand for all time in the annals of 'Royal London' history.*

Executive Council, Royal London Staff Association (June 1930)[2]

Most observers of the events since Mr Blythe challenged the conversion of the Royal Co-operative Collecting Society probably expected Royal London to seek immediate approval from the court for the business being conducted as at 3 August 1910, leaving it open for further approvals to be sought as and when extensions of the Society's business were contemplated. The Board, however, had been working on a more radical approach.[3] They preferred to address the difficulty by resurrecting the 1905 proposal and immediately putting in place a proprietary company to stand beside the Society and to use the Society's agents, administration and infrastructure. The great attraction of this was certainty – a new company could be given the widest insurance powers from the beginning without the need for any court approval then or in the future. The certainty would be achieved, however, at a cost to most of the members of the Society because the profits of the business of the company would accrue, not to the membership at large, but to the shareholders of the company. Another attraction to the Board was that they could be amongst those shareholders.

In fact this approach had already been put in place. The chain of events had begun on 8 July 1908, between the special and the confirmatory general meetings that converted the Society to a company, when the Committee of Management of the Royal London Friendly Society resolved to draw a cheque for £40,000 in respect of the deposits that had to be lodged before the Society could transact all the business that was contemplated after conversion. Of this, £20,000 was for fire and accident insurance. In December 1908 the Board issued an invitation to members of the newly converted Society to subscribe for 100,000 certificates of £1 each. Subscribers were to pay 4s for each certificate. The document explained that the Society had decided to establish a new department to carry out non-life insurance and to create "a special fund for the working of the new department, so as to leave the existing insurance fund of the Society, and any accretions thereto, for the life insurance and endowment businesses".

The recipients of this document (it is not clear how widely it was circulated) were invited to invest in a fund, which came to be called the Auxiliary Fund, to finance the Society's new businesses. It was probably no coincidence that the amount to be raised by the issue of the certificates (100,000 at 4s each) was £20,000, the sum deposited in relation to fire and accident insurance.

The certificates, which were neither shares nor debentures,[4] had been created by a trust deed dated 3 December 1908 that established a scheme for the business of the new department under which:

- the Society's agents sold its policies and collected the premiums
- the premiums were paid into the Auxiliary Fund

- all the expenses incurred by the department (for example claims under the policies, the agents' commissions on the sale of its policies, and the remuneration of office staff working exclusively on its behalf) were paid from the Fund
- the Fund paid the Society 1 per cent of the premium income and 5 per cent of the profit of its business to cover the use by the department of the chief office and the district offices and to reimburse the Society for expenses incurred on its behalf that could not be specifically attributed to the department
- the certificate holders were entitled to the balance left over in the Fund.

The effect of the scheme was to make the new department a stand-alone business, the profits of which accrued, not to the Society, but to the holders of the certificates. Between them the directors held more than 16,000 certificates and it seems likely that most of the other certificates were owned by Royal London staff. The payment of £20,000 by the Society in relation to fire and accident insurance was contrary to the Life Assurance Act 1870 which provided that life funds must be preserved for life policies. Accordingly, it was entirely proper that steps were being taken to refund it although a loan from the Society's bank, that would surely have been available if requested, would have regularised the position without the need for any complex investment scheme.

Essentially what the directors were proposing in August 1910 was an extension of the certificates scheme, with a newly incorporated proprietary company being substituted for the Auxiliary Fund. The plan to launch a company to stand beside the Society had, by modern standards, at least two flaws. It conflicted with the repeated assurances of the Board, which had campaigned in 1908 on the basis that after the conversion there would be no shareholders and that the profits of the future business of the Society would belong to the members. This had been stressed in any number of documents issued by the Committee of Management, not to mention the statements made by Edward Smith at the special general meeting at which the resolution to convert was passed.[5] Secondly, the company would be paying nothing for the use of the Society's established and well-respected name, its existing infrastructure and its extensive customer contacts. In the open market, a company starting up in business would have had to pay for these benefits over and above the reimbursement of future expenses, such as commissions payable to agents for selling its policies and claims made under them. All that was to be required of the new company was to reimburse the Society for direct costs incurred by the Society on its behalf and to pay to the Society 2 per cent of its premium income to cover expenditure incurred by the Society in providing services to the company that could not be specifically attributed to the company.

It is unlikely, however, that these flaws alone would have prompted any objection. Creating a company owned by the directors and staff to transact business that the Society could not undertake might offend modern governance standards but seems to have provoked little criticism at the time, *The Policy-Holder* commenting that "the creation of an allied company to operate in those fields from which the parent concern is excluded... is open to no objections".[6] This rather overlooks the fact that the membership had voted for the conversion two years earlier on the basis that there would be no shareholders. If, however, *The Policy-Holder* was genuinely reflecting public opinion, this suggests that, if the activities of the company had been restricted to general insurance (such as buildings and contents insurance) and life policies for more than £200, the Society and its allied company may have satisfactorily co-existed for many years. Both *Post Magazine*[7] and *The Policy-Holder* reported that the new company had been formed only to transact business that the Society was not competent to undertake and that was the view of the Board on 25 July 1910 when they resolved to form a new company "to transact such business as the [Society] cannot accept".

Shortly after 25 July the directors changed their mind on this point and in so doing created the flaw that would in due course prove disastrous. Letters to all the staff dated 3 August were approved by the Board on 4 August and circulated in the days that followed. The letters criticised both the judges, suggesting that the decision in *Blythe v Birtley* was "opposed to the intention of the Act of Parliament", and the Government that had "resolutely declined, despite repeated applications, to go beyond legalising" the business permitted under the Friendly Societies Act, and explained that:

> *In order to continue the business of the Society and maintain the interests of the staff therein, the Directors are about to immediately register an Auxiliary Company which, by agreement with the Society, will confine its business in the United Kingdom to Ordinary Life, Fire, Accident, Burglary, Plate Glass, Fidelity Guarantee etc. the Society continuing to transact the Industrial Life and Endowment Assurance business.*

In 1909 the Society had produced a handsome ordinary branch prospectus. There were 23 different policies on offer and the Society had sold 10,000 ordinary life policies in the two years since the conversion. Premiums were paid annually, half-yearly, quarterly or monthly, Careful readers of the 3 August letters would have realised that the Society was about to revert to its original industrial assurance role, selling only policies involving weekly collection of premiums, and that in future it would be the company rather than the Society that would undertake ordinary business.

The document signed by Henry Ridge and Joseph Degge on 2 February 1861 in which they agreed to form and promote the Royal London Life Insurance and Benefit Society.

Joseph Degge

Henry Ridge

William Hambridge

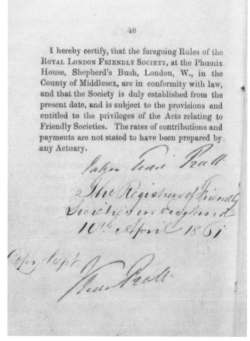

49

I hereby certify, that the foregoing Rules of the
ROYAL LONDON FRIENDLY SOCIETY, at the Phœnix
House, Shepherd's Bush, London, W., in the
County of Middlesex, are in conformity with law,
and that the Society is duly established from the
present date, and is subject to the provisions and
entitled to the privileges of the Acts relating to
Friendly Societies. The rates of contributions and
payments are not stated to have been prepared by
any Actuary.

What the founders were waiting for –
the certificate signed by the Registrar of
Friendly Societies.

The Committee of Management out and about in the 1860s. Henry Ridge (straw hat) and Joseph Degge (top hat) are in the driving seat with William Hambridge standing at the rear.

The Committee of Management between September 1875 and March 1877. Left to right: Frederick De La Bertauche, Joseph Barnes Degge, Laurence Barrett, William Hambridge (secretary), Dr Thomas Forster, Henry Ridge, James Birnie, Augustus Beane.

51 Moorgate Street (1861)

5 Aldermanbury Postern (1866)

28 Finsbury Place, later 70
Finsbury Pavement (1876)

108 (later 6) Paul Street (1886)

Representations of chief office and the coat of arms often featured in the impressive policy documents.

"To my surprise I got the job and started work [at 6 Paul Street] on the following Monday... I was shown into a glass roofed room about 30 feet square..." (April 1904)

(Left) William Hambridge in the 1890s

(Below) The Committee of Management at the turn of the Century.
Left to right: Edward Hambridge, Edward Smith, William Bowrey (secretary), John Price, Frederick De La Bertauche, Thomas Byrne, George Atherton, Horace Duffell.

Agents relaxing on their annual outings: a south London office (probably Penge) in 1889 (above) and a Sheffield office in 1893 in front of Robin Hood's tree in Sherwood Forest (below).

The first phase of Royal London House, Finsbury Square: a magnificent building *"with its handsome elevation, its beautiful architecture, and its towering erection of massive stone and granite"* that will *"not only be worthy of its name as head offices of a great and prosperous Institution, but will be a credit and improvement to the City of London."* (1904)

The annual outing to Henley-on-Thames was a memorable event for head office staff in the summers before World War I.

By 1911 the first extension along the north of Finsbury Square had been completed.

HANDS OFF

THE PEOPLE'S FRIENDLY SOCIETIES.

THE

London Trades' Council

Calls upon all Trades Unionists
who are Members of the

ROYAL LONDON
FRIENDLY SOCIETY

TO ATTEND THE

CONVERSION MEETING

AT THE

Royal Albert Hall, Kensington, W.

On WEDNESDAY, JUNE 24th, at 6 p.m.

AND

VOTE AGAINST
THE CONVERSION

Of your Friendly Society into a COMPANY

ATTEND IN YOUR THOUSANDS
And Save Your Society from the
COMPANY AGITATORS.

Don't Forget to Bring your Premium Receipt Book.

All over 16 years of age, Male or Female, who have been members for
12 months may attend.

ISSUED BY THE ROYAL LONDON ANTI-CONVERSION COMMITTEE.

| President— | Treasurer | EDWARD WRIGHT, 28 Penrith Street, Streatham, S.W. | Hon. Sec. |
| Mr. JOHN STOKES. | Mr. E. HESKETH. | HY. BROWN, 15 St. John's Church Road, Hackney, N.E. | |

Printed by The New Goswell Printing Co. (T.U.), 220 Goswell Road, London, E.C.

The great debate of 1908 – to remain a friendly society or convert to a company.

The Royal London Cricket Club, winners of the Insurance Companies Cricket League in 1912, photographed with the chairman.

Royal London were at their strongest just before World War I – in the 1912/13 season they won both cup competitions of the London Insurance Offices' Football Association.

"*Sir Edward Smith… arranged for an Army Tank to appear before the Society's main entrance and from the top of this addressed us all in stentorian tones, damned all Germans and urged us to contribute liberally towards War Loan.*" Finsbury Square, winter of 1917/18

Lawrence Millage

William Bertie Newman

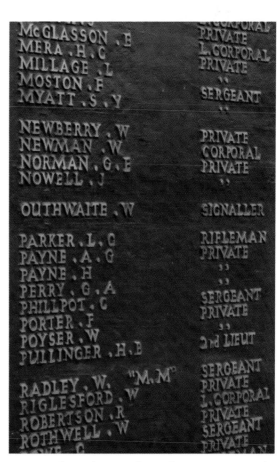

William Radley

Extracts from the Royal London war memorials
now at the Wilmslow office.

(Left) Sir William Llewellyn's portrait of Sir Edward Smith (1918).

Smith and his colleagues beneath the portrait in the magnificent boardroom of Royal London House. To Smith's left are Horace Duffell (joint managing director) and Alfred Skeggs (secretary) and to his right John Price (joint managing director) and Ernest Hambridge.

Evan Hayward, soldier, solicitor, Member of Parliament, Auxiliary Company litigator, Consultative Committee member and Royal London's first in-house lawyer.

Benjamin Braham, agent, director and courageous whistleblower.

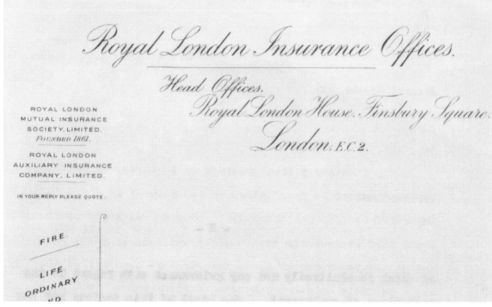

Royal London's letterhead during the years of the Auxiliary Company.

(Right) Sir Edward Smith
Member of the London County Council,
chairman of the Tower Bridge magistrates,
vice-president and chairman of the managing
committee of the National Liberal Club and
chairman of The Royal London Mutual
Insurance Society, Limited (1908–1920)
and The Royal London Auxiliary Insurance
Company, Limited (1910–1922).

(Below) The Board of 1921 – all new
appointments, following the mass
resignations after the Auxiliary Company
arbitration. Note the absence of the portrait
of Sir Edward Smith (see the previous Board
photograph). Back Row: George Sorrell,
Evan Hayward (member of the Consultative
Committee), John Wiseman, John White,
Thomas Williams, William Missett
Front Row: William Stanbury, William Lowe,
Frederick Baker, Alfred Skeggs, John Skinner
(secretary), Ernest Thomlinson, Henry Parr.

The legislation permitted the Society to undertake all life business (industrial and ordinary) up to the £200 ceiling and so the Society was in a position to compete with the company in relation to life policies where the sum assured was less than this. The directors of the Society were to be the directors of the company and, by allowing an area where the two businesses overlapped, they were creating a conflict of interest and putting themselves in a position in which they could not properly perform their obligations as directors of the two companies. The conflict would be made worse by the fact that they were about to acquire substantial shareholdings in the company. As counsel put it during the subsequent litigation:

> If [the directors] *had no pecuniary interest in the matter, the only charge must have been one of unutterable folly because they were putting themselves in a position in which they could not perform the duties they had undertaken; they had put themselves in a position where they could not possibly perform both duties. When in addition there is pecuniary interest turned to getting the business for the Auxiliary Company they then expose themselves to the censure that anyhow the Judges give although gentlemen who apparently confine their activities to the insurance world may not think the censure justified.*[8]

The Royal London Auxiliary Insurance Company, Limited (referred to subsequently as 'the Auxiliary Company') was incorporated on 6 August 1910 with full powers to do all classes of insurance and on 11 August it entered into two significant agreements with the Society. The holders of the certificates would have been particularly concerned by the turn of events following Mr Blythe's intervention because the practical effect of the 1910 Act was that the Society could no longer issue fire and accident policies and this would have rendered the certificates virtually worthless. Help, however, was at hand. The first agreement provided that the Auxiliary Company would take over the whole of the Society's fire and accident business and the certificate holders would be allotted 100,000 fully paid shares of 10s each in the Auxiliary Company. So holders received, without any further payment, a 10s share in the Auxiliary Company for each certificate that they owned. The certificate holders had done rather well for themselves – they paid 4s for a rather strange certificate in a mutual company, received a dividend of 4½ per cent in the first year and ended up with a fully-paid 10s share in a proprietary company with a ready-made business. The legality of this swap of certificates for shares was questionable because the trust deed provided that, if a decision was made to wind up the Auxiliary Fund, the balance, having paid off the creditors and the certificate holders, had to be paid to the Society. The directors, of course, held more than 16,000 certificates.

In the other agreement, the Society granted the Auxiliary Company ("which has been formed to co-operate with the Society and to carry on *inter alia* the classes of insurance business hitherto carried on by the New Department of the Society") the joint use of the Society's offices, office staff and stationery. In the agreement, the Auxiliary Company agreed not to compete with "the industrial business of the Society". The significance of the two agreements was such that they were conditional upon the approval of the members of the Society. At the extraordinary general meeting called on 30 August 1910 to authorise them, Edward Smith adopted an informal eloquence more suited to the smaller audience of the 150 members who were present, most of whom would probably have been staff who had strolled across the City on a summer's evening from Finsbury Square to Old Broad Street where the meeting was held. Effective as the speech may have been in achieving the required majority, it did not make clear that the Auxiliary Company and not the Society would in future be selling ordinary life business, neither did it address why the Board had rejected the alternative solution of temporarily suspending the new business until an application to the court could be made to permit the Society itself to carry it out. No member present at the meeting thought to ask Smith why this was not being done.[9] The resolution was passed and the agreements became effective.

Smith and his colleagues probably preferred the Auxiliary Company route for three reasons, although he would, no doubt, have only referred to one of them at the meeting if the question had been asked. The public reason was certainty – it enabled all insurance business to be transacted without the need for any court authorisations now or in the future. But there were two rather more personal reasons. The Auxiliary Company provided a means by which the strange certificates in a company could be converted into the altogether more recognisable and marketable shares in a proprietary insurance company. More importantly, if the Society itself had sought authorisation, this would have focused attention on the Royal London Auxiliary Fund because the judge hearing the application would have had to have been satisfied that the life funds were not being used to finance fire insurance. A judge of the Chancery Division – not to mention the members of Royal London at the general meeting that would have to precede the court hearing – could well have been unimpressed by the action of the directors in setting up a scheme that provided that the certificate holders rather than the members were benefiting from the new business, especially as the directors were significant holders of the certificates. It was arguable that, by creating this situation, the directors were already in breach of their duty to the members of the Society.[10]

The Auxiliary Company was to have two classes of shares: 100,000 shares of 10s, all of which were issued to the certificate holders, and 450,000 shares of £1 of which 80,000 were to be issued, although only 10s was to be paid (by instalments) per share. On 31 August a share prospectus for the £1 shares was circulated. The response was overwhelming and the shares were nearly four times over-subscribed. Letters of allotment and regret were sent to all subscribers on 14 September. There were to be more than 1,900 shareholders, most of whom were superintendents, agents and clerks employed by the Society with holdings of a just a few shares. Initially, the directors held a little more than 20 per cent of the shares by virtue of their director qualifying shares, those obtained on the conversion of their certificates and those for which they successfully subscribed. In time their holdings were to rise to nearer 30 per cent (and perhaps even beyond) as several directors enthusiastically acquired further shares as other shareholders wished to dispose of them. By 1919 Smith, Duffell and Price held, in their own names, some 14 per cent of the issued shares of the Auxiliary Company, and they may well have held many more shares through nominees and connected persons.[11]

When the Auxiliary Company opened for business, it did not limit itself to fire, accident and any other branches of insurance business not previously undertaken by the Society but offered an extensive range of life and endowment policies. Whatever the true meaning of "industrial business of the Society" in the non-compete clause of the 11 August 1910 agreement, and there was to be much debate about this, the Auxiliary Company was competing with the Society by promoting and issuing life policies for sums of less than £200 and then £300, to which the ceiling was increased in 1911.

The Liverpool Victoria Insurance Corporation Limited floundered after a promising start. An agreement had to be entered into with the Commercial Union that guaranteed all its life, fire and accident policies, but this proved insufficient, and the corporation collapsed into liquidation in 1914 with the Commercial Union taking over its policies.[12] The Royal London Auxiliary Insurance Company, Limited, however, flourished – by 1913 its income exceeded £116,000, much of which related to life assurance policies that the Society was permitted to transact. The Auxiliary Company had issued its own ordinary branch prospectus. All but two of the policies referred to in the Society's 1909 prospectus appeared under the same number in the Auxiliary Company's prospectus together with 27 further policies, although most of these were variations on the existing policies, rather than genuinely new products. Advertisements failed to distinguish between the two companies and the notepaper was headed 'Royal London Insurance Offices' with the names of both the Society and the Auxiliary Company appearing in smaller print below. Almost the whole of the Auxiliary Company's business was obtained through the agents of the Society, and much of it from existing customers of the Society, few of whom would have understood the distinction between Auxiliary Company and Society. The administration was carried out at the Society's offices. And yet, the Auxiliary Company was owned by and its profits accrued to its shareholders and not to all the members of the Society. As early as its second and third years of trading it was able to pay 2½ per cent dividends to its shareholders.

One director was becoming increasingly concerned with developments. Benjamin Lorne Braham joined the Society as an agent in 1872 and had been a member of the Committee of Fifteen and president of the Royal London Staff Association in 1905. Early in 1909 he was appointed a director of the Society and divisional manager of the north-eastern districts based in Newcastle. He did not have an easy relationship with Smith and the two managing directors, believing that the London triumvirate were assuming powers that should be exercised by the Board as a whole. He had dissented, for example, from the resolution in June 1910 authorising the triumvirate to take "all necessary steps parliamentary and otherwise" in relation to the lawsuits being brought against the Society following *Blythe v Birtley* and again in November 1911 when they were authorised to negotiate and enter into a provisional agreement in relation to an acquisition. A resolution that Braham himself proposed in December 1912, that litigation be discussed by the Board before counsel was instructed, was defeated by his colleagues.

Braham had never been comfortable with the concept of a proprietary company standing beside the Society and had tried to have no part in it.[13] Smith persuaded him that the appearance of Board unanimity was important and Braham was appointed a director of the Auxiliary Company on its formation. He was required under the articles of association to hold 250 director's qualifying shares but never applied for, or acquired any further shares. In February 1913 he resigned as a director of the Auxiliary Company and sought to propose resolutions at a Board meeting of the Society. He was persuaded to agree that this be deferred to a meeting at which all the directors were present. There then occurred an unusual event. On 13 March Alfred Skeggs, the Society's secretary, formally applied to be appointed to the vacancy that then existed on the Board. He had been nominated by four members of the Society, one of whom was Major Evan Hayward who, as well as being a member of the Society, was the Liberal MP for South East Durham and a solicitor.[14] It seems unlikely that Skeggs would have taken this action unless he believed that he had support from at least some of the directors but, early in April, Smith reported that Skeggs had withdrawn his application.

There would seem to be two possible explanations for Skeggs' action. He may have believed that the time had come for him to be a director and, disappointed that no invitation was forthcoming, persuaded the most influential member he knew to lend his name to the application. The conversion had, in fact, demoted Skeggs. At the annual general meeting in February 1908, he had been appointed the secretary of a friendly society, a role that was somewhere between chief executive and company secretary. By July in the same year he was the company secretary of a company that had a chairman and two managing directors. Another interpretation is that Hayward had already become (or been made) aware of problems within Royal London and nominating Skeggs for a place on the Board was his first step in seeking to address them.

On 5 April 1913 Braham, concerned that his resolutions had still not been discussed, wrote to Smith. His letter in immaculate longhand ran to eight and a half pages of thick, lined, foolscap paper. He wrote:

> *The way that we, as Directors of the Mutual Society, have been allowing ourselves as Directors of the Auxiliary Company to more and more absorb the business and the sphere of action of the Mutual Society has been troubling me for a long time past. I protested against such action when a [life policy for as little as £25] was adopted by the Auxiliary Company, and since then I have been considering more and more our action in this respect, and I feel that perhaps I should have made a more energetic protest earlier. I was loath to do so because when unfortunately I have before taken any line opposed to that of yourself and the Managing Directors I have found myself in a minority of one and things at times have been made not too pleasant for me as you are aware. There comes a point, however, when a man must have the courage of his convictions and when I realised more fully than before what we have done and what we are doing I felt that it had come for me.*[15]

He referred to the 'pledges' given by the Board that the business of the Society would not be carried on by a proprietary company and that the Auxiliary Company should not take away any work from the Society and complained about even the smaller business of the Society increasingly being encroached upon by the Auxiliary Company until "practically all the business of the Mutual Society except its weekly business is catered for by the Auxiliary Company". The policy prospectuses of the Auxiliary Company, he complained, were far grander than the Society that had to manage with bad print on flimsy paper. He objected to the managing directors authorising special surrender values on Society policies on the basis that the policyholder would take out a new policy with the Auxiliary Company, and the ways in which the agents have been encouraged and incentivised to promote ordinary business for the Auxiliary Company rather than industrial in the Society.

He continued:

> *The Auxiliary Company is not only competing with the Mutual Society but is doing so unfairly through the Mutual Society's own staff and with the Mutual's Society's own money and the Directors are whipping and spurring the one and hobbling the other.*

He complained of the Society being required to grant mortgages at concessionary rates that were secured by Auxiliary Company policies and commented:

> *Another extraordinary thing is that while the Auxiliary Company is taking away the business which the Mutual Society can and should do, it is being housed by the Mutual Society in its offices, and run by the Mutual staff at a percentage of cost which is wholly inadequate.*

It was not until 28 July that an opportunity could be found to hold a special meeting of the Board to consider Braham's resolutions. They were specific and related to issues referred to in his letter. He proposed that the Society should be offering policies up to £300, that where a Society industrial branch policy was surrendered with a view to taking out an ordinary policy up to £300, the new policy should be issued by the Society and that the Society should not advance mortgages on property where the endowment policies were taken out with the Auxiliary Company. The minutes of the meeting read: "These propositions were discussed at great length and were negatived".

Benjamin Braham had two options – resign as a director of the Society, sell his 250 shares in the Auxiliary Company and walk away, or 'go public'. He was reluctant to resign, feeling that he could do more from the inside to protect the members of the Society, which really left only the latter. He chose to do so at the annual general meeting of the Auxiliary Company in December 1913 where he made a speech explaining why he had resigned as a director earlier in the year. The few shareholders there who were, no doubt, expecting another rather boring meeting were in for a shock. Braham repeated many of the points made in his letter He talked of his role as a director of the Society requiring him to carefully watch its interests, guard its business and protect its funds that belong to the members; he complained that the Auxiliary Company:

> *... was reaping untold advantages, quite out of proportion and beyond all reason, exercising vast competing tables with monthly premiums and for sums assured as low as £25, leaving the Society*

helpless to transact much of its legitimate business which it has
power to do under its constitution.

After the meeting, Braham sent a copy of his speech to *The Policy-Holder*. It was published in the correspondence section of the 24 December edition under the disclaimer "We do not hold ourselves responsible for the opinions of our correspondents".[16] Braham also sent copies to a number of people including Major Hayward, who wrote at once to Smith indicating that, as what seemed to be serious charges were being made, he felt that he had to look into the matter on behalf of those of his constituents who were also members. He asked Smith to let him know what substance (if any) there was in the charges and to provide him with a copy of the agreement between the Society and the Auxiliary Company. Smith suggested that, instead, Hayward should have a meeting with Kingsley Wood, the Society's solicitor, but Hayward insisted on a reply from Smith. On 22 January 1914 Smith wrote to Hayward that he was "pleased to state that there is no substance in the statements made, and no infringement of the agreement has taken place". He enclosed a copy of the agreement.[17]

More information came to light, however, and in May 1914 the firm of solicitors of which Hayward was then a partner issued a writ against the directors of the Society and the Auxiliary Company. The plaintiffs were three policyholders, William Lovett, William Ackland and Selina Mary Ann Jennings. Their claim was expressed to be on behalf of all the members and they relied upon 'a procedure' said by their counsel to exist by which, where there are a number of persons with the same complaint, a few of them may bring a representative action without the need to obtain any authorisation or approval from the membership at large.[18] A statement of claim was served in July. The plaintiffs sought the removal of all the directors of the Society and claimed damages on behalf of the Society from the directors and the Auxiliary Company. They alleged that the entering into of the two agreements of 11 August 1910 by the Society, and the Society's consent to the use by the Auxiliary Company of 'Royal London', had been procured by the fraudulent conspiracy of the directors and thus the Society was not bound by the agreements. If the agreements were held to bind the Society, then they claimed that the Auxiliary Company was in breach of the clause not to compete with the Society. The directors soon received a sharp reminder that this would not be a private debate when *The Policy-Holder* of 1 July 1914 contained this brief paragraph:

> *We hear that an action is pending between some members of*
> *the Royal London Mutual and the Royal London Auxiliary, the*
> *subject of dispute being the treatment of the former concern since*
> *the latter came into existence.*[19]

A short defence that denied everything was served in November 1914. By then the country was at war, and the governance of Royal London understandably became rather less significant to those involved. Little progress was made in the case, but the plaintiffs' solicitors were able to extract some relevant documents from the Society, and probably from Benjamin Braham who, as one of the defendant directors, could quite properly respond to the plaintiffs' requests for disclosure of documents in his possession. The business of the two Royal London companies continued. The atmosphere at Board meetings must have been very difficult. The last meeting that Braham attended was in July 1915. He asked for four weeks leave of absence at the end of July and medical certificates forwarded by his wife were tabled at subsequent meetings. He had to retire by rotation under the Society's Articles of Association at the annual general meeting in April 1917 and did not seek re-election because of ill health.

There had been other developments during the war years that may well have been linked to the litigation. The 11 August 1910 agreement, by which the Auxiliary Company agreed to pay 2 per cent for the use of the Society's office staff, provided that after three years there would be paid "such sum as a fair compensation as shall be determined by" an independent actuary. The agreement is not well drafted: "compensation" seems a strange word to use but this payment was apparently intended to be in substitution for the 2 per cent, no obligation was imposed on the parties to appoint an actuary and, if no appointment was made, the 2 per cent would continue to be payable indefinitely, and it must have been difficult for a third party to determine what was fair without any guidance in the agreement on the factors to be considered.

A referral was made and on 22 July 1914 the independent actuary recommended modifications to the agreement that were "fair and equitable". They were to be back-dated to 1 October 1913 and to run for five years. Now the Auxiliary Company had to pay £2,650-a-year and 4.5 per cent of the gross premium income, less the cost of any reassurance. This certainly seems to have been an improvement so far as the Society was concerned, although the payment was also to include the cost of advertising. Five years later, the process was repeated and from 1 October 1918 a rather more complex regime was put in place involving a payment of 6.25 per cent of the premium income of the major policies and percentages varying between 0.5 and 1.75 per cent for the others.

The war may have ended but 1919 was a stressful year for the Board of Royal London. In May an amended statement of claim in the lawsuit was served by the plaintiffs, whose lawyers were now better able to formulate the claim in the light of the documents they had received. The seriousness of the situation must, by now, have been dawning on the directors. Then the

Board was requested to provide a witness to give evidence to a Government committee recently appointed under the chairmanship of Lord Parmoor to look into industrial assurance companies and collecting societies.[20] The concern was that Major Hayward was a member of the committee. The Board could hardly expect him to put out of his mind his knowledge of Royal London and they would have been worried that he would have mentioned something to the other committee members if only to avoid the criticism of conflict of interest and to warn them not to stray into areas that were *sub judice*.

Edward Smith dealt adequately with the various issues being put to him and all the industry witnesses.[21] He was additionally questioned at some length about the conversion from friendly society to company. This was surprising – it had taken place 11 years before and conversions were, at best, on the fringe of the committee's terms of reference. He was asked outright if any benefit had been derived from the conversion. His response that "I do not know in what sense the question is put, but I think that the object of the directors in converting into a Company has been attained, though the experience we have had since the conversion has been somewhat unusual" was hardly compelling and did not seem to have convinced the members of the committee. Smith reiterated that the reason had been to move Royal London beyond the restraints of the friendly societies legislation. The low point in his evidence came when Lord Parmoor took exception to a somewhat rambling reply in which Smith seemed to be suggesting that approval or encouragement for the conversion had been given by various government departments and numerous politicians and civil servants, the names of whom, Smith 'dropped' in his evidence. The list included Lloyd George, Winston Churchill, both the attorney and solicitor generals and the chief registrar of friendly societies. In the end, chairman and witness agreed that the decision to convert had been that of the Committee of Management having taken advice and consulted, and having established that there would be no objection from the authorities. As Smith put it: "I have found it is far better to have the agreement or concurrence of Government departments before you commit yourself rather than find you are objected to afterwards". The committee asked no questions about the aspects of the conversion that had prompted the setting-up of a proprietary company to stand beside the Society.

In the same month the members' case came to court, but only so that Mr Justice Sargant could approve an agreement between all the parties to refer the matter to arbitration. When the members brought their action in 1914, the Board had turned to Kingsley Wood whose firm found itself acting for the Society, the Auxiliary Company and the directors, although he instructed different counsel for each party. The arbitration agreement that Wood negotiated with the plaintiffs' solicitors provided something for both parties – arbitrations are conducted in private, and so the directors would not have their conduct scrutinised in open court, but in return the Society and the Auxiliary Company accepted responsibility for the plaintiffs' costs (and those of the Royal London Staff Association who were to be represented by counsel at the arbitration) both prior to and after agreement. The directors would have welcomed the fact that in the agreement the plaintiffs withdrew all charges of fraud or conspiracy, although they were to discover that a narrow interpretation was to be placed on the terms as the case developed. The involvement of the Royal London Staff Association, the in-house trade union, suggests that they may have been funding the plaintiffs' case up to then – the three policyholder-plaintiffs were clearly not paying themselves and Hayward's role probably did not extend to that of wealthy benefactor. On the other hand, the many members of the staff association who held shares in the Auxiliary Company may not have been totally committed to an initiative that could only do harm to their investment.

The arbitration opened on Tuesday 27 July 1920 in the Bar Council Room at 5 Stone Buildings, Lincoln's Inn. The arbitrator was George Talbot KC,[22] a much-respected barrister who, it was felt, would soon be appointed to the High Court bench. An impressive array of counsel had been instructed. Representing the plaintiffs was Malcolm Macnaghten KC,[23] the son of a law lord and former president of the Cambridge Union who had just been knighted for his unpaid services during the war as director of the Foreign Claims Office.[24] Artemus Jones KC[25] was acting for the Auxiliary Company. Four years earlier he had been junior defence counsel in the trial of Sir Roger Casement for treason and had been called upon to make the final speech when his leader collapsed. The Society was represented by A F C C Luxmoore KC,[26] a fine all-round sportsman who had played rugby for Cambridge University, Richmond and England. Described as a "hard-working, thrusting forward", it was said that Luxmoore's style of advocacy was similar to his forward play: "restless, eager, forceful but never unfair".[27] Benjamin Braham had instructed Henry Cautley KC, MP who had been a member of the Parmoor Committee, Owen Thompson KC acted for the directors and Henry Kemp KC, the Recorder of Hull, for the staff association.

When the case adjourned for the weekend the plaintiffs' counsel had still not concluded his opening speech. Sir Malcolm Macnaghten was not simply outlining his clients' case but was also taking the arbitrator through the documents. It would not have been an enjoyable four days for those of the directors who were present. Macnaghten was an impressive and, they might have felt remorseless, advocate. He had begun on the Tuesday describing the aborted efforts to set up a proprietary company in 1905. The directors had denied that there had been any such attempt, and could produce no minutes of any of the meetings, but the notes of the staff association, including a transcript of the deputation's meeting with the Committee of Management, had survived. By Friday the arbitrator was aware of the events before, during and after the conversion, the trust deed and the certificates, the legal threat and the 1910 Act, the setting-up of the Auxiliary Company, its immediate success and Benjamin Braham's letter and statement. The relevant documents had been read to him by Sir Malcolm who had added his own observations on behalf of the plaintiffs.

It is a fundamental of any litigation that the parties disclose to each other, well before the trial, all the documents that they have in their possession that are relevant to the case. This process, called 'discovery', is not inserted solely to provide work for lawyers, although it certainly achieves this end. An awareness in advance of all the relevant documents (especially where documents will form a significant part of the evidence) enables the parties and their advisers to see the case that they can present, and to anticipate the case that can be presented against them. This assists in ensuring that the trial focuses on the key issues and also means that an informed view can be taken of the merits of the dispute. Discovery in this case, however, had not gone according to plan – many documents had only been disclosed by the Society just before the hearing and some only became available during Macnaghten's speech. The transcript of the arbitration suggests that so many vital documents had been disclosed so late that it was only by the Friday evening of the hearing that those involved in the proceedings were aware in any detail of the plaintiffs' case and the evidence that supported it. This probably applied even to their own counsel, as Macnaghten at times found himself reading documents to the arbitrator that had only just been put into his hand.

There must have been much careful reflection over the weekend and on the Monday morning, counsel for the Society and the Auxiliary Company told the arbitrator that they could no longer participate in the arbitration because the instructions that they were receiving were coming (and could only come) from the directors of the respective companies who not only were identical but were themselves parties to the proceedings in their own right. The concern was clearly valid, the only surprise being that it took counsel until the fifth day of the hearing to express it, although the impossibility of their position had become rather more obvious as the evidence unfolded during the previous week. The position of the Society's advisers was particularly difficult because their instructions needed to come from the members but excluding the plaintiffs and the directors. The whole arbitration appeared to be under threat when directors' counsel indicated that he could not continue if the Auxiliary Company was unrepresented. Mr Talbot adopted the standard approach of judges and arbitrators in difficult situations and adjourned the proceedings until 2 o'clock. Much must have been discussed in the meantime because after lunch the Auxiliary Company's counsel indicated a willingness to proceed and

Sir Malcolm resumed his opening speech, the Society having withdrawn from the proceedings.

The mutiny by counsel may have finally persuaded the directors that their position, too, was impossible. At the start of the following day's proceedings, Sir Malcolm told the arbitrator that certain suggestions had been made that he felt were likely to prove fruitful. Mr Talbot was again prepared to adjourn until 2 o'clock to give more time for the discussions to be continued. When the sitting resumed, it was clear that the battle was over. The directors of the Society agreed that four of them would resign at the next board meeting and that the remaining four would resign at the end of 1920. They acknowledged that all the life assurance business of the Auxiliary Company ought to have been transacted by the Society. They agreed that the Auxiliary Company would transfer to the Society all its life assurance business and would cease transacting life business. All agreements with the Society would be terminated. If the Auxiliary Company was to continue undertaking non-life business it would change its name. The plaintiffs agreed that when the terms of the settlement had been carried out, they would withdraw all claims for damages against the directors and all charges affecting their personal honour and integrity.

One of the first decisions of the new Board was to increase Benjamin Braham's annual pension to £436 13s 4d, the maximum permitted, representing two-thirds of his final salary, payment to be back-dated to the date of his resignation. For reasons not disclosed in the minutes, the Board in 1917 had fixed his pension at £300, increased in May 1920 to £400. Later the staff association explored ways of "perpetuating the name of Mr B. L. Braham". For various reasons, a portrait in oils for the boardroom at head office was ruled out and it was decided that "bearing in mind his lifelong principles" the most fitting tribute would be to establish a fund bearing his name for Royal London workers needing convalescence. The scope of the 'Braham Convalescence Fund' was later widened to include dependants of staff and other benefits when it was re-named the 'Braham Benevolent Fund'.

Much had to be done after the arbitration to implement the terms of the settlement. New directors were appointed to both boards so that the interests of the members and the shareholders could be represented in the negotiations by directors who had no personal involvement. Kingsley Wood's firm was replaced as the Society's solicitors to remove another area of potential conflict. Not all the points could readily be agreed and there were to be more days before the arbitrator, and several short hearings in the High Court. A second set of High Court proceedings were commenced and, after patiently listening to counsel for nearly a day and a half, Mr Justice P O Lawrence[28] asked how two companies, having competing businesses, could "sit in the same office and use the same staff and have the same Board?[29] When no satisfactory answer was forthcoming from the rows of counsel in front of him, the Judge (who was regarded as an eminently practical man of the world as well as a scholarly lawyer[30]) indicated that, given the impossibility of this situation, he was surprised that the parties wished to continue spending money on litigation. He was pleased to learn later in the day that discussions were going on outside his court and in due course it was agreed that the Society would acquire all the business of the Auxiliary Company, which would then be put into liquidation immediately afterwards, leading counsel for the Auxiliary Company to comment that the result of the acquisition "of course, will be to put an end to the almost impossible situation in which the parties have found themselves owing to one Board controlling the affairs of the two Companies."[31]

The arbitration hearing had been held in private and so those present in Mr Justice Lawrence's court on the 22 and 23 February 1921 were the first and only outsiders able to gain a first-hand impression of the true nature of the claims although, as no judgment was given, their knowledge would have been based on what they could understand of the dialogue between counsel and judge and without having access to the documents. The correspondent from *The Policy-Holder* who may perhaps have benefited from some inside information probably understood more than most. His report of 2 March[32] under the heading "Friendly conclusion to law suit" (was irony intended? – 'friendly' is hardly the word that the directors would have used) went out of its way to congratulate "the members of the Royal London Mutual, who had the courage and tenacity to tackle and carry through a difficult and thankless task, upon the success of which has attended their efforts, and which if rightly handled should result in great advantage to the Society".

It was at the Society's annual general meeting on 26 April 1921 that an explanation of why no less than eight directors had resigned since the last meeting would have to be given to the members. No chairman had been appointed to succeed Sir Edward and so Alfred Skeggs, now managing director of the Society, would have that difficult task. The privacy of the arbitration room gave him rather more flexibility than would have been available if Sir Malcolm's narrative had been delivered in open court. Skeggs was not a man who lacked confidence but he could be excused for feeling mildly apprehensive as he rose to his feet in the Kingsway Hall in the presence of "a very large attendance of members". His skilfully crafted speech was a huge success. He began by reminding the members that this was the Society's diamond jubilee and talked of the "boundless energy and faith in the mission" displayed by the founders and the "early years of struggle demanding strenuous work, abundant faith and great fortitude".

He reviewed the 1920 accounts in some detail – as usual they displayed substantial progress from the previous year. Having created this general feeling of wellbeing he commented, almost in passing, that members would have observed from the directors' report that "eight members of the old Directorate had retired after many years' service" and continued:

> The reason for the resignation of those Directors was in consequences of difficulties which arose in the working of the business of the Mutual Society and the Auxiliary Company under one management. It was felt by everybody that there should be independent Boards and the Directors mentioned as having retired during the year being members of the Auxiliary Company resigned in order to allow the appointment of an entirely independent Board for the Mutual Society.

And that was that. He then recommended to the members that they confirm the appointment of the directors appointed during the year before briefly commenting on the legislation on industrial assurance that was expected in the light of the report of Lord Parmoor's committee. Notice had been received nominating six gentlemen for appointment to the Board in place of the existing directors, but those proposing them had overlooked the fact that five of them were agents and thus ineligible for appointment to the Board. The meeting reappointed all the existing directors and failed to elect the one remaining external nominee. Little, if any, opposition seems to have manifested itself from the floor of the meeting and Skeggs was confronted with no difficult questions.

At last all the details had been agreed and on 16 August 1921 a conditional agreement was entered into by which the Society agreed to pay 15s a share for the Auxiliary Company's business. The agreement in fact provided that the sum was "Ten shillings together with such sum for interest from the Sixth day of August One thousand nine hundred and ten down to completion of the sale as [the arbitrator] shall consider reasonable". Smith told the extraordinary general meeting of the Auxiliary Company that the price agreed upon provided a minimum sum of 15 shillings per share and this presumably included the interest.[33] The total consideration paid was £112,510 – around £4.4 million in today's money. The agreement was conditional upon the approval of the members of the Society, the shareholders of the Auxiliary Company and the Court.

The Auxiliary Company held its extraordinary general meeting on 9 September 1921. Sir Edward Smith (he had been knighted for public services in 1916) rather made light of it all. He referred to an agreement between the Auxiliary Company and the Society, suggested that after it had been in operation for some years, difficulties of opinion arose as to its true meaning and scope and that, in consequence, litigation was commenced. The agreement, he suggested, was to avoid further litigation. The resolution to approve the conditional agreement was carried, almost unanimously. Sir Edward was much in debt to the confidentiality of arbitration.

The extraordinary general meeting of the Society took place on 12 September 1921 and Alfred Skeggs proposed the resolution to approve the agreement. After a lucid review of the history, he concluded:

The existence of the two companies, with similar names, occupying the same offices, using the same staff, and having largely the same objects, but one of which was a Company making profits for private shareholders, while the other was a Mutual Society limited by guarantee, the object of which should have been to make profits for its members, and both of which were governed by the same body of directors, was bound to bring about injustice and friction. It is manifestly to the interest of the Society to do the Life business which the Auxiliary Company has been doing and also to do the Fire and other general business, if it can obtain power from the Court to transact it. Obviously, however, the Mutual Society could not expect the Auxiliary Company to transfer all this business to it for nothing. Although the business was obtained through the connections of the Mutual Society, it had to be obtained by the use of capital put up by the shareholders of the Auxiliary Company, and the shareholders were entitled, in fairness, to receive, not only their capital, but something by way of interest for the use of it.

The resolution was passed and in due course Mr Justice Astbury gave his approval. At a hearing in November 1921, he extended the Society's powers to enable it to undertake life business without any restriction as to the sum assured and fire, burglary, accident and general insurance business that was required before the Society could take over the business of the Auxiliary Company. If a similar application had been made with the same outcome in 1910 there would have been no need for the Auxiliary Company.

Another agreement had been entered into on 16 August 1921 that needed no external approvals. It was made between the directors, the original plaintiffs and the Society and provided that, in satisfaction of the damages claimed against them, each director would recover only his original investment in the shares and the certificates that went before them, and would forego the profit on those investments being enjoyed by the other shareholders on the sale of the Auxiliary Company's business to the Society. The directors were also required to pay some of the costs of the litigation and arbitrations. The two agreements were implemented and the unfortunate interlude of The Royal London Auxiliary Insurance Company, Limited was at an end.

The actions of the directors must be considered in context and judged against the standards of the day. Forty years before the incorporation of the Auxiliary Company, Charles Bretherton, Royal Liver's solicitor, gave evidence to the Royal Commission investigating friendly societies. He referred to collecting societies as "trading Friendly Societies" and considered that, as long as they had the funds to meet all claims that may fall due on the death of all the members, "the rest of the funds of the society practically belong to" the management of the society. He continued:

> I think the real means to adopt is to make the creators and originators of these Friendly Societies, that is, the persons by whose industry and by whose talents the institutions have been made into large institutions, the proprietors of those institutions, and, as long as they discharged the contracts with the assured, whatever profits they might develop beyond that by their efforts should be their own property. Therefore I advocate... the conversion of existing [trading friendly societies] into proprietary companies, so that those gentlemen who have developed the societies to the extent they have, and who, as far as I know, are generally persons of unusual talent, and who, if they had devoted themselves to any other walk in life would have met with the same success as has followed their exertions on behalf of the societies, should have whatever profits might accrue from their good management, without being subject to the public obloquy they now receive; the existing funds to form a guarantee capital, and those gentlemen becoming responsible personally for the good conduct of the societies, and discharging their obligations toward the insured.[34]

Bretherton was speaking before paying bonuses to industrial branch policyholders had been introduced, and his evidence may have lacked detail, but what is clear is that the concept of collecting (or trading) societies being converted into proprietary companies owned in part by their hard-working directors, whose skill and energy had made them so successful, had long existed. It is unlikely that this evidence would have been given (even by an industry witness) if it was abhorrent to public thinking at the time and indeed this was confirmed by the Commission. The men who had given Degge such a hard time on expenses and lapsing merely commented that a "careful consideration of the [Bretherton] evidence shows that his theory is not a singular one. The proprietary principle seems more or less consciously to be accepted and acted upon by the managers of many of this class of societies, and sensibly affects their administration".[35]

The thinking may well have changed in the intervening years, but Bretherton's evidence, and the Commission's reaction to it, indicates that a view had once existed that would see little wrong with the basic approach of the Royal London directors. A proprietary company had been the outcome of the Liverpool Victoria's attempt at conversion, and one would have come into being if Royal Co-operative and City of Glasgow had been allowed to convert. Although prevented by the courts on what might be seen as technical grounds, there did not seem to be an objection to the basic concept of converting to a company with shareholders and after all, many industrial assurance providers had been proprietary companies from the very beginning.

The directors of Royal London never gave evidence in the Auxiliary Company litigation and no detailed statement was made by them or on their behalf (or if one was, it has not survived) by way of explanation, defence or plea in mitigation.[36] The minutes of the special Board meeting in July 1913 at which Braham's resolutions were 'negatived' are silent on the arguments advanced in favour of the majority view. The directors were undoubtedly confronted with a difficult situation in 1910 and a new company with wide powers provided an attractive immediate solution. They could hardly claim, however, that they were forced by pressing circumstances into this arrangement because the basic concept of the Auxiliary Company had been put in place late in 1908 by means of the certificates. Neither could it be suggested that the Auxiliary Company had stumbled into competing with the Society. During the first nine weeks of its trading, the Auxiliary Company received over 1,500 proposals for ordinary branch policies with a total sum assured of £152,000. The average sum per policy was £97 suggesting that all (or virtually all) of these proposals were for less than £200 and that the policies could have been issued by the Society. The directors might have argued that the Society was benefiting from the Auxiliary Company's business. The payments under the 11 August 1910 agreement, however, amounted to no more than a reimbursement of expenses and there was no attempt to share profits, while the increases in 1913 and 1918 may well have done little more than reflect the additional workload that the Auxiliary Company was generating. The directors would also, no doubt, claim with some justification that their actions had been entirely open – the invitations to invest in the certificates and later in the shares of the Auxiliary Company had been widely circulated, and the availability of life policies from the Auxiliary Company was clear from the beginning, and yet no objection had been raised at the time.

Before purporting to pass judgment on the directors, we would also need to know more of the legal advice that they received. They were advised that the certificates scheme was lawful, although counsel was not asked to advise in the context of the pre-conversion assurances given by the Board that there would be no shareholders and that profits of the new business would accrue to members, and it also appeared the documentation that was adopted differed from that approved by counsel.[37] They were advised too, that the court would be unlikely to approve an extension of powers in August 1910 but the instructions sent to counsel were misleading and he was never asked to advise on seeking limited authorisation to cover only the business being carried out on the day the Act became law.[38] They were advised in 1914 that there would be great difficulties in merging the Society and the Auxiliary Company but counsel was not told about the allegations that had been made or that litigation was being commenced.[39]

Throughout the period, Kingsley Wood, or his firm, is shown in the annual reports and accounts of both the Society and the Auxiliary Company as solicitor to both companies, the appointment generally being shared with another sole practitioner or firm, and his role in the sorry saga raises some interesting questions. He was undoubtedly a man of great ability – one of the best law students of his year,[40] he set up his own firm in the City almost as soon as he was admitted and was quickly the lawyer of choice for the industrial assurance offices, both individually and collectively. He acted for Royal London on the conversion, and then in addressing the subsequent threats posed by *Blythe v Birtley*.[41] It was largely due to his skills in negotiating with the Government in 1911 that the offices retained a role in national insurance via the approved societies.[42] By 1920 he had written a textbook for industrial assurance agents,[43] served with Edward Smith as a member of the London County Council, been knighted for his public services (as deputy chairman of the London Pension Authority, chairman of the London Insurance Committee, chairman of the Faculty of Insurance and member of the National Insurance Advisory Committee), been elected to Parliament as the Conservative member for West Woolwich and been appointed parliamentary private secretary to the Minister of Health. He was later to serve as Postmaster-General, Minister of Health, Secretary of State for Air and to die in office as Chancellor of the Exchequer in 1943. Winston Churchill referred to him as "amiable, experienced, competent, efficient, [and] accessible".[44] An MP from the East End of London admired him for reaching "his great position without any social influence, purely by hard work, application and industry" and "liked his genial smile and lack of pomposity".[45] The entry in the *Dictionary of National Biography* noted that "to any task he… brought great thoroughness and energy of mind [and] shrewd judgment."[46]

The fundamental question, of course, is how could it possibly come about that, with an adviser of this calibre involved, a situation so serious could arise that all the Society's directors had to resign? Although technically acting for the companies, and not for the directors in their personal capacities, it seems inconceivable that Kingsley Wood did not express his view on the legality of the directors' position, and repeat or develop it as the matter progressed. For all we know, he may clearly and emphatically have advised against the course they were taking from the very beginning and the directors may simply have declined to follow his advice. That seems unlikely – there is no mention of this in the Board minutes, and Braham makes no reference to legal advice supporting the concerns that he was expressing in his April 1913 letter. So, based on the information of which he was aware, did Wood believe that the directors' position was sound and that they had discharged their duty by ensuring that the Auxiliary Company was contributing to the Society's expenses?

By 1913 Wood had probably ceased to be a full-time lawyer, and was devoting more of his time to public affairs, local government and then parliament, but it is difficult to believe that he could have come to a radically different view from the one shared a few years later by Mr Justice Lawrence and (one suspects) all the lawyers engaged in the arbitration. These gentlemen, however, had the benefit of being aware of the facts of the case. Wood would merely have known what he had been told by his clients. Did he know anything about the 1905 attempt to create a proprietary company? Was he fully aware of the extent of the overlap of the business of the Auxiliary Company and the permitted business of the Society? Alternatively, perhaps Wood had become more of a 'co-venturer' than an independent legal adviser. He had been allotted 1,223 of the 80,000 £1 shares of the Auxiliary Company and his father and wife held a further 266 and 166 shares respectively.[47] The holdings were hardly material – to put them in context, by the end Smith held in his own name more than four times as many £1 shares – but it may suggest that Wood had become close to his clients, or at least to the triumvirate with whom he would have had most of his dealings. As a result, his advice may have been rather more ambivalent – can we perhaps hear Smith saying, "Dear old Kingsley has always been a bit concerned, but then he's such a pessimist", or words to that effect? Was a belief allowed to take hold that all that the directors had to do to discharge their legal duties was to ensure that the Society received a sum that reimbursed it for the costs that it incurred on behalf of the Auxiliary Company?

The comment of one of Wood's successors as solicitor to the Society is that, while none of these theories seems entirely plausible, it is possible that one, or perhaps a combination of them, coupled with the attitudes prevailing at the time, may provide an explanation of what went on up to the point when it became clear that Braham was not going to let matters rest. At that moment, however, the Board required formal legal advice from a lawyer who had been made aware of all the facts… and then, assuming the advice highlighted the danger of the directors' position, they needed to act upon that advice. Instead, they just carried on, business as usual, with dire consequences.

The new managing director seems to have felt that Wood had

contributed to the outcome. Following a notice of motion sent by Alfred Skeggs to his colleagues, the Board resolved at the meeting on 13/14 October 1921 to rescind a resolution passed on 5 Aug 1908 "appointing Mr (now Sir) H Kingsley Wood as one of the solicitors to the Society". The minutes give no reasons for the decision and it is just possible that it was inspired more by Wood's conversion from lawyer to politician rather than by any past failings when acting for the Society.

What is certain, however, is that the Society remained dominant throughout the period (in 1920 the premium income of the Society was £2.1 million and the Auxiliary Company's less than £450,000), that no individual policyholder suffered and that there was no material loss to the Society's funds. The dispute would probably have come to trial much sooner but for the war and it may have been possible to achieve a less traumatic solution if, when the parties assembled in the court or arbitration room, the Auxiliary Company had existed for five rather than ten years.

On 25 May 1922 the Board held a private dinner at the Savoy Hotel for Sir Malcolm Macnaghten and Major Evan Hayward. The menu suggests that it was an agreeable evening that began with dry martini cocktails and concluded with port and champagne. Sir Malcolm would, no doubt, have been persuaded to say a few words in response to the toast of 'Our Guests'. Sadly no record exists of what insights he provided in that relaxed and informal atmosphere. Hayward was to remain closely involved with the Society for another 20 years.[48] Macnaghten became a MP, representing North Derry and then Londonderry as a Unionist, and Recorder of Colchester. In December 1928 he was appointed a High Court judge and was regarded by the Bar as a kindly and courteous man who, while not responsible for great developments in any particular area of law, made very few mistakes.[49]

Few members of the Society would have heard of either man, but their roles were crucial in restoring Royal London to a mutual organisation owned by all its members. Macnaghten told the arbitrator that "if these charges are established, and this wrong is put right, it will be mainly, if not entirely, due to the courage and initiative of Major Hayward that this has been done."[50] But without Benjamin Braham there would have been no case for the lawyers to fight. 'What if?' is a question that can prompt interesting answers when applied to many historical situations. If there had been nobody on the inside who realised that what was going on was wrong, and who was prepared to take bold action that would alienate him from his colleagues, the Auxiliary Company may have survived, especially if no complaint had been made before war broke out. Without Benjamin Braham the subsequent history of Royal London would have been very different.

CHAPTER 8

The Mutual Company

1908–1936

London, the birthplace of life assurance, has reason to be proud of giving its name to the largest British mutual life office – Royal London Mutual. Seventy years have passed since a friendly society was started to provide small assurances for people earning a weekly wage, and from this beginning there has developed an organisation which in 1929 handled premiums to the extent of over £5,000,000.

The Policy-Holder (12 February 1930)[1]

A powerful sentiment influencing the customs and practices of the industrial classes is a desire to show what they regard as a proper respect to their dead. This is not merely confined to the actual burial, but it is considered an obligation and a duty to visit the dying whenever possible, to attend the funeral and to wear mourning. Although there may be no legal compulsion, every person, with few exceptions, would feel his (or her) responsibility to pay the whole or a portion of the cost of the funeral expenses of a father, mother, brother or sister or other relative, rather than allow any one of them to be buried by the parish.

Memorandum of the Association of Industrial Assurance Companies and Collecting Friendly Societies Offlces to the Treasury Departmental Committee chaired by Sir Benjamin Cohen KC (1931)[2]

The previous chapter took the governance of Royal London into the 1920s and told of the time when there were two Royal London companies. Many of the events were known only to the participants and the more perceptive or informed observers. This chapter returns to the time of the conversion and examines the public face of The Royal London Mutual Insurance Society, Limited and the environment in which it was operating from 1908 to the mid-1930s.

The conversion from friendly society to company took place during the welfare reforms of the Liberal government. Free school meals, medical inspection of schools and additional protections for children were already in place; the Old Age Pensions Bill was passing through Parliament at the time; and the introduction of labour exchanges, boards to fix minimum rates of pay for certain trades, the use of public funds to generate employment and improvements to town planning were to follow. In 1910 the talk was of Lloyd George's 'People's Budget' and of the Government's plan for a system of national insurance. Basic income tax was held at 3.75 per cent, but a higher rate of 5 per cent was introduced for annual incomes of over £2,000 with an additional surcharge of a further 2.5 per cent on the amount by which incomes of £5,000 or more exceeded £3,000. As average earnings were less than £100 a year, there was no public outcry.

Historians still debate what prompted these reforms. Some regard them as displaying a genuine commitment to social justice, and recognition that a government must intervene to address poverty. Others see them as having been prompted by a fear of social unrest and working-class power, now strengthened by direct involvement in national and local politics through the widening of the franchise. Another view is that the Liberals were only interested in Britain's efficiency and that the welfare reforms were introduced because the Government was afraid that a sick and badly educated workforce would leave Britain behind other countries, such as Germany. After 40 per cent of recruits during the Boer War had been found unfit to serve, a Government committee reported in 1903 that the health of large sections of the urban population was being undermined by poverty, ignorance and neglect.[3] Another investigation suggested that 28 per cent of the male population displayed such an "obvious want and squalor [that it was] impossible for them to be economically efficient".[4] Whatever prompted them, and even if the immediate results were limited, these measures marked the opening of a new chapter in the history of British social policy. Edward Smith was a leading Liberal who was to chair the managing committee, and later become a vice president, of the National Liberal Club. No doubt, his inside views were of considerable interest to his colleagues around the board table at Finsbury Square.

A point of immediate concern to the directors of Royal London in 1910 was Lloyd George's plans for national insurance. There were rumours that the Government measures would virtually replace industrial assurance. Lloyd

George was speaking of the relief of pauperism in the context of the scheme and this was the language of the friendly societies, and more recently the industrial assurance providers. There was a widely held view that industrial assurance would collapse if the Government's scheme were to include a death grant or widows' pension. The industry mobilised. Royal London was an active member of the Association of Industrial Assurance Companies and Collecting Friendly Societies and a meeting was arranged with Lloyd George. The Chancellor was not best pleased by what he was told. He had envisaged that widows' pensions would be included in the scheme and found that he was confronted with two equally unattractive options: pay adequate compensation to the offices and the agents for the loss of the business, or confront considerable opposition.

Ahead of the general election due to take place on 19 December 1910 the offices sent a circular to all candidates that asked:

> *Will you pledge yourself to oppose any measure of State Insurance which is likely prejudicially to affect the interest of the great affiliated orders and friendly and collecting societies and companies, or to jeopardise the livelihood of the very many thousands of persons engaged in the business of industrial life assurance, and will you oppose any exceptional treatment of any order, society or company to the prejudice of others?*

Pledges were, in due course, obtained from 490 of the 670 members of the newly elected House of Commons. Before then, however, Lloyd George had come to the pragmatic view that he did not wish to add the industrial assurance industry to the other opponents of the scheme that included advocates of *laissez faire* who found this level of state intervention unacceptable. On 1 December he wrote to the *Daily News* denying that the Government's proposed scheme included a form of death benefit and confirming that "the proposals which the Government have in view... are not likely, so far as I can judge at present, to interfere in any way with the business now carried on by industrial life assurance companies or societies". The letter was reprinted in the *Insurance Times*. Needless to say, the qualification implicit in "so far as I can judge at the present" caused concern at the time but Lloyd George was as good as his word and there was to be no death benefit or widows' pensions within the scheme.[5]

Under the first part of the National Insurance Act 1911, manual labourers and all those over the age of 16 earning less than £160 a year were required to insure against ill-health and its consequences. With average earnings of less than £100 a year, most of the working population was included. Contributions were paid by the employed men and women, their employers and the state. The insured were entitled to medical treatment from a designated general practitioner with access to a sanatorium if they were suffering from tuberculosis (but to no other hospital treatment) and to limited financial benefits to compensate them for income lost through ill-health. The second part of the Act dealt with unemployment insurance, which was again funded by contributions but applied only to some 2.25 million workers in specific trades. The Government looked to the expertise of the industry and outsourced the administration of the health insurance to 'approved societies', approval coming from the Government's National Insurance Committee. Contributors were obliged to belong to one of the approved societies, non-profit-making organisations to which the Government would pay a modest sum per member for their services and that, at least nominally, were to be under the control of the members.

The directors initially felt that Royal London should go it alone – in their report for 1911 they indicated that approval had been sought for "a separate Section of the Company to administer the Sickness and Invalidity Benefits under the Act". This was adopted by the Prudential, which eventually operated four approved societies. A year later it was clear that this had been abandoned by Royal London in favour of a combined approach:

> The National Insurance Act of 1911 came into operation on 15 July last, and, after careful consideration, we decided that our Assurants should be granted the undoubted facility of transacting their State Sickness Insurance through the members of our own Staff. We therefore joined in the amalgamation of many of the Industrial Life Offices, and are pleased to report that so largely has this action been approved that most of our Assurants have become members of the National Amalgamated Approved Society, with our own Staff as Agents. This has entailed enormous labour, but we hope that in the future it will tend to a large expansion of our business.

Steve Else, from whom we have heard before, was part of that 'enormous labour':

> About this time I had graduated to the position of 'preparer', my duties being to examine six hundred proposals a day. Also the [National Insurance Act] which at first insurance offices refused to operate (a decision from which they later retracted) was about to become operative. The procrastination... made a last minute grab for this class of business necessary. The Government had fixed a date... So great was the rush for membership that we were

on overtime for many months and ultimately finished by working all night, and enjoyed a condition of comparative affluence until our supplementary income was spent.[6]

The efforts of Steve and his colleagues were worth it – Royal London agents would soon be calling on more than half a million Royal London policyholders on state insurance business for and on behalf of the National Amalgamated Approved Society, the other members of which included Pearl, Refuge, Britannic, British Legal and London & Manchester. Carrying out work on behalf of the Government gave status to these offices and provided them with an opportunity to discuss with their customers other aspects of insurance that the state did not provide. The involvement in the health of the nation encouraged the Society into modest philanthropy and from the mid-1920s regular donations of ten guineas (today: £450) were made to hospitals in London and other areas in which Royal London was active: the Brompton, St Bartholomew's, Charing Cross, King's College, the London (there was no 'Royal' in its name then) and St Mary's all benefited, as did the Hospital for Sick Children at Great Ormond Street, the City of London Maternity Hospital, the Elizabeth Garrett Anderson Hospital, the Royal National Orthopaedic Hospital, the Royal Infirmaries at Liverpool and Sheffield, the Royal Victoria Hospital, Manchester, the Birmingham and Royal Manchester Children's Hospitals and many others.

In 1909, the first complete year after the conversion, the Society's total income was £1.23 million (today: £95.5 million) with total funds of £2.67 million (today: £207.3 million). The Report of the Directors for 1914 records the progress over the intervening five years and refers to the impact that World War I was already having on the Society:

The TOTAL INCOME for the year amounted to £1,514,257 10s 11d.

PREMIUM INCOME. In the Industrial Branch the total amounted to £1,336,434, representing an increase of £51,377 over 1913, whilst in the Ordinary Department the sum of £37,973 was received. The increase would probably have been considerably larger but for the detrimental effect of the War upon trade generally during the last five months of the year. In response to the appeal of our King and Country, 478 members of the Staff volunteered for Active Service, and are now serving with the Naval or Military Forces at home and abroad. The noble sacrifice by so large a number of the working Staff has called forth our unstinted praise, and though it must have affected the work of the Society, yet we gladly join in this common service to our Country.

War had been declared on 4 August 1914 when the British Army had a total strength of only 250,000 men supported by an Army Reserve of around 200,000 former soldiers and a territorial force of 270,000 volunteers. By December 1914 a million had enlisted and volunteers continued to come forward at the rate of 20,000 a month until early 1915. By April 1916 "no less than 2,139 of the Outside and 198 of the Inside Staffs [of Royal London had] responded to the Country's call, being over 72 per cent of the men eligible for service".[7] Conscription was introduced in January 1916.

The statistics of World War I – ten million military deaths, twenty million wounded and possibly as many war-related civilian deaths – are such that our comprehension is numbed. The experiences of those with whom we feel some affinity is perhaps more effective in demonstrating the horror and futility of war. Photographs of sports teams have an ageless quality. We, of subsequent generations who donned our kit, stood or sat on benches and looked towards the camera and probably differ very little from the players in the photographs. We would have laughed at similar jokes, complained about decisions of umpires and referees and relived games in the bar afterwards. The Royal London Cricket Club won the Insurance Companies Cricket League in 1912 and the team was photographed with the chairman and some of his colleagues. Sitting on the ground in front of Edward Smith and proudly holding the trophy was William Radley. He was 20 and lived in Kentish Town with his parents and two elder brothers: Frank worked for Maple & Co, whose Tottenham Court Road furniture warehouse was recognised as one of the sights of London, and Arthur was a clerk at a firm of upholsterers. Lawrence John Millage who was 18 and lived with his mother, three sisters and two younger brothers in Romford, was standing in the second row to the left of the chairman. There were eight men in the back row – seven of them in suits and William Bertie Newman in cricket kit. Newman was 23, born in Stoke Newington and lived near the Elephant & Castle with his wife Beatrice Mary and their young son, John.

The year 1915 was one of disasters for the Allies on the Western Front. On 9 May an offensive at Neuve-Chapelle achieved nothing but heavy losses – in several places the enemy line had been broken but the attackers did not seem to know what to do next. On 15 May, an attack was launched to the south around the village of Festubert, preceded by a four-day artillery bombardment. By the end of the battle on 27 May, the village of Festubert had been captured although territorially the Allied forces had gained less than a kilometre at a cost of 16,000 casualties. After the battle, Private Lawrence Millage of the 15th (County of London) Battalion, London Regiment (Prince of Wales Own Civil Service Rifles) was missing.[8] His body was never recovered. He is commemorated at the Le Touret Memorial to the Missing above the entrance of which are inscribed the words:

*To the Glory of God and in memory of 13,482 British officers
and men who fell fighting in this neighbourhood from October
1914 to September 1915 whose names are recorded but to whom
the fortune of war denied the known and honoured burial given
to their comrades at death.*

Little progress had been made on the Western Front by November 1917
when the Battle of Cambrai was fought. Military historians regarded the
battle as the dawn of a new epoch – it illustrated that tanks could be used in
a combined operation while the German counter-attack showed the value of
their new infantry tactics. The Allies' objective was to surround the town and
capture Bourlon Ridge. During fierce fighting, not far from the woods on the
Ridge, Private William Newman of the East Surrey Regiment was seriously
wounded. He died on 26 November and was buried at the Orival Wood
Cemetery at Flesquieres. Each side suffered casualties of around 45,000. By
December most of the British gains had been abandoned. Beatrice, Newman's
wife, had collapsed and died in April 1915 – at the inquest, evidence was
given that she had suffered from valvular disease of the heart. John Newman
was an orphan at the age of seven.

William Radley was a sergeant in the 12th (County of London) Battalion,
London Regiment (The Rangers) that landed at Le Havre in December 1917.
The casualties in resisting the German spring offensive were so heavy that two
battalions merged. By August the offensive had been halted and the Allied
advance to the Rhine had begun. The German commanders realised that the
war could not be won and were considering the basis upon which an armistice
could be sought. On 12 September 1918 Radley, who had been awarded
the Military Medal for bravery in the field, was one of nine members of the
Regiment to lose their lives as the Allies advanced through Picardy and Artois.
He is commemorated on the Vis-en-Artois Memorial that records the names
of 9,903 officers and men who were lost between 8 August and the Armistice
on 11 November and whose bodies were never recovered.

Also on the Western Front was Bertram Simpson, that promising clerk
in the Agency Department at the turn of the century who left industrial
assurance to study for the Church. He had been ordained in 1908, was Vicar
of St Peter's Harrow and had joined the Army's Chaplains' Department in
1916. He was renowned for his insistence that he be allowed to carry out
his work in the front line and, following an incident in August 1918, he was
awarded the Military Cross.

The citation read:

*For conspicuous gallantry and devotion to duty. Whilst visiting
the most advanced line he was injured by the burst of a shell but*

carried on with his duty. He has always carried out his daily task regardless of all fire.

By the end of the war, 147 Royal Londoners had been killed on active service. More almost certainly died after they left the Services as a result of their injuries and other members of staff may have been killed as civilians. An example of the former appeared in the second edition of the *Royal London Head Office Staff Magazine* in 1920: it reported that William Beecroft had died on 29 July 1920, aged 24. He had been with the Royal London for nine years, enlisted in 1914 and went to France early in 1915, serving with the Lewis Guns. He was taken prisoner early in 1917 and his death was due to illness contracted whilst a prisoner of war in Germany. He, and many others like him who died after the war, would not generally have been included in the lists of those killed on active service. The older generations suffered too, without appearing on any memorials – parents who never came to terms with their grief and others, like W G Grace, the world's first sporting superstar, whose death in 1915 was probably accelerated by depression prompted by the thought of so many young men with whom, or with whose fathers, he had played cricket being mowed down on the Western Front, and by the bombs being dropped from Zeppelins near to his south London home.[9]

Research has been able to identify with some certainty 125 of the 147 deaths and within the Society's archives are details of their families, the battles in which their units were engaged, the date and place of death, the location of the graves and (where no grave exists) the name of the memorial on which the death is commemorated.[10] Of the 125, 74 were killed in action, 29 died of their wounds, 3 died at sea and 19 are simply described as having 'died'. Inevitably, the greatest loss of life was on the Western Front – 99 died in France or Belgium, of whom 41 have no known grave. The names of Royal Londoners appear on the great memorials at Arras, Cambrai, Loos, the Menin Gate (Ypres), Thiepval (the Somme) as well as Vis-en-Artois and Le Touret. A memorial to the 147 was erected in Royal London House in 1921 – fittingly, it was the Reverend Bertram Simpson, now Rector and Rural Dean of Stepney, who gave the address at the unveiling.[11]

During the war, the work of the Society had to continue. Many industrial assurance policies contained a provision by which the sum paid would be reduced if death occurred as a result of war. This would have been intended to apply only to regular soldiers and it had never been envisaged that it would be relevant to more than a million policyholders. The industrial assurance offices agreed early in the war that they would not apply this exclusion. In due course, a Royal London policy was designed for serving soldiers and sailors. Full benefit was payable where death occurred 'on Home Service' (even during an invasion) or in any part of the world as a result of disease or accident (other than drowning at sea). A quarter benefit was allowed in the first year, and a half benefit subsequently, where the policyholder was killed in action, died from wounds or drowned at sea. For a weekly premium of 2d (today 42 pence), a soldier or sailor under the age of 30 could assure himself on these terms for £10 (today: £500) The offices also had to deal with the Courts (Emergencies Powers) Act 1914 which provided that assurance effected before the outbreak of war for sums not exceeding £25 could not be forfeited without leave of the court. This provision was a concern to the offices as they had to maintain cover despite the removal of the requirement to pay premiums. All they could do was deduct the arrears of premium when a claim was made. They would have been even more concerned had they known that the legislation would remain in force until 1924. In practice it did not prove too troublesome as the great body of policyholders maintained their payments.

Edward Smith had given some startling news at the Board meeting on 29 January 1915 – in consequence of the partial depletion of the head office staff through the war, it had been found necessary to engage a number of girl copyists and typists. Steve Else, as we have come to expect, had a rather more personal view:

> Up till then there were no ladies employed on the staff. Such correspondence as was necessary was dealt with from brief notes written as reminders on documents and later punched out by male two-fingered typists on old Empire machines. Great excitement occurred when it became known that a limited number of girls were to be employed to write policies. This excitement was due more to the fact that some of us thought we were about to lose our jobs than to the amorous possibilities arising from the proximity of the girls. Anyway, those in charge, viewing the position from their own moral standpoint, considered that the young members of the Staff would be totally unable to restrain their lascivious tendencies and imposed restrictions by which we were prohibited from going anywhere near what was then called (the title being somewhat marred by its association with other places) 'The Ladies'. Ultimately it became clear that the attractions offered by this small concentration of young females (although I have no doubt favourably comparable with any other group of young women) were insufficient to detract the average young man from his alternative choice of the wide world outside the Office, and the ban was removed, without any disastrous results.[12]

The fact that extensive immorality had not broken out, at least not within the office, encouraged the management to extend the recruitment of women, and shorthand typists and clerks appeared later in the year. Away from head office, wives, sisters and mothers collected on behalf of absent agents and by 1916 the joint managing directors were empowered to exercise their discretion as to the acceptance of suitable women (and men over 50 years of age) to take over vacant agencies. As one of the managing directors had worked for Mary Ann Davies in Stepney, he at least should not have needed convincing that women could play an important role in industrial assurance. At the end of the war, the Society had 3,267 male and 568 female agents.

In November 1917 the National War Savings Committee saw the success of tanks at the battle of Cambrai, a year after they were first used in the battle of the Somme, as a fundraising opportunity and initiated a 'Tank Bank' campaign. A battered tank named 'Egbert' was recovered from the battlefield and installed in Trafalgar Square where passers-by were invited to buy war bonds and certificates, and to queue up so that their bonds could be stamped by young women seated inside the tank. Politicians, churchmen, war heroes and theatrical celebrities were invited to perform and address the crowds from the top of the tank. The campaign was hugely successful and was soon extended with a number of tanks touring the country. One, called Juliet, made it to Finsbury Square.[13] Steve Else takes up the story:

> *Sir Edward Smith* [who had been knighted for his public service as a magistrate and member of the London County Council] *arranged for an Army Tank to appear before the Society's main entrance and from the top of this addressed us all in stentorian tones, damned all Germans and urged us to contribute liberally towards War Loan. The fact that I was then being paid only thirty-eight shillings a week[14] limited to some extent my ability to help the Country out of its financial difficulties.*

Steve need not have worried. The minutes of the Board meeting on 14 December read:

> *It was reported that a cheque for £50,000… payable to the Bank of England for purchase of War Bonds had been drawn on 7th inst and it was Resolved that same be confirmed.*

The directors seem to have been inconsistent in their attitudes to money and the war. They saw it as their duty to assist the country, and by the end of the war 32 per cent of the Society's funds were invested in war loan stock. In total, the industrial assurance offices invested £57 million in British Government securities (today: almost £2 billion). The same generosity was not displayed to the Society's head office staff absent on active service. Initially they were entitled to half pay, although later payment seems to have been limited to married men who were already employed before the outbreak of war. Then a complicated formula was introduced that had to take into account what the member of staff was being paid by the army or navy, with the Society paying only what was necessary (up to a maximum of half) to take the individual's total earnings up to his Royal London salary. At Finsbury Square overtime was generally available at 4½d per hour with 6d tea money except on clear nights with a full moon when a Zeppelin raid was likely. A marquee was set up at the Honourable Artillery Company, just over the road from the office, where for the payment of 2d for admission, the relics of Zeppelins shot down near London could be viewed.[15]

Among the 1914 claims were those paid "upon the death of 825 Assurants who have bravely fallen in Active Service" and by 1919 the total claims paid by the Society as a direct result of the war exceeded £500,000 (today: £17 million). In total, the war claims paid by the offices exceeded £10 million (today: £340 million) while the life expectancy of many other 'Assurants' had been reduced by their wounds and other experiences, including exposure to poison gas.

The death of Frederick de la Bertauche on 2 March 1919 at his home in Gerrards Cross brought to an end the last link with the founders and the early days of the friendly society. He was born in 1846, the son of a policeman in Hackney, and at the age of 15 was working as a groom in nearby Stratford. In 1868 he was recruited as an agent of the Royal London Friendly Society. He became a member of the Committee of Management in September 1875 and remained on the Board until his death, serving for nearly 44 years as a director. He was long-remembered as a tall man with a long grey beard who would often tell of the early days, when pockets had to be turned out to pay claims.

The strengths and weaknesses of industrial assurance had been much discussed at the time of the limited introduction of national insurance in 1910 and the Fabian Society commissioned Sidney Webb[16] to make an investigation, the results of which appeared in the *New Statesman* of 13 March 1915. Of rather more concern to the offices was the appointment in 1919 of a Board of Trade committee under the chairmanship of Lord Parmoor[17] to investigate industrial assurance and collecting societies. Sir Edward Smith gave evidence and experienced at first hand the concern of the committee that no attempt had been made by the companies, other than the Prudential, to give industrial assurance policyholders a share of the profits. Smith made two points. Although it was true that no bonuses had been declared since the conversion, policyholders were participating to a degree because of the practice of the Society to reflect its increasing financial strength by issuing tables for new policies that provided for more generous payouts and then to make these payments on existing policies. As he put it: "A person may come with a policy that has £10 or £12 on it, issued under the old table, and under the new table it may be £12 or £13. The money is paid like that; and during the last ten years we have paid £136,000 in that way over the policy-value of the policies."[18]

Secondly, Smith suggested that the Board had, in fact, displayed great prudence in not paying bonuses and their approach had been amply justified by the costs to the Society of the war and the influenza epidemic of 1918–19. Fifty million people died in the worldwide influenza pandemic, several times more than had been killed in the war, including 250,000 in the United Kingdom, with many of the victims being healthy young adults. The next valuation revealed a surplus in the Industrial Branch fund of £736,000 (today: £24.3 million) and the Board resolved to "make an addition to the sum assured" on all policies issued prior to 1 January 1911 of 5 per cent. This generous bonus absorbed 59 per cent of the surplus – some might have felt that this was an over-reaction to the committee's criticism.

The data collected and published by Government committees is as interesting today as their findings and recommendations. The Parmoor Committee required offices to complete a questionnaire that enabled its members to acquire a detailed knowledge of the business of the offices. The committee calculated that the average weekly premium on all industrial assurance policies was under 2½d and that the average sum assured was between £11 and £12 (today: £400).[19] The lapsing of policies was as much a concern to Parmoor and his colleagues as it had been to the Royal Commission in the 1870s. In 1913, the last complete year before the war, 910,818 Royal London policies were issued and 659,664 policies lapsed of which 525,815 had only been taken out in 1912 and 1913. So for every 100 new policies put on the books, 73 existing policies were lost because payment of the premiums had stopped. The lapse ratio (adopting the definition that was later to become the standard that included only policies lapsing within the first two years) was 57.7 per cent. This experience was typical, the Parmoor Committee reporting in 1920 that:

> *Taking all the offices together it is probable that lapses of polices in the year of issue or in the year following reach an annual total of 5,000,000. This vast figure can only mean that there is a section of the population which is repeatedly induced by the pressure of agents and canvassers to take out policies and which discontinues payment immediately that pressure is removed, having lost nearly the whole of whatever premiums it has paid, since the benefit assured at the outset is a mere fraction of the full sum named in the policy. So long as heavy procuration fees are allowed, it will always pay the agents to devote themselves to the ceaseless pursuit*

*of new business among this class of the community regardless of
the value of the policies to the assured or of the probability that
they will be kept up.*[20]

Royal London agents were receiving commission on new sales of ten
times the amount of the first premium (or the first 13 weeks of the premium
as collected) and 25 per cent of all subsequent premiums collected. Further
payments were due quarterly and half yearly based on the amount by which
they had increased their total weekly collections. The average weekly earnings
of agents were between £2 and £3. Over and above this, they had the right to
sell their collecting books to a successor, who they could nominate.

The report of the Parmoor Committee prompted the Industrial Assurance
Act 1923 that created the office of Industrial Assurance Commissioner, and
provided him with considerable powers of supervision, laid down principles
of valuation, established minimum standards of free policies and surrender
values and introduced a number of other policyholder protections, including
the right to request the commissioner to investigate complaints.[21] As amended
from time to time, the 1923 Act was to provide the regulatory regime for
industrial assurance.[22] It strengthened the 1875 Act by providing that, before
a policy could be forfeited, a notice had to be issued setting out the amount
of premiums in arrears and allowing a further 28 days for payment. Notices
could not be issued until premiums were at least eight weeks in arrears, and
so a policyholder was allowed a period of at least 12 weeks to pay the arrears
before the policy could be forfeited during which the life cover remained in
place. In practice, the notices were rarely served promptly which gave the
policyholder a longer period of grace. A lapsed policy could be reinstated
within a year of the notice providing it had not been surrendered.

The Act ensured that where the policyholders who had paid premiums
for a while before allowing the policy to lapse would receive some benefit.
It provided that, where a policy was discontinued after at least five years, a
free paid-up policy had to be issued, under which the policyholder remained
covered for an appropriately reduced sum and with no further premiums
being due. Many offices had adopted this approach long before 1923, and
subsequently offices often exceeded the statutory minimum and issued free
policies after two years and sometimes after one year.[23]

On 2 March 1921, *The Policy-Holder* concluded its report on the
settlement of the Auxiliary Company litigation with some perceptive and
prophetic comments on governance:

*We understand the Royal London rearrangements involve several
vacancies in the directorate of the Mutual, and we cannot help
thinking it would be wiser, although there is a very capable*

*and experienced managing director, to take this opportunity
of securing the co-operation upon the board of men of a wider
experience of business and knowledge of affairs and finances,
than can be recruited from the ranks of the agents and staff
alone. We know the difficulty lies in the fact that through the
apathy and indifference of the policyholders, the control of the
friendly societies and mutual companies has passed very largely
into the hands of the staff. We believe in the fair and adequate
representation of the staff on the board, for, after all, the success
of the undertaking must to a large extent depend upon their
efforts. There is, however, a vast difference between this and the
complete control which the agents have secured in some of the
offices.*[24]

This suggestion was a bridge too far at the time but later in the year
steps were taken to meet this concern, at least in part. In September 1921
the extraordinary general meeting was held to approve the settlement to
the Auxiliary Company dispute and to approve changes to the Society's
memorandum and articles of association. Clearly the latter were all part of
the settlement – some of the excesses of the earlier articles were removed and
there was some necessary updating. Over and above these changes, there was
evidently a wish to put in place some mechanism that would reduce the risk of
a similar situation arising again. The independent non-executive director had
yet to be conceived but a similar approach was adopted in the new articles
that created a Consultative Committee of not more than three or fewer than
two members of the Society who essentially had three roles:

- to attend Board meetings and "to make representation to the Directors
  if they think fit" although as they were not directors they could not vote
- if and when requested by not less than 500 members "to make
  investigations into the affairs of the Society or to appoint an Inspector
  or Inspectors" to do so
- "generally to interest themselves in and keep themselves acquainted
  with the affairs of the Society".

Alerted by the notice of meeting, several members had put themselves
forward for appointment to the committee but a few days later the Board
appointed Major Evan Hayward and Sir Harold Elverston.[25] Hayward, a
solicitor and MP, had been a member of the Parmoor Committee and played a
major role in the Auxiliary Company litigation. Elverston was the proprietor
and editor of *The Policy-Holder* and had been MP for Gateshead from
1910 to 1918. The author of the "Friendly conclusion to lawsuit" article in

The Policy-Holder of 2 March 1921[26] seemed particularly well informed – Elverston, who would have known Hayward from the time when they were both in Parliament, had probably become interested in the case and may have written the article himself. It is unlikely that such worthy gentlemen were appointed by chance and the membership of the committee was probably all part of the settlement. The two men became regular attenders at Board meetings until 1931, when it was decided to create an internal legal department and Hayward, no longer an MP, accepted the invitation to head it up. As an employee, he could hardly remain on the committee and Elverston was joined by Sir Alfred Brumwell Thomas,[27] an architect renowned for grand civic buildings in the baroque revival or 'Wrenaissance' style, including the Belfast City Hall, (considered to be the finest example of Edwardian baroque in the British Isles), Stockport and Plumstead (now Woolwich) town halls and the Deptford public library. Hayward continued as the Society's legal adviser until 1941 when he retired, aged 65, to his family home at Wotton-under-Edge in Gloucestershire. One of his final accomplishments was to motivate and train young Billy Skinner who, many years later, would not only be solicitor to the Society but would move on to be its chief executive and chairman.[28]

The Consultative Committee survived until 1949 when, as part of an exercise to bring the articles of association "up to date and more in conformity with modern law and practice", the opportunity was taken "to abolish the offices of the Consultative Committee and the Trustees, these offices being considered to be now redundant".[29] To the extent that the committee brought independent outsiders into the Board's discussions, it was ahead of, rather than behind, the times. It would not be until 1980, when the first independent non-executive director was appointed, that anybody other than past or present executives would be involved in the Board's deliberations. The inclusion of trustees in the 1908 articles had been a strange decision. There was a role for trustees in a friendly society but not in a company[30] and there is no evidence of the tasks performed by Sir Edwin Cornwall[31], Sir Henry Dalziel[32] (both Members of Parliament) and Sir Edmond Browne, a barrister, although it may have been felt that their presence amongst the officers served to add substance to the Society. Alfred Skeggs' son, Dr Basil Lyndon Skeggs, a GP from Stevenage, was a trustee from 1928 until 1941 and then a member of the Consultative Committee until it was abolished.

Great Britain won nine gold medals at the 1924 Olympic Games in Paris. The film *Chariots of Fire* will keep alive the success on the track of Harold Abrahams and Eric Liddell in the 100 and 400 metres, while Douglas Lowe won the 800 metres. Harry Mitchell was a clerk in Royal London's Valuation Department who had seen active service in France, Salonika and Egypt. He was a member of the Polytechnic Boxing Club and, as the Amateur Boxing Association's light-heavyweight champion, it was no surprise when he was selected to compete at that weight in Paris. His first three fights went well: his Dutch opponent was disqualified, he comfortably outpointed a Frenchman and in the first round of the quarter-final knocked-out another Frenchman. He had a tough battle in the semi-final against an awkward Italian, and there was nothing between them after two rounds, but Mitchell had the better of the final round to win the verdict of the judges. In the final, Thyge Petersen of Denmark also tried to keep the fight at close quarters. It was a disappointing spectacle but Mitchell was the comfortable winner.

Today, Harry would have been a national hero – open-deck bus tours, media interviews, advertising contracts, sponsors and meetings with the great and good would have followed. As it was, he just returned home with his gold medal and got on with his work in the Valuation Department, where he remained until he retired as a first-class clerk in November 1955. As an Olympic gold medallist and ABA champion for four successive years he must have received encouragement to turn professional, if only from those who saw themselves benefiting financially from his success. We will never know if he was tempted and whether it was perhaps the security of Royal London that played a part in persuading him not to do so. He was 28[33] when he won the gold medal and probably felt that by then he was too old to make the conversion. A sad letter from the secretary of the Head Office Pensioners' Association appeared in the Head Office News in July 1979.[34] It printed a photograph of Mitchell, then a fit looking 83-year-old, and reported that he was living in a rented room in Twickenham and had been forced to sell some of his cups and trophies. He had never married, but a girl he had known had recently looked him up and confessed that, 50 years ago, she was longing for him to propose. Harry Mitchell died on 8 February 1983.

The offices were increasingly providing sporting and leisure activities for those working in their head offices in London. They saw it as a means of attracting and retaining staff. Subscriptions and match fees were generally kept at a nominal level, with the offices paying for the acquisition and upkeep of sports grounds, and providing space within their offices for sporting and cultural activities. Industry-wide sporting associations were formed to provide fixtures and competitions for the offices and in some cases to field a team representing the industry. The first of these was the Insurance Chess Club, formed in 1893, followed in 1906 by the Insurance Rifle Club, with Field Marshall Lord Roberts firing the first shots.[35]

In 1908 Royal London was a founder member of the London Insurance Offices' Football Association. The association played a few representative fixtures against such sides as the Public Schools and the London Banks and operated a league with four (later six) divisions and three cup competitions, providing regular fixtures for 61 teams, the larger offices fielding two XIs. Royal London, with a ground at Bloemfontein Road, Shepherd's Bush, were at their strongest just before World War I – they won both the Senior and Charity Cups in the 1912/13 season having been the losing finalist in the Senior Cup in the two previous seasons. Sydney Webb, later a director of Royal London, was general secretary of the association for many years and Alfred Skeggs took his turn as president and donated a trophy for the winners of the third division.[36] By now finals of the Charity Cup were being played at Chelsea's Stamford Bridge ground, and one year when the final was drawn after extra time (this was long before penalty shoot-outs), Arsenal made Highbury available for the replay.

The success of the football association encouraged the insurance industry to expand into other sports with the formation of many similar organisations including the Insurance Offices' Amateur Swimming Association (founded in 1913), the Insurance Golfing Society of London (1914), the Insurance Boxing Club (1920), the Insurance Athletic Association (1922), the Insurance Offices' Lawn Tennis Association (1925), the Insurance Offices' Rugby Football Union (1927) and the Insurance Offices' Table Tennis Association (1931). Royal Londoners were active in many of the associations. In the early 1920s the Royal London was one of the few offices to have a rowing section.

The activities were not limited to sport. The Insurance Musical Festival Society was formed in 1923 and the Insurance Orchestral Society of London in 1924. It was claimed that the insurance profession could boast one of the finest amateur orchestras in the world.[37] At one stage, Royal London contributed both the principal flute and the principal oboe to the orchestra, and for many years had its own orchestra and dramatic and operatic society. The Insurance Brokers' Debating Society (1928) was soon opened to all engaged in insurance and 'Brokers' was dropped from the title. In 1930 the Insurance Flying Club was formed at the London Air Park, Hanworth, although the increasing congestion in the air around London soon prompted its relocation to Gatwick. There, members could learn to fly and obtain a pilot's license for as little as £10 (today: £520).

The life of an agent had hardly changed. Some went on foot, and others cycled. The insurance man (and sometimes woman), complete with cumbersome collecting book, was a familiar sight on the streets. They would often be carrying considerable sums of cash and, as their presence could be predicted because it was important to collect from policyholders at the same time each week, there was a constant risk of being mugged in some inner city areas. The attributes demanded of an agent were the same as ever: integrity, strength of character, self-motivation and self-discipline, energy, drive, perseverance, determination and ambition coupled with common-sense, good mental arithmetic, an ability to plan and sound administration.

Basil Sanders, one of ten children, born in Bethnal Green in 1906, was to become a much respected representative of Royal London agents. He left school at the age of 14 and in 1930 was working in an ironmonger's shop in Fetter Lane, earning 50s a week, and engaged to Ellen. His fiancée was horrified when she found out how little Basil was earning and told him in no uncertain terms that they could never get married on that. Both Basil and Ellen were actively involved in the Nichol Street Mission, the superintendent of which was Dickie Pearson, whose day-job was superintendent of Royal London's Islington district. Through him, Basil acquired a collecting book. In *The Simple Annals*, Peter Sanders wrote of the acquisition and his father's life as an agent:

> His book cost him £325. He had £65 available, mainly from my mother's savings, and he borrowed £260 at 7½ per cent interest. Since he had to pay this back at £1 a week, and since his income on the book was only about £3, at first he was earning less than before. But there were possibilities, which he realised, of gaining new business, and by the war he had paid off the loan and was earning £5 a week.
>
> Most of his clients had life or endowment policies in which they paid a shilling or two a week, and his round was concentrated in Highbury, Stoke Newington, Stamford Hill and Hoxton. He went out collecting on Mondays and Tuesdays, and on Friday evenings and Saturdays, when people had just been paid, and he travelled by tram on an all day ticket which cost a shilling a day. On Thursdays he paid his money to the branch office at Islington. He took Wednesdays and Sundays off, and for the rest of the time he tried to get new business. He enjoyed his work and became very friendly with many of his clients. For some of them he was the only white collar worker they knew, and they would ask him to write letters for them to the local council; or to fill in a form or draw up a will.[38]

The success of industrial assurance was based on agents like Basil Sanders. They were trusted by their clients and seen very much as the family's adviser. They took their responsibilities seriously and were respected in their communities. Many were active in local government or voluntary organisations. Dickie Pearson, for example, became Mayor of Bethnal Green and a member of the London County Council while Sanders devoted much of his spare time to the Nichol Street Mission and the scouting movement and later to trade union matters. Agents were able to provide a personal and local service. When a death occurred, the district office was in a position to calculate the sum payable and there would be cash available there to meet the claim. Sometimes the agent would act as the intermediary taking the death certificate, policy (or frequently policies) and premium books to the district office and returning to the family, often on the same day, with the cash. Alternatively the claim could be paid over the counter at the district office on production of the documents. Invariably some of the payment went straight to the funeral director.

The term 'district office' conveys a grandeur that was not always present. At the time of his retirement as a director of Royal London in 1980, Stanley Goodall recalled the events following his father's appointment as a superintendent just after World War I:

> *When my father was made Superintendent at Staveley, he was required to let our front room to the Society for use as the Branch Office... We had a brass plate on the front of the house. To complete the Office furniture, it was necessary to fetch a large square table from Snig Hill, Sheffield. I was ten at the time and I accompanied the Assistant Superintendent... on the journey to Sheffield which took all day. We went by horse and dray ... With a signed photograph of the then Chairman – Sir Edward Smith – this table graced what was regarded as an up-to-date Branch Office, complete with a letter-press used for making copies of the then all handwritten correspondence!*[39]

And all of that in the front room of the family home. Stanley followed his father into Royal London and there were many families who, over the same or successive generations, provided several Royal Londoners. The archives contain little personnel data, but the record is probably held by the Endersbee family, ten members of which collectively had some 340 years of service as agents and superintendents, beginning in March 1903 when Thomas joined as an agent in London, quickly followed by his three brothers. Fred soon set off for pastures new but Tom, Harry and George were to achieve collectively over 100 years of service. And then came Harry's three sons, George's one son and Fred's two sons, all of whom became Royal London agents.[40]

The period that followed World War I was grim for many of the population. After the horrors of the war, there was extensive unemployment in the older industries – steel, shipbuilding, textiles, and coal – and throughout the areas in which they were located. There was an air of helplessness and hopelessness, disillusion and despair, with hunger marches and other demonstrations by the unemployed. The miners' strikes early in the 1920s were followed by a nine-day General Strike in May 1926 when Britain was at a virtual standstill. Wall Street crashed in 1929, leading to a worldwide slump in demand. In the UK there was industrial stagnation with over-manning, inefficient work practices and a shortage of investment. Wages were cut and the industrial and manufacturing base contracted. By late 1932 there were three million unemployed. The Government seemed unable or unwilling to act. But industrial assurance defied what was going on and continued to operate in its own successful vacuum. In 1913, the last complete year before World War I, the Society had reserves of £3.3 million and its agents collected premiums of £1.3 million and sold policies with a total sum assured of £8.6 million. By 1936, the reserves were £38 million, the premiums had increased to £6.6 million and the sum assured by new policies had grown to nearly £22 million.[41]

Good progress was not limited to Royal London and a similar pattern was seen across the industry. In July 1933 a Government committee observed that:

> It is a striking fact that during the long years of industrial depression through which the country has been passing the total amount of the premiums paid under policies of industrial assurance has been steadily mounting. In 1920 it was somewhat short of £36 millions; by 1930 this figure had increased to £54 millions, i.e., by 50 per cent. The magnitude of the sum devoted to industrial assurance and its constant increase, in face of the downward course of wages and of the wide extension of unemployment, indicate that, for good or ill, this business is an element of vast importance in the economic structure of the community.[42]

There were several explanations for the constant increase. Industrial assurance was of great importance to the significant proportion of the population who took up the service that it provided. The need to be able to give a decent funeral to every member of the family, and to avoid the consequences of not being able to do so, was as real now as it had been in the middle of the previous century. The pauper funeral was as distressing as ever:

> [A] grave [is] dug ten, fifteen or twenty feet deep and the bodies are put in one after another. There will be about eight adult persons in that grave, and they will finish off the top with a layer of four children, so there may be twelve to sixteen people in one grave.[43]

But even where a family's finances were such that there would be no question of a pauper's grave, many felt strongly that their relations should not be out of pocket, nor should a modest inheritance be reduced, by the cost of the funeral. So they took out policies on their own lives that were there, so the families were told, 'so that you won't have to pay to bury me'. There were parents who, although they would probably be able to scrape together the cost of a funeral, felt more comfortable knowing that, if anything terrible happened to one of their children, funds to pay for the funeral would be available from the insurance company.

During the war, the willingness of family members to collect on behalf of absent agents, the availability of work at reasonable wages to fuel the mighty war machine and the reluctance to let the assurance lapse in difficult times enabled premium income and reserves to increase. After the war, much of southern England and the Midlands experienced increased prosperity. For those employed in the new industries (motor car, electrical engineering, chemical), and for the white-collar administrative and professional groups that had so expanded between 1880 and 1918, the period between the wars was not such a bad time, with prices starting to fall, houses more freely available on easy terms, and more leisure interests to pursue. This was the market for the newer types of policies now available from the offices that provided a means of saving and repaying a mortgage.

It seemed that no sooner had the offices finished dealing with one government committee than they were confronted with another. A committee of enquiry appointed by the Chancellor of the Exchequer to examine industrial assurance and assurance on the lives of children under ten years of age, chaired by Sir Benjamin Cohen KC, reported in 1933.[44] It made a number of detailed recommendations but concluded that:

> ... while improvements of varying degrees of importance may be expected from the adoption of these proposals, the defects of the business, and their consequences to the assuring public, call for remedial measures of a much more substantial character than can be secured by the changes in the statutory provisions which have been submitted by us.

The committee suggested four such measures but immediately rejected three of them as being unworkable (nationalisation, transfer of all industrial assurance business to "a public utility company" or "grouping the larger companies and societies into a limited number of compact bodies") which left only the suggestion of a statutory limitation of expenditure.[45] There was no immediate response from the Government to the committee's report.

Funeral policies still remained a significant part of industrial assurance business. These were not confined to the family member who would probably have to pay for the funeral. What occurred millions of times over, was illustrated in an article in the *Assurance Agents Chronicle*. It appeared on 29 August 1931 but the events that it described could have taken place at any time between the 1860s and the 1940s.

In the fall of last year, after a long and painful illness, I lost my dear mother. My eldest brother, who is in the building trade, and in addition to having sickness in his home, was only working short time, was called upon to travel from Torquay to Birmingham [for the funeral]. He lost nine days from work, had to clothe himself decently, and in addition naturally desired to assist in the actual cost of the funeral... What applied to him applied to a lesser degree to a sister who had to travel all the way from Bournemouth...

The writer and his brother and sister would each have taken out a life-of-another policy under which they assured the life of their mother and paid the premiums. Mother need not have known (in most cases the life assured did not know) that her family had taken out policies on her life.

Evidence given to the Cohen Committee suggested that more than half, and probably much more than half, of the policies issued by the offices in the early 1930s were for funeral expenses.[46] There were two inherent problems with these policies. It was not entirely certain that insuring against the indirect costs (such as those incurred by the brother and sister in travelling to the funeral) was permitted under legislation that had been in place since 1909.[47] Also, this type of policy was open to abuse – policies could be taken out as a pure speculation on the life of an elderly family member where there was no reasonable prospect that the proposer would incur any expense in relation to the funeral. For all we know, Mother's life may have been insured many times over by other relations who incurred little or no expense when she died and to whom the insurance money would have been at best a windfall and at worst the winnings from a successful bet.

The *Royal London Staff Gazette* of September 1927 included a brief report from one of the London district offices of the extremes that could arise:

At 2 minutes to 1 o'clock the Saturday before the August Bank Holiday, a cart drew up at our Old Kent Road Office, containing part of a large Deptford family with claims upon their mother and grandmother. An old lady had died, leaving ten surviving sons and daughters, 150 grandchildren and great grandchildren. The first contingent mentioned above had fourteen policies between them and as they looked a pretty fierce lot, I thought discretion the better part of valour and paid out at once, rather than hold over until after the holiday. On the Tuesday following, six more policies were presented making twenty in all. After this, who says the birth rate is falling in South London?

Even allowing for an element of exaggeration in the report, the proceeds of these 20 policies, no doubt, comfortably exceeded what was required to give the old lady a decent burial. The offices disputed the suggestion by critics that gambling on lives was rife, although they had to concede that it was not unknown. Where it did occur, life-of-another policies fell outside the scope permitted by legislation and were illegal. Nevertheless these policies, properly used, continued to provide a valuable service to families who had no means of dealing with a sudden, out-of-the-ordinary, expense. They continued, at least for a while, to form an integral part of industrial assurance.

It had always been the Board's aspiration to expand along the north side of Finsbury Square. The 1904 building had been extended in 1911 but the war had delayed further expansion. In 1926 the Society obtained a lease from the Church Commissioners of the whole of the north side of the square and in 1928 work began on what would be the central section. The architect was J J Joass, John Belcher's partner, who had taken over the firm when Belcher died in 1913.[48] The ten-storey building, opened by Sir William Waterlow, the Lord Mayor of London, on 5 February 1930, was (according to *The Policy-Holder* of 12 February) distinctive even in comparison with the many splendid buildings erected in London since the war:

> *The most prominent feature is the tower which surmounts the main building. From the basement to the top of this tower the height is two hundred and fifty feet, the loftiest commercial building in the City of London.*[49] *Crowning the tower is a figure representing Mercury, the God of Prudence, which was exhibited at the Royal Academy last year. There is a total floor space of one hundred and fifty thousand square feet… British materials had been used throughout, with the exception of the marble-work, and here the famous Travertine – the material so freely used in Ancient Rome – has been adopted. Solid Travertine blocks of great thickness have been used for the entrance hall, and the result gives an effect much superior to the appearance of marble-lined structures. The imposing appearance of the entrance hall is also enhanced by the massive bronze work, and the main front doors – finished with an antique green patina, as in famous examples of Ancient Rome – weigh fully two tons, and are virtually unequalled in the City.*

The sculptor of Mercury and the two Tritons at the front of the building was James Alexander Stevenson, a regular exhibitor at the Royal Academy, who signed his work 'Myrander' a combination of his wife's first name and part of his second name.[50] Mercury was the apex of the building's lightning conductor, although workers on the site were unconvinced by the identification – they felt that the figure represented the centre forward ('striker' in the modern idiom) of one of the London football clubs.[51] In October 1930, Joass presented a bronze of the figure to the Board.

The directors' offices were panelled in Cuban mahogany, decorated in gold leaf, with walnut borders to the parquet floors. Once again, the builders were Walter Lawrence & Son Limited whose competitive quote of £371,738 had won them the contract – a £16.5 million project by modern standards.[52] Joass' design was described as "harder and more angular" than Belcher's original building "with an American-looking jagged clock tower".[53] Joass favoured towers – at this time he was also designing Abbey House, Baker Street, the tower of which is all that survives today. Several hundred of the Society's staff and an impressive array of distinguished guests attended a lunch at the Connaught Rooms immediately after the opening. There on the top table was the Reverend Bertram Simpson, now Vicar of St Peter's, Cranley Gardens, and Chaplain to King George V. In his speech, the Lord Mayor referred to Royal London as "one of our great insurance institutions".[54] Sir William was probably unaware of a family connection with Royal London – his great-uncle Sydney, who had also been Lord Mayor, was one of Joseph Degge's interrogators when he gave evidence to the Royal Commission in 1872.

Lord Dalziel of Kirkcaldy, a trustee of the Society and a former journalist, MP and newspaper proprietor, was in some difficulty in proposing the toast of the Lord Mayor and the Sheriffs because (as he acknowledged) "some 40 years ago I made quite a respectable living in Fleet Street by writing articles showing why the Corporation and Lord Mayors and Sheriffs should be abolished".[55] He and his colleagues at the time had plans then to capture the City, although he could not recall what they were going to do with the Mansion House and Guildhall. There was a gracious exchange between Dalziel and the Lord Mayor in which Dalziel praised the Corporation for the great public service that it performed and Sir William suggested that these early writings of Lord Dalziel had been one of the very few unsuccessful incidents in an otherwise very successful career.

On grand occasions such as these, the Society's coat of arms could not fail to impress, although it had to be conceded that, with the cross of St George and the sword of St Paul, it bore a startling similarity to the coat of arms of the Corporation of the City of London, and indeed the motto 'Domine Direge Nos' (Lord direct us) was the same. The explanation was simple – just as the founders had adopted 'Royal' as a sign of respect for their sovereign, they had copied the City's coat of arms to represent the 'London' in the title of their new friendly society. In neither case had they thought that any permission was required. Royal London had been using its coat of arms for more than 70 years but then an objection was raised. There were perhaps some technical arguments – the long usage and the fact that no grant had ever been made to the City, although that was only because its coat of arms had been in use before the College of Arms was founded in 1484.

The matter was resolved in January 1934 when the College of Arms granted the Society its own coat of arms that was quite different from the City's – the motto was now was *Sustentet Nos Deus* (God sustain us).[56] "Why do we have to change now, after all these years?" somebody may have asked. The answer was probably that an 'insurance institution' warranted much more public attention than an industrial assurance life office.

CHAPTER 9

Smith, Skeggs and the Royal London of 1936

Sir Edward Smith and Messrs W.H. Coombes and W.C. Martin tendered their resignations as Directors of the Society. It was Resolved that same be accepted, with an expression of regret for the necessity, after so many years of valuable service.

Minutes of a Board Meeting of the Society held on 3 January 1921

Mr Skeggs always had great faith in the better qualities of his fellow-men, enabling him to bring the best out of those he was called upon to lead, and throughout his service with the Royal London he had the full confidence, loyalty and co-operation of the staff and the esteem of all with whom he came into contact.

Obituary of Alfred Skeggs, The Insurance Mail (29 September 1937)[1]

Edward Smith was chairman of the company from 1908 to 1920. He had been the dominant force for rather longer because, during the decade before the conversion, he seems to have been chairman in all but name of the friendly society. He was a natural leader, with a commanding presence and a 'hale fellow and well met' personality, who was popular with most of his colleagues and the staff. The dinner he gave in the National Liberal Club to the Royal London Football Club to mark the 1st XI being losing finalists in the London Assurance Offices Charity Cup and the 2nd XI winning the Minor Cup in 1919–20 was remembered as "one of the most enjoyable and happy evenings it has been the lot of any of us to attend".[2] The words of the Board are interesting when paying tribute to him on his knighthood in 1916 – they spoke of "the unvarying kindness, impartiality and ability at all times shown by him in the discharge of his duties as Chairman of the Society". His impartiality was demonstrated when, on two occasions, he voted against increasing his own salary.

The announcement of his knighthood in *The Times* of 22 December 1916 referred to him as chairman of the Standing Joint Committee of the Justices for London and a member of the London County Council and County of London Appeal Tribunal. Smith, a member of the Progressive Party, had been elected in 1901 to represent Bethnal Green North East in the London County Council and was deputy chairman in 1909 and 1910.[3] The Board rather overlooked the fact that his knighthood had been conferred for public services. In a circular to staff dated New Year's Day 1917 the managing directors, directors and secretary felt "that this new dignity will be appreciated by every member of the Staff throughout the Country who will realise that the 'Royal London' shares in the reflected honour of the Knighthood of its Chairman". It was hoped that it would serve as an incentive "to all 'Royal London' workers to unite in their endeavour to make the ensuing year an epoch in the progressive histories of the Companies". Surviving the horrors of World War I would have been rather more in the minds of many of those workers. The Auxiliary Company was in evidence – by the reference to 'Companies' and the fact that the document was headed 'Royal London Insurance Offices'.

Smith developed wide political and social contacts that were of value to the Society and the industry. He encouraged his colleagues to 'think big' – to realise that by the turn of the century Royal London was a significant organisation that could expand further, that a substantial purpose-built head office was consistent with the status it had acquired and that thoughts should be turning to throwing off the shackles of the friendly societies legislation. After the conversion he was keen to expand the business by means of acquisitions: there were discussions with the City of Glasgow Friendly Society and the London, Edinburgh and Glasgow Assurance Company in 1909, with the Church Burial Society in 1910 and with London & Manchester Industrial Assurance Company in 1911. None of these came to fruition, although a provisional agreement was entered into with London & Manchester but this was terminated by the Society in the light of advice received from its actuary. (Benjamin Braham had been against the deal from the beginning.) Smith sought to improve the efficiency of the head office and presided over a reorganisation in 1911. There were now 11 divisions: agency, accountancy, cashier, claims, fire, general, investments, ordinary, policy, inspection and valuation. The divisions were divided into departments and then (if required) sub-divided into sections. The larger divisions were headed up by a chief clerk, assisted by a principal assistant clerk, and the smaller ones by a first-class clerk.

The confident, convincing (and at times domineering) manner of people like Edward Smith is an asset so long as their ideas are good but can be a liability when they are bad. It is probable, although by no means certain, that the idea of the certificates or the proprietary company solution to the problems in 1910 came from Smith or advisers encouraged by Smith. The records do not indicate how readily these proposals were accepted by his colleagues, apart from Benjamin Braham's wish to have nothing to do with the Auxiliary Company. They do show, however, that when objections were forcefully and lucidly expressed by Braham in 1913, no change of policy was felt necessary. The traumatic events that followed might have been avoided even then if Smith had belatedly realised the dangers and done two things: encouraged the Board of the Society to put in place the reforms along the lines suggested by Braham, and appointed some directors onto the board of the Auxiliary Company who were not directors of the Society. Simply ignoring Braham's warning probably made unwelcome consequences inevitable and meant that Smith's huge contribution to Royal London would be tainted by his errors in relation to the Auxiliary Company.

Smith resigned as a director of the Society at the end of 1920 amongst the second batch of resignations agreed at the arbitration. Early in 1926 he suffered a pulmonary embolism and died later in the year during surgery to remove a kidney stone. He was a month short of his 69th birthday. His obituary in *The Times* of 21 September (the day after his death) described him as being active in magisterial and municipal life in London, and referred to his chairmanship of the Tower Bridge Magistrates and membership of the Lord Chancellor's Advisory Committee and the London County Council. His knighthood, and roles as vice-president and chairman of the managing committee of the National Liberal Club, were all mentioned, as was his involvement in the Crystal Palace and Surrey County Cricket Club. There was no reference, however, to his 43 years working in industrial assurance or the fact that he had been a director of the Royal London Friendly Society and a director and chairman of The Royal London Mutual Insurance Society,

Limited and The Royal London Auxiliary Insurance Company, Limited.

Alfred Skeggs had joined the Society as a junior clerk in 1882. He was chief clerk when early in 1908 he was appointed secretary of the Royal London Friendly Society. He was the first secretary of the converted Society and became a director in April 1920 and managing director four months later when John Price and Horace Duffell, the joint managing directors, resigned following the arbitration. He was appointed chairman (retaining the role of managing director) in 1932, retired in December 1936 after more than 54 years in the service of the Society and died the following September, aged 74.

In the late 1950s a number of long-serving staff and pensioners were invited to reminisce. Henry Helliwell joined the Society as a branch office clerk in 1905, became a district superintendent in 1923 and was a director from 1946 to 1961. He spoke of Skeggs' outstanding qualities of leadership and remembered him as a quiet, polite man, not big in stature, a Londoner with a polished London accent, who could stand on a platform with an air of control and who was an exceptionally good judge of men. Another's recollection of him was as being a real gentleman, greatly admired by the outside staff, who was "severe with a velvet glove". Skeggs' life was Royal London – a pensioner remembered Skeggs as a good businessman who "liked to have his own way and got it", while another commented that Skeggs "thought he was Royal London and that the Royal London was Alfred Skeggs". He had risen from humble beginnings to the top of what had become a significant company and, no doubt, appreciated the status that this gave him and the circles in which he could now mix as an equal. He was described by one as "snobbish and standoffish but good to the staff" and dismissed by another as a social climber. Perhaps Helliwell was too diplomatic to refer to Skeggs having acquired his polished London accent.

The archives reveal little about Skeggs' role during the period when the Auxiliary Company was active. Skeggs was secretary of the Society and the Auxiliary Company but was never a director of the Auxiliary Company, and became a director of the Society only a few months before the arbitration. His shareholding in the Auxiliary Company was negligible.[4] His abortive application for the vacancy on the Board of the Society in March 1913 may have been significant, and in particular the fact that he was proposed by a solicitor-MP – hardly the archetypical Royal London member. This indicates that the influential Hayward was involved in the Society's affairs before Braham's December 1913 statement and that this was via Skeggs. This may suggest that Skeggs was uncomfortable with the approach being adopted by the Board and encouraged Hayward's interest. It may also explain why observers noticed that Skeggs and Smith had a somewhat strained relationship. Skeggs must have become concerned during the arbitration that his proximity to the directors would drag him down with them because, at the end of the fifth day, counsel representing Braham told the arbitrator that he was now representing Mr Skeggs as well. His new client's name had, during the hearing:

> ... been coupled with the other Defendants, apart from Mr Braham, in this action as if they were all on the same footing. Whatever the result of the case may be, very serious charges have been revealed against these Directors. Mr Skeggs feels that his position, so far as his own character is concerned, is very much jeopardised.[5]

Skeggs would probably have been present throughout the hearing and realised by then that an outcome favourable to the directors was unlikely. He would have been looking not only to protect his name, but also to align himself with Braham and distance himself from the directors. As the arbitration was settled, he was never required to expand upon his role during the period when there were two Royal London companies. After the resignations that followed the arbitration, Skeggs came to the sound and pragmatic view that it was in the interests of the Society to bring to an end the unhappy saga as quickly as possible and the impressive speeches he made at the two general meetings in 1921 seem to have satisfied those attending and the wider audience.

Alfred Skeggs was a highly effective steward of the Royal London business. He was successful in both containing and moving on from the issues around the Auxiliary Company and the resignations. He presided over the site acquisition and designing and building of the grandest part of Royal London House. New business and the reserves increased steadily and the reputation and status of Royal London was enhanced. He achieved stability after a difficult period.

There was further evidence that Royal London had become an institution. Scarcely a photograph exists of Ridge, Degge or Hambridge but eminent portrait painters were now being commissioned so that subsequent directors would be inspired by the presence in the boardroom of images of past chairmen. Sir William Llewellyn,[6] who had painted the State portrait of Queen Mary in 1910, presented Smith, with part of his distinguished features in shadow, looking imperiously towards the distant horizon. Skeggs, wearing a natty bow tie and with pince-nez and a rather quizzical expression, appears in Richard Jack's[7] portrait, about to chair a board meeting. Jack had painted portraits of King George V and Queen Mary and interiors of Buckingham Palace. The top men of Royal London had come a long way since Ridge and Hambridge had visited those "fever invested districts"[8] to sell policies and Degge had demanded that everybody empty their pockets at 51 Moorgate Street so that a claim could be paid.

Alfred Skeggs was chairman and managing director throughout 1936

– the year in which George V died, Edward VIII abdicated and Hitler invaded the Rhineland – but he retired on 31 December. He was replaced by two joint managing directors: John Skinner and John Wiseman. Skinner, a head office man, had joined the Society in 1893 as a junior clerk. Fifteen years later he became agency manager, succeeded Skeggs as secretary in 1920 and was appointed deputy managing director in 1932. Wiseman's career began in 1894 at the age of 12 as office boy ('junior clerk' was the official title) at the branch office in Bow Road presided over by Edward Hambridge. In due course he became a clerk at the branch office and was promoted in 1902 to assistant inspector and in 1913 to superintendent. He was president of the Royal London Staff Association in 1917 and became a member of the Board at the very early age of 38 in 1920 when he was appointed divisional manager of the London C Division. Under his "forceful personality and wise leadership" the premium income for the division grew from £200,000 to £850,000.[9]

No chairman had been appointed, and Skinner was seriously ill, so it fell to Wiseman to present the directors' report and accounts for the year at the 76th annual general meeting on 27 April 1937. As this is the mid-way point in the story of Royal London, it is worth considering in a little detail the business that he described on that spring evening in 1937. The articles of association provided for the meeting to be held at the registered office but, as was the case at various times during the Society's history, there was no room there large enough there to accommodate a members' meeting. So after formally opening the meeting at Royal London House, Wiseman adjourned proceedings to Winchester House in Old Broad Street and it was there that he rose to address his colleagues and the very large number of members who had assembled.

After paying a generous tribute to Skeggs, the joint managing director was able to report that 1936 had been a good year for Royal London with a premium income of £6.6 million and funds of £38 million.[10] So by modern standards the Society had premiums of £336 million and funds of £1.93 billion. The impression that Wiseman sought to convey in his speech was that the Society was moving beyond funeral expenses and small industrial branch life policies and was now a company to which members turned to save for their old age, to make worthwhile provision for their dependents and to provide mortgages so that they could buy rather than rent their homes. He did not shy away from promoting the products – he advised that the "best form of policy in the great majority of cases is an endowment assurance maturing at the prospective age of retirement [that provides] a large amount of assurance as a provision for dependents [and] if the assured survives to 65 he receives a capital sum, which at his own option he can convert into an annuity as a pension for himself, or himself and his wife."[11] This was "a safe and profitable form of investment: the stability and security of British Insurance Offices is proverbial; it provides a large amount of insurance as a provision for dependents; it offers an excellent yield on a policyholder's money; and it carries with it the right to a rebate in the amount of income tax payable, which is a distinctly valuable privilege in these days." Wiseman was "glad to be able to say that for some time past this form of policy has formed a substantial proportion of our new business." He was enthusiastic too about the role of the Society in the mortgage market:

> Under the Society's House Purchase Scheme advances are made to assist people to become house-owners. The scheme is a simple one; the amount advanced being redeemed over a period of years by means of an endowment assurance policy. Tenants can thus use their rent to buy their house. The scheme is popular, the number of advances and the amount advanced showing an increase last year. Tenants would be well-advised to use our scheme to buy their own homes.[12]

Industrial branch was moving forward in its own way and in recent years, there had been "a welcome tendency to effect larger assurances on the life of the bread-winner, as distinct from policies taken out with the more limited object of meeting expenses arising out of a funeral" so that industrial assurance was "becoming more and more the means of helping the family to tide over the difficult time following the loss of the weekly wage on which the maintenance of the home depended."[13]

A member who had arrived early for the meeting and spent the time studying the *Directors' Report with Statement of Accounts for 1936* may well have felt that these statements were aspirational and misleading to the extent that they were understood as suggesting that these new and exciting policies were now dominating the Society's activities. A quick glance at the document would have revealed that in 1936 the Society issued 947,580 industrial branch policies assuring the sum of £15,454,957, and 41,919 ordinary branch policies for the sum of £6,313,628. If the early arrival was good at mental arithmetic he would have realised that more than 95 per cent of the new policies were industrial branch with an average sum assured of £16. Most industrial assurance customers would have been earning between £2 and £3 a week and so the average sum assured was no more than a couple of months' wages. Many of the policies would not have paid for a basic funeral that then cost about £20 in most towns, a little more in London and half that in many rural areas.[14] No doubt, as Wiseman suggested, some 'larger assurances' were being taken out but much of Royal London's new business was still at traditional levels.

The same could be said of ordinary branch. If endowment policies were being used to support mortgages, a sum assured of more than £400 would have been typical, at a time when the average house cost £550[15]. In fact the average sum assured by ordinary branch policies issued by Royal London during the year was only £151. Nevertheless the comments of Wiseman are interesting as they indicate the direction in which the Board wanted the Society to move, and in which it was moving, even if progress seems to have been slower than they would have wished. The ordinary branch service offered by the industrial assurance offices was a modified one because the premium renewal notices, instead of being sent in the post to the policyholder, were still delivered by the agent who was responsible for collecting the premiums.

Members may well have been interested in the extent of the life policies then available from the Society. If the member who arrived early for the meeting, bored with mental arithmetic, had asked to see the latest industrial and ordinary branch prospectuses, and started to scribble down a list of the policies, he would probably not have finished the task by the time the meeting began. There were more than 30 policies, although many were variations on the same theme. Essentially the Society was offering a range of 'whole life' (the basic life policy) and endowment policies with premiums being paid weekly, four-weekly, quarterly, half yearly or yearly, to suit the customer.[16] As might be expected, given the expense of collecting, better terms were obtained where premiums were paid less frequently: a young person, just short of his 20th birthday, who wanted to assure his life for £50 would have to pay:

- 5d a week (260d a year)
- 1s 4d every 4 weeks (208d a year)
- 4s 1d a quarter (196d a year)
- 7s 11d a half year (190d a year).

So if he could only trust himself not spend all his hard-earned wages, and to pay the insurance man only twice a year, he would only have to put by 3½d each week, and then find an extra penny every month, for his £50 policy. If he felt that this discipline was too much for him, he would have hand over to the collector 5d a week.

Wiseman said little at the annual general meeting about the context in which Royal London was operating. Perhaps this was because everybody at the meeting would have known of the significance of industrial assurance – at a time when the population of the United Kingdom was just below 45 million, there were more than 96 million industrial assurance policies in force. No less than 11 million industrial assurance policies were taken out in 1936, with an average sum assured of £19 14s in the case of companies and £16 3s in the case of collecting societies (today: £1,000 and £820). The premium income of the industrial assurance offices exceeded £66 million and their funds exceeded £385 million (today: £3.3 billion and £19.4 billion).[17] Industrial assurance had come a long way from its tentative beginnings in the middle of the previous century.

Towards the end of his statement, the joint managing director turned to the Society's funds:

> The Balance Sheet shows that the assets total £38,211,169, an increase of £2,610,377 over the previous year. Stock Exchange securities represent 72.5 per cent of the total, the remainder consisting mainly of mortgages, loans on public rates, freehold and leasehold properties, and ground rents. British Government Securities and Securities guaranteed under the Trade Facilities Acts represent 19.5 per cent of the total... Of the Stock Exchange securities, 81.2 per cent are made up of investments in Great Britain and Ireland, and 13.2 per cent in India, the Dominions and Colonial Dependencies. The total within the British Empire is thus 94.4 per cent. Investments in foreign countries amount to 5.6 per cent.[18]

The 1936 balance sheet showed how the assets were invested:

- £7.4 million in British Government Securities
- £3.7 million in UK mortgages
- £4.1 million in loans to public bodies
- £2.0 million in UK municipal and county securities
- £2.1 million in Indian and colonial government securities
- £4.3 million in debentures
- £5.2 million in preference and guaranteed stocks
- £3.1 million in ordinary shares.

A member with any reservations about the investment strategy would have been reassured by the next edition of *The Policy-Holder*. It noted that there did not seem to have been any material change in the investment policy adopted by the Society and commented that it had "been wise to select a considerable proportion of preference stocks and shares among the recent investments, as this type of stock exchange security offers the highest yield at the present time, commensurate with security, and along the same line of thought the increase in carefully selected ordinary shares is entirely justified."[19]

A perceptive member would have realised that what matters in a life company is not the extent of the reserves but rather the surplus determined following an actuarial valuation. The latest quinquennial valuation of Royal

London had been carried out as at 31 December 1935 and the Society's actuary had determined that there was a surplus of £3.16 million in the industrial branch and £1.57 million in the ordinary branch (today: £163.5 million and £81.2 million). As this had been reported at the previous annual general meeting, there was no need for Wiseman to mention it again, although he did refer to the generous bonuses to policyholders that were permitted by these surpluses. There was no contractual right to a bonus in industrial branch policies but bonuses had been declared after the 1925, 1930 and 1935 valuations. Initially these applied only to policies that had been in existence for some years, with the 1925 bonus, for example, applying only to policies issued before 1911, but after the 1935 valuation a bonus of 5 per cent of the sum assured was declared on all policies issued between 1871 and 1930 and 10 per cent on policies issued prior to 1871. The accumulated bonuses meant that pay-outs were now significantly exceeding the sum assured. A claim or maturity in 1936 under an industrial branch policy taken out in 1906, for example, paid 15 per cent more than the sum assured and one taken out in 1916 paid 10 per cent more. The ordinary branch declaration in 1935 was 2 per cent of the sum assured for each year since the last valuation. These declarations, according to *The Policy-Holder*, put Royal London "among the very select band of mutual societies which are famous for their splendid bonuses".[20]

By the mid-1930s, the promotional material of the Society suggested that the range of insurance that it offered was virtually unlimited:

- Fire
- Consequential loss
- Personal accident and sickness
- Burglary, larceny and theft
- Comprehensive insurances for private dwellings
- Motor car
- Workmen's compensation
- Fidelity guarantee
- Plate glass
- Sprinkler leakage
- Storm, tempest and flood
- Property owners' liability
- Boiler, engine and electrical plant
- Livestock
- Third party including general public liability and driving risks.

The joint managing director dealt briefly with this.[21] In 1936 the premium income of the Fire Department was £74,000 and the Accident & General Department was £31,000. Collectively they contributed £18,000 to the profits of the Society (today: £3.7million, £1.6 million, and £911,000). Both had satisfactory claims records. All insurance relating to workmen's compensation, employers' liability and motor was reinsured – in other words, the Society issued the policies, but the risk was accepted by another insurance company to whom the premiums would be paid, the Society receiving a share of the profit of the business in the form of commission. In 1941 an agreement was to be entered into with London and Lancashire by which all general insurance was reinsured with them.[22] Reinsurance enabled Royal London agents to offer as wide a range of insurance as any of their competitors without requiring the Society to undertake business with which it was unfamiliar, in volumes that would have been uneconomic.

Wiseman said nothing about the extent of Royal London's operations. Seven hundred people were now employed at head office and there were over 6,500 agents and 300 superintendents in the field, that was divided into nine divisions – six outside London (Lancashire, Midlands, Northern, Yorkshire, Southern and Western) and three in London. In addition to the grand building at Finsbury Square, the Society had a City office at 52 Queen Victoria Street, 73 branch offices in London (more than a third of which were east or north-east of the City), 10 principal provincial branch offices and more than 250 provincial branch offices with 16 of them in Manchester, 12 in Birmingham and 6 each in Liverpool and Sheffield. At the time of the conversion in 1908 there had been a mere 170 offices. When Alfred Skeggs joined Royal London in 1882 there were less than 25 staff at the chief office and fewer than a thousand in the field.[23]

Wiseman explained that the vacancies on the Board caused by the death of Frederick Baker and the retirement of Skeggs had been filled by appointing Arthur Houlding and Charles Spencer. These were hardly controversial appointments as both gentlemen were "men of character and ability, who have had a wide experience of the business of the Society and have served it faithfully and well".[24] The articles of association provided that appointments by the Board had to be confirmed at the next general meeting, and this was duly done, but Wiseman did not explain how the Board went about selecting new directors. Members who were not employees of the Society may have been uncomfortable with the answer. The Royal London Staff Association was the trade union for Royal London employees. It had been founded in 1900 and was now affiliated to the Trades Union Congress through the National Federation of Insurance Workers. Most of the major industrial assurance offices had their own self-contained trade union affiliated to either the National Federation or the National Amalgamated Union of Assurance Workers. The merger of the two in 1964 would create the National Union of Insurance Workers.

By 1936 the association had acquired a significant role in the life of the Society. It had over 200 branches and nearly 6,000 members – most of the field staff were members and there was one branch for the head office. It was the role of the association to represent the interests of the staff and, given the breakdown of the membership, the interests of agents were always likely to be paramount. The association submitted to the Board (that they consistently referred to as 'B.O.D' – board of directors) on an almost monthly basis formal requests to which the Board formally responded. After the association's annual conference, a long list of resolutions would be sent to the Board. Deputations from the association 'waited upon the B.O.D' from time to time when vital issues emerged and the executive council of the association was consulted when changes were to be made, for example alterations to the articles.

The Royal London Staff Association also had a role in the appointment of directors. When the Board intended to make an appointment it informed the executive council of the association. The council then organised a ballot of the members of the association and provided the Board with what amounted to a shortlist from which the Board made the appointment. Houlding and Spencer had been appointed in this way, and indeed both had to resign their membership of the council of the association to take up their directorships. This process may be hard to defend by modern governance standards but it did produce men of the calibre of Braham, Skeggs and Wiseman, all of whom had, in their time, been president of the Royal London Staff Association.

Some members at the meeting may have wondered where Royal London featured in the league table of industrial assurance providers. In 1936 there were eight industrial assurance providers whose premium income exceeded £3 million, one of which led the field by a long way with an income of more than £20 million. The top eight comprised four proprietary companies ('PC'), two mutual companies ('MC') and two friendly societies ('FS').[25]

Table No. 4

The top eight industrial assurance offices in 1936 (by premium income):

	Status	Premium Income £m	Fund at year-end £m	Agents and canvassers[26]
Prudential	PC	21.46	176.70	11,264
Pearl	PC	8.42	41.89	10,675
Liverpool Victoria	FS	6.13	33.07	8,312

	Status	Premium Income £m	Fund at year-end £m	Agents and canvassers
Refuge	PC	5.69	24.38	4,974
Royal London	MC	4.83	24.89	7,770
Co-operative	MC	4.20	13.36	3,352
Royal Liver	FS	3.86	19.72	6,369
Britannic	PC	3.78	14.26	3,665

Well-informed members would probably have been interested in how the Society was faring in the two areas that had prompted criticism over the years – expenses and lapsing. The Society's performance on the former was poor even allowing for the standards of the time. In its report in 1933, the Cohen Committee had singled out Royal London for its disproportionately high expense ratio – 31 per cent of all industrial branch premiums received by the Society in 1930 were paid as commissions to agents and canvassers and salaries to the superintendents, and another 12 per cent of premiums were required to cover the other expenses of running the Society. The Committee offered its own explanation as to why Royal London's expenses were so high:

It is worthy of remark that in [Royal London] *the terms of remuneration of all classes of employees who were in the service of the Society at the time of its conversion, from the directors downwards and including the agents, are prescribed by the memorandum of association and are not to be less than those paid by the Royal London Friendly Society... Further, the memorandum provides that the rates of remuneration of the then existing agents shall apply to all their successors not only in respect of the tables under which assurances were granted when the Society commenced business as a company but also in respect of any future tables which may from time to time be introduced in lieu of them. Whatever there was of extravagance in the old system is thus perpetuated, with the additional disadvantage so far as the assured members are concerned that while they would have found it extremely difficult to alter the rules of the old Society in order to secure any needed reforms, they are now up against a memorandum of association deliberately designed (as it appears to us) to protect every interest but theirs. It is not for us to estimate the legal efficacy of this device.*[27]

It seemed that the Board of the Society would never be free of the consequences of the conversion. Members at an annual general meeting today would expect to be told what progress had been made in addressing complaints such as these but the expense of running the Society was not a topic that Wiseman felt had to be addressed by him or covered in the report and accounts. The latter were disarmingly simple but short on explanations, and exactly what expenses were covered by the various headings was not always clear. Nevertheless a member who made a few calculations in the margin of the report and accounts as he was waiting for the meeting to begin would have sensed that there had been little improvement in the industrial branch expenses, although the overall ratio was brought down by lower ordinary branch expenses. In due course the data published by the Industrial Assurance Commissioner confirmed those fears – Royal London's industrial assurance expense ratio in 1936 had increased to 44.1 per cent.[28] This was significantly higher than the three proprietary companies in the top eight – the Prudential was as low as 25.9 per cent – and even higher than that of the friendly societies, with the Liverpool Victoria and Royal Liver both at just below 40 per cent.

The other area of concern was, and always had been, lapses – the large number of policies where premiums ceased to be paid and the policy was forfeited. The Society's evidence to the Parmoor Committee revealed that for every 100 new policies put on the books in 1913, 73 existing policies were forfeited. The position had improved slightly by 1929 – now 62 existing policies lapsed for every 100 new policies.[29] This was in line with Royal Liver (59 per 100) but lagged behind Liverpool Victoria (44 per 100). The figures for 1936 have not survived – we can only hope the progress was maintained, although it seems unlikely that there was any material change until the 1950s. By modern standards, a disturbing number of policies were still going off the books, most of them within two years of being taken out.

So what progress had Royal London made in the 75 years since Ridge and Degge had their chat in the coffee shop in City Road? The reports on the opening of the central part of Royal London House in 1930 provide part of the answer. There were lengthy articles in both *Post Magazine*[30] and *The Policy-Holder*,[31] written no doubt with some assistance from the Society. The sheer size of the business was beyond doubt, *Post Magazine* reporting that:

> *Mr Alfred Skeggs was appointed to the secretaryship of the Society in 1908 when the income was £1,243,925 and the assets £2,437,682. In 1920 Mr Skeggs was appointed managing director, and thereafter giant strides seemed to galvanise the Society to greater successes. Succeeding steps in progress were: 1920, income £2,412,187, assets £6,721,355 and 1929 income approximately £6,100,000 assets nearly £22,000,000. And in the*

latter years' developments one may visualise the organisation and driving force of Alfred Skeggs.

The status that the Society had achieved was evidenced by the Lord Mayor's reference to Royal London as one of our great insurance institutions. The *Financial Times* was so impressed that it granted Skeggs a knighthood, repeatedly referring to him in its report as 'Sir Alfred'.[32] Sadly for Skeggs this proved to be an embarrassing error and not one prompted by inside knowledge within the *Financial Times* of who would feature in the next honours list. Its correspondent must, however, have seen Royal London as the type of organisation that warranted a knighted chief executive and regarded Skeggs as a worthy candidate for that elevated role. Nobody on that momentous day would have seen fit to mention the Auxiliary Company but it seems that no long-term damage had been suffered as a result of that unfortunate interlude.

The Policy-Holder pointed out that Royal London was the largest British mutual life office and continued:

> *A member may take out a policy to provide a cash sum at his death, or when he reaches a ripe old age, or he may insure his house and furniture against fire, or himself or his employees against accidents. He may cover his livestock, protect himself against the risks arising from the use of electric plant, engines and boilers, or from the perils of the road while driving his car! In fact there is hardly an insurable risk that this progressive mutual fund will not handle, and on all the risks to which the ordinary man is liable the Royal London Mutual can offer valuable advice as well as sound protective contracts.[33]*

One senses that the Royal London of the 1930s was making much, perhaps a little too much, of the extent of the Society's diversification. These claims were true in the sense that the insurance services were available but as Wiseman's speech at the 1937 annual general meeting indicated, these policies played only a limited part in the life of the Society. The report and accounts also revealed that the sum assured under many of the new life policies remained modest and there had been limited progress into ordinary assurance.

The Royal London of 1936 had achieved a size and position in the community that would have exceeded the wildest dreams of Ridge, Degge and Hambridge. It was managed by men of ability and integrity. Its reserves could inspire nothing but great confidence in the minds of members and potential members. Good bonuses were being paid and its assets were well managed. A variety of policies were now available. And yet, the fundamental business, although hugely expanded, had changed very little over the years. The basic product continued to be small industrial assurance policies, many of which were taken out so that there would be money available to pay for a decent funeral for the policyholder and members of his or her family.

An obvious question is, why would the Board even think of changing so successful a business? An answer is that the expenses involved in canvassing and collecting would always appear high in proportion to the modest premiums and, given the market in which they were operating, persistency was always likely to be an issue. The report of the Cohen Committee, that was so critical of industrial assurance, was still on the table, and seemed to be having some impact on liberal middle-class public opinion, if not on Parliament or on industrial assurance customers.[34] The offices needed to reduce their reliance on the traditional policies, as the Board clearly accepted by its wish for the Society to be seen as a company to which one turned to save for old age, to make worthwhile provision for dependents and to provide mortgages so that homes could be purchased rather than rented.

By 1937 thoughts were inevitably becoming preoccupied with events in Europe. Had this not been so, the Board might well have been worried that some of the criticisms could one day be reflected in the statute book, and if they were, wondered what impact this would have on the Society's business. They would have been right to anticipate the need for change.

CHAPTER 10

The Middle Phase

1937–1960

The Englishman's concern for his corpse is as strong as ever it was, as can be seen by the slow progress which the movement for cremation is making, by the universal reluctance to allow bodies to be used for scientific purposes, and particularly by the introduction, nearly two hundred years ago, of the wooden coffin and the marble tombstone (which have resulted in our over-crowded and ever-spreading graveyards). In Protestant England, where religion has ceased to have any meaning for the majority of the people, the fantastic expenditure on funeral arrangements is almost incomprehensible. But it exists; it is a fact which has to be accepted and allowed for.

Harry Henry, The Insurance Man and his Trade (1938)[1]

Whereas in the old days industrial life assurance consisted mainly of policies for funeral expenses, the trend now is for a type of policy which includes a means of saving. The Society has encouraged this trend by the issue of a wide variety of endowment assurance policies secured by weekly or monthly premiums, collected at the home of the policyholder. So complete has this change been that almost three-quarters of the premiums on new policies issued by the Society in the Industrial Branch in 1953 were in respect of endowment assurance policies of one kind or another.

Christopher Shuttleworth, Chairman & Joint Managing Director,
annual general meeting of Royal London (27 April 1954)[2]

In 1937 *Industrial Assurance: an historical and critical study* was published.[3] Its authors were Sir Arnold Wilson and Professor Hermann Levy, a MP and an academic[4] and the book was an attempt to address the lack of attention paid, both inside and outside Parliament, to the report of the Cohen Committee.[5] The authors had been provided with data by W E Mashford of Hull, a self-appointed champion of aggrieved policyholders, who many years earlier had been an agent of the Prudential until he was dismissed.[6] He had given evidence at some length before both committees – the Parmoor Committee was "not equally impressed by all the cases [he] brought forward"[7] while the report of the Cohen Committee, having referred to devoting two and a half days to his evidence commented that:

> *It is proper to say that while, for a variety of reasons, he failed to convince us in regard to a number of his submissions, we were much impressed by his sincerity and by his desire to protect the policyowners especially those who are ignorant of their rights.*[8]

At the request of Sir Arnold, the Prudential and the Industrial Life Offices Association agreed to pay for a review by independent accountants of 157 of Mr Mashford's cases but the papers were never forthcoming from him and no review ever took place.[9]

'Comprehensive' is an inadequate word to describe the book by Wilson and Levy. It begins its review in the fourteenth century and runs to nearly 500 pages that give:

> *... a full account of the various committees and commissions which have for the space of a century considered and reported upon industrial assurance, of the various attempts at legislative control of abuses from 1828 to 1923, of the work of the great early Registrars, Tidd Pratt and Ludlow, and of the Chief Assurance Commissioner of to-day.*[10]

Not content with summarising the reports, the authors refer extensively to the evidence given to the committees, endorsing the critical findings of both.

For better or for worse, "scholarly, comprehensive, thorough and constructive" works rarely activate public interest and a reviewer suggested to the authors of this mighty tome that they produce an abridged version so that their message could be brought to "the more articulate sections of the assured public".[11] Such a book was to appear in November 1938, not by the same authors but by Harry Henry, a recent graduate from the London School of Economics where he had edited the magazine of the students' union.[12]

Described as a "succinct, fact-rich account"[13] and titled *The Insurance Man and his Trade*, it was based on *Industrial Assurance*, Henry referring to the work of Wilson and Levy as "the most comprehensive and masterly survey ever made of the subject".[14] Henry certainly achieved the objective set by the reviewer, and any articulate and interested member of the assured public who had access to this slim, 80-page monograph would have acquired a working knowledge of the criticisms of industrial assurance.[15] There is little doubt that the reports of the Parmoor and Cohen Committees, augmented by these two books, made a considerable impact on those who would be developing government policy a few years later. In the meantime, tragic international events were to intervene.

The directors of Royal London had the satisfaction of reporting substantial progress in both 1937 and 1938 but, by the 1939 annual general meeting, John Wiseman was fervently hoping that "wise statesmanship will avert the catastrophe which hangs like a threatening cloud over Europe".[16] Even as he said the words, he may have sensed that the time for statesmanship was past. Any hopes there had been the previous September, when Neville Chamberlain made the "Peace for our time" speech and waved his agreement with Hitler to the crowd at Heston Aerodrome, had been shattered by Hitler's invasion of Czechoslovakia in March. In August Britain signed a defence treaty with Poland, on 1 September Germany invaded Poland and on 3 September 1939 a state of war existed between Britain and Germany.

Few can have thought that the actions taken in World War I would, within a quarter of a century, serve as useful precedents and lessons for the Government and the industrial assurance offices in another conflict. The legislative protection was an improvement despite its cumbersome title. The Industrial Assurance and Friendly Societies (Emergency Protection from Forfeiture) Act 1940 provided that a pre-September 1939 policy could not be forfeited where the lapse of premium payments was due to circumstances arising directly or indirectly from the war. In practice, the legislation proved to be practical and effective. The majority of pre-war policies contained restrictions against active service risks but at the outbreak of war the directors decided that war claims would be paid in full where the life assured was a civilian at the time the policy was issued. Policies issued during the war posed more of a problem – in due course, a standard approach was developed by the offices that provided limited life assurance cover for service personnel and civilians who died as a result of the war.

Early in May 1940 Germany invaded and rapidly conquered the Netherlands, Belgium and Luxembourg. The Allies were expecting France to be attacked in the north but instead the invasion came through the Ardennes, the German army crossing the River Meuse near Sedan on 13 May and advancing quickly into the heart of France. On 10 June the French government left Paris for Bordeaux, on 14 June the Germans marched into Paris, and on 22 June the French Second Army surrendered, essentially bringing an end to hostilities. The French Government signed an armistice with the Germans on 25 June. In the meantime, over 300,000 British and French soldiers had been rescued from Dunkirk between 26 May and 4 June. During June the British Government decided that, as the Channel Islands were of no strategic significance, they would not be defended which made a German invasion of them inevitable. Unsuccessful attempts were made to organise a co-ordinated evacuation although many islanders did leave.

Most of the collecting societies and industrial assurance companies were represented in Jersey.[17] Royal London's superintendent was Ben Whiston who had joined the Society as an agent in Southampton in 1931 and relocated to Jersey three years later. Not unnaturally, Whiston contacted head office at Finsbury Square for instructions and was told that, unless ordered by the authorities to evacuate, staff should remain at their posts. The archives do not indicate when in June that decision was made, who made it (the issue is not referred to in the Board minutes) or the knowledge of the situation in the Channel Islands possessed, or that should have been possessed, by those making the decision. On 28 June, Whiston was in the district office in St Helier writing a report to head office when his work was interrupted by an air-raid on the nearby harbour. Within a few days, all the Channel Islands had been occupied by the Germans.

Whiston was not the only insurance man on Jersey and discussions began at once amongst the representatives of the offices. They must have been in a state of shock – two months ago the war had seemed remote but now they had to come to terms with the enemy occupying their island, uncertainty as to their own personal future, and in particular whether they would be allowed to go on living there or be sent as prisoners to Germany. It was clear that no contact with the mainland would be permitted and indeed an attempted invasion of the mainland seemed imminent, while the ineffective evacuation before the invasion had left Jersey in a state of chaos – as Whiston was later to report:

> Houses were abandoned, with unwashed dishes and scraps of food on the table of dining rooms and kitchens. Domestic pets were left to starve or to be destroyed by the hard-working staff of the Animals Shelter… Many shops with all their stocks were simply locked up and abandoned by their owners. Licensed premises and even farms, in some cases, were left unattended.[18]

Life, however, had to go on and there were policyholders on the island from whom premiums had to be collected. In due course, claims would be made but it would not be possible to transfer funds to or from Jersey and there was no guarantee that recently collected premiums would be sufficient to meet the claims. The early discussions also revealed considerable disparity between the offices – some were well below strength, with staff having left earlier in the war to join up or as part of the recent evacuations. Whiston and his colleagues from the other offices were keen to find a way to maintain business as usual and to safeguard the interests of all the offices, the welfare of their policyholders and the staff. A meeting was held on 3 July attended by representatives of every office on the island. An approach was agreed and a small committee appointed to draft a document for approval by the post-invasion government of Jersey. The inability to contact their head offices provided those on the ground with a rare freedom – the drafting proceeded quickly, the approval from the States of Jersey Finance Committee and Superior Council soon followed, and the new arrangements became fully operational within two weeks of the invasion.

The scheme involved a pooling of resources and the creation of the Associated Life Offices Central Fund (Jersey). Premiums from all industrial assurance policies on the island were collected and paid into the fund. Claims were paid out of the fund subject to some restrictions – payments of endowments were deferred until the cessation of hostilities and other claims were capped. Staff were paid a weekly wage of £2 5s 0d. The scheme with minor modifications operated for the five years of the occupation and was so successful that by 1941 limited new business was being accepted. A meticulous record was kept of all payments into and out of the fund so that after the war there could be a reconciliation with the appropriate sums being paid to the participating offices who would then resume responsibility for their own policies.[19] The original committee that had created the scheme became the committee of management.

The fund was operated from the Royal London office in La Motte Street, St Helier, and Whiston was the secretary of the committee and the supervisor of the fund. The main point of contact was with the Finance Committee although periodically the German authorities requested information. As a point of principle, Whiston never completed any form or return sent by Germans but played them at their own game by providing them with a mass of data and paperwork (that avoided disclosing confidential or sensitive information and was often not entirely relevant to their inquiry) which seemed to satisfy them. He made much of the fact that this was a Jersey association rather than English companies doing business there, an interpretation that was apparently accepted.

A constant fear was deportation and in September 1942 the Germans inserted a notice in the *Evening Post* to the effect that all English nationals were to be evacuated to Germany. Several members of the committee and a number of agents were evacuated and the future of industrial assurance on Jersey was uncertain. Papers were served on Whiston, but with the support of the Finance Committee, he was granted an exemption by the Germans on the basis of the necessity of the insurance work. A considerable re-organisation of the operations was required following the loss of so many agents and committee members. An intense feeling of isolation prevailed, with no communications being permitted outside Jersey although in time it was possible to get messages back home via the Red Cross. These were primarily of a personal nature, and the Red Cross, no doubt, stopped short of communicating budgets and new business figures, but there was some contact with Finsbury Square. At the Board meeting on 28 April 1943, for example, the "Acting Secretary read a letter which had been received from Mr B C Whiston of Jersey, through the German Red Cross, the contents of which were noted with pleasure."

After the D-Day landings in June 1944 the German supply lines for food were severed and both the islanders and the occupiers were soon on the point of starvation and having to rely on the Red Cross for food and medical supplies. When Germany at last surrendered, Whiston was to have early visitors – amongst the British forces that liberated Jersey were the Society's assistant superintendent at Croydon and Lieutenant Howard Jones, whose father was superintendent at Brighton. Whiston was invited to attend the Board meeting at Finsbury Square on 4 July 1945. The minutes read:

> At this juncture, Mr B C Whiston (Superintendent of the Channel Islands) was called into the Board Room to receive the congratulations and thanks of the Board for the efficient and loyal manner in which he had carried on the work of the Associated Offices, and particularly that of Royal London, during the difficult and trying period of the German Occupation. Mr Whiston suitably responded.

For the period up to 28 April 1945, £326,425 was paid into the fund and claims of £213,780 were paid-out (today: £10.5 million and £6.9 million). The fund stood at £109,313, of which £70,000 had been invested by means of a loan to the States of Jersey (today: £3.5 million and £2.2 million). Ben Whiston left Jersey later in 1945 to take over as superintendent at Bristol (where Howard Jones was to become his assistant superintendent) and later became divisional manager of the Chester and Midland Division and then the South Wales and Western Division. He retired in November 1968.

The greatest problem for the Society on the mainland was maintaining the service. Of the 8,150 people employed by the Society at the outbreak of war, 3,892 were released for the armed forces, civil defence or other war work. Temporary staff were much in evidence both at head office and in the field where larger agencies were created to improve efficiency of administration. Women joined the workforce as they had done in World War I. Pre-war, the industrial assurance offices employed 90,000 men and 10,000 women but by July 1943 there were 47,000 men and 41,000 women. It was a challenge to retain contact with policyholders during a time of great movement of the population. This was not limited to those in the armed forces. During August and September 1939, for example, many children, mothers and expectant mothers were evacuated from London to safer rural areas. When there was no immediate attack on London some drifted back, but there was further evacuation after the fall of France, at the beginning of the Blitz and with the arrival of the flying bombs in 1944. Agents in London, Birmingham, Cardiff, Coventry, Liverpool, Manchester and the other cities that were bombed could be confronted with a destroyed or severely damaged building that on their last visit had been the home of a policyholder.

Basil Sanders' collecting book was worth £5 when in 1940 he was called up to join the War Department Constabulary and posted to the security force at an armaments factory at Waltham Abbey.[20] His wife Ellen took over the round, often having to push or carry her bike through the rubble during the Blitz, and while Basil was away bought a new book and paid off the loan on it. She had doubled the family income by the time he returned. Industrial assurance had become so embedded that premiums continued to be paid and new policies issued regardless of the trauma being suffered by policyholders and the disruption within the offices. Between 1938 and 1946 the Society's premium income increased by more than 25 per cent and its funds by nearly 40 per cent.

In September 1939, 30 members of the ordinary branch and claims departments and many of the Society's important documents were evacuated from Royal London House to Peverel Court, a country house standing in its own grounds at Stone, near Aylesbury, in Buckinghamshire. It had been built in 1862 for the Bartlett family who were High Sheriffs of Buckinghamshire. The Society's archives contain a collection of 'Box Brownie' type photographs that capture cramped offices and rather basic bedrooms and bathrooms in the main building, a kitchen that resembles those on view today in National Trust properties, huts in the grounds, a tennis court, vegetable garden, local agriculture (two horse-power meant exactly that), leafy Buckinghamshire lanes and 'the local', the Bugle Horn Hotel.[21] The huts fulfilled many functions: they were used for work, recreation (billiards and table tennis), meals and, for those not eligible for a bedroom in the house, as dormitories. Steve Else was not evacuated:

> *I was not so fortunate – I stayed at HO, worked hard during the day, and, as a Warden, most of the night. Although Royal London House is adjacent to the City's most devastated areas, we did not*

suffer serious damage. Many incendiaries were dropped on and around during the great fire blitz and the HE [high explosive] bomb that destroyed a large part of Smithfield Market gave us a bad shaking but we never received a direct hit.[22]

In December 1940 a 35-acre area in the City had been laid waste by incendiary bombs – every street from Moorgate to Aldersgate Street was destroyed – and by the end of the war a further expanse as far south as Gresham Street had been devastated. Yet Royal London House, just a few hundred yards away, sustained only minor damage although other properties in Finsbury Square and Worship Street were destroyed.

At first the war was referred to in the minutes of Board meetings only in relation to logistical matters, such as the move to Peverel Court, although in fact little occurred during the 'phoney war' period between September 1939 and April 1940 that would have merited attention. For a while after that it may have been felt that acknowledging the war was inconsistent with the 'business as usual' approach that was so strenuously adopted.

From 1943, however, the minutes do provide glimpses of wartime life. For example:

It was reported that the Distinguished Flying Cross had been awarded (posthumously) to Flying Officer C C A Fuchs who was formerly a clerk in the Premises Department. This was noted with great pleasure combined with regret at the untimely death of Mr Fuchs.

(28 April 1943)

Copy of a post card received by Divisional Manager Mr E C Thomlinson from an agent of the Channel Islands who is now interned in Germany was read and noted with interest.

(13 May 1943)

Mr Thomlinson mentioned that he had received a letter from Superintendent Mr Farthing (who is now with the Army in India) in which he tendered his respects to the Board.

(10 June 1943)

The Secretary reported the death of Lt Frank Howells (a clerk attached to the Ordinary Department) who while stationed at Catterick Camp was accidentally shot and a verdict of misadventure was returned. A letter of condolence was dispatched to the Family and the local Superintendent attended the funeral on behalf of the Society. A wreath was sent from the Directors and Chief Officials of the Society.

(25 November 1943)

It was resolved to close the Head Office so far as the Clerical Staff are concerned (Claims Office excepted) on Saturdays the 8th and the 15th July 1944 in view of the present enemy activity against London.

(6 July 1944)

It was reported that Head Office Clerk Mr D E Sidwell had been discharged from the Royal Air Force owing to ill health [he was suffering from tuberculosis] and that he was now an inmate of a Sanatorium. This was noted with regret and it was Resolved to continue payment of half salary for a period of six months subsequent to the date of his discharge from the R.A.F.

(17 August 1944)

The Secretary reported that Flying Officer Mr Barter, a clerk at Head Office, who had been missing for some months, was now presumed to have been killed in action which was noted with regret.

(19 December 1944)

The case of Head Office Clerk Miss Darkens (Claims Department) who sustained serious injuries in October 1944 as the result of Enemy Action was submitted and it was resolved to continue payment of salary (less Government Compensation) for the present. The matter to be reviewed 3 months hence.

(1 February 1945)

It was reported that Mr M Reid (Clerk Agency Department) had died while a Prisoner of War in Japanese hands and noted with regret.

(13 December 1945)

Mabel Darkens had stayed working late one evening at Royal London House in October 1944 and the train taking her home was bombed. She was badly injured and was never able to return to work. She did not have the length of service to entitle her to a disability pension from the pension fund but the Board resolved that, in all the circumstances, the Society itself would pay her a 'compassionate allowance'.[23]

The extent of civilian casualties was for Britain one of the most immediate differences between the two wars. The first bomb fell on London in 1915, dropped from an airship. It killed six people and by the end of World War I the death toll had risen to 600. In World War II nearly 30,000 were killed in London and 50,000 seriously injured. A third of London's housing stock, 1.4 million homes, was damaged or destroyed. By the end of the war the Society paid claims of £1.12 million (today: nearly £40 million) under 55,306 policies where the death was war related, of which more than 35 per cent involved the deaths of civilians.[24] The Society's experience was similar to other offices whose strength was such that they were able to cope without serious damage to their financial position. As in World War I, the offices played their part in funding the war effort. By 1945 the Society had invested £23 million in War Loans – its total holding in Government securities exceeded £34 million (today: more than £1 billion), half of its total assets.[25]

Ninety-three members of staff were killed during the war and their names are recorded on a memorial that was placed and has remained beside the memorial for those lost in World War I – 33 were serving in the Army, 30 in the Royal Air Force, 9 in the Royal Navy, 4 in the Civil Defence and National Service and 17 were civilians. How cruelly short a period it was between the two wars is illustrated by the fact that the dedication of the memorial on 11 May 1954 was by the Right Reverend Bertram Simpson, former clerk in the agency department and Army chaplain, now Bishop of Southwark, who had given the address when the World War I memorial was unveiled some 30 years earlier.

When the war was over, the re-absorption of returning staff and the release of temporary staff was a major concern for the offices. This was more than a logistical exercise as it raised fundamental long-term issues. Advancement by those who had stayed behind was resented by those who had been away fighting for King and Country. Many of the latter, already scarred by their experiences, soon became disillusioned by the post-war Britain of shortages, rationing and bomb sites. Others had changed in a different way – they had left as clerks and returned as officers. The industrial assurance offices had not always seen it as their role to identify those with potential and to give them special training so that they could assume a management role ahead of their contemporaries. The services, however, had been constantly on the look out for officer material. Jobs were scarce, and Royal London and the other offices had clerks who had commanded men on active service now back in the huge departments carrying out the same routine and often repetitive jobs day after day, and in some cases being paid less for doing so than they were earning in the services at the end of the war. There was no career structure – new joiners were assigned to a department and remained there for life, their advancement depending entirely upon the retirement or death of those above them. It was not uncommon for men who joined at the same time to work at adjoining desks for the next 30 years. The way in which the work was organised was such that there was rarely a need to leave your own department. Pay was hardly generous. Many stayed only because of their pensions – deferred pensions were not introduced until 1975 so that leaving involved losing all pension entitlement that had built up with the Society. Steve Else commented:

> When at last the War ended and the future could be calculated with greater certainty, improvements were made in salary scales and year by year the Society's assets crept up and up. [An] imposing addition was made to the existing building and arrangements were made for still further additions at a later date. We, the older members of staff, were given more responsible jobs and ultimately became Chiefs of Departments and were generously referred to by the Management as the Junior Executive.

This is Steve's last contribution to the story – he retired as chief clerk of the General Department on 31 December 1948.

In 1941 the Government asked William Beveridge, the Master of University College Oxford, a former civil servant and director of the London School of Economics, to undertake a survey of the existing national schemes of social insurance and allied services, and to make recommendations. His report to Parliament was published in 1942.[26] He suggested that ways had to be found of fighting the five 'Giant Evils' of want, disease, ignorance, squalor and idleness, and proposed that all people of working age should pay a weekly national insurance contribution and, in return, benefits would be paid to those who were sick, unemployed, retired or widowed. The system was intended to provide a minimum standard of living below which no one should be allowed to fall. The Society's directors welcomed the extensions and improvements but deprecated the proposal to set up a vast new bureaucracy. It believed in improvement within the present framework that would have involved the retention of the approved societies.[27]

In 1944 the Education Act raised the school leaving age to 15 and provided free secondary schooling for all after selection at the age of 11, and in 1945 the Family Allowance Act gave mothers 5s a week for every second and subsequent child. But it was only after the general election in July 1945, when Labour led by Clement Attlee defeated the Conservatives, that Beveridge's proposals were implemented and the basis of the modern welfare state put in place. The National Insurance Act 1946 provided for old age pensions and sickness, unemployment and death benefits and the National Health Act 1948 created a free medical service for all. Both Acts envisaged that the compulsory contributions alone would be insufficient to provide the benefits and that a significant subsidy from general taxation would be required. In 1948 the Poor Law was abolished.

An article in the *Modern Law Review* in April 1947 suggested that the "boldest feature of the new scheme is the death grant, because this challenges the orgy of industrial assurance in which the British people have hitherto indulged in order to enable them to meet the cost of a funeral and thus avoid the hated pauper's burial".[28] The death grant varied according to the age, ranging from £20 for an adult to £4 for a child under three years of age. The deceased had to either have paid his or her national insurance contributions or have been at the time of death the husband, wife, widower, widow or child of the family of a person who did so. Before the grant was paid, the potential recipient had to show that that he or she had incurred or intended to incur the funeral expenses.

The industrial assurance offices came to the view that the surge of public opinion in support of the Beveridge proposals was unstoppable and that mounting a campaign to exclude death grants would be pointless. This was intended to be a comprehensive and unified scheme, was fundamental to the beliefs of the Government of the day and had the support of a population that had suffered in the 1920s and 1930s and fought two world wars within the previous 30 years. The war had been won and implementing Beveridge was seen as part of winning the peace. Wiseman, who was now chairman as well as joint managing director, gave his grudging support when the proposals were being discussed in Parliament – he agreed at the annual general meeting in April 1946 that if "the cost of the scheme is within the financial capacity of the country, and it is administered on sound lines, it will ultimately have a stabilising effect".[29] But he felt obliged to place on record the views of the offices. It was a matter of regret that "the Government have seen fit to include a death grant amongst the benefits of the scheme, as the expenses it is intended to cover by such a grant are already adequately and practically universally provided for, for the present population, by means of existing insurance policies." The decision to abolish the approved societies that had "contributed a great deal to the success of the national insurance system since its introduction 35 years ago" was also "much to be regretted".[30]

The offices were promoting the view that the benefits under the National Insurance Act were a minimum only and that there remained a need for private voluntary insurance to supplement these benefits. In broad terms this was undoubtedly correct, but it soon became clear that widespread selling of funeral policies by the offices to augment the death grant would not be permitted. In July 1949 the Industrial Assurance and Friendly Societies Act 1948 came into force. It brought to an end all the existing statutory powers that offices had to effect life-of-another funeral policies,[31] and all the uncertainties and abuses that went with them, and replaced them with one simple and restrictive provision. Proposers could now insure only their parents or grandparents for a sum not exceeding £20. This was an aggregate maximum – offices could not issue further assurance on any parent or grandparent who was already insured for £20 under existing policies with any office. In 1958 the maximum of £20 was increased to £30.

If Benjamin Cohen had survived (he died in 1942) he would probably have been satisfied that the main finding of his committee had been implemented by the introduction of the death grant in 1946 and the severe limitation subsequently imposed on funeral expense policies. In 1937, Wilson and Levy had seen a simple solution to the problems of industrial assurance – a sum sufficient to pay for a basic funeral should be paid by the state as an integral part of national health insurance. They felt, however, that there would be formidable difficulties to achieve this. Within a decade, the death grant had been put in place with virtually no opposition.[32]

The offices were philosophical, Wiseman suggesting that although policies to provide for funeral expenses had formed the original basis of industrial assurance, the character of the business had so changed that this particular type of policy was now of minor importance.[33] He was probably overstating the position but an advantage to which Wiseman could hardly refer was that this brought to an end business that had attracted so much criticism especially over the previous 25 years.[34] Nor was it quite correct that funeral policies were at an end. Life-of-another/funeral expense policies were severely restricted but there was nothing to stop Royal London customers from taking out policies on their own lives, the proceeds of which would be used to augment the death grant. Many millions of industrial assurance policies were still to be issued for sums of a size more consistent with funeral expenses than making any real provision for the future of those left behind.

This attitude of the industrial assurance offices to funeral policies may have been influenced by the fact that they had a far bigger worry – the threat of nationalisation. Beveridge had been highly critical of industrial assurance in his report and suggested that it should be converted into a public service, supervised by a board that would have the monopoly of life assurance up to £300, and it was one of the industries that the post-war Labour Government was keen to nationalise. Both Beveridge and the Labour Government had clearly been influenced by the findings of the Cohen Committee. No action had been taken until consideration within the Labour Party turned to the programme with which it would go to the country at the general election in 1950. On 12 April 1949 the Labour's Executive published *Labour Believes in Britain*, which contained a bold statement about its plans for industrial assurance:

Only one major recommendation of the Beveridge Report has not yet been carried out: the proposal to convert industrial insurance into a public service. A minimum standard of life in illness and old age is now ensured for all by National Insurance, and a grant is to be provided for burial expenses. But this minimum can and should be added to by voluntary thrift. One of the best ways for the individual to save is through insurance. The nation's social security plan will be completed when industrial assurance itself becomes a great social service... Splitting off industrial assurance from the remaining business of the companies would lead to confusion and inefficiency, Labour therefore proposes that all the industrial assurance companies, the biggest being Prudential and the Pearl, and the larger collecting societies, should be taken over as they stand.

Wiseman was chairman of the Industrial Life Offices Association (ILOA), which had already submitted a memorandum to Labour's Executive Council arguing against state ownership of industrial assurance. At a press conference at the Savoy Hotel on 31 May, he stressed that the offices had no desire to be drawn into the political field but would resist an attempt from any quarter to nationalise the industry. History tells us that Labour narrowly won the 1950 election and that a majority of only five limited its ability to introduce controversial legislation. The Party was defeated in 1951 and did not return to power until 1964. Accordingly the proposed state involvement in industrial assurance was never taken forward. In fact enthusiasm within Labour was far from unanimous especially as it became clear that the majority of policyholders and collectors were opposed and so the proposal could lose rather than gain votes. The ILOA was active in seeking to influence public opinion and its efforts may have assisted some policyholders to come to that view. By the time of the 1950 general election, 'nationalisation' had been dropped in favour of 'mutualisation', although this would still have allowed considerable state intervention. Hindsight is a wonderful thing and it is easy to regard nationalisation of part of the insurance industry as too far-fetched to be of any real concern, but for a while it did pose a serious threat that would have remained if the electorate had come to a different view in 1951.

The extent of industrial assurance was such that it was inevitable that the offices would receive claims arising out of post-World War II hostilities around the world and catastrophes at home. More than 60 lives assured with the Society were lost in Korea, Cyprus, Malaya and Egypt. The claims were paid in full despite provisions in the policies that limited the amount payable where death occurred on active service. Eighty miners died at the Creswell colliery in September 1950 and 14 of them were assured with Royal

London. Thirteen of the 300 who died in the east coast floods in January 1953 had Royal London policies as did eight of the crews of the *Roderigo* and the *Lorella*, two Hull trawlers that sank in appalling conditions off Iceland in January 1955, and four of the victims of the terrible rail crash in dense fog at Lewisham in December 1957. To provide some small comfort to the bereaved, the practice developed of paying out on the basis of press reports of the deaths and not waiting until death certificates were available.

On 25 January 1951 a luncheon was held at the Connaught Rooms to pay tribute to Wiseman, who had just completed 56 years' service. Three hundred staff and pensioners attended and he was presented with two portraits of himself by Maurice Codner.[35] Wiseman duly returned the larger one to the Society to join those of Smith and Skeggs on the walls of the boardroom. The artists' Royal connections were maintained – Codner painted what proved to be the last portrait of George VI. "His portraits [were] pre-eminently what are called good likenesses, a superficial representation of features being more in demand than a penetrating analysis of character." Perhaps for this reason, he "was extremely successful and his work was especially in demand for the boardroom of businessmen or company directors".[36] Clearly greater perception was not felt necessary for such subjects. In proposing Wiseman's health, one of the chief clerks at head office referred to his "high integrity, strict discipline of himself and his subordinates, pertinacity and a broad outlook on affairs".

Wiseman was active outside the Society. He had for many years been a trustee of the National Amalgamated Approved Society, was appointed to the executive of the ILOA in 1937, serving as chairman in 1947 and 1949, and was a member of the Industrial Assurance Council. He was a director of a building society and an investment trust, a member of the management committee (and chairman of the finance committee) of the Forest Group Hospital, chairman of the Essex Executive Council under the National Health Scheme and a member of the committee of the Executive Council's Association of England. On 12 September 1951, while spending a few days on holiday at Windermere on his way to the annual conference of the Chartered Insurance Institute in Edinburgh, Wiseman suffered a fatal heart attack. He was 69. Talking about him some years after his death, James Wall, who had joined the Society as an agent in 1908 and served with him on the Board, suggested that there was not a man who in his day was more highly esteemed or more sought-after for his advice than Wiseman, and that no other man had Royal London so much at heart or sacrificed himself so much for the Society. Some notes on Wiseman were found in the archives, setting out details of his career and external appointments, probably put together immediately after his death for the purpose of tributes and obituaries. The unknown author had written at the bottom in his or her own hand: "Great leader. Unrelenting energy and determination. Inspired respect and loyalty." His son, Leonard, was secretary of the Society from 1950 until 1976.

When this phase of the Society's history began in 1937, Wiseman and John Skinner had just been appointed joint managing directors. Skinner, two of whose sons were killed on the Normandy beaches the day following D-Day, died of a heart attack in December 1944. The decade that followed saw many changes at the top, prompted in part by what seems to have been a tendency to regard the role of joint managing director as a reward for services rendered possibly due, in part, to the identity of those making the appointments. In the modern era it is the non-executive directors who appoint the chief executive. They generally have no personal interest in the job and are keen to get the best person, regardless of age. But Royal London was not to have a non-executive director until 1980, and it would be a while after that before they were present in numbers. Human nature being what it is, executives appointing a chief from amongst themselves are likely to be aware of the implications for them before casting their vote. It is a noble director who supports a contemporary or junior colleague, thereby effectively eliminating the chance of ever holding office himself.

Ernest Thomlinson, who had been appointed to the Board in 1921 after the mass resignations that followed the Auxiliary Company litigation, succeeded Skinner as joint managing director. He retired in 1948 after 54 years' service and was replaced by Christopher Shuttleworth. When Wiseman died in 1951 Shuttleworth was additionally appointed chairman and Robert Lundie, who had nearly 50 years' service, became the other joint managing director. Lundie retired, aged 70, in April 1955 and was replaced by Ernest Haynes, the actuary. Then Shuttleworth died of a heart attack on his way to Finsbury Square on 13 February 1956. He was well-liked and respected both within the Society and outside – he had just been appointed chairman of the ILOA – and his sudden death came as a great shock.[37] He had joined the Society as an agent in 1911 and in his tribute Haynes spoke of his "high conception of duty and a quality of human kindliness which endeared him to all".[38]

On Shuttleworth's death, Haynes became chairman as well as joint managing director and Stanley Goodall was appointed joint managing director. Haynes was 51 and Goodall 46; a period of stability at the top of the Society was about to begin. Haynes was born in Brixton in 1904 and brought up in Camberwell, the son of a Post Office sorter, and educated with his elder brother Tom[39] at Alleyn's School, Dulwich, thanks to scholarships from the London County Council.[40] Both he and Bertram Simpson were Alleyn Old Boys. He joined, left and later rejoined the Atlas Assurance Company (which was to merge with Guardian Assurance in 1957 and is now part of Aegon) and began studying for his actuarial examinations. Between his two spells at Atlas, Haynes worked for various companies in the City and was unemployed for a few months during the 1930 depression. Qualifying in 1936, he joined Royal London in March 1937 as head of the actuarial department and became assistant actuary in 1939, deputy actuary in 1946 and actuary in July 1947. He was appointed a director in December 1952 and for a while was in charge of the Society's M Division with its divisional office at Bristol, in addition to his actuarial role.

Stanley Goodall followed his father Harry onto the Society's Board. Six months after Stanley's birth, his father had left the Pearl in 1909 and moved from Tyneside to Normanton in Yorkshire to join Royal London as an agent. It proved a good move – Harry's career flourished, culminating in February 1939 when he was appointed a director and divisional manager of G Division. When Stanley left school in Staveley, near Chesterfield, in 1924 he was keen to go to sea with the White Star Line but they had no job for him and so instead he joined Royal London as a clerk. He was paid 12s 6d a week. For an extra 2s in winter he left home at 6 am six days a week and walked two miles to light the boiler in the landlord's chemist shop. After four years, he bought his first collecting book and became an agent in Derby. By 1934 he was an assistant superintendent in Birmingham. He spent three years as a branch inspector and had just been appointed superintendent at Walsall when war was declared. He joined up, spent 18 months in the ranks before being commissioned and by the end of the war was a lieutenant-colonel attached to the General Headquarters, India. Early in 1951 Harry indicated his wish to retire – his resignation took effect on 28 February – and on 12 March, Stanley (now back as superintendent at Walsall) was appointed a director with responsibility for H Division based in Sheffield. Apart from these eleven days, a Goodall was on the Board of Royal London from 1939 to 1980.[41]

Doris Franklin was born in 1911 and left school at 16 to join Royal London. She made a huge contribution to the actuarial department during the war years and in 1955 was appointed assistant actuary, at a time when there were very few women in senior positions in business. Then in October 1957 she announced that she had been married for some months and was pregnant. Her daughter Eve was born in April 1958. Doris returned as Mrs Guest on a part-time basis and was a valued member of the actuarial team until her retirement in 1976. In February 1970 the *Financial Times* suggested that the Commercial Union had made history by appointing Teresa Fortescue as an executive assistant: "The Company believes there is no other woman in a major insurance company holding a post of equal responsibility to Miss Fortescue." Peter Taylor, then Royal London's joint actuary, took great pleasure in alerting the editor to Doris Franklin's appointment 15 years earlier.

World War I and the depression that followed had made little or no impact on the expansion of industrial assurance. Confirmation that this trend had continued was provided by the first report produced by the Industrial

Assurance Commissioner after World War II. The paper shortage meant that there had been no report since 1938 (and the report for that year had been a brief, two-page document) so much updating was required in the introduction to the report for 1952:

> *During the years 1937–1952, the number of industrial assurances in force (including free policies) has increased from 96,225,000 to 121,937,000, the premium income from £66,390,000 to £137,605,000 and the industrial assurance funds from £385,056,000 to £918,992,000. The amount paid in respect of claims on death during the same period has increased from £21,550,000 to £32,836,000 and, in respect of claims on maturity, from £6,579,000 to £34,502,000. The latest valuation returns available show that the aggregate of the sums assured by industrial assurances in force (including free policies) was £2,804,333,000. The corresponding figure in 1937 was £1,495,099,000.*[42]

Royal London had made good progress both during and after the period referred to by the Commissioner. The premium income, that had been £6.6 million in 1936, was £16.3 million in 1960 and the reserves had increased from £38 million to nearly £162 million.[43] There had been a significant reduction in the number of industrial branch policies being issued each year from nearly 950,000 due in part to the outlawing of most funeral policies and to the more prosperous policyholders converting to ordinary branch. By 1960 it was clear that, in terms of the sum assured, sales of ordinary branch policies would soon exceed industrial branch. That said, more than 320,000 industrial branch policies were still being issued in 1960 with an average annual premium of less than £4 10s. The quinquennial valuation as at 31 December 1960 showed healthy surpluses of £17.4 million in industrial branch and £6.6 million in ordinary branch (today: £300 million and £114 million) and this financial strength enabled competitive bonuses to be declared – where a claim was made in 1961 under an industrial branch policy taken out in 1950, for example, the effect of the bonuses was that 115.75 per cent of the sum assured would be paid. For a policy issued in 1940, the pay-out was 125.25 per cent of the sum assured.

Some interesting new policies were being introduced. The 'Rising Generation Policy' was designed to enable a father (the documentation did not envisage mothers with incomes) to safeguard his child's future. This was an endowment policy that additionally provided, on the death of the father, for an income for the child up to the age of 21 or 24 as well as a capital sum payable then, and included "an option to take at the maturity date a policy on the life of the child named in the contract, at a guaranteed rate of premium irrespective of the health, occupation or residence of the child". 'The Comprehensive Family Income Policy' was an endowment policy with additions. It provided an immediate cash payment on the death of the policyholder, an income from death to the end of the term and a capital sum payable then. The 'Carefree' policy provided a pension and life cover in the meantime – for a premium of £10 18s 4d a quarter, a 29-year-old man would be entitled to a pension of £10 a month at age 60 and be insured for £1,540 until then.

There had been improvements in both the expense ratio and persistency.[44] Royal London's 1936 expense ratio of 44.1 per cent had by the 1950s been reduced to the mid-thirties, placing the Society towards the bottom of a much narrower band of the leading industrial assurance offices. For example, in 1960 when Royal London's expense ratio was 36 per cent, there was less than 12 per cent between top (27 per cent) and bottom (38.4 per cent). Reliable comparative data on lapsing became available from 1953 when the Industrial Assurance Commissioner included in his reports the lapse ratio for each office.[45] In 1913 the Society's lapse ratio[46] had been 57.7 per cent and there had been a great improvement over forty years although, with a lapse ratio of 25.9 per cent in 1953, the Society had not been as successful as some of its competitors in reducing the number of policies that went off the books because payment of the premiums soon stopped. By 1953 the Prudential, Co-operative, Pearl and Liverpool Victoria all had lapse ratios below 15 per cent. Royal London was able to maintain, but not better, a lapse ratio in the mid-20s throughout the 1950s during which other offices achieved some further improvements with the Prudential cutting its ratio by 1960 to less than 10 per cent. Nevertheless, even with a lapse rate of 25.9 per cent, the number of Royal London policies forfeited after only a few premiums had been paid was now at a very much more respectable level.

Ever since the Committee of Management of the Royal London Friendly Society identified Finsbury Square as the site for its head office, it had been the directors' objective to create a building that occupied all the northern side of the Finsbury Square. But for the war, this would have been achieved much earlier and it was not until January 1958 that the Lord Mayor opened the final section. The Society had no operational requirement for more space – it had always been intended that the 93,500 square feet of offices space would be let. Later in 1958 the Society acquired the freehold of the entire Royal London House from the Church Commissioners.

As the 1950s closed there was a growing awareness that the Society's centenary was approaching and that this momentous landmark should not be allowed to pass unmarked. Ernest Haynes, while well aware that there were issues within Royal London that would have to be addressed, was convinced of two things – the significance of the industrial assurance offices and their potential for expansion. He spoke at the 1957 annual general meeting of the "large funds for investment arising from regular collection of small amounts at millions of homes" assuming an increasingly important place as providers of capital that was essential for the development of the economy, and "without which the country would inevitably fall into a state of stagnation and decay". He regarded the fact that the total amount spent on life assurance in the country was less than a quarter of the sum spent on drink and tobacco – and less than half the corresponding figure in Canada or the USA – as presenting a challenge and pointing "clearly to the fact that opportunities for expansion are virtually unlimited". That this would be to the advantage of the individual as well as the national economy was "beyond doubt to anyone who has spent his working life in the business and has first-hand experience of the social benefits which life assurance confers".[47]

CHAPTER 11

Centenary and the Haynes Reforms

1961–1972

Indeed let us be frank about it: most of our people have never had it so good. Go around the country, go to the industrial towns, go to the farms and you will see a state of prosperity such as we have never had in my lifetime – nor indeed in the history of this country.

Harold Macmillan, Prime Minister, speech at Bedford (20 July 1957)

The Britain that is going to be forged in the white heat of this revolution will be no place for restrictive practices or for outdated methods on either side of industry. In the Cabinet room and the boardroom alike, those charged with the control of our affairs must be ready to think and to speak in the language of our scientific age.

Harold Wilson, Leader of the Opposition, speech at the Labour Party Conference

(Scarborough, 1 October 1963)

... the high hopes of the mid-sixties curdled into the disillusionment with which Britain entered into the seventies.

Dominic Sandbrook, historian and writer (2006)[1]

Few corporate celebrations can have matched those to mark the Royal London centenary in 1961. The year began with two banquets – the first at the Dorchester on 2 February for distinguished guests and the second at Grosvenor House a week later attended by over 1,300 Royal Londoners representing the head office and every district office. During the year, more than thirty banquets, dinners, dances, lunches and outings were held so that every member of staff could share in the celebrations. Head office staff were entertained to lunch at the Tavistock Banqueting Room in Charing Cross Road, followed by a matinee performance of *The Amorous Prawn* at the Piccadilly Theatre. The event had to be repeated three times to accommodate everybody. The sales divisions' celebrations included white-tie dinner dances at the City Hall, Cardiff and the Old Assembly Rooms, Newcastle, a coach trip to Woburn Abbey for lunch with the Duke of Bedford and then back to London for the Royal Tournament and trips on trains specially decked out with the Royal London centenary motif from Liverpool Street to Southend, and from Manchester and Liverpool to Morecambe for lunch at the Winter Gardens, an afternoon enjoying the local facilities, tea and a visit to the Charlie Chester show *Pot Luck*. During the year places as far afield as Belfast, Birmingham, Brighton, Bristol, Glasgow, Llandudno, Porthcawl, Ross-on-Wye, Scarborough, Sheffield, Skegness, St Andrews, Torquay and Windermere were visited by celebrating Royal Londoners.

A nursery in Hertfordshire was invited to breed a dahlia to commemorate the centenary. Named *The Royal London*, it featured on the 1961 Christmas card. A history of the Society was commissioned and complimentary copies were widely available.[2] A lavishly illustrated souvenir edition of the *Royal Londoner* was produced. "We set out to make this a year of years", wrote Ernest Haynes, the chairman and joint managing director, in the introduction "and, judging by the reports that reach me from all sides, I think we have succeeded".[3] Staff benefited financially, with everyone who had more than one year's service receiving a bonus of between 1 and 8 per cent (depending on length of service) of their 1960 earnings. All celebrations have to be paid for and the 1961 accounts revealed that the cost of the centenary exceeded £250,701 (today: £4.2 million). In presenting the accounts at the 1962 annual general meeting, the chairman explained that the cost of the staff bonuses represented the greater part of the item and said that he was sure that the members would agree that this expense was well justified. As virtually all the members attending the meeting were staff, the lack of any disagreement was not altogether surprising.[4]

The Dorchester banquet, held 100 years to the day after Ridge and Degge met and agreed to form a new friendly society,[5] was a grand white-tie occasion – over 500 attended with Reginald Maudling, the President of the Board of Trade, as guest of honour.[6] The City, the industry, the professions, and local government were all represented at the highest level and the guest list included the grandsons of Henry Ridge and William Hambridge, and the great-grandson of Joseph Degge.[7] Bertram Simpson, the former Bishop of Southwark, said grace. He must have been one of the very few diners who had worked at 6 Paul Street when Royal London was still a friendly society and could remember the death of William Hambridge. During the evening, entertainment was provided by Jacqueline Delman, a soprano whose recordings are available today, Joseph Cooper, a concert pianist who was to become better known as the chairman of the BBC's long-running television panel game *Face the Music* and the Arthur Salisbury Quartet. Preceded by a fanfare from trumpeters from the Royal Horse Guards, a cake in the form of the head office with a hundred candles was cut by Mrs Haynes.

What was being discussed as the guests worked their way through turtle soup, sole, Aylesbury duck and lemon soufflé? Conversations would probably have started on safe ground – perhaps the possible impact on the world of John F Kennedy, who had just been inaugurated as the youngest president of the USA, or whether the recently reconvened constitutional conference on Northern Rhodesia would achieve anything in view of the boycott by the African parties. Londoners may have wondered if Tottenham Hotspur would be able to maintain their form to the end of the season, while others would have bemoaned the quality of British rugby following the success of the South African tourists who were then unbeaten after 29 matches in the British Isles.[8]

Ernest Haynes was proud of the changes made since the early days when the main business of the Society had been funeral expense policies. The emphasis, he said, was now on savings – "on ensuring a good start in life for the children, on provision for old age; in short on planning for a better standard of life".[9] One factor, however, was unchanged. Home service, the rock on which Royal London was founded, was, said Haynes, as essential a feature in 1961 as it had been a century earlier:

> The wage-earner, who represents some eighty per cent of the working population of this country, is accustomed to budgeting on a short-term basis. Even in today's much improved conditions, he finds it difficult to accumulate funds to meet substantial and intermittent payments. Principally for this reason Ordinary life assurance, under which premiums are paid quarterly, half-yearly or yearly is not favoured by many wage-earners. The benefits of life assurance can only be fully brought within the reach of this section of the community by means of a system which is specially designed to meet their own personal financial arrangements.[10]

The typical wage-earner to whom Haynes was referring was earning £10 to £15 a week. He was paid weekly in cash and did not have a bank account.[11] In 1961 there were more than 20 industrial assurance offices and an insurance man (or sometimes, but not very often, an insurance woman) from one or more of them was calling on ten million homes. Royal London had almost nine million industrial branch policies on its books.

Haynes was aware that major changes had to be made if Royal London was to continue to thrive but if he had been expecting a benign economic environment in which to make them he would have been disappointed. In his speech at the centenary banquet, the President of the Board of Trade touched upon a topic that was increasingly being debated – the role of Britain in the world. World War II had set in motion processes that brought to an end the European empires and established the two superpowers. By 1961 many former British colonies already had their independence and others would shortly follow. The Suez Crisis in 1956 had demonstrated a decline in Britain's diplomatic power and prestige. Few were convinced that Britain's future lay in a closer involvement in Europe, a view shared by many Europeans. Maudling commented on the changes in the previous hundred years including "the change in enormous powers such as the United States and Russia, so much stronger than we are in military force, and the shifting emphasis of the importance of Britain from that of a military power to a moral and economic power".[12] The pace had been quicker than Maudling suggested with many significant changes taking place during the lifetimes of the guests, some of whom may have been unsure as to exactly what was expected of "a moral and economic power". Looking to the future, Maudling believed that we were a country requiring a new impulse:

> After all, we have made great progress in recent years. We have shaken loose from the war and the aftermath of war. We have freed our economy. We have built up remarkably, and we have in recent years developed steadily our living standards at a rate sufficient to double our standard of living in a quarter of a century. But the question is: are we going fast enough? Although we are progressing should we not perhaps progress even faster? There is no doubt that we have made good progress, but a new effort is needed in which all of us must join, and that new effort must be to promote a more rapid growth in our community.[13]

Unfortunately neither political party proved able to provide that new impulse and difficult times were ahead. In the late 1950s there was full employment and rising incomes and nothing appeared seriously wrong, although there were concerns below the surface. British industry was struggling to produce quality goods at a price that was competitive and too much of the new-found prosperity was being used to buy foreign goods, to the detriment of the balance of payments. The Conservative Government favoured a Stop/Go economic policy – a credit squeeze in 1960 and a pay pause in 1961, soon to be replaced by a wage restraint policy.

In 1963 Maudling, now Chancellor of the Exchequer, introduced a budget that was designed to seek expansion without inflation. The balance of payments deficit that confronted Harold Wilson's Government following the general election in October 1964, however, was so bad that the country was forced to undergo a period of increasing taxation, reduction in public spending, high interest rates, restrictions on credit, hire-purchase and exchange control, and mandatory wage and price restraints. Sterling was chronically unstable and by November 1967 devaluation could be avoided no longer. Inflation had been low at the beginning of the Sixties but was up to nearly five per cent by 1968 and was over 9 per cent in 1971. Industrial action was an ever increasing concern – there was a rail go-slow in 1968 and strikes by seamen (1966), postal workers (1971), miners (1972) and dock workers (1972) and numerous other actions at a local level. Harold Wilson abandoned attempts to restrict the power of trade unions and when, following the general election in June 1970, Ted Heath's Conservative government expressed its intention to do so, one and a half million workers came out on a one-day strike. By the late 1960s, immigration and Northern Ireland had become important issues on the political agenda. Fears began to be expressed that the country was ungovernable.

An attractive booklet for newly appointed Royal London agents had been produced in the late 1950s. It extolled the virtues of "Book Interest":

> *When you were appointed you bought the Nominating Right in your agency; this gives you the privilege of nominating your successor (who must, of course, be approved by the Directors), and is commonly referred to as Book Interest. Whenever an agent disposes of the Nominating Right in the whole or part of the business on his agency he must agree a price with his successor just as your predecessor agreed a price with you. The Society is not connected with this transaction in any way. Every time you sell a policy you will improve the capital value of your Nominating Right. This increase in capital value is tax free and is additional to your remuneration. The privilege of Book Interest which you enjoy is, therefore, of great value to you.*[14]

The booklet made much of the directors' link with front-line insurance work: "Without exception the Directors have risen to their present high office from the ranks of the insurance industry; thus they are fully alive to the problems and difficulties which must inevitably face members of the staff from time to time." In fact Haynes was convinced that change was needed at Royal London in both the structure of the sales force and the composition of the Board.

In 1961 there were some 3,400 agents, based at 320 district offices each managed by a superintendent assisted by a team of assistant district managers, inspectors, travelling assistants and clerks. The country was divided into seven divisions each under the control of a director and divisional manager, often assisted by area superintendents. Sales management in any other industry would take it for granted that they could assign to a salesperson an area in which he or she must exclusively operate knowing that no other agent from the organisation would be doing business there unless authorised to do so. It would be fundamental that management could alter the assignments of sales staff as and when required to meet changing circumstances.

These basic principles did not apply. From the very beginning Royal London (and most of the other collecting societies) had operated on the basis that agents for all practical purposes owned their collecting books. This had always caused some unease. When Joseph Degge gave evidence to the Royal Commission in 1872 he was asked if the collecting books were the property of collectors. He replied: "I could never reconcile myself to that idea, but some offices allow them to assume that privilege: I always contend that the business belongs to the institution itself".[15] The dangers inherent in this system had been forcefully expressed by Harry Henry in *The Insurance Man and his Trade*:

> [Book interest] *is now mainly confined to the societies. It gives the agent what amounts to full proprietary rights over the business which he handles. Suppose, for example, the amount of 'debit' on his 'book' – that is, the amount of premiums he collects each week – is worth £15 a week. The commission he draws in consequence will be about £5 a week, and the society will not permit any other agent to handle this business. The agent is then permitted to sell these rights (his 'book') to anyone he can get to buy them, and for any sum he pleases – the sale price in the example we have taken would be about £450. In consequence, the agent is not so much a wage-earner as a small capitalist; so long as he keeps up his business his capital is secure, for the 'book' can always be sold again. The essence of this system is that the agent is given control, not of a fixed area, but of a certain number of policyholders; in getting new customers for his office he is competing not only with the agents of other societies and companies but also with*

*other agents from the same society. In consequence we get all
the evils of unrestrained and ferocious competition, particularly
where an agent has purchased 'debit' at an excessive price and is
compelled feverishly to build up further business at all costs, for
fear of losing his capital.*[16]

The system had been devised with the best of intentions: it was seen
as a means of motivating agents to build up a large book of sound business
from which the Society as well as the agent would benefit. Critics of industrial
assurance, however, had long since suggested that this approach was wasteful
and a key contributor to the high expense ratios. It was becoming increasingly
clear to those within the industry that the inability to reassign responsibility for
collecting from particular customers from one agent to another, or to assign
specific geographical areas to agents, was standing in the way of creating an
efficient and cost-effective sales force. Often a number of Royal London agents
would be operating in the same street or even the same building. Elsewhere
premiums were not being collected where the agent was ill or had moved on
without being able to sell his book. This may have been because there was
little to sell or because few were attracted to the job. In difficult economic
times, potential successors were sometimes unable to obtain a loan sufficient
to acquire large and profitable books. Where this occurred, it fell to the local
superintendent to put in place some temporary collecting arrangements.
There was no retirement age and, although some elderly agents' collecting
and selling was unimpaired, this was not always the case. Neither was there
an argument that the sum obtained on the disposal of an agency represented
the agent's pension because a pension scheme for agents had been introduced
as long ago as 1923.[17]

A decade earlier, Liverpool Victoria had introduced a scheme by
which the society would buy the books from agents who wished to leave
the employment of the society. Newly recruited agents were not granted
a nominating right and were referred to as 'new terms agents'.[18] A similar
proposal from the committee of management of Royal Liver in 1952 had been
greeted with absolute opposition from the trade union, especially in Ireland
where Royal Liver had significant business and where the books remained a
valuable commodity. Despite continued opposition, a voluntary scheme was
introduced in 1955 and over the next two years, Royal Liver spent more than
£1.2 million on buying out book interest agents.[19]

Haynes could see that continuing with book interest agents would
severely impact upon the viability of the sales force and make it increasingly
difficult to resist external criticism. Direct selling was the Society's only business
– anything that threatened this threatened the survival of Royal London. He
was able to convince his colleagues on the Board, and the executive council

of the Royal London Staff Association accepted that change was inevitable. There was agreement too, that the right approach would be for the Society to purchase the collecting book for a fair price when an agent left the Society's service, with all future agents being recruited on the basis that they would receive a salary and commission but would have no right to nominate a successor. What had to be agreed was the basis on which that fair price would be determined.

Discussions between the Board and the association began in 1962. Presidents of the association, who held office for only a year, came and went as the negotiations dragged on and it was the association's general secretary, Basil Sanders, who provided the continuity. After the war Sanders could have gone on and become a superintendent but he found that he could earn more as an agent. Later he decided to seek office in the association. He had been a member since he joined the Society:

> In 1952 he was elected as the Association's Treasurer, and in the following year as General Secretary. There were only about 2,000 members, and at that stage it was only a part-time job. But in 1966 it was made full-time, and he spent the rest of his working life as a trade union official. In the meantime, in 1959, the Association had become the Royal London section of the National Union of Insurance Workers, but he had retained the title of General Secretary.[20] He was happy in the job, just as he had been happy as an insurance agent. As the only full-time official of the Section he acquired an expertise and held a status that no other member could match. He enjoyed the challenge of negotiating, he enjoyed travelling round the country and attending meetings, and above all he enjoyed the annual conference, which was usually held at a seaside town like Eastbourne or Blackpool. He also attended the TUC's annual conference.[21]

After numerous negotiating sessions on extinguishing book interest, Haynes wrote to every agent in July 1964 setting out detailed proposals. At an extraordinary general meeting on 1 December 1964 the Society's memorandum and articles of association were altered to accommodate the changes and on 29 December 1964 there was a signing ceremony in the boardroom at which Haynes, Goodall, Sanders and the president signed an exchange of letters to which was annexed the agreed scheme under which nominating rights would be purchased from agents who were leaving the Society's service. The scheme provided a set of rules that enabled a value to be placed on every industrial branch policy in an agent's collecting book and on all in-force ordinary branch policies that the agent had sold. So, for example, a payment equal to two years' commission was due in the case of an ordinary branch policy. A simple approach could not, however, be applied across the portfolio and many complications were introduced with the aim of achieving a fair balance between agent and Society. So the payment in the previous example reduced to one and a half years' commission where the policyholder would be between 61 and 65 on his or her next birthday and to one year's commission when over 65. In industrial branch, all books had to be audited, certain policies where the policyholder was in arrears were disregarded, and a 5 per cent deduction was made from the total value. Where an exceptionally large amount of new business had been entered into during the final six months, the scheme gave the Society the right to satisfy itself as to its quality.

Recruitment of salaried (or 'new terms') agents and consolidation of agents' areas began at once. As might be expected there were some teething problems. In what one senses was a masterly understatement, Haynes commented at the 1966 annual general meeting that:

> ... *tradition runs very strongly in British institutions and nowhere was this more the case than the tradition of Book Interest in the Royal London. To change to what is in these days a more practical system of agency organisation has given rise to a number of problems which have disturbed the normal day-to-day working of the staff in some areas.*[22]

Gradually issues were resolved but progress was always going to be slow as long as conversion could take place only when an agent left. In 1971 the scheme was extended to enable the Society to purchase the books of all remaining agents who still had nominating rights and to continue to employ them on salaried terms.

Haynes regarded the extinction of agents' nominating rights in their books as the most fundamental change in Royal London's history. Consolidation enabled policyholders to be grouped in areas that made sense geographically and took into consideration local factors, some as mundane as avoiding the time wasted by an agent who frequently had to cross a busy road to reach policyholders on both sides. Collecting times were reduced, often considerably, leaving more time for prospecting for new business. Consolidation served to trigger other changes. Fewer branch offices were required and by 1972 the 320 had been reduced to 200. Recruitment of agents was a problem that was to confront successive managements, and there were years when those recruited barely exceeded the number promoted or who had left. A report to the Board in 1971 bemoaned the fact that "in spite of the unfortunate percentage of unemployment in the country, it would seem... that the type of man sent from the Ministry of Employment Exchanges is rarely suitable for, and they are seldom interested in, agency work".

The other area on which Haynes focused was the Board itself. At the time of the centenary, the collecting and selling operations of the Society (by now generally referred to as 'the Field') were divided into seven divisions each headed by a divisional manager, who lived within the part of the country covered by his division. The Board comprised these seven divisional managers, Stanley Goodall (joint managing director) and Haynes. Whatever the Board lacked by way of modern governance standards, it was not short of experience of the Society's business. Haynes himself was the newcomer, with a mere 25 years' service. Three of his colleagues had begun their careers with Royal London before World War I and five joined between 1919 and 1925. No new director had been appointed for five years and four of the directors had been on the Board since the 1940s. All the directors apart from Haynes had been recruited as agents or clerks and worked their way up to the boardroom.

Haynes had several objectives. Not only was he looking for new blood but for a wider range of skills and experience around the boardroom table. He also wanted directors to concentrate on complex issues involved in running the Society, and to be free of day-to-day operational responsibility for a division. He was keen for them all to be based at Finsbury Square so as to create a senior management team. Haynes left chairing most Board meetings to other directors except when vital issues came up on the agenda. He took over the chair on 26 April 1961 to lead a discussion that was to change the Board of Royal London forever. Momentous decisions were made that day. It was agreed that in due course all the directors would be located at the head office and would no longer have a direct divisional role. A new type of divisional manager who would not be a director would be created to manage each division and to be responsible for new business. All future directors would be required to agree on appointment that they would retire at 65 unless requested to stay on until 70. It was hoped to create in the course of time a Board comprising managing directors, senior managers responsible for new business and the management of the Field staff, head-office officials who would continue with their executive roles and 'part-time directors' who previously had executive roles. In other words, Royal London was to adopt a more conventional board composition with sales and marketing having their representatives but no longer dominating. It would not be until 1980 that an independent non-executive director was appointed.

Gradually the long-standing directors and divisional managers retired – Samuel Swetnam and Henry Helliwell (who together had nearly a hundred years' service) in 1961, Charles Ashling in 1962, Sydney Webb in 1965 and Hubert Massey in 1966. Webb and Massey had a mere 99 years' service between them. Webb joined Royal London as a clerk at head office in 1911.

After 21 years he fancied a change and became a head-office inspector. He was a superintendent in south London before being appointed a director and divisional manager in 1951. Massey, an accomplished organist and artist, and a local councillor, joined as an agent in Stalybridge in 1921, just after the mass resignations of the Board following the Auxiliary Company litigation, was a superintendent in Manchester and was appointed a director and divisional manager in 1948.

Head-office officials were now being appointed to the Board: Arthur Russell Firth (solicitor), Tony Lamb (actuary), George Cannell (on his retirement as property manager) and Donald Overy (investment manager). When Russell Firth, Haynes and Goodall retired, they all became non-executive directors. Haynes remained chairman and Jim Bailey, the only survivor of the 1961 directors and divisional managers, was appointed chief general manager. He had joined the Society as an agent in Nottingham in 1925 and, after time as an assistant superintendent, ordinary branch inspector, superintendent and area superintendent, was appointed director and divisional manager in 1956. The last Board chaired by Haynes in 1972 illustrates how the 1961 objectives had been achieved. In addition to Haynes himself, there were three other non-executive directors (Goodall, Cannell and Bailey, who was now the non-executive deputy chairman), two senior Field executives (Tom Cowman and Leslie Poll) and three head office executives: Lamb, who had taken over from Bailey as chief general manager, Overy and Billy Skinner, the son of John Skinner, the former joint managing director, who had succeeded Russell Firth as solicitor.

There were changes too within Field operations. A training scheme for agents had been established in 1962 and there was an ever-increasing emphasis on training. Two other decisions would have been significant at the time. In 1962 it was decided that BIC ballpoint pens rather than traditional pens and ink would in future be issued to district offices. This was when the secretary of Royal London still recorded minutes of Board meetings in ledger-type minute books in immaculate longhand, using a fountain pen.[23] In 1969 it was decided to follow the example of the banks and not to open district offices on Saturday mornings. Policyholders often paid premiums at the local office when their agent was unable to call or made claims there over the counter, and reducing the hours when the offices were open cannot have been an easy decision.

The first 'Chairman's All Star Dinner' was held at the Hyde Park Hotel in 1969. Until then, districts were rewarded for outstanding performance by a lunch to which the superintendent, the office staff and all the agents attached to that office were invited. These may have fostered team spirit but rewarded those who had contributed little. At the suggestion of Jim Bailey, they were replaced by inviting those Field staff whose performance in their various roles during the previous year had been outstanding to a grand dinner attended by the chairman and a deputation of directors at which awards were made. The first was to be a stag dinner but Rita Elliff, a widow with three children from Thanet who had only recently joined as a salaried agent, was amongst the qualifiers. She duly attended. The 'All Star' event was to become an important part of Field culture – in time, the dinner expanded into a weekend to which spouses were invited, first at British hotels that had luxurious facilities and a relaxing atmosphere[24] and then at exotic international settings that included Guernsey, Marbella, Sorrento and Villamoura.

Change was needed at head office where work and working conditions had changed very little over the years. Pay was hardly generous and most staff were still being remunerated on the basis of age-related scales that assumed a gradual increase in pay to match a gradual increase in responsibility, so that pay depended more on age than performance or the market rate for the job. This atmosphere could be frustrating to the ambitious whose progress depended upon when those senior to them were due to retire. On the positive side, the staff at head office enjoyed almost absolute job security – nobody was ever made redundant or dismissed on grounds of competency, and the dismissals for what now would be termed gross misconduct were few and far between. The Society was a long-established, highly reputable company and this increased the sense of security and bestowed upon the staff a form of vicarious status. There was a good pension for those who made it to retirement and staff mortgages were available at preferential rates of interest. The work was not too demanding and a prompt exit at five o'clock was possible for most people on most days. Excellent sporting and recreational facilities funded or heavily subsidised by the Society were available. A sports ground at Mill Hill had been acquired in 1952 that had two football pitches (one of which doubled up for hockey), a cricket square, tennis courts, a netball court and a well-appointed pavilion. Apart from a minimal subscription by staff to the Royal London Club, all of this was paid for by the Society – there were no subscriptions or match fees, and the beer was cheap. The football section fielded two teams in the London Insurance Offices Football League. League cricket came to the south of England much later but Royal London had a good fixture list of friendly matches with many clubs keen to enjoy the facilities at Mill Hill. Sport was not the only social activity – as one former member of staff told the author: "the sports ground played its part too as an unofficial marriage bureau".

At Finsbury Square there was a club room on the top floor. It was men only, the ladies having their own room that was out of bounds to male staff. The club room was equipped with two full-size snooker tables and a lounge area complete with newspapers and magazines supplied by the Royal London Club and *Post Magazine* and *The Policy-Holder* provided by the

Society. Chess and bridge were popular and the inter-departmental snooker competition was keenly contested. There was a table tennis table permanently in place in the basement of the building for use at lunchtimes, with evening table tennis and chess matches taking place in the lounge area of the club room, with five table tennis teams and a chess team competing in leagues with other insurance offices. The club room was used for the dramatic society's rehearsals and for meetings of the committee of the Royal London Club. A swimming gala was held every year at the Ironmonger Row Baths where the inter-departmental competition was intense. Bowls was played, initially at Mill Hill and then in the middle of Finsbury Square. The two flower shows organised by the Royal London Horticultural Society were very popular. The autumn show was the larger of the two and, as in 1962 there was "ample scope for flowers, fruit and vegetables, plus arrangements and cookery", the club's magazine felt that it was safe to "assume we shall have the usual crush".[25] Mrs Haynes presented the prizes to the successful exhibitors – her husband was on parade at the Handicraft Exhibition the following May when the judges "thought the knitting was not up to our usual standard".[26] The productions of the Royal London Dramatic and Operatic Society, under its chairman Norman Hambridge, a grandson of William, were eagerly awaited, although a reviewer of the *The Touch of Fear* in the Cripplegate Theatre in May 1961 was disappointed that, despite the title, "there was only one moment of high emotional tension induced by attempted physical violence in the whole of the play".[27]

Sport and recreation were left largely untouched but during the 1960s, with the assistance of external consultants, jobs were evaluated and appraisals undertaken. By 1971 a new structure was in place and age-related wage scales had virtually been abandoned. Traditionally Royal London had primarily recruited 16-year-old school leavers ('we grow our own timber' as it was put) and recruitment policies were made more flexible to cope with the increasing numbers who were staying on at school for A-levels with perhaps university to follow. The way in which the head office operated and the various departments interrelated with each other (or in some cases did not do so) was reviewed and a number of efficiencies introduced.

Attention was also given to the working environment after years of neglect. The lower ground and basement areas of Royal London House were a warren where a huge amount of historical documentation, proposal forms, policy registers, old magazines and the like were stored. New recruits tended not to be sent down there unaccompanied in case they went missing. Part of this area was reclaimed in 1963 and 'the theatre' was created. This was where the drama society produced plays but the principal use of the theatre was to hold the annual general meeting and other large meetings. The exterior of Royal London House was badly in need of a facelift. The

Portland stone had almost disappeared under the coating of soot and grime that covered so much of London until the smokeless zones of the Clean Air Acts of 1956 and 1968 reduced pollution and provided an incentive to clean the exterior of buildings and landmarks. In January 1968 the scaffolding came down and the front of the head office had been restored to its former glory. The interior was more problematic. The unnamed author of an article in the *Royal Londoner* of May 1969 could not resist reminding readers of how branch offices (the openings of which featured regularly in the magazine) presented a smart, modern image to the insuring public and provided pleasant working conditions for the staff. In head office, however, the siting of departments had become a critical problem:

> Over the years, some departments had grown out of all recognition, others had dwindled or even ceased to exist. Where a department had become too large and unwieldy, and space was available (often in an entirely different part of the building) it had been necessary to hive off the overflow. This meant that over a period of time some departments had been divided and sub-divided into rooms on several floors. In addition nearly forty years of wear and tear on the machinery and equipment used in everyday work was reflected in rising repair bills and in unavoidable delays in the efficient running of our business.[28]

A major refurbishment was started that took over two years to complete. Departments were relocated to improve efficiency, the building was decorated throughout, new desks, furniture and equipment were purchased and over a thousand feet of cupboards installed. Six thousand square yards of carpeting replaced the wooden floors, making working conditions quieter, cleaner and much more pleasant and avoiding the risk of splinters when recovering an item that had been dropped onto the floor. The carpets delivered an unanticipated benefit as filing clerks did not mind using bottom drawers now they could kneel in comfort. Management philosophy at the time, and this was not confined to Royal London, was that if a job had to be done on a regular basis it was better done by an employee than an outsider. Outsourcing was not yet seen as an option. Virtually all the refurbishment work was carried out by employed carpenters, electricians, engineers and painters. Three-quarters of the printing required by Royal London was undertaken in-house at Finsbury Square where a chief printer presided over a team of nearly 30 who used between three and four tons of paper a week.

What today would be called 'data management' had always been a challenge for life offices. The difficulty was the number of purposes for which the information relating to each policy was needed. A multiplicity of records was required to enable the offices to:

- collect premiums, and where necessary take action for non-payment
- account for the premiums received
- pay commission, often where different terms of remuneration (including claw-back where the policy soon lapsed) were in place
- deal with any special arrangement (such as an additional benefit) included in the policy
- calculate and credit bonuses
- pay claims – the right amount to the right person
- value policies
- provide statistical information to management and a regulator
- ensure that information required locally was available at the district offices
- provide underwriting information to assist in the calculation of future premiums.

A dozen different filing systems were required to meet all these objectives.[29] Cards were replacing ledgers and other volumes as the preferred storage medium. There were two types – written or typed cards and punched cards. The latter were made of stiff cardboard, and information was represented by the presence or absence of holes in predefined positions. In the first generation of computing from the 1920s to the 1950s, they were the primary medium for data storage and processing. Data was entered by a key punch that was similar to a large and noisy typewriter. Accuracy was essential and each card had to be verified. Errors could not be corrected and, if a hole was punched in the wrong place, the card had to be discarded and the operator had to start all over again. Electromechanical equipment enabled the cards to be read.

A paper discussed by an actuarial society in 1962 pointed out that every new policy involved "writing, typing, calculating, checking, punching, sorting, tabulating, transporting [moving documents from place to place] and filing; most of these operations taking place several times for each new policy... The correction of errors is also an important 'time waster' and involves more costly labour".[30] Just one process gives a flavour of life before computers:

> Accounting for premiums has, for many years, been done by means of a punched card system. Two files of master punched cards are maintained for premium accounting. These are the 'account cards' in due date order, and the 'cash' cards in policy number order... Cards from the 'account' file are processed in

batches shortly before the due date. The batch is used to list cases due for payment and is then filed 'awaiting payment'. As premiums are paid, the corresponding cards are pulled from the 'cash' file and matched to cancel cases 'awaiting payment'. If the cash paid is the same as the amount due, the 'account' card is filed in a 'paid' section. It is subsequently reproduced with the next due date and filed ready to deal with the next premium when it becomes due. If the cash paid is different from the amount due, a temporary card is punched and processed with the 'account card' to obtain the arrears due.[31]

The paper was dealing with ordinary branch policies and the records were different for the traditional industrial assurance policies. Some of the key documents of record were not even at head office – premium receipt books were with policyholders and the collecting books with agents. The agent recorded every premium payment in the former and the latter listed all his or her clients and details of their policies. Periodically the district office officials accompanied agents on their rounds to check the premium receipt books against the collecting books and sometimes premium receipt books were borrowed from policyholders for audit purposes. A receipt had to be issued and the book returned within 21 days.[32] Audit teams from head office spent most of their time on the road visiting district offices.

The original proposal form for every industrial branch policy was (or should have been) filed at the head office – as the number of policies ran into the millions, this was a massive operation in terms of both storage space and labour. The only record of industrial branch policies maintained at head office was the barest minimum required for valuation purposes – policy number, type of policy, date commenced, age at entry and sex of policyholder, premium, sum assured and status: active, fully paid up, or partly paid up. It was not deemed cost-effective to store this data on a punched-card system and so the information was contained in policy registers – first ledgers and then hand-written cards.

Their skill at mental arithmetic, perhaps augmented by a scrap of paper, was all that staff could rely upon for simple calculations. The more complex ones tended to be undertaken by the actuaries who were skilled in the use of logarithms and slide-rules. Then came mechanical calculators complete with handles to crank, carriages to shift, cogs that whirred noisily and bells that rang when a certain point had been reached. Later electrically powered mechanical versions were introduced. Towards the end of the day, as their attention began to drift, it was apparently not unknown for actuarial students at some companies to amuse themselves by setting several machines off to divide a number by zero. Once started, the cogwheels would clatter away forever, and could only be stopped by pulling out the plug. The noise was deafening. Typewriters too were present in numbers – everything had to be typed manually, often in triplicate with carbon copies. Once again, errors could not easily be remedied and often a whole document had to be re-typed. Sometimes handwriting was more trustworthy. The notice that had to be served before an industrial branch policy could be forfeited for non-payment of the premiums was a printed form on which the name of the policyholder, and the details of the policy and arrears, was inserted in long-hand.

Royal London installed its first computer in 1962, one of the first assurance companies to do so, but Ernest Haynes was insistent that the Society proceeded with care. "In the early years," he explained, "we were learning how to use the machine economically and we deliberately restricted our rate of development until we felt that we appreciated the scope and the limitations of a computer system".[33] Sound progress was made and by 1964 the computer was being used extensively in the preparation of ordinary branch renewal notices and receipts. A new computer with greater capacity was installed late in 1967.

Those responsible for the computerisation of Royal London gradually began to realise the extent to which the computer could be put to use within an assurance company and were soon thinking of an even bigger and better machine. This raised some difficult issues. The next generation of computers were large and it was difficult to see how one could be accommodated within Royal London House, especially as a controlled air-conditioned environment was demanded with constant temperature and humidity, stable electric power and anti-static and dust-proof floor-coverings. Modern office accommodation was needed in which to install a computer suite, but this would be expensive in the area around Finsbury Square. Another requirement was for the computer to be running as long as possible. This pointed to shift-working that was not easy for those commuting into central London by public transport. Gradually the solution emerged – relocate the computer to a modern office within reasonable reach of London, but far enough away to benefit from lower rents, and where there was a local labour market to meet Royal London's demands. A number of areas were investigated and in due course Colchester was selected. Little did they know but the team of early computer experts who moved to Colchester in 1972 were to be the advance party for an altogether larger relocation.[34]

This was also the time when the copying of documents in the office was revolutionised. The originator of a typed document who knew that copies would be required had long-since had three options: carbon paper; a duplicator that involved the cutting of a stencil and wrapping it round a drum, that was turned manually by electricity; or printing – either at external printers or by means of a small printing press in the office. But that was no help for the recipient of a document who needed a copy. Photostat machines had been around since before World War I. They contained a camera that photographed the document, initially producing a negative image, that itself was then photographed to produce the positive copy document. The process took five minutes per copy, was expensive and not particularly reliable. The traditional method of a clerk with a pen and later a typist producing a 'new' copy continued to be much in evidence. The first copiers produced copies on chemically treated, photosensitive paper but copy-quality was mixed, the paper was expensive and durability of the copies was a concern. But then came the xerography process invented by a US patent attorney. The first Xerox plain-paper copiers, introduced in the US in 1960, soon found their way over the Atlantic, and copying, and indeed the entire office landscape, was changed for ever.

A topic being advanced by the Government and others was decimalisation, although the prospect of converting 12 pennies to a shilling and 20 shillings to a pound to a system of decimal currency worried many people. The concern within the life assurance industry was that converting the vast number of low-premium industrial branch policies to any new currency would be a massive job of itself but it would be vastly more complicated if, as was always likely, there was no exact equivalent to the old penny. Two proposals were being floated in the early 1960s – create a new decimal pound worth half an old pound, so that a decimal penny would be worth only slightly more than an old penny, or leave the pound as it was so that a decimal penny would equal 2.4 old pennies. In 1963 the Government's committee of enquiry recommended the latter, but only by a split decision of four to two. It took until 1966 for the Government to accept that recommendation, with legislation being passed in 1967.

A committee was formed to prepare Royal London for Decimalisation Day – 15 February 1971. The Society had over a million and a half policies with a weekly premium of one (old) penny. The official table issued by the Government converted one old penny to half a new penny. To replace one old penny with half a new penny would, however, involve increasing the weekly premium by 20 per cent and the committee felt that this could not be justified without increasing the benefits. Some offices did increase benefits, but the majority, including Royal London, left the benefits unchanged and instead marginally reduced the premiums. So the premium for a traditional (old) penny-a-week policy became 1½ new pence, payable every four weeks, representing a reduction of a tenth of an old penny every four weeks. This may not have run off the tongue as easily as 'a penny a week' but it was a fair and equitable solution.

The conversion involved a huge amount of work, and matters were not helped by Decimalisation Day falling in the middle of a postal strike, although it proceeded as smoothly as could be expected, but at a price. Every business had to make changes to prepare for decimalisation, including reprinting its price lists and other documentation, and to incur the cost of doing so, but the presence of millions of existing contracts, each one of which had to be converted and a new premium receipt book issued, meant that the process was particularly onerous and disruptive for the industrial assurance offices. As many of them were mutuals, the cost could only be borne by the policyholders.

New business performance during the Haynes years was mixed, with the Field reorganisation having an adverse impact in the short term.[35] New business was flat during the early 1960s and it took longer than anticipated for ordinary branch to overhaul industrial branch. From 1968 there was a steady ordinary branch improvement that compared well with the competition. Industrial branch sales also improved towards the end of the period although this was less uplift than that enjoyed by many competitors. Although the number of policies being issued was dropping, the total sum assured by the new policies was increasing significantly. In terms of the sum assured, ordinary branch was now well ahead, although industrial branch still represented more than 86 per cent of the new policies sold in 1972, with Royal London issuing nearly 188,000 industrial branch policies with an average premium of little more than a £1 a month.

The financial strength increased, in part due to a change in the basis of valuation. Until the late 1960s the Society had understated its assets by showing them in the annual accounts at book value, usually the price paid for them, with no credit being taken for any increase in their value. This approach was adjusted in stages. In the light of the actuary's advice following the 31 December 1965 valuation, the Board decided "that the margin between the market and book values of the Society's investments is such as to enable them to dispense with the Investment Reserve Funds which have been built up over the years".[36] These were transferred into the life funds. After the 1968 valuation, the Board "decided that the margin between the market and book values of the Society's investments is such as to enable them to write up the book values by £11,000,000".[37] By the 1970s assets were being valued at middle market price or by the directors in accordance with regulations that applied to all insurance companies.

Progress was at last being made in relation to expenses and lapses. The industrial branch expense ratio was maintained at around 37 per cent during an inflationary period. This did not put the Society with the companies at the top of the league (in 1968, for example, the Co-operative had an expense ratio of 29 per cent, Pearl 32 per cent, Prudential 32.8 per cent and Royal London 36.7 per cent[38]) but was a great deal better than the 44 per cent of pre-war years and below that of the major friendly societies. The Society's lapse ratio had nearly halved since the early 1950s – by 1968 it was 16.5 per cent. Again the Prudential (10.5 per cent) and Pearl (12.7 per cent) led the way but the Society compared well with Liverpool Victoria (17.6 per cent) and Royal Liver (21.8 per cent).[39]

The Board, the Field operations and head office had been modernised. New business was improving as were investment returns in the light of greater exposure to shares and property. There was a healthy surplus in both the industrial and ordinary branch funds permitting bonuses to be paid that were amongst the best available. The computer was becoming embedded in the Society's operations. Under Haynes' wise leadership, Royal London had made an excellent start to its second century despite all the uncertainties of the economic and political environment.

On 16 July 1971 Bertram Simpson died, aged 87, his obituary in *The Times* suggesting that a strong case could be made for the claim that he was the greatest preacher of the generation and commenting that he "had a gift (rare amongst Bishops) of answering letters by return and toiled at routine office work which others would have delegated".[40] The training he had received at Royal London between school and university had clearly stayed with him throughout his career.

In January 1972 Basil Sanders retired. His son wrote:

> *My father would not have risen to the top in a union committed to the politics of the Left. But most members of his Section had Conservative sympathies, and there was little call for confrontation and struggle. There were inevitably contentious issues and hard individual cases, but relations between management and the staff side were very good on the whole. When my father retired in 1972 the company magazine recorded of him that he could 'smile his way through any crises' and paid tribute to his 'constructive' negotiating: 'A kindly man, he represents all that is best in British trade unionism.' His farewell dinner was attended by several company directors, and the guest speaker was Len Murray,[41] himself a Methodist, who placed him in that tradition of the union movement which 'owes more to Wesley than to Marx'.[42]*

In July 1972 Reginald Maudling resigned as Home Secretary. He had been involved in the business of John Poulson, an architect who was subsequently convicted of fraud and imprisoned, and felt that he could hardly remain as the minister responsible for the Metropolitan Police while they were investigating a business with which he was connected. He died in 1979, aged 61.

In August 1972 Ernest Haynes suffered a massive stroke and resigned early the following year. He was to live, severely paralysed but unimpaired mentally, until 1987 and continued to take a keen interest in the Society.

Royal London was fortunate to have somebody of his calibre in charge at this critical time. He had the approach of modern business leaders. Fifty years after Haynes was appointed, Tim Melville-Ross, the current chairman of Royal London, was quoted in a series of articles about leadership in business. He spoke of the loneliness inherent in that role:

> The more national your role, the more impact over a longer period of time your decisions have. So you have to make yourself get away from dealing with the day-to-day. You have to have people around you who you trust, who will deal with the day-to-day so that you can think through where your organisation is trying to get to over the long term and make decisions that respond to that.[43]

Although never losing his attention to detail, Haynes was probably the first chief executive of Royal London who would readily have subscribed to this view. His predecessors are to be much admired – Alfred Skeggs for leading the Society away from the trauma of the Auxiliary Company, and John Wiseman for coping with the war and the years that followed, and for his representation of the industrial assurance offices at Whitehall and Westminster. Both dealt well with the many difficult issues that arose during their stewardships and saw huge growth in terms of new business and assets. The Royal London was seen as a well-run organisation. Haynes, however, realised that displaying competence with the day-to-day issues would not be enough to steer Royal London through the 1960s and beyond. He recognised that, unless the sales force could be reorganised along more efficient lines, the expense ratio would reach unsustainable levels and new business would suffer because there was no means of quickly addressing vacant agencies. The right of agents to sell their collecting books to a successor who they nominated was a bar to any reform and as such had to be removed. He saw that his fellow directors needed to be free of direct day-to-day responsibility for the Society's business in their part of the country so that they too could think about the strategy of the organisation and changes that would have to be made to achieve it. He realised that the Board would benefit from a wider range of skills and experience.

On first meeting, Haynes could appear forbidding, and he certainly did not suffer fools gladly, but he was hugely respected and a sound judge of people. Haynes' critics (and even some of his admirers) suggested that he had a tendency to bully and that there were times when, with a more conciliatory approach, he would have been able to generate considerable support, especially amongst the younger 'middle management'. There were times, however, when a combative streak was essential. He made it quite clear to those representing the sales force that Royal London was run for the benefit of policyholders, not agents, and suggested more than once that if they continued to pursue what he regarded as excessive demands, the best action for the Board to take on behalf of the policyholders would be to shut down the business.

On other occasions he must have displayed quite extraordinary powers of persuasion. Minute books traditionally recorded only decisions and said little or nothing about the discussions that preceded them. One of the most frustrating omissions is the arguments advanced by Haynes in April 1961 that persuaded the other directors, all of whom had come up through the ranks of the sales force, to give up the dominance that the Field had always enjoyed on the Board. After all, they would surely have argued, it was quite possible to benefit from the input of actuaries, investment managers, lawyers and property managers by inviting them to attend meetings when particular issues were being discussed – there was no need to give them a role in the making of decisions. Perhaps as a result of his part-time role heading up one of the sales divisions, the Field directors regarded Haynes as one of them. Alternatively what he learned from that role may have provided him with arguments that were irrefutable. Whatever it was that he said, Ernest Haynes succeeded in breaking the mould of the traditional Royal London Board.

Those who won Haynes' confidence discovered a considerate, fair-minded person who challenged rather than intimidated, and was capable of displaying both charm and compassion. He was popular with staff, in a respectful way – the journal of the Royal London Club referred to the excellent speeches that he had made at the two centenary banquets, and was "sure that the reception he received when he rose to speak at Grosvenor House will remain long in his memory. As a spontaneous example of regard, it could not have been bettered".[44]

Haynes was active outside the Society – at various times he was chairman of the Life Offices Association, the Industrial Life Offices Association and the Industrial Assurance Council, president of the Insurance Orchestral Society of London, treasurer of the Soldiers, Sailors, Airmen and Families Association and vice-chairman of the trustees of the Yvonne Arnaud Memorial Theatre in Guildford. On his death, Bill Forsey, a subsequent chairman, wrote:

> *Mr Haynes was an inspiring figure and was the driving force in the Society's development and growth in two critical decades of our history. There is no doubt that the present financial strength of The Royal London has been created from the firm operating base that Mr Haynes was so instrumental in helping to create.*[45]

CHAPTER 12

Colchester

1972–1999

Colchester's second castle, The Royal London Mutual Insurance Society's splendid new headquarters in Middleborough is now about [to be] completed and opened to the first of its force of 800 or so employees in October. This remarkable turreted structure, centred on two courtyards, took about 3½ years to build and, equipped to the highest standards of modernity, looks beyond the onslaught of the 1980s into the 21st century. If it looks imposing from the outside, the impression of size inside is even greater.

Essex Countryside (1982)[1]

Triton Court set the expensive tone for Finsbury Square. A monumental yet graceful Art Deco block refurbished in 1984, Triton Court holds not only 26 offices and the Rouxl Brittannia Restaurant but also an award-winning greenery-filled atrium, the newest kind of City garden. On a chilly spring day, the atrium felt almost Mediterranean, with a glass roof, terraced interior walls hung with trailing greenery, and large fig trees clustered around an ornamental pool below.

An American visitor to London (1994)[2]

The stroke suffered by Ernest Haynes heralded a period where retirements and deaths conspired to create an almost constantly changing Board. Between 1972 and 1983 there were seven chief executives (or chief general managers as they were now being called throughout the industry), five of whom went on to become chairman.[3] William Forsey, one of Haynes' successors, referred to this as a period when nobody "was in harness long enough. Whereas in the 50s and 60s, for example, Ernest Haynes had effectively been the saviour of the Society and played a leading part in our successes for so long, in the 70s we were cruelly deprived of the talents of a whole succession of experienced men".[4] The years immediately after Haynes' retirement were dominated by relocating the head office to Colchester. The business continued to develop and grow but, by the closing years of the century, the home service sector was having difficulty in coping with regulation, and with the additional financial burdens imposed both by it, and by the high inflation that had prevailed for much of the period.

In the 1970s many companies were considering relocating their head office out of central London. They were often in buildings that could not be further expanded, or felt their efficiency threatened by the extent of overspill offices acquired over the years. Traditional office space was ill-suited to the increasingly important demands of technology and there was a fear that the rising costs of living and working in London would make expansion there difficult and expensive. Royal London was not immune from this debate. The concept of moving the computer and those who operated it out of London had been approved by the Board back in November 1970 when they authorised a search for "somewhere where we could accommodate our Data Processing equipment and Department and where there is expansion to cope with other Departments of Head Office if this was thought desirable in the future; the Society would wish to own such a property, not rent it. The Society might also consider building such a property". The precise wording is interesting – "if" it was thought desirable and the reference to "other Departments" rather than the whole of the head office.

A paper had gone to the Board in March 1971 indicating that Colchester in Essex could meet both requirements – suitable leasehold office space was available and nearby was a site on which to build. It was also easily accessible by train from Liverpool Street station, just a few minutes' walk from Finsbury Square. Other possible locations including Ipswich, Peterborough and Southend had apparently been investigated, and perhaps discussed informally with the Board, but no alternatives were included in the paper. Colchester, 56 miles from London and with a population of 75,000, certainly met the immediate data processing requirements of lower rents and local labour, and the Board authorised the taking of a lease of three floors of a building in the course of erection in St Peter's Street.

Other companies which left London chose New Towns that, although financially attractive, often did not appeal to staff who were considering re-locating. Royal London adopted a different approach by moving to the oldest recorded town in Britain – there is thought to have been a Bronze Age settlement as early as 1100 BC on the ancient ridgeway, along which the High Street now runs, and in AD 44 the Emperor Claudius established there Colonia Camulodunum, the first Roman colony in Britain, which was stormed by Boudicca, Queen of the Iceni, in AD 60. After Boudicca's defeat, Colchester was re-established as a Roman garrison and later became a Saxon stronghold. William the Conqueror ordered the building of a Royal fortress there, Richard the Lionheart granted Colchester a Royal Charter in 1189, and a parliamentary army besieged the town for many weeks in 1648. An influx of Flemish and Dutch refugees in the late sixteenth century had made the town a centre of the cloth trade, although by the early nineteenth century this had died out as a result of competition from the north of England.

The Colchester that greeted Royal London provided services to the surrounding rural area, was a garrison and university town, and had a strong engineering presence. The computer was lifted by crane out of Royal London House and moved to Colchester in 1972. A new one was installed there later in the year. Planning began for the huge task of putting onto the computer the details of every industrial branch policy. By 1973 the 43 staff at the computer centre were forming a Colchester branch of the Royal London Club – there were hard-fought football matches between Programming/Analysts and Operations and three table tennis teams were entered in the local league.[5] No progress could be made on a new office building, however, because the borough council decided not to sell the site referred to in the Board paper.

Back at Finsbury Square, thoughts were turning towards a possible extension of the move to Colchester, but it was a much changed Board that would have to make the decisions. In March 1973 Tony Lamb,[6] who had been chief general manager for only a year, died in an accident, Ernest Haynes recognised that he would never be able to return after his stroke and resigned, and George Cannell retired. Jim Bailey was appointed chairman, Tom Cowman became chief general manager and three new directors were appointed: Peter Taylor (the actuary since 1970), Bill Forsey (assistant general manager, Field staff, who was appointed deputy general manager), and Michael Pearce (the investment manager). Cowman had joined as an agent in 1934 at Wallsend, and four years later was superintendent of the newly established district of Hawick, later Galashiels. After spells at Blyth and Newcastle he became area superintendent in Scotland and then Lancashire before being appointed a director and divisional manager in 1961. The new Board decided that the exodus to Colchester would continue and in 1974 the ordinary branch (new business and claims) and staff departments moved. By the mid-1970s there were 350 Royal Londoners in leased premises in Colchester.

Friday 28 February 1975 was a tragic day for the Royal London head office and for many others who worked in the Finsbury Square area. Liverpool Street and Moorgate were the local stations and, when news reached the office of a crash at Moorgate during the morning rush hour, there were immediate concerns that Royal Londoners might be involved. The 8.39 am from Drayton Park to Moorgate on the Northern City Line (Highbury Branch) of the London Underground had sped past the platform and ploughed through the buffers into the wall at the end of the tunnel. Mary O'Brien, a part-time clerk in the claims department and mother of four children, and Vera Bray of accounts often travelled in together. They were chatting in the second coach as the train entered Moorgate. The impact crushed the first three coaches of the train, killing 43 people and injuring over 70 in what was the worst peacetime loss of life on the London Transport system until the London bombings of 7 July 2005. Mary was killed instantly and Vera suffered a fractured pelvis and other injuries. The cause of the accident was never determined.[7]

Still no final decision had been made to move all the head office to Colchester, although during 1975 the former cattle market at Middleborough was identified as a possible site. The local community was generally welcoming, the Chamber of Commerce regarding the Society as the sort of business they wanted to bring into the area, although, as the local press reported, the responses from the members of the planning committee to whom preliminary plans of the building were submitted in December 1975 were not unanimously encouraging: one considered that the vast and futuristic complex would be more suitable for Heathrow Airport, another compared the building to Alcatraz and a third felt that it was one of the weirdest buildings they had ever seen.

It was hardly surprising, given that large parts of the building at Finsbury Square were standing empty, that there were rumblings amongst the staff who were still based there, and these increased when it was announced that the Government had granted the office development permit for the Colchester building required before planning approval could be sought. A voluntary redundancy programme was introduced in April 1976[8] and uncertainty prevailed, although in June the Board was still stressing that no decision had been made on further moves to Colchester. The assurance was, however, rather weakened by the comment that in any event a new building could not be ready for occupation before 1980.[9] On 1 September 1976 after "full and careful consideration of all the factors involved... the Board decided that it will be in the best interest of the Society, its staff and policyholders for the whole of the Head Office to be located in one building in Colchester".[10] As well as the concern of the rising costs in London, it was felt that the move would enable Royal London to develop into more of a community than would be possible in London, provide staff with first-class amenities – social, working and living – and further strengthen the Royal London family tradition.

Outline planning permission was obtained in early 1977 and the time had come to consider purchasing the Middleborough site. By now there had been yet more changes in the boardroom. After three years' stability, Bailey retired in April 1976 after 50 years' service and Cowman became chairman. He was succeeded as chief general manager by Leslie Poll who had been a director and deputy general manager since 1968. Poll had a similar background to Bailey and Cowman – his career began in 1936 as an agent at Bow and, after spells as a superintendent in and around London, he became area superintendent and then divisional manager in Liverpool. In October 1977 Poll died of cancer and a year later Cowman too died after surgery. As a result Billy Skinner unexpectedly found himself chief general manager and later chairman. He was the son of John Skinner, the former joint managing director. His loving parents decided that he was to be named after a close family friend, who would also be his godfather. The friend's name was William, although he was known as Billy, and it somehow came about that the Skinners' sixth child was christened Billy, the apparent informality of which was to cause difficulties throughout his life. It just did not seem right for 'Billy' to appear on official documents that often referred to him as 'W Skinner' or 'B Gerald Skinner', while some of his close friends adopted the American fashion and called him 'BG'.[11]

Skinner had joined the solicitor's department in 1932 and his early days were spent as assistant to the office boy. He was later articled to Major Evan Hayward. His father made it quite clear to young Billy from the beginning that he was on his own. Over half a century later Skinner wrote, "[I] always stood in awe of my Father in the office and very rarely encountered him. Indeed, if ever I saw him coming I turned and ran like hell. It appeared that he was regarded as a real Victorian character, always a familiar sight in his frock coat around Royal London House. His word was to be obeyed! Nevertheless [he was] very much respected and liked by all". Skinner appreciated that he was fortunate in his mentor: "The Major was principally responsible for my tuition in the law and he being a splendid man and lawyer himself, I like to feel that many of his qualities and much of his expertise eventually rubbed off on me. He certainly got me very enthusiastic about the law and determined to make the grade".

The war clouds were gathering when Skinner qualified and he was amongst a number of Royal Londoners to enlist in The City of London Yeomanry, the local territorial regiment. As a result, he was called up as soon as war was declared and, after various postings in batteries around London, spent three years in India and Burma as an artillery officer in the 14th Army as it halted the Japanese advance, and then drove them back to Rangoon.[12]

After the war he commanded a territorial regiment, retiring with the rank of colonel. He had returned to Royal London on demobilisation and was gradually promoted through the ranks of the solicitor's department. He played cricket and football for the Society and was a member of the chorus in several productions of the Royal London Dramatic and Operatic Society. He succeeded Russell Firth as solicitor in 1967, served for many years on the legal committee of the Industrial Life Offices and was chairman of the Life Assurance Legal Society. He was appointed a director in 1972. Skinner regarded this as the zenith of his career, with retirement only seven years away. But the deaths of Lamb and Poll caused something of a void in the Society's hierarchy and in October 1977 he was appointed chief general manager at the age of 63. A year later when Cowman died he was appointed chairman as well, a role that he retained until April 1983, having retired as chief general manager in July 1979. Between them, he and his father had over a hundred years' service.

William Forsey took over from Skinner as chief general manager. Major Forsey had served at Normandy and was later on Montgomery's staff. He had become a fire specialist and when he was demobbed with no clear idea of what he wanted to do it was suggested that somebody with his experience was ideally suited to insurance. He went along to the Royal London office in Bristol in 1948 and was interviewed by the superintendent, Ben Whiston.[13] The interview went well and Forsey was hired as an agent. Whiston was instrumental in Forsey's early appointment as an assistant superintendent, and he regarded this as his best contribution to Royal London.[14] Forsey was a superintendent by 1954 and then area superintendent. He spent two terms in South Wales and two in the West Midlands before becoming divisional manager in 1967. He came to head office in 1970 as the Society's first production manager and developed the role into that of a national sales manager. He was appointed a director in April 1973.

The decision had been made before they were in office but it fell to Skinner and Forsey to mastermind the final move to Colchester. They were without their 'right-hand man' John Gann, the secretary and former head office manager, who had been responsible for organising the staff moves to Colchester. He was made a director in 1978 but died in January 1980, aged only 59. In his tribute Forsey wrote of Gann starting with Royal London as a young lad of 17 and rising to the position of secretary with a seat on the Board.[15]

The site for the new office was between the wall of the Roman town and the River Colne. With the assistance of a grant from Royal London, the Colchester Archaeological Trust was permitted to excavate before work began and revealed a magnificent 14 square foot mosaic pavement. Restored, it was originally intended for display in one of the courtyards of the new head office but it was later decided that the museum in Colchester Castle would be a more appropriate venue. The brief to the architects – Cruickshank & Saward, who were Royal London's tenants in Manchester – was to design a building that was functional and in which the staff would be pleased to work, while at the same time blending in and harmonising with the natural charm of the small-scale buildings of Colchester. What they produced was Colchester's second castle: a striking, five-storey turreted structure, centred on two courtyards, surrounded by roads that served as a moat, and that was linked to a multi-storey car park by a drawbridge-like enclosed footbridge on which were emblazoned the coats of arms of Royal London, Essex County Council and the Borough of Colchester. The building covered more than two acres, comprised 150,000 square feet, accommodated 800 staff (two-thirds of whom had been recruited locally), cost £14.5 million and took three and a half years to build.

Royal London were required to build the multi-storey car park on the other side of the road, part of which had to be made available for public parking, and this provoked more opposition than the head office itself, the owners of the properties beside the River Colne feeling that it would devastate a pleasant and unspoilt corner of the old town. The county council could not be persuaded to change the local road scheme, and the office building was to remain on the centre of a roundabout. This was not a problem for staff, who could enter via the footbridge from the car park or through the restaurant, but locating the entrance and negotiating a safe passage provided a constant challenge for visitors. Not quite everybody was to be on the one site – printing and stationery services and the bulk of the Society's archive filing were located half a mile away in a leasehold building at Clarendon Way, near to the railway station.[16]

The new head office was not Royal London's only construction project in Colchester. On 27 July 1981 the Royal London Sports Centre was opened. On an 18-acre site in Mill Road, three miles away to the north-east of the town, it was said to be the best privately owned complex of its kind in East Anglia.[17] On the ground floor were four badminton courts and two squash courts, and courts for basketball, netball and volleyball. Upstairs were snooker and table tennis rooms, a bar and a lounge. Outside were tennis and netball courts complete with floodlights, a cricket square and football and hockey pitches. All of this was available to staff on payment of a very modest subscription to the Royal London Club. No longer were Royal Londoners making their way every weekend to the sports field at Mill Hill that had been so integral a part of the Society's social life for nearly 30 years. The ground was let to the Post Office for a while and later, after planning permission had been obtained, was sold for residential development. This was, as a senior executive said on visiting the fully developed site many years later, a splendid result for the policyholders but an awful vision for someone who had spent many happy hours there.

By autumn 1981 every department had relocated to temporary accommodation in Colchester except the equities and bonds teams within asset management who had moved next door to 22 Finsbury Square. The original decision had involved all of asset management moving to Colchester (and indeed Michael Pearce, the director then in charge of investments resigned as a result) but it was later decided that the City-dealing part of the operation would remain in the City. The construction project experienced its fair share of problems but at last the new building was finished. During September and October 1982 the temporary offices were vacated and everyone moved into the new building which was opened by the Duke of Gloucester on 29 October.

A distinguished company had been invited to join the Board and other Royal Londoners to watch the proceedings, including the Lord Lieutenant and High Sheriff of Essex, the High Steward and Bishop of Colchester, the Major General commanding the Eastern District and senior representatives from the insurance industry, the borough council, and from the contractors and professional team who had worked on the building. Wives were included in some of the invitations and the organisers had clearly made an important executive decision indicating in advance that ladies would not wear hats and gloves. Skinner made a short speech of welcome, the Duke unveiled the plaque and said a few words and Forsey thanked the Duke for participating in a day that "marks the occasion when the whole of the head office administration, after a decade or so of a splintering into a number of locations, is once again housed under one roof and operating as a family unit". After a tour of the building, the Duke hurried off to the annual Colchester Oyster Feast in the Moot Hall. The Colchester move had at last been concluded. The new head office, said Forsey in his 1982 Christmas message, "symbolises the faith of management for the long-term future. Let us all share in that pride, hope, ambition and achievement".

An attractive brochure was produced to mark the opening, although this did not please everybody. It purported to list the 162 district offices but provoked this response from an agent in Essex:

> Today we received a glossy book
> Within which I chose to look
> How sad it was for me to find
> That out of sight and out of mind
> Southend office does not exist.
> But we at Southend do insist
> That here we are and here we remain
> Just look at your list after each campaign.

In another ceremony a couple of weeks later, the war memorials that had been moved from Finsbury Square were rededicated by the Bishop of Colchester. Present was James Duffell, aged 93, the son of Horace, one of the joint managing directors through the Auxiliary Company years. Jimmy Duffell joined Royal London in 1908 and was appointed assistant actuary in 1912. He was actuary from 1921 to 1947 and secretary from 1946 until 1949, when he retired. His father's resignation following the litigation must have been a very difficult time for him. Here was the man who should have been interviewed when the centenary history was being written but if he was, no notes of that interview have survived. His visit to Colchester was recorded by a photograph with the Society's current, previous and subsequent actuaries – collectively these gentlemen held that high office for more than 50 years.[18]

The phased move gave the sports teams a difficult transitional period but in due course they were assimilated into local leagues. The Royal London Dramatic and Operatic Society, founded in 1931 and later renamed the Royal London Drama Group, suffered only limited disruption as a result of the re-location of the head office. There was no production in 1972, 1974 or 1975 but they were soon back to two productions a year – *This Happy Home*, for example, was a sell-out in 1978 and their performances continued well into the 1990s.

On Friday 16 October 1981 Royal London House, Finsbury Square had closed for business for the last time. From late 1976 it had been clear that the day would come when the status of the building would change from head office and symbol of the Society to a non-performing asset. There was no prospect of letting the building in its present condition or with minor improvements – the demands of City tenants had moved far beyond the internal environment created by Belcher and Joass. The Society had two options: sell, leaving it to the purchaser to carry out a development; or develop the building itself. Commercial property development is risky and involves considerable crystal ball gazing – success depends upon the availability of tenants willing to pay the required rent when the development is completed, perhaps several years into the future. The question was whether the Society was prepared to run that risk, in exchange for the rewards that would be available if their predictions of the market proved correct. The Board took the bold decision and committed £30 million to a major redevelopment of the former head office.

The work took 30 months and, when it was finished, an open day was held for past and present staff with nearly 600 taking up the invitation to see the transformation.[19] The external façade had been retained but (to quote the letting agents) inside a "court yard had been formed in the centre of the buildings where there was originally a light well, and a glazed roof has been added to form an atrium with gardens and waterfalls on the three lowest levels. Wall-climbing lifts, balconies and planting provide further interest and

the principal office accommodation at all levels overlooks the atrium area".
An imposing archway, two storeys high had been created to provide access
from Finsbury Square into this central atrium of more than an eighth of an
acre in size, where there was a restaurant, a Japanese water garden and a
viewing gallery overlooking two squash courts. The 200,000 square feet of
air-conditioned offices had been "constructed or upgraded to cater for present
and anticipated demands of communication and environment".[20] Careful
thought had been given to the name of the building. Triton Court was finally
agreed, inspired by the two brass Tritons that had been placed at the front
of building in 1930, no doubt to keep Mercury company.[21] Royal London
House was retained for 22–25 Finsbury Square – the 1950s extension to the
east of the main building that had been built to let and was not included in
the redevelopment.

By the end of 1985 Triton Court was virtually fully let. City rents had
been rising significantly and the quality of the building, reflected in awards
from various bodies for architectural and aesthetic merit, attracted good
tenants. The Toronto Dominion Bank relocated its UK headquarters to Triton
Court, leasing 24,500 square feet and the Stock Exchange took nearly 18,000
square feet. The development was masterminded by Rodney Pollard, the
head of property investment, ably assisted by Colin Cannings, the Society's
solicitor.[22] The Board's decision had been vindicated. Triton Court was an
impressive and profitable redevelopment of which those involved at the time
could be proud – it won a number of awards and long retained a modern feel.
This was an exciting time to be working in the City of London – 27 October
1986 was 'Big Bang Day', which changed everything for ever. The distinction
between brokers, who traded shares on behalf of clients, and jobbers, the
market makers, was abolished, fixed rate commissions were eliminated and
foreign ownership of UK brokers was permitted, with electronic trading
rendering face-to-face share deals obsolete.

Forsey provided the continuity at the top of Royal London that had
been lacking during the previous period but, by the time he was presenting
Triton Court to the market in the autumn of 1984, he had already relinquished
the chief executive's duties. Michael Pickard became chief general manager on
1 May 1983 and, when Forsey retired as chairman on 31 December 1987,
Pickard assumed that role as well. He was educated at Christ's Hospital[23]
where there was a tradition of boys with mathematical ability turning to the
actuarial profession; he attended his interview in 1957 wearing his distinctive
school uniform of long blue coat with a leather belt, knee breeches and yellow
stockings, a sight long remembered by Stanley Goodall, the joint managing
director, who happened to pass the applicant in the corridor on the way to the
interview.[24] It was a chance meeting to which Goodall would refer from time
to time as the young man's career progressed. He survived a couple of years of

boredom working on industrial branch surrenders, celebrated the centenary with a visit to *The Amorous Prawn*, passed his actuarial examinations, took three months' leave of absence to undertake social work in Jersey City, New Jersey and was on the fringe of the project to convert the Society's agents from book interest to salaried. He was an asset on the sports field, the staff magazines of the day referring to a "very good movement [that] resulted in M. Pickard crossing for a try which we failed to convert"[25] and scoring 72 for the Sunday XI out of a total of 101.[26] His professional ability was soon recognised – by 1967 he was assistant actuary and three years later became deputy actuary, following the promotion of Tony Lamb from actuary to chief general manager. He was appointed actuary in 1974 and a director in 1977.

Michael Pickard was recruited at a time when anybody with any seniority was still 'Sir' and he was 'Pickard'. In a speech at the Actuaries Club in March 1988, he talked of his visits to the paralysed Ernest Haynes in the nursing home after his enforced retirement:

> *He was, of course, of a different generation to me and on my first visit he said to me: 'Pickard, I'm sorry, but I can't do anything other than call you Pickard', which was how he had always referred to me at the office. And of course he was 'Sir', or 'Mr Haynes', to me. Mr Haynes kept an interest in the Royal London and indeed insurance affairs right to the end, and when my present appointment was announced a year or so ago, he dictated and sent to me a letter of congratulations and good wishes which began – and this gave me an enormous amount of pleasure – 'Dear Michael'.*

At the time that the head office was relocating to Colchester, changes were taking place within the Field and these continued throughout the period. The successful agents continued to demonstrate their genuine, in some cases verging on passionate, belief in the service they were providing – insurance for working-class people who would otherwise be unprotected, as well as a safe and practical way by which the better off amongst them could save. But there was so much administration: collecting books had to be balanced weekly and rewritten every year and there were numerous forms to be completed in relation to every sale, claim, surrender, lapse or change of address. Computerisation may have been so advanced that it prompted the move of the head office out of London but at the end of the 1970s the administration of the Society's sales operation remained as it had always been. There were more than 1,700 agents and 150 district offices but the processes put in place by Degge, Ridge and Hambridge were still being operated. Agents deducted their earnings from their collections, utilising laborious and time-consuming procedures, and paid over the balance in cash every week at the district office. Each district paid claims and office expenses from these payments and then accounted to head office with the balance. The documentation required to support each payment had to be completed, checked, sent off, delivered, read, (often queried and sometimes corrected), actioned and filed. There just had to be a more efficient and economical way and one that would readily provide information required to manage the business and to comply with legal and accounting requirements.

In 1980 the Society's computer-planning department was tasked with finding it and a project was set up called the General and Life Branches Accounting and Sales Staff Remuneration Review, or GLASS for short. Close contact was maintained with local offices and a full-scale pilot scheme was run at the Colchester district office. A 'closed shop' agreement was in place with the Royal London Section of the National Union of Insurance Workers in relation to agents and several other grades of Field staff. Discussions with the trade unions, the *Royal Londoner* reported, had "of necessity been very involved" and in fact they were rather more contentious than this. In October 1980 the union withdrew its support for the programme and instructed its members not to arrange or attend any meetings or training, not to supply regional or head office with any data on sales and not to post branch office accounts to head office until Mondays, and then by second-class post. Good sense in due course prevailed and the issues were resolved. In time, union members came round to management's view that the implementation of GLASS streamlined the Society's administrative and accounting systems and left staff with more time for productive work.

The agents' remuneration had already been simplified. Now they were paid a salary dependent upon the size of their agency rather than commission based on the premiums collected. Procurement fees were paid on new industrial and ordinary branch business, but ordinary branch renewals were reflected in the form of an addition to salary at the beginning of the year. Agents could now pay their gross collections directly into a bank or post office that was convenient for them – they did not have to go to the district office – and a payroll system calculated and itemised their remuneration, taking account of procurement fees and making deductions such as tax, national insurance, trade union subscription and any loan repayments. The net payment was credited to every agent's bank account every month. All claims and district office expenses were now paid centrally. At the time of his retirement, Forsey regarded the introduction of the agency computerised accounting system as the most significant change since the war. In fairness to Ernest Haynes, it is probably more accurate to say that the abolition of the agents' rights to nominate their successor coupled with GLASS, the latter only being possible as a result of the changes brought about by the former, were the two key developments.

The structure of the Field operations was evolving too – the last of several reorganisations in the 1960s had established 11 divisions. In 1973 they were consolidated into eight divisions that, by 1979, had been reduced to six regions.[27] In the early 1980s the Field staff exceeded 2,600, including 1,600 agents, operating out of 160 district offices. Gradually much of the administration formerly carried out in the district offices was eliminated by the use of technology and by the mid-1990s there was a move away from the high streets into 62 area offices, generally situated in business parks or on the outskirts of towns, laid out as sales and training centres. A residential training centre was opened at Dedham, near Colchester, in 1995.

New job grades were introduced: district managers, assistant district managers and life specialists ultimately replacing superintendents, district inspectors and life and ordinary branch inspectors. Differences were appearing between the north and south of the country and between the remaining book interest agents and those recruited more recently on salaried terms, and these trends were to continue. Many book interest agents had massive agencies that (especially in the north) were almost entirely industrial branch. Their new business was largely 'top-ups' on existing clients, extended family referrals and neighbours, with collecting still taking up much of their time.

This may have been the traditional life blood of the Society. By 1980, however, 60 per cent of the adult population had a bank account and, with earnings increasingly being paid directly into them monthly rather than weekly, agents were finding that some industrial branch policyholders were handing over cheques when they called to collect premiums. This was seen as a positive development by many of the newly recruited agents who were encouraging both existing and potential customers to take out ordinary branch policies where payment of the premiums was by standing order. This was more suitable for many customers and better terms were available that reflected the cost savings achieved by not having to make weekly calls. This new breed of agent was not convinced that collecting every week to maintain contact was an efficient use of time, believing that there were other ways of keeping in touch with customers, such as discussing with them their general insurance requirements. Nor were they convinced by the traditional concept that one had to collect every week otherwise the insurance money would have been spent on other things. Their view was that the Society did not want new customers whose ability to pay was this fragile. Another advantage of an ordinary branch policy to the agents was that sales were less geographically restricted – agents could only sell an industrial branch policy if it was practical for them to call regularly to collect the premiums but there was no such restriction where payment would be by standing order. Where this change of emphasis was successful, Royal London found itself in competition with 'new' life assurance companies with their large direct sales forces – for example, Abbey Life (founded in 1961) and Hambro Life, later Allied Dunbar (1970), and with Sun Life of Canada which had significantly expanded its UK operations, as well as with the traditional competitors such as Prudential, Pearl and (more in the north of England) the Co-operative.

The Society advertised on television for the first time in 1980, as much to motivate staff, particularly the agents, as to influence customers. The advertisement featured the guards at Buckingham Palace, a modern housing estate in Maidenhead and a bus with "The Royal London" emblazoned on its side driving round Finsbury Square. The shooting was interrupted when the bus broke down and had to be repaired by one of the film crew. New policies were launched. In April 1981 Royal London entered the unit-linked market with its 'UnitPlan' policy that required the creation of the Royal London Capital Accumulator Trust and the incorporation of The Royal London Unit Trust Managers Limited to manage the unit trust business.[28] The benefits from a unit-linked life assurance policy depend on the performance of a portfolio of investments. Each premium paid by the policyholder is split – part is used to provide life-assurance cover, while the balance (after the deduction of costs and expenses) is used to buy units in a unit trust. This enables a small investor to benefit from an investment in a managed fund without making a large financial commitment.

In 1984 there occurred one of those events which had long been feared and was greeted with consternation when it happened, but in the end had only a very limited impact. Since as early as 1799 tax relief had been given on the premiums of most life policies. 'Tax effectiveness' was seen as an advantage of saving, or repaying the mortgage, by means of an endowment policy. A policyholder who could afford £20 a month would be encouraged to take out a policy with a premium of £24 or even £25 on the basis that the tax man would be paying the difference. This increased the policyholder's cover, the insurance company's income and the agent's commission. All three would suffer if the tax relief was abolished. The industry had long realised that this benefit was under threat. It lasted until March 1984 when Nigel Lawson, the Chancellor of the Exchequer, announced in his budget speech that it would be withdrawn immediately. There was gloom and despondency within the Society. The chief general manager rushed out a circular to the entire organisation that spoke of regretting the development but having to accept the new challenge. He expressed his confidence that in view of its many home service contacts, strong financial reserves, competitive portfolio of policies and "above all a highly trained and able staff" Royal London was "admirably equipped to respond positively and effectively to the new situation". His confidence was not misplaced.

Home loan activities were expanded. A £50 million loan, or more accurately 'a syndicated revolving cash advance facility', was obtained in July

1985 to re-finance the Society's existing mortgages, which had previously been advanced from the life fund, and to finance new mortgages. Later in the year the Society announced the launch of its home mortgage scheme, 'Royal London Homebuy'. This represented a significant development in the Society's objective of providing an enhanced service to customers. The terms on which mortgages were available provide an interesting comment on the times and indeed, on a much later period when unwise lending on residential properties pushed the world to the brink of financial meltdown. The initial rate of interest was 13.25 per cent; loans could not exceed 95 per cent of the value of the property and were limited to 2.75 times the applicant's annual income or, where two applicants were involved, 2.75 times one income and 1 times the other income. Demand for mortgages and the endowment policies that accompanied them was high, and a year later what was now termed a syndicated revolving underwriting facility had to be increased to £100 million.

The 1980s saw an increasing use of the Society's logo. Until 1978 the only Royal London emblem was the coat of arms granted to it in 1934. But in 1978 a logo was unveiled – known as the 'hand around the family', it showed a hand enclosing a diagrammatic mother, father and child. At first it was used only in a sales and marketing context – the coat of arms remained much in evidence, for example, at the time of the opening of the Colchester office, and appeared on the front cover of the annual report and accounts until 1987. By the late 1980s, the logo had taken over for all purposes although, along the way, the supporting wording had been shortened to 'Royal London Insurance' and the father had been given dark hair.

For most of the Society's existence, general insurance had been outsourced.[29] Although policies were issued in the Royal London name, the risk was accepted by another company that dealt with the administration and claims handling and paid commission to Royal London for the business. It had been decided to bring this in-house when the agreement with Norwich Union expired in 1980. This was a huge task, that would take time to carry out, and so an agreement was entered into with Norwich Union that provided for the handover to be completed by the end of 1985. The Royal London General Insurance Company Limited, a wholly owned subsidiary, was created and the business was transferred to it in phases during 1984 and 1985. RLG, as it came to be called, was no shell company but a real and fully staffed general insurance company.

Late in 1985 the Society acquired The Lion Insurance Company, a motor insurer, based in Chelmsford, whose products were marketed through brokers, with the object of extending the business of Royal London's non-life account by diversifying into this different method of distribution. For the same reason, a London underwriting room was opened in February 1986 on the ground floor of Plantation House, Fenchurch Street at which Royal London

General accepted property and liability insurance through a panel of brokers. They were part of the London insurance market – "a tightly knit business community comprising several hundred insurers and brokers and Lloyd's, between them handling international and UK insurance and reinsurance business in excess of £7 billion premiums in 1985".[30]

The broadening of the Society's business was prompting discussions in the boardroom about the auditors: "In view of the Society's growth and expansion into wider fields of activity in recent years, the Board felt it an appropriate time to consider whether the policyholders might be even better served if a large firm of international auditors, with wide experience of the insurance industry and extensive ancillary facilities, were appointed."[31] Frank Brown, FCA, and William Peet, ACA, who had already audited the friendly society for several years, had been appointed the first auditors of the company in 1908. They were members of the firm of Brown, Peet & Tilly and the firm rather than the individuals was soon shown as the Society's auditors. Tilly had first appeared in the context of the Royal London audit in the 1880s when Tilly & Company were joint auditors, a role later assumed for a few years by John Tilly in a personal capacity.

Brown, Peet & Tilly remained the Society's auditors until 1972 when, as a result of a merger, the firm became Howard, Tilly & Co. The new firm – or rather broadly the same firm but with a different name – was appointed at the 1973 annual general meeting. Given that the predecessors of the existing incumbents had been in place for a hundred years, the decision to make a change was not taken lightly, but taken it was, and in 1986, after a beauty parade, Peat, Marwick, Mitchell & Co were appointed the Society's auditors. Within a decade, a worldwide merger and various name-changes had converted the new auditors into KPMG.

In 1986 the Society celebrated its 125th anniversary. The celebrations provide an interesting comparison with 1961, reflecting the move out of London and a change of attitude to formal and corporate socialising – there was not a white tie in sight. Every member of staff received a commemorative vase and was invited to a lunch, at the conclusion of which a birthday cake was brought in, generally to the accompaniment of trumpeters or pipers. There had to be repeat functions: there were three head office lunches at the Garden House Hotel, Cambridge, while the Cavendish Hotel, Eastbourne suffered a surfeit of Royal Londoners entertaining three regions during May. The usual format was that a local official proposed the health of the Society, Forsey, Pickard or Brian Knights (the director in charge of the Field) responded, another director proposed the health of the region and a local official responded. The finale was a buffet supper at Colchester Castle to which a hundred guests including local civic, academic and commercial leaders were invited.[32]

Lion and the City underwriting room did not prove to be successful. The former found it difficult to operate profitably in what was becoming a highly competitive market (Direct Line opened for business in 1985) and neither generated the income to justify their survival as stand-alone operations that had no impact on the Society's main business. RLG was moderately successful as the provider of general policies for Royal London customers via the sales force, although having control of all aspects of a business has to be balanced against the economies of scale achievable within a larger operation.[33]

Although not every development was a success, they were all prompted by the best possible motives, and the directors should be admired for taking the initiatives, on the basis of 'nothing ventured, nothing gained'. In its desire to broaden the Society's business, the Board skilfully avoided any major catastrophes. The disaster of choice at the time was estate agency. The estate agents industry was transformed in the 1980s from one dominated by small local firms to one where the major participants were large national financial institutions. By the end of 1987, for example, the Prudential Property Services had more than 600 residential branches, having rebranded all the firms that they had acquired. Other institutions, fearing being left behind, entered the market. The rationale was that they would provide further points of contact with customers and enable institutions to market other services through them. This proved a flawed strategy – estate agents sold houses, not insurance policies, and in the property slump could not even do that. In 1990 the Prudential closed all its branches. It had been a costly venture for those who undertook it and a matter of great relief to those who did not.

The Society remained a significant employer – in 1998, 950 were working at the head office (a third more than in 1936) but the sales force had reduced significantly from pre-war days, largely as a result of the consolidation and reorganisations that was possible after the abolition of Book Interest agents. The 6,500 agents in 1936 had shrunk to 1,700, although, by the time they had been managed, administered and trained, there were still more than 2,500 people working in the Field.

The new business figures for the period suggest that Royal London had continued its impressive advance, and in many senses this was true. Home service was demonstrating the immunity to external influences previously experienced by industrial assurance. Even when world wars, depressions or recessions were impacting on the lives of so many customers, new policies continued to be taken out and the premium income to increase. The decades before and after the Colchester move saw their fair share of difficulties. In 1973 the Arab–Israeli conflict was causing oil prices to soar and, with the miners working to rule, coal stocks were dwindling. A nationwide voltage reduction was imposed and, in an effort to prolong fuel stocks as long as possible, the Government limited commercial consumption of electricity to three days a week. (The lighting for Royal London House, Finsbury Square was provided by a ten kilowatt diesel generator in the basement, by hurricane lamps on the stairs and by a combination of natural light and candles in the offices. Nearly 300 candle holders were in use, all made by the in-house carpenters.[34]) Ted Heath called a general election on the basis of 'who governs Britain' but the electorate was unsure and there was no overall majority. Heath resigned, Harold Wilson formed a Government, the miners accepted a pay rise of around 35 per cent and returned to work in March when the three-day week ended.

The Stock Market gave little comfort to the government in 1974, with the FTSE All Share falling 55 per cent during the year, and inflation continuing to rise, reaching an alarming 26.9 per cent in 1975. By 1978 inflation had been halved but protests were increasing against the Government's continued insistence that pay increases must not exceed 5 per cent. The winter of discontent of 1978/79 saw lorry drivers and many public sector workers, including ambulance drivers, ancillary hospital staff, gravediggers and waste collectors, on strike and a series of 24-hour strikes on the railways. The Conservatives, now led by Margaret Thatcher, came to power in May 1979. After an initial increase, they succeeded in reducing inflation but at the cost of high interest rates and increasing unemployment – by 1982 over three and a half million people were out of work. Conditions improved during the 1980s but by the end of 1990 the UK was in recession.

Despite the occasional disappointing year, there was a dramatic increase in Royal London's premium income and funds during the period. A premium income of £26 million in 1972 had grown to more than £500 million by 1998.[35] Single premium policies were a major contributor. Single premium endowment policies, unheard of until the final quarter of the century, were proving very popular – in 1998 premiums exceeded £138m. Many of these policies had a five-year term and were essentially investments, the policyholder looking to receive, when the policy matured, a good return on the premiums that he had paid. Single premium pension policies contributed a further £40 million. Royal London's involvement in pensions dated back to 1956 when the Finance Act granted tax concessions to those in business on their own account, or in non-pensionable employment, who chose to provide for their retirement by means of policies taken out with a life assurance office.[36] In response to this opportunity, the Society introduced two pension policies that provided a specified pension, related to the policyholder's age when he took out the policy and when he chose to take the pension. They differed from later personal pension policies, where a fund is built up during the life of a policy and used to acquire an annuity and provide a tax-free lump sum on retirement, so that the size of the pension cannot be determined until then. In 1978 a personal pension policy was introduced that included "many attractive features such as a 'notional fund' build-up of contributions and the flexibility to make special contributions on top of the regular payments".[37] Soon this new policy was contributing 15 per cent of ordinary branch new business.

Other contributors to the premium growth at the close of the twentieth century were the gradual switch from industrial branch to ordinary branch, and the introduction of some shorter term industrial branch policies, both of which tended towards higher premiums. By 1998 the Society was selling a five-year industrial branch policy, with a minimum four-weekly premium of £10 – very different from the penny a week that had been the staple industrial branch policy earlier in the century. General insurance was an additional source of income.

The Society's reserves had grown from £296 million in 1972 to £6.84 billion by 1998. A combination of the growth of the Society's reserves, the skills of its investment team and improved economic conditions provided an income from investments in 1998 of £263.2 million. The bonuses were the envy of competitors. Every year *Money Management* surveyed the performance of with-profits policies looking at 10, 15, 20 and 25-year terms. So in a five-year period, 20 league tables were produced. The 1998 survey revealed that over the previous five years, Royal London had appeared in the top ten in 18 of these tables and had been first no less than 11 times.[38] A *Money Management* survey the previous year had found that Royal London was the top life company in the UK in terms of financial strength.[39]

The concern over the expense ratio remained, however, and was as valid as it had been in 1872 when Joseph Degge was interrogated by the Royal Commissioners, just 11 years after the founding of the Society. In 1985 industrial branch premiums were £53.4 million and expenses £28.2 million, producing an industrial branch expense ratio of 52.9 per cent.[40] So in industrial branch more than half the premiums collected were being spent on providing the service. The more economic ordinary branch operations brought the Society's overall ratio in 1985 down to 41 per cent. By 1998 the overall ratio had dropped to 34.4 per cent. The shift towards ordinary branch continued with the average sum assured broadly reflecting the annual average earnings, suggesting that in many cases insurance was being taken out to provide a year's income on the death of the breadwinner. Industrial branch may have been in decline (43 per cent fewer policies were issued in 1998 than in 1972) but nearly 81,000 new policies were put on the books in 1998, with an average sum assured of less than £3,400. Many of these would have been top-ups where an existing policyholder felt able to increase the total cover, and so would not have involved an extra home visit from the agent, but when this was not the case, the Society was committing itself to call and collect premiums of less than £15 a month for many years.[41]

The future and cost-effectiveness of industrial branch, however, was to be swallowed up in a greater trauma. On 19 March 1999 the Board decided temporarily to stop selling life and pension policies, an event that was not overlooked by the following day's newspapers. Under the heading "Royal London suspends sales force on FSA probe", the *Independent* reported that "Royal London, the mutually-owned insurance firm, yesterday suspended its sales force after an investigation by the Financial Services Authority, the financial services watchdog. The firm said it was stopping its 1,900 financial advisers and managers from selling its life insurance and pension products and has ordered them to undergo a retraining programme. The move follows spot checks carried out during a routine visit of the firm by FSA inspectors in January." The sales force would be off the road for at least eight weeks and the "training will focus on improving the levels of compliance with the tougher standards being imposed on the industry…".

An extensive training and accreditation programme was put in place and the sales force returned to action in phases between July and the end of the year. Due process was followed within the FSA and in July 2001 the Society was fined £400,000 for breaches of rules relating to the sale of investment products primarily for the period between April 1996 and February 1999, the FSA acknowledging that Royal London had undertaken a radical and thorough overhaul of the business since the failures were identified – as well as the new training and accreditation programme, there had been a complete overhaul of the sales process, a sales monitoring unit had been introduced, commission-based sales had been abolished and the compliance function restructured. More than 80,000 sales had been reviewed and compensation offered to customers where appropriate.[42]

These problems were not unique to Royal London. Liverpool Victoria and Prudential in 1997, and Britannic in 1998, had all suspended their sales forces for retraining, and the Personal Investment Authority (PIA) had fined Liverpool Victoria £900,000 and Britannic £525,000. How had all this come about? One day a definitive history of the regulation of life assurance and pension companies under Financial Services Act 1986 (and later the Financial Services and Markets Act 2000) may be published, no doubt based upon a review of a massive amount of data. In the meantime, any conclusions can only be provisional.

The 1986 Act that came into force early in 1988 was the first comprehensive financial services legislation. It created self-regulation within a statutory framework. The overall regulator was the Securities and Investment Board (SIB) below which were self-regulating organisations that each regulated particular types of business. It was an offence to conduct investment business without being authorised by SIB or the relevant self-regulating organisation – IMRO dealt with those managing investments on behalf of others, and was RLAM's regulator, while life assurance and unit trusts were initially regulated by LAUTRO and FIMBRA, although they later merged to form the PIA.[43] The Financial Services and Markets Act 2000 replaced all of this with a statutory regime and the Financial Services Authority (FSA), a single regulator that also acquired the Bank of England's power to regulate banks and the prudential regulation of insurance firms under the Insurance Companies Act, previously exercised by the Insurance Directorate of HM Treasury.[44] Further radical changes in regulation are on the way because the Conservative/Liberal Democrat Coalition Government has announced that it plans to abolish the FSA by 2012.

The home services offices would have to concede with hindsight that they were slow in coming to terms with regulation. They had long since had training programmes for agents – the Society, for example, had introduced in 1977 a new and improved programme that was seen as a planned and systematic approach to ensure that all staff achieved the highest possible degree of competence and professionalism.[45] They believed that they had already done much of what would be required and in the early days, there was a feeling that the legislation was directed more at the activities of others. When the offices realised that they too were involved, they took time to grasp the fundamental nature of the changes that the regulators were by now demanding. When that too was understood, it was too late – the correct orders were coming from the bridge but the ship was already on a collision course. It is difficult to disagree with Howard Davies, the first chairman of the FSA, when he said in a speech in 1997:

> In retrospect, it would appear that the insurance industry did not take regulation particularly seriously in the early years of the Financial Services Act. Of course they appointed compliance officers and the other outward and visible signs of regulatory observance. But it is apparent that, by and large, organisations did not adjust their behaviour significantly to match the demands of the new environment and did not appreciate the consequences that might flow from their failure to do so. In other words, they did not appreciate the need to manage regulatory and reputational risk.[46]

The regulatory environment of the late 1990s was set by the so-termed 'pensions mis-selling' of the late 1980s and early 1990s. Major changes made to pensions in 1988 had the effect of enhancing any deficiencies that may already have existed in the selling of private pensions. Concerns had grown within Government during the 1980s about the long-term cost of state pensions and how occupational pension schemes disadvantaged workers who changed jobs frequently. The 1988 pension environment involved a phased cutback in the State Earnings Related Pension Scheme, the introduction of a new system by which an individual could contract out of SERPS in favour of a personal pension, and receive benefits from the Government for so doing, and a prohibition on making membership of a pension scheme a condition of an employee's service.[47] As a result, personal pensions tended to be a major contributor to the new business of life companies in the years that followed.

The industry (the issue extended far beyond the home service offices) ought to have been more alive to the risks being run by any member or potential member of an occupational pension scheme who decided to opt or transfer out of the scheme in favour of a private pension. These risks should have been fully explained to everyone who was contemplating doing so. That said, many of the customers were probably aware of the risks and the extent of the business was obvious to all, but there was no objection from the regulator for more than five years, a failing acknowledged by Howard Davies: "How on earth could the new regulators, put into place after the Financial Services Act 1986, have allowed this scandal to occur right under their freshly minted noses?" He went on to reply to his own question: "At the same time, the regulatory system put in place to oversee the industry was immature, and the regulators themselves were in many cases inexperienced and feeling their way. This did not foster a robust approach to policing compliance".

There were also grounds for believing that every working person having his or her own portable pension was an aspiration of the Conservative Government. To quote Howard Davies again:

> At the same time, the Government's reforms to the pensions framework created the structural conditions for rapid growth in private pensions sales which the industry was not slow to exploit. And the positive climate which surrounded the growth of private pensions certainly had an impact. Of course many of the arguments advanced for personal pensions – the importance of portable provision which matched the growing mobility of the labour force, the importance of pension frameworks which coped with periods in and out of work, etc. – all points valid in themselves, tended to encourage people to look less critically than they might have done at personal pension products.

Despite these mitigating factors, the outcome of the pensions review was that the providers of personal pensions (including Royal London), and independent financial advisers who had sold them during this period, were required to review all their sales and to put those who had opted out or transferred from an employer's scheme into the position that they would have been if they had joined or never left their employer's scheme. This involved buying them back into the employer's scheme (where this was possible) or topping-up the personal pension, or (where the individual had retired) augmenting the pension.

The scene was set and the pensions review was still fresh in the memory as regulators went about their business in the late 1990s. Regulation under the Financial Services Act required a conversion from agent to quasi-professional adviser. This was a huge step for many home service agents, however effective the training programmes provided by their employers. Perhaps it was a step too far. Many were dismissed for failing to achieve accreditation but some of those who were successful still experienced real difficulties in practice. They were used to exploring the customer's finances informally as part of the sales process but to demand detailed answers to a number of questions, and then to record them in writing was seen by many as an unnecessary intrusion into the customer's financial affairs, and they found it difficult to respond to customers who objected to providing this information.[48] The concept of recording in a letter to the customer reasons for a sale and the advice given did not come naturally to many and this was brought into sharp focus as regulators increasingly adopted the view that every sale was a mis-sale unless the documentation proved otherwise.[49] Some sales were compliant. Some, it had to be conceded, clearly were not. The debate was around the middle area – those sales that may well have been sound but that could not be demonstrated to be so because of the absence or inadequacy of documentation. Supporters argue that many of these met the customers' requirements and provided them with valuable benefits or protection. The critics are not convinced. Wherever the truth lay, one point could not be denied. Regulation was imposing significant additional financial burdens on the home service offices. This gave yet further weight to warnings, articulated long before the Financial Services Act, that the home service offices would need to adapt and change in the light of the cost of running the business.[50]

The 1990s ended with the retraining programme complete and the Royal London accredited sales force back at work delivering financial advice into customers' homes, and without the collapse of all computer systems worldwide that had been predicted by many as 1999 became 2000. The technology was still working as people returned to their desks after the New Year festivities. The need for the Society to adapt and change was somehow heightened by the arrival of the new millennium.

CHAPTER 13

Today's Fundamentals Begin to Appear

Provision of a national service on the doorstep of each home is expensive… Although inflationary pressures on expenses exist for ordinary life assurance, they are a greater problem in industrial assurance since the physical collection of a large number of relatively small premiums means that the business is labour intensive. Most companies have seen fairly significant rises in expense ratios in recent years and this has highlighted the need not merely to adopt very strict house-keeping methods but also to consider radical changes in structure and organisation to keep operating costs to a minimum.

William Forsey, Chief General Manager, Royal London,
address to the Chartered Insurance Institute, London (1981)

Royal London Asset Management operates externally as well as managing policyholder funds of Royal London. It has enjoyed its best year ever in the external market, winning seven new clients with total funds of £85m. It now has 29 pension fund clients with funds under management of nearly £774m out of a total £7.6bn. Key to the business's success is its long track record of strong investment performance.

Royal London, Report and Accounts (1998)[1]

In the years following the move to Colchester, over and above the developments referred to in the previous chapter, four of the fundamentals of Royal London today were put in place: a recognition that there are times when companies must be prepared to make radical changes; the presence on the Board of experienced independent non-executive directors; an asset management subsidiary that managed external as well as internal funds; and the Group chief executive.

The need to change had been articulated in a perceptive address given by William Forsey to the Chartered Insurance Institute in London early in 1981. An article based on the address appeared in *Post Magazine*[2] and a potted version was included in *The Royal London News*.[3] The messages it contained were such that he felt obliged to state that the views were entirely his own "and, whilst they may reflect to an extent the general views of my company, they certainly do not purport to speak for the industry as a whole". Although "the present industrial branch market is a very healthy one", Forsey felt that "the current period [was] a watershed for IB companies [industrial assurance offices]."[4] His audience was left in no doubt as to what he regarded as the biggest challenge: inflation was harmful to all industries but that was particularly so for life assurance that was unable to reprice its products except for new sales.[5]

Forsey's view was that the concept of home service would remain for the foreseeable future, and that there would continue to be a demand for savings by way of cash collected at the home. He felt that there would be enough cash for the next decade or so, even with the technological advances towards cashless transactions, the increasing use of credit cards and the increase in payment of wages direct to banks. He was convinced, however, that the nature of the organisations would have to be very different in ten or 20 years' time and that "the future for the industrial assurance companies was one of need to adapt and change". These words may appear unexceptional to the modern reader – of course an organisation needs to adapt to cope with changes in the environment in which it operates – but Forsey was speaking of an industry that had made only limited changes in over 120 years. He was going further and suggesting that industrial assurance (and perhaps even home service) might not survive beyond the foreseeable future.

Bill Forsey may have feared that since the retirement of Ernest Haynes too much management effort had been devoted to the relocation of the head office and that this, coupled with the untimely deaths and retirements, had slowed up the modernisation of Royal London. He worked tirelessly to continue Haynes' work, and on his retirement, the baton was gladly accepted by Michael Pickard and those who followed. The thinking of the Board clearly evolved – the language of the 1970s had been about rationalisation and making maximum use of modern administrative methods, suggesting that reform was seen as improving the current business. Gradually 'diversification' became an acceptable topic for discussion, with ways being explored of reducing Royal London's dependence on home service and the risk attached to operating in a narrow segment of the market. The various initiatives referred to in the previous chapter are indicative of the Board's awareness that the traditional Royal London model might not continue for ever to be in the interest of policyholders and members. As was reported in the press at the time, there were talks in 1996 between Royal London and Liverpool Victoria about a merger of the two organisations. They came to nothing but this was evidence that the Board did not feel itself restricted to tinkering with the existing operations but was prepared to consider radical measures.

The composition of the Board, the second of the fundamentals, had been evolving. Haynes had inherited in the 1950s the traditional Royal London model of a Board dominated by directors who were directly responsible for running the sales divisions. The impact of the changes that he encouraged the Board to make was seen by 1972 when there was a non-executive chairman and three other non-executive directors (all four of whom were retired executives), two senior managers from the Field but with no direct divisional responsibility, and three head office executives (the chief general manager, investment manager and solicitor). Stanley Goodall who had retired from executive duties in August 1969 remained on the Board as a non-executive director until 29 April 1980, the annual general meeting after his 70th birthday. When Goodall died in 1994, Michael Pickard wrote of his engaging manner and encyclopaedic memory of Royal London people and events: his "style was individual and intuitive. He cut a somewhat larger than life figure whose presence always enlivened an occasion".[6]

Lewis Cooke, the first independent non-executive director, was appointed in late 1980. This was a major departure from the way in which Royal London was managed and staff had to be reassured – a letter was sent to all of them by the secretary telling them that the directors felt "that the introduction to the Board of experience and knowledge from a wider reservoir will be advantageous in framing policy and monitoring progress" but that this would not "preclude the continued appointment of executive Directors in the future, nor indeed the appointment of non-executive Directors, from within our own ranks as hitherto".[7] This was particularly directed towards the Field where agents were recruited on the basis that those who did well could make it to the boardroom. For some, this was highly motivational. They had not welcomed the reduction of the number of seats on the Board available to them following the Haynes reforms and would have been even more concerned to learn that now they were also competing with people who they would have seen as total outsiders who knew nothing about the business. Cooke was a former director and general manager of National Westminster Bank who was awarded the OBE for his charitable work in connection with mental health.[8]

By the end of 1989 Pickard, as executive chairman, was presiding over a board that included three independent non-executive directors with a wide range of experience: Norman Wooding was a former deputy chairman of Courtaulds,[9] Bob Erith, a stockbroker and, like Wooding, a director of several companies,[10] and Tom Slee an accountant and finance director of Costains.[11] They brought different perspectives to the management of the Society which Wooding saw as "a rather enclosed regime" that, at least by the standards he had experienced in industry, tended to the hierarchical, formal and paternalistic: "Bob Erith and I sought to inject other attitudes and practices, and I have to say that the Board was on the whole receptive, if sometimes a little shocked at the open style which we adopted." They were able to influence the composition of the Board:

> *When the last of the former executives who had later been a non-executive director retired the question of a successor arose.[12] My colleagues were minded to seek a retired insurance person; I on the other hand, felt that someone with personal experience as a finance executive in business would be an asset. The response was that we already have four actuaries on the Board; my rejoinder 'that is the reason for my recommendation' was greeted with cold dismay.*

Wooding was a persuasive man and in due course Slee, who had been a finance director of two public companies, was appointed – he "brought new insights to our affairs and was a great success". Modern governance standards meant that Wooding and Erith both retired after nine years in 1996 when "the Chairman, Michael Pickard, was keen to find new non-executives who could be candidates for Chairman when he retired a few years later. Bob and I had the satisfaction of helping in the search and playing some part in what has turned out to be a strengthened Board, and the Society has gone from strength to strength".[13]

The lunching arrangements at Colchester provided a good example of the hierarchical, formal and paternalist tendencies. Over and above what was an excellent staff restaurant, there were three dining rooms. The directors lunched within the executive suite on the fourth floor, the officials lunched on the first floor (junior officials at 12.15, senior officials at 1.15), while the assistant departmental managers and departmental managers lunched in a third room, again at different times. There was no intermingling. Nor was it a case of grabbing something off the buffet at a convenient moment and finding a space to sit, but rather assembling at the appointed hour, sitting in the seat to which your seniority entitled you, and being served a three-course meal by waitresses. Attendance was not compulsory – the informality of the staff restaurant was always available as an alternative. Similar arrangements were not uncommon in other long-established British institutions but they probably survived in Royal London longer than elsewhere. The 'messes' were finally abolished in the late 1990s.

The third of the fundamentals was first mentioned in the 1989 annual report and accounts:

> *The Society's investments are now managed by a wholly owned subsidiary, Royal London Asset Management (RLAM). The success of the Society's investment performance over the years across the full range of our insurance and unit trust funds has led the Board to the view that RLAM is well equipped to offer its services in the wider marketplace. Accordingly we can offer the investment services of RLAM to outside bodies with confidence, and are actively seeking external funds for investment management.*

The story had begun in August 1987 when Cyril Brill, the investment manager and a director since 1978, had informally canvassed the idea with his Board colleagues. Brill had joined Royal London in 1957 when Friends Provident, where he had qualified as an actuary, relocated from London to Dorking – a move that did not appeal to him. After two years as head of the actuarial department, he transferred to the investment area. This was to be for only a year, but he never returned to actuarial – he had found his true role. As he explained:

> *Investment presented me with a fascinating challenge. I learned about many different industries and products, to the extent that no matter whom I met I was able to talk with some knowledge about their own industry. The main challenge was having to follow events worldwide in both politics and economics. Anything which might affect the market, for example the Cuban Missile Crisis, had to be monitored and I then had to predict the outcome and make my decision to buy or sell on the basis of that prediction.[14]*

Brill's proposal for an investment management subsidiary that managed external as well as the Society's funds gradually found support and in January 1988 the Board agreed to the basic principle. It was felt that the service should be capable of generating a profit for the benefit of the members. The basic infrastructure was already in place and the extra costs involved in acquiring and managing external funds would be marginal. The Board would also have the opportunity to seek a Stock Exchange quotation for the asset management company at some stage in the future. There was concern at the time that the Society's ability to expand by acquisition might be hampered by its mutual status, and the fact that share options could not be used to incentivise staff. A quoted asset management company was seen as a way of addressing these perceived concerns. History proved them to be misplaced, and RLAM remains a wholly-owned subsidiary to this day.

After the Board's approval, further details had to be resolved, computer systems installed that were capable of administering external funds and providing the information that clients would require, and a marketing executive recruited. It was envisaged that the initial focus would be on property – the performance of the property investment team under Rodney Pollard had been particularly impressive and the success of the Triton Court development had given them a presence in the market.

The search for external clients began in early 1989. At first it was an uphill struggle. The multi-stage process initially involved persuading actuaries and pension fund consultants to allow RLAM to come and talk to them about the impressive performance of its team of investment managers. When pension funds and other institutional investors were considering appointing a new asset manager, they turned to these intermediaries for advice, and the hope was that they would be sufficiently impressed by RLAM to include it on lists of potential managers they submitted to their clients. For a long time, this did not happen – as the marketing executive reported to the RLAM board, the opinion seemed "to be that they would rather someone else's clients were first to try us out". Then at last RLAM appeared on some lists, although at first this led only to more abortive work and frustration. The client generally asked all the listed managers to complete a comprehensive questionnaire, and based on the replies, established a short list of those who would be invited to attend 'a beauty parade' and make a presentation to the trustees. After all the time spent completing the questionnaire, rehearsing the presentation and preparing the answer to every question that could possibly be asked, it was little consolation to learn that, although the trustees had been very impressed by RLAM, they had been beaten into second place and another manager had been appointed.

It was August 1990 before RLAM acquired its first external client – a £10 million property portfolio for the pension trustees of the Devonport Royal Dockyard. This was not a good time to be out looking for new business and by December 1990 the UK was in recession: GDP recorded its sharpest drop in ten years, retail sales were falling away, inflation was in double figures, interest rates had been as high as 15 per cent, unemployment was rising and property prices were crashing, exposing many to negative equity, repossessions and bankruptcy. But RLAM persevered with its marketing, more new clients gradually followed, and in 1994 it was able to pay its first dividend to the Society. By 31 December 1994 RLAM had ten property clients – four direct and six with investments in a property unit trust established by RLAM for institutional investors who wanted exposure to the commercial property market without direct ownership – and eight securities clients, six direct and two invested in funds managed by RLAM. Just four years later RLAM had 29 external clients providing funds under management of nearly £774 million. A successful diversification from home service had been achieved and a link with the past re-established – RLAM's City office was at Triton Court.

The fourth fundamental was the group chief executive. Mike Yardley was born in Maldon, Essex in 1956 and, from the local grammar school, won a place at Cambridge to read natural sciences. He decided on a gap year and, when the money ran out, took a temporary job with Pearl Assurance in Southampton. His first day was spent locating files in the basement. He was promoted to issuing general branch policies, although this demanded little more than transferring the data from the proposal onto the policy document. He began to have doubts about university – a degree, even from Oxbridge, was no guarantee of a job and he had no serious aspirations to be a scientist. His manager at Pearl, realising that this trainee administrative clerk might be destined for bigger things within the industry, suggested that he consider becoming an actuary. The idea appealed to Yardley: "Although I had never come across an actuary while I was at school, I believe in fate and there was an opportunity that opened-up. Having decided not to go to university, I needed to get a profession. Actuaries were and still are highly regarded."[15] So he relocated to Pearl's actuarial department in London and started studying for the profession's examinations. But calculating surrender values and the other tasks assigned to the students was little more stimulating than issuing general branch policies, although being asked to analyse the success of a TV advertising campaign was a welcome diversion.

As a part-qualified actuary, he was attracted in 1978 by an advertisement for a trainee investment analyst at Royal London. He took the job, and was at once enthused by the work. "After I joined the investment business, I found it fascinating. I was 21 years old and sitting across the table from a chief executive of a major company quizzing him about his business and his strategy. It was a foundation course in business."[16] His role was to research and write reports on sectors and companies so that decisions could be made on shares to be bought or sold. The investment team at Royal London was small, and young Yardley was soon dealing as well as analysing. In time he crossed the divide altogether and became a fund manager. He qualified as an actuary and was appointed deputy investment manager in 1985. He was active in the creation and expansion of RLAM, and a director from the beginning, taking the lead in many of the early meetings with external actuaries and consultants and participating in his fair share of beauty parades.

At the time, it was rare for external applicants to be considered for senior positions in companies like Royal London. This meant that by the late 1980s the next chief executive was probably already employed by the Society. Many who had worked with Yardley saw him as a strong candidate. Directors were impressed by what he had learnt from his discussions with chief executives and hearing so many of them talk about their businesses, strategy and plans. Here they felt was somebody who saw and articulated the big picture and was not diverted by irrelevancies.

The fear was that this high-flier, City investment manager would be enticed away and lost to Royal London. Yardley was appointed a director of the Society in November 1989 in the hope that this would encourage him to stay. It also meant that the Board would have the benefit of his input on the wide range of issues discussed by the directors. The appointment came as a great surprise to him – he was only 32, and there was no obvious vacancy as Cyril Brill, the investment director and his boss, was remaining on the Board. When Brill retired on 31 January 1993, Yardley became chief investment manager of the Society and chairman of RLAM. The early promise was confirmed and, when the time came, the Board was satisfied that he was indeed Michael Pickard's successor. Mike Yardley was appointed deputy chief executive in 1997 and chief executive in April 1998. This all happened, he suggested, "because of a few decisions I took fairly casually when I left school".[17]

While Royal London had been putting in place these fundamentals, there had been some interesting developments elsewhere in the industry.

CHAPTER 14

The Transformation

1999–2001

One of the greatest challenges which we face is how to build on the strengths of Royal London's past and ensure that what we are doing is still right for customers today. This applies as much to what Royal London stands for as the products and services which we offer.

Mike Yardley, Chief Executive, Royal London Group (February 2000)[1]

The transformation which the Group has undertaken leaves us well positioned for the ongoing challenge of increasing the value of the business. We are more broadly based in terms of our income and distribution and we have strengthened our capabilities as a manufacturer of products. We will continue to pursue opportunities to develop our business and are confident that the Group will be able to deliver enhanced value for members.

Hubert Reid, Chairman, Royal London Group (March 2002)[2]

The summer of 1996 saw England lose to Germany on a penalty shoot-out at Wembley in the semi-final of Euro 96 and Redgrave and Pinsent win the United Kingdom's only gold medals at the Atlanta Olympics.[3] It also saw much corporate activity in the insurance industry – following on from General Accident's acquisition of Provident Mutual the previous year, Royal Insurance was merging with Sun Alliance and the Halifax Building Society was taking over Clerical Medical. But on Friday 9 August 1996 the only topic of conversation in the corridors of power of the home service offices was the news that Refuge and United Friendly were planning to combine. The merged company, to be called United Assurance Group plc, would have a premium income of £445 million and assets of £6.5 billion, making it the fourth largest participant in the home service sector.

The factors that prompted the merger came as no great surprise, the Listing Particulars in due course explaining that:

> *Refuge and United Friendly are major participants in the home service sector in the United Kingdom, which is characterised by the sale of life assurance, pensions and savings products through a network of agents and advisers calling at policyholders' homes. The target market of the home service sector covers over 60 per cent of households in the UK. The home service sector, in common with other areas of the life and pensions market, is having to address the challenges created by greater competition, increased regulatory costs, the requirements for fuller disclosure and, until recently, declining new business volumes, particularly in industrial branch business.*[4]

The boards of both companies believed that the merger would create a more competitive business, with enhanced prospects for the benefit of both shareholders and policyholders.

The *Independent* felt that the merger highlighted the long-running contractions being suffered by the insurance industry, which was being hit by rising costs and over-supply in an increasingly competitive market, and quoted George Mack, the chief-executive-in-waiting of the new organisation: "We intend this merger to obtain significant economies of scale".[5] While shareholders, competitors and the financial press were debating the perceived merits of the proposals, the staff were confronted with rather more personal issues. It was envisaged that the United Friendly head office near Southwark Bridge, where there was a workforce of 650, and many of the 279 district offices of both companies would close, and that around a quarter of the 7,122 employees of the two companies would lose their jobs.[6] This was not a good time to be working in insurance – 4,000 jobs in the UK were to be lost as a result of the Royal Insurance and Sun Alliance merger and *The Sunday Times* suggested that up to 100,000 jobs in the insurance industry would be axed over the next five years as the sector experienced an unprecedented 'shake-up'.[7] How times had changed from when insurance was seen as a job for life.

To the premium paying public in the mid-1990s, Refuge, United Friendly and Royal London were similar organisations – all three sold life assurance, pensions and savings products and general insurance policies through employed agents who called on policyholders' homes. At one time, Refuge had been the largest – in 1938, for example, Refuge had premium incomes of £6.0 million (industrial branch) and £4.7 million (ordinary branch) compared with Royal London's £5.1 million and £1.9 million – but by 1995, Royal London was larger than either of the merging companies.

Table No. 5

Comparison of Royal London, Refuge and United Friendly in 1995

	Life & pensions premium income £m	Assets £bn
Royal London	400	5.2
Refuge	217	3.5
United Friendly	228	3.0

There were, however, significant differences in the histories and corporate structures of the three companies. Refuge was one of the earliest industrial assurance offices.[8] It had been formed in 1858 in much the same way as Liverpool Victoria and Royal Liver when a group of "men of quite ordinary stature, whether socially, industrially or intellectually"[9] came together in Manchester and, for reasons that are not recorded, decided to form a friendly society. The driving force behind the venture seems to have been James Proctor, born in Preston in 1820, a 'general agent' (travelling salesman) and journeyman tailor. His colleagues were from as far afield as Broadbottom, Dukinfield, Oldham, Pemberton, Stockport and Wigan. Little is known about them, although there is no evidence that anyone had any insurance experience or that Refuge was a breakaway from another society. Proctor was on the committee of management from the beginning but did not appear to have any wider responsibilities until 1870 when he became general manager and later managing director. The Robins brothers, who were grocers and corn dealers, were the first officers of The Refuge Friend in Deed Life Assurance and Sick Fund Friendly Society – Joe was treasurer and George secretary – and the office was George's home at 15 Hart Street, Manchester.

With one exception, the development of Refuge closely resembles that of Royal London. Severe financial problems in the early years – without generous contributions from the Robins brothers, Refuge would have failed – were followed by a period of great expansion toward the end of the century. By 1900 the premium income exceeded £1.2 million, more than 20 per cent of which was ordinary branch. Like Royal London, Refuge began by offering sickness cover but soon closed the sickness department, and later was keen to mark its ever-increasing success by creating an imposing head office. A site on the corner of Oxford Street and Whitworth Street in Manchester was acquired and in 1890 Alfred Waterhouse, the best-known architect of the time, was retained.[10] Waterhouse, whose work included the Natural History Museum in South Kensington, Manchester Town Hall and the Prudential's head office in Holborn, produced a magnificent red brick and terracotta building, later extended along Oxford Street by his son with a 217-foot tower. The building, now the Palace Hotel, is of a "very large and ornate eclectic design with French Renaissance accent and some Baroque features" and represents a "conspicuous landmark and probably the apogee of 'Manchester style' late C19 commercial architecture".[11]

Where Refuge differed from Royal London was the timing of its conversion and its structure. Even as a friendly society, Refuge had flirted with a more corporate status and raised capital by issuing shares of 2s 6d to its founders. In 1864 Refuge converted from friendly society to proprietary company with, so far can be seen, little or no opposition. The members of the committee of management became the first directors and significant shareholders. As a consequence:

> ... quite soon after its foundation the Refuge became a family concern in that not only the work itself but also the controlling interests became the province of a number of individuals whose successors carried on in their place. Some very large shareholdings came to be built up, which tended to become unwieldy; and it was thought wise to broaden the basis of ownership by putting the shares on the market, which meant, of course, obtaining a Stock Exchange quotation.[12]

The family concept was seen at the top of the company. At the time of its centenary in 1958, when the annual premium income exceeded £20 million and reserves were approaching £140 million, the board of Refuge included three great grandsons of James Proctor and the grandsons of Henry Thornton and Robert Moss, two of the pioneers of Refuge who had joined in 1862 and who together had 86 years' service on the company's board.[13] Until the appointment in 1966 of Hal Sever, the managing director had always been a member of one of the five founding families. Sever, who spent all his working life at Refuge having joined as an actuarial student, was well known outside life assurance circles. He had played football at school but a friend persuaded him to turn out for the 3rd XV of the local rugby club. With his speed and weight, he was an immediate success: within two weeks he was in the 1st XV, joining Sale the next season and scoring seven tries in his first two games. He was to play ten times for England, scoring a try in the first ever victory over New Zealand, and scoring in every match of England's Triple Crown winning team of 1936–37.[14]

The second half of the twentieth century saw Refuge expand its product range to incorporate general insurance business in the 1950s and unit-linked business in the 1980s. General insurance was transacted, initially through the acquisition of Federated Employers Insurance Association but later by Refuge itself.[15] Unit-linked policies were successfully added to broaden the range of products available from the sales force. They were a success but Refuge was beginning to feel the pressures to which all home service companies were subject and by the late 1980s regulatory burdens were making industrial branch uneconomic for both customers and the company. To facilitate the provision of additional products, the structure of the group was changed with the formation of Refuge Group plc, which became the quoted holding company. This heralded the formation of RLJ Finance Limited which was to provide loans to policyholders and the acquisition of a chain of estate agents, with the intention of creating a one-stop-shop for all the financial needs of clients. Like many others trying to go down this route, Refuge found that clients still preferred to pick and choose their adviser for a particular service, and neither venture flourished.

Waterhouse's Victorian masterpiece had become increasingly difficult to modernise and it was decided that the time had come to discontinue its historical association with Manchester and to move to a new purpose-built office. Fulshaw Hall, a 300-year-old property alongside the A34 between Wilmslow and Alderley Edge, was acquired in 1983 and, amongst the trees and grassy banks of its parkland grounds, a three-storey, 100,000 square foot, head office complex was built. Extensive landscaping ensured that the building did not intrude on the local environment and provided attractive working conditions. The move into the award-winning building took place in November 1987.[16]

To help the sales force and spread the name-recognition of the company, Refuge made it first venture into sports sponsorship in 1983 when Refuge Assurance National Tennis Championships came into being. There were then two one-day cricket competitions – the Gillette Cup, introduced in 1963, a knock-out competition with the final at Lord's in early September, and from 1969, the John Player League in which the first class counties competed in a league on Sunday afternoons. In 1987 Refuge became the sponsor of the Sunday league and an end of season play-off was introduced, known as the Refuge Assurance Cup. At the peak of sponsorship, an estimated two million viewers watched the matches every week on BBC2 and were exposed to the Refuge name. In 1992, however, the TV contract was switched to Sky, then in its very early days, and with the audience dropping to less than 50,000, Refuge discontinued the sponsorship at the end of the season.

United Friendly, Refuge's future partner, was formed on 15 January 1908, at the height of the Royal London conversion debate.[17] A company from the very beginning, it was a breakaway from Royal Liver although the concerns in Liverpool may have been mitigated by the fact that initially United Friendly offered only general insurance and was not authorised to issue life policies until 1919.[18] Edwin Balding, the founder of United Friendly, joined Royal Liver as a deputy collector in 1893 at the age of 17 and ten years later was district manager at New Cross. His father was a Royal Liver agent and his grandfather had been sent by Royal Liver to manage the London office at 77 Bridge Road, Lambeth in 1861 when Joseph Degge left to found Royal London.

In June 1906 Edwin Balding was one of the three founders of the Reliance Fire & Accident Corporation Limited with offices in Farringdon Street, although he only resigned from Royal Liver a year later – a letter sent to him from his co-directors suggests that in the meantime he had been recruiting Royal Liver agents to work part-time for Reliance.[19] He soon left Reliance, however, in part because he did not feel that he had been given a free hand as agency manager and, encouraged by letters from Reliance staff regretting his departure, decided to form a company that he would be allowed to manage. To do so, he would need to attract investors – the only capital that he possessed was the proceeds of the sale of his Royal Liver collecting books. Only 6,165 of United Friendly's 20,000 shares of £1 each were taken up in the first year and only half of those were fully paid. Balding's fellow directors were an insurance manager, an umbrella manufacturer, a printer, a solicitor and a 'gentleman'. There were 50 shareholders, with most holdings ranging between £1 and £500, although Balding acquired 778 and John Wood, the gentlemen director, 1,000 shares. Among the other shareholders was a hop factor, a clerk, a pork butcher, a steamship broker, an auctioneer and a couple of licensed victuallers. The company opened for business with a staff of seven but the policies were well received – the premium income for the first year was £2,851 and this had risen by 1915 to £18,866.

The historians of United Friendly reported that physically:

> Edwin Richard Balding was a striking man. Of medium height, stocky in build, the first impression he gave was that of a military man, with his air of authority, straight-backed carriage

and carefully waxed moustache. He exuded an air of complete self confidence, and encouraged others to do the same, even if sometimes it was a confidence neither he or they really felt. A man meticulous in his own appearance – he was never seen out-of-doors without a hat – he insisted upon the same standards not only from his family, but later from his employees. Despite his sometimes bristly, almost ferocious, appearance he was a kindly man. From even a very early age he displayed a knowledge and understanding of human nature, coupled with a deep compassion and respect for the less fortunate members of society.[20]

Balding's compassion and extrovert personality were well illustrated during those grim days of World War I when London experienced its first air raids. The policies provided no cover where the property damage was caused by enemy action but Balding would visit areas that had suffered over-night from a bombing raid by Zeppelins "with his pockets full of pound notes, gathered from goodness knows where" so that every United Friendly policyholder had something to relieve his loss and provide his family with shelter.[21]

In 1930 United Friendly moved into 42 Southwark Bridge Road, its head office until the merger, although when the building could not be further extended it was demolished and rebuilt in the 1980s. Premium income tripled between 1921 and 1931, and 1934 was the year, according to the *Insurance Mail*, "when United Friendly emerged from its teething period, reached healthy youth and could look forward to successful manhood".[22] During the 1930s Balding acquired a Rolls Royce and a uniformed chauffer of such bulk that engineers had to modify the steering column to enable him to perform his duties. By 1939 United Friendly had an office in every city and major town and between 1946 and 1958 the turnover increased from £10 million to £58 million.

United Friendly had only four managing directors. Edwin Balding remained in post until his death in 1941 and was succeeded by his son, Richard Courtney Balding ('RCB') whose brothers, Noel and Donald, were also on the board. At United Friendly's core was its ethos as a family company. Dinner dances for the staff were regular events up and down the country and were always attended by the directors. It was not unusual for successive generations of a family to give the whole of their working lives to the business. Until he was finally persuaded to make way for more efficient methods, RCB made it his practice to hand out the weekly pay packets to his head office staff with a personal 'thank you', even when some hundreds of staff were employed and regardless of the length of the queue up the stairs to the wages office. In contrast with his more flamboyant father, RCB was a quieter personality, even shy in his early years, although this hid his strength of character and astute understanding of people. His steady leadership was exactly what was required to consolidate the company after the first precarious decades. He had taken to heart some ungenerous remarks made about his upstart company at an Industrial Life Office Association meeting and carried a small notebook in his breast pocket in which he recorded year by year the progress of premium income for United Friendly and its competitors. He took quiet satisfaction every time United Friendly moved up a place in his private league table of ILOA offices, sharing this information in his speeches at staff functions, where the news would be received with much pride and cheering.

RCB retired in 1978 after 37 years as managing director and was succeeded by John Rampe, a grandson of Edwin Balding. RCB could look back on a business very considerably expanded and now on a sound and secure footing. He remained chairman until his death in 1980 and was as keen as ever to see the latest weekly figures for each branch. Rampe maintained the traditions of the company while promoting the introduction of modern management methods. The business continued to expand – from 1982 its shares were quoted on the unlisted securities market and in 1991 it was floated on the London Stock Exchange. In 1986 Richard Edwin Balding ('REB'), RCB's son, was appointed managing director. Like all family members before him, REB enjoyed a good grounding in the business, serving in head office departments and in the field as an agent in Croydon, an assistant manager in Epsom and manager of the Maidstone and Sevenoaks districts. REB continued the process of modernisation, assisted by George Mack whom he recruited as finance director. By 1996 the company had made good progress, but the management was confronted with the problems that beset the industry: the cost of providing a door-to-door collection service was proving harder to justify while the regulatory tightening of the sales process was making the sale of relatively small premium policies increasingly uneconomic. Despite the inevitable dilution of the proud traditions of this family company, the United Friendly board agreed that it was time for change.

United Assurance Group plc came into being on 16 October 1996 when the merger offer contained in the Listing Particulars 'went unconditional' following the passing at special general meetings of the required resolutions, acceptances having been received from most of the shareholders. John Cudworth, the chief executive of Refuge, became chairman of United Assurance, Arthur Ewen, the chairman of United Friendly, was deputy chairman and REB was vice-chairman. Initially, Refuge and United Friendly had equal representation on the board. George Mack, the group finance director and deputy chief executive of United Friendly, was appointed chief executive although a little over a year later he left to pursue opportunities elsewhere. He had come under heavy pressure from investors irritated by the Group's slow handling of the merger: sales were falling, the share price was significantly underperforming the sector and consensus was lacking in the boardroom where it was proving difficult to establish a common understanding of the way forward.

As soon as successors with wide industry experience had been recruited, Cudworth followed Mack out of the company, and the board was restructured. Andrew Longhurst, a former chief executive and chairman of the Cheltenham & Gloucester Building Society and director of Lloyds Bank and Lloyds TSB, was appointed chairman and Alan Frost who, after roles with London & Manchester and Sun Life, had been investment director and then managing director of Abbey Life, became chief executive. Early in 1999 United Assurance was employing more than 3,300 in its field force, nearly 2,000 less than when the companies merged, 200 of which were temporary staff. On 16 April it was announced that a further 1,000 jobs would be cut, spread across the 110 branches. From 1 May the sale of industrial branch policies ceased and the field force was restructured into separate sales and collection operations and, as pressures of scale progressively favoured the larger general insurance providers, United Assurance decided to outsource its general insurance.

Changes were continuing to take place at Royal London. In January 1999 Stephen Shone was appointed group finance director. Born in 1957 in Wallasey on the Wirral, not far across the Mersey from where Joseph Degge spent his teenage years, he was always 'good at sums' with a feel for numbers, and it was probably no surprise that accountancy emerged from a careers discussion at Wirral Grammar School. With a degree in accountancy and economics from Hull University, he joined KPMG. The article in *Connections* that welcomed him to Royal London reported that:

> *Since qualifying as a chartered accountant with KPMG, Stephen's career has been spent within the life industry, including the Prolific Group, which he led through their demerger from Provincial Insurance. Over the last nine years he has worked for Irish Life, splitting his time between St Albans and Dublin, and managing a variety of subsidiaries including the second largest bank in Hungary. More recently [as group chief finance officer] he was key architect in merging Irish Life with Irish Permanent to form one of the largest financial services companies in Southern Ireland.*[23]

He had stressed to the author of the article that his job was more than simply chief accountant: "It's a much broader role, working closely with Mike Yardley on strategic development to make the company more profitable for the future". He was to waste no time in proving the accuracy of this statement.

On 9 July 1999 Michael Pickard retired after almost 42 years with Royal London, 22 of them on the Board, five as chief executive and 11 as chairman. When he joined the Society, the premium income was less than £14 million and the reserves £121 million. When he became a director, they had risen to £35.7 million and £426 million. In 1998 the premium income was £514.7 million (including general branch premiums of £31.9 million) and the reserves were £6.8 billion. Pickard had been deputy chairman of the Association of British Insurers, and chairman of its Life Insurance Council, and vice-president of the Chartered Institute of Insurers. He was chairman of the Colchester Business Enterprise Agency and a member of the council of the University of Essex and the board of the local health trust. Mike Yardley praised his predecessor for the very high standards that he set for himself, his management team and Royal London as a whole. Sir Norman Wooding referring to the increasingly unfashionable combination of chairman and chief executive – for 10 of the 11 years Pickard had combined the two roles – and suggested that:

> *Michael's tenure was characterised by two features which mitigated against the criticisms often voiced about such a combination of roles. He was more than usually attentive to the views of all his Board colleagues; and his approach to decisions was invariably conditioned by the answer to the question 'what is in the best interest of the society and its members?'*[24]

Pickard's sporting career had continued into senior management – in 1992 he won the Royal London squash tournament for the sixth time.

Hubert Reid was appointed chairman – he had been a non-executive director since April 1996 and deputy chairman from January 1997. A former managing director and then chairman of the Boddington Group, he was chairman of Enterprise Inns and a non-executive director of several other companies. The discussions around the board table during the autumn of 1999 were dominated by two topics – issues arising from the retraining of the sales force following the suspension of selling[25] and the future of Royal London. At the review of the Group's strategy undertaken by the Board in the autumn of 1999, Reid recalled:

> [We] *identified Royal London's key strengths – a strong financial position, investment returns which regularly exceeded those of its peer group, excellent product performance and a long tradition of providing advice to customers in their homes. Our analysis also highlighted matters which needed to be addressed – a strong asset management capability which was under-utilised, a cost*

base which was too high relative to the level of sales, and an over-reliance on the direct sales force as the only method of distribution. The Board's conclusion was that without action Royal London's financial strength would be placed under a strain.[26]

It was important to involve the management in the challenges that had to be faced, and one of the most significant meetings in the history of the Society was held in the University Arms Hotel, Cambridge, in November 1999. The 140 senior managers who attended received a stark message from Yardley and Shone: the future of Royal London was at stake. The challenges facing the Society were described in a video shown to all employees as part of the cascade of information after the meeting, and the December edition of *Connections*, which had replaced the *Royal Londoner* as the house journal, carried a post-meeting interview with the chief executive and finance director. The message was simple and no punches were pulled:

> *Royal London has considerable capital strength. In finance terms we have a strong balance sheet – in layman's terms you could say that we have a lot of money in the bank. It is that capital which supports our good product performance, and means that we can continue to say to policyholders that Royal London is among the most financially strong insurance companies in the UK... But our operating performance is weak. In financial terms, our profit and loss account each year is showing a loss. We are having to take some of that money out of the bank each year, if you like, using our free assets to cover our operating loss. What we must all remember is that our capital – our free assets – belongs to our policyholders. We are in business to add value for our policyholders. If we are to continue to add value then we must ensure that we eliminate our operating loss [that] occurs because of a gap between our costs and our income. So, simply put, we need to reduce our costs and increase our income. It is the combination of both that will deliver results.*[27]

Every manager left Cambridge knowing that he or she had to seek more cost-effective and efficient ways of operating. It was recognised that this might prompt job losses. Most of those at the meeting had attended many management meetings during their careers but there was a consensus that this was different, the position was serious and that action needed to and would happen.

At the time of the Cambridge conference, there had been some press reports linking Britannic Assurance with a possible bid for United

Assurance, but in due course it was announced that there would be no bid at present. So far as the public was concerned, things went quiet. In fact early in October 1999 Mike Yardley had dinner with Alan Frost to discuss common problems and the possibilities of joint ventures between United Assurance and Royal London. Following on from this, there were further meetings that also involved Stephen Shone and his opposite number. A rapport had been established and these discussions proved to be the groundwork for something more than a joint venture. From early January 2000 highly confidential negotiations were taking place between Royal London and United Assurance. The Royal London team was led by Stephen Shone – there were countless meetings in crowded rooms full of lawyers, investment bankers, consulting actuaries and tax advisers. The Financial Services Authority was consulted. By 18 February the basics of a deal by which Royal London would acquire United Assurance had been agreed and this was approved by the Royal London Board, subject to a number of outstanding issues. Secrecy had so far been maintained, but later that day a rumour about the deal appeared on an internet site for private investors. The *Sunday Telegraph* had become interested in the story and reported on 20 February that a deal was imminent. On 21 February, the day on which the purchase of Norwich Union for £7.5 billion by CGU (the company created when Commercial Union and General Accident merged in 1998) was announced, United Assurance issued a stock exchange statement confirming that talks were taking place. Those talks and a great deal of detailed work had continued throughout the weekend and shortly before midnight on 21 February the deal was finalised. An announcement was made at 7.30 the following morning.

In the formal recommended offer document that was sent to United Assurance's shareholders on 7 March 2000, Longhurst referred to the new business strategy and reorganisation and acknowledged that, although progress had been made in a number of areas, sales performance had been "adversely affected by the reorganisation and training programmes necessary to meet tough regulatory requirements".[28] The *Wall Street Journal* was rather more direct:

> *Investors and analysts hailed the deal as the best solution for the troubled United Assurance, the result of what its own chief executive, Alan Frost, called the 'disastrous' merger between door-to-door insurers Refuge Assurance and United Friendly in 1996. A bungled integration of the two companies' sales forces halted new business and even left many premiums uncollected, leading to a tumble in sales. Over the past 12 months, its share price has dropped by more [than] half to as low as 220 pence.[29]*

The United Assurance board had considered a number of alternatives for enhancing shareholder value and unanimously recommended shareholders to accept the Royal London offer. In due course they did, and the transaction – the largest takeover of a listed company by a mutual – was finalised on 19 April 2000.[30]

The enlarged Royal London now had a premium income of around £800 million, total assets of some £18 billion and over three million customers.[31] There was also great potential to benefit from substantial economies of scale and synergies – the head offices, administrative functions and investment management teams of Royal London and United Assurance could be combined; it was hoped that a reorganisation of the merged sales force of 1,750 advisers and 175 area offices would be able to produce a more cost-effective structure; and, subject to having obtained the appropriate approvals, the life funds could be merged that would create further administrative and financial efficiencies. The increased scale of funds under management gave RLAM a stature that could only enhance further growth, and this strong investment capability would support a wider range of products for the sales force.

In return for the £1,557 million paid for United Assurance, Royal London acquired assets and the potential to create further value by integrating the two businesses. Included within the assets of United Assurance were nearly five million in-force policies and Royal London would now be entitled to charge the Refuge and United Friendly life funds for administering these policies. The assets including the future profits from administering the in-force policies were valued at £1,611 million, £54 million more than the price paid for United Assurance. In his review in the report and accounts for 2000, the group finance director addressed the value being created:

> Immediately following the acquisition, we set about planning the integration of the two businesses identifying total potential annualised savings of approximately £97m. The integration programme is now well into implementation phase and our latest forecasts and plans show potential savings of at least that level. Of the total cost savings planned, approximately £51m represent savings to the cost of servicing existing policies. Using the same valuation methodology as is applied to the valuation of the present value of in-force business, we estimate the value of these servicing cost savings to be approximately £250m over a 10 year period. In addition to the above, Royal London will benefit from enhanced revenues from the asset management and general insurance businesses acquired. The Board has estimated the value of this enhanced revenue to be in the region of £50m.[32]

So the Royal London policyholders saw a benefit of £350 million from the acquisition – £1,557 million of their money had been invested and they received assets of £1,611 million, cost savings worth £250 million and the potential to enhance two areas of the business to the tune of £50 million.

The offer document said little about redundancies, merely commenting that some were to be expected. *The Times* provided its readers with an estimate: "United employs 3,000, while Royal London employs 3,100. The industry benchmark for job losses in such mergers is between 25 per cent and 35 per cent, analysts said, which would see up to 2,100 of the combined work force axed".[33] As Mike Yardley later acknowledged:

> ... [a] *particularly troubling aspect of the year was the redundancies which followed on from the integration of UAG into Royal London. The analysis of cost savings arising from the integration led us to the conclusion that a number of redundancies were inevitable if we were to deliver benefits to policyholders. However, that did not make it any easier to make the decision, nor did it reduce the distress for those directly affected. We endeavoured to give the greatest possible support to employees, particularly through the provision of extensive careers counselling and advice services.*[34]

One of the two areas that would particularly suffer had already been heralded – by March 2001 the 1,750 agents had been reduced to 1,000 and the 175 offices to 40, with 18 smaller satellite offices. The agents were backed up by four regional directors, 40 area managers, 240 sales managers and development supervisors and 160 sales support staff. The other area came as a terrible shock to most of the employees involved. The functions carried out in Royal London House, Colchester and Refuge House, Wilmslow were almost identical – sales management and marketing, the issue of new policies, servicing and dealing with claims under existing policies and the various staff groups (such as compliance, finance, actuarial, human resources, IT and legal), all presided over by the senior management in the executive suite. Both were modern purpose-built head offices but if Royal London was serious about integration and the creation of one cost-effective combined company, then this duplication had to be addressed.

The Board, expanded by the appointment of Longhurst as deputy chairman and Frost as deputy chief executive, considered as a priority the handling and processing of business. The first thought was to have this partly at Wilmslow and partly at Colchester, but the view quickly emerged that, if the company was to meet its goal of achieving the most efficient operation possible, all processing and servicing should be put together on one site. But which one? This was a desperately difficult decision but in the end the Board determined that all servicing would be at Wilmslow and that there would be no customer services at Colchester. This was on the basis that within "Wilmslow's servicing functions there is the right blend of skills and efficiency, together with the capacity to grow. This does not mean that there are not skilled and experienced people in Colchester. However at Wilmslow there is experience of dealing with a more complex and diverse product range and a more efficient, lower cost operation".[35] This decision would mean that 180 permanent and 80 temporary jobs would be lost at Colchester and around 100 new jobs created at Wilmslow. It was also decided to follow the United Assurance example and outsource printing which would mean closing the printing and stationery function at Colchester. This would involve a further 36 permanent and 12 temporary job losses.

When these decisions involving more than 300 job losses were announced on 25 May 2000, there was surprise and outrage at Colchester where many staff had clearly felt that jobs would only be lost in the acquired company. The Colchester *Evening Gazette*, under the banner heading "Royal London Axes 300 Jobs" reported that the "unexpected announcement has sent shockwaves through the town".[36] The *Essex County Standard* referred to the stunned "Royal London staff [who] were yesterday struggling to take in the news of the job losses".[37] "Some staff at the company's landmark headquarters at the bottom of North Hill broke down in tears, others saw it as an opportunity to move on to something new".[38] Colchester's Liberal Democrat MP Bob Russell was widely quoted – he told the *Essex County Standard* that he found it "appalling that a company that came into Colchester with all flags flying is now dispensing with a third of its workforce. It is bad news for them and bad news for Colchester".[39] It was all the worse for the area because only two months before, Trebor Bassett, a subsidiary of Cadbury-Schweppes, had closed its factory on a Colchester industrial estate where it had manufactured Refreshers and Extra Strong Mints, with the loss of more than 200 jobs. Trebor Bassett was reducing its six manufacturing sites to four to make it more competitive and other plants in the company would benefit from closures at Colchester and Maidstone. It was little consolation to the staff at Royal London that similar situations arose in other industries.

The Royal London response to the criticism was entirely consistent – the message was the same whether it was the chief executive or a spokesman. The head of corporate communications, told the *Evening Gazette*:

> We are in a very competitive market, and we have got to be as competitive as possible. Naturally last week's news was very distressing for those concerned, and it is our friends and colleagues who are affected. But this is in the long term interests

of the company – the alternative is that the business doesn't have a future at all. We have been very honest from the outset and it was a very difficult decision which had to be made.[40]

It had been announced as early as 20 April that the two asset management teams would merge and the combined operation would be based near the Monument at 55 Gracechurch Street, United Assurance's office. By 1 July RLAM had vacated the basement of Triton Court, although the irony of leaving the first Royal London House (aka Triton Court) at a time when the future of the second Royal London House was under discussion would have been lost on those engaged in the traumatic events of the time.

The Colchester community was not reassured by the statement on 25 May that the head office would remain in Colchester because it was coupled with comments to the effect that the location of other functions was still under review. On 26 May the *Evening Gazette* suggested that these job losses could be the first of many, quoting a 'union representative' who believed more were to follow: "The true extent of the damage will not be revealed for some time. It is absolutely devastating for the staff. It is the biggest kick in the teeth imaginable".[41] The review had been completed by 6 July when a further announcement was made. There was more bad news, because it had been decided that Wilmslow would in future be the operational base for almost all the core Royal London functions, in addition to customer services, and that all asset management activities would now be in London, so the team responsible for property investments would relocate to Gracechurch Street. Colchester would continue as head office but would be limited to corporate strategy and development, central financial control, legal and some aspects of regulatory work. Royal London House would in due course be vacated, the 120 survivors from the head office moving into Royal London Court, a compact office block built and owned by the Society on the other side of the road, previously occupied by Royal London General.[42] In due course it was to be renamed 'Royal London House' and the building in the middle of the roundabout, which had served the Society for little more than 20 years, became 'The Octagon'.

The decisions announced in early July involved a further 450 job losses at Colchester, although a team charged with developing new ways of distributing products would be established there, creating 20 new jobs. The fact that the 270-strong pensions review team (located nearby in short-term leasehold premises) was to remain in Colchester was good news although many were temporaries and everyone recognised that these jobs would go when the review was completed. The effect of these decisions was that all or the greater part of compliance, finance, actuarial, human resources and IT of what was increasingly being called The Royal London Group would in future be located at Wilmslow. This would involve an increase in job numbers there although redundancies had occurred in sales management and legal.

Expressions such as 'Jobs Disaster', 'Chill news shocks our community' and 'Jobs Shock' reappeared in the local press, but there was an element of resigned acceptance when this second wave of redundancies was announced on 6 July. The branch chairman of the Manufacturing, Science and Finance Union had been expecting the worst and was not surprised by the news. As he told the *Evening Gazette*:

> *... there is a feeling of shock and upset in the building. The bottom line is money but it should not be. Salaries are between eight and 30 per cent cheaper in Wilmslow. We were told skill levels and service levels would be taken into account but in the end it came down to the calculator.*[43]

As it had promised to do, the Society offered all possible assistance to those who would be losing their jobs. A large part of the ground floor of Royal London House was given over to a resource centre, with trained external advisers from a specialist company on hand from 8.00 am to 6.30 pm every day, available for individual counselling and advice on all aspects of job search, including CV production, application letters and interview technique. The centre contained a library with books and newspapers related to job hunting and a bank of personal computers that could be used to help with the job search. All of this was funded by the Society. Staff were given reasonable time off to attend interviews. It proved to be a hugely successful outplacement programme – within six months more than 90 per cent of those seeking a job had found one. Some had to take a drop in salary but others, especially those who were prepared to commute to London, found better remunerated roles. Many who were over 50 took the early retirement option because of the generous pension and redundancy terms.

Work continued throughout 2000 and into 2001 integrating the two businesses. The priorities were to achieve cost savings by eliminating duplication, to identify and put in place improvements to business processes, to bring together the sales force into a single team operating under the Royal London brand and to maintain all existing business alongside the integration programme. Ahead of their redundancies, many of the customer service staff from Colchester spent time at Wilmslow helping with the transfer of the Royal London policies.

The acquisition of United Assurance did nothing to address Royal London's over-reliance on the direct sales force as the only method of distribution. By the summer of 2000 the Board was looking northwards for the solution. The Scottish Life Assurance Company had funds under management in excess of £9.7 billion, 500,000 policyholders and 1,200 staff, of whom 900 were based in Edinburgh. Its primary business was providing individual and group pension products that were distributed exclusively through independent financial advisers.

Scottish Life had been founded in 1881 when the entrepreneurial David Paulin, who was then the superintendent of agencies at the Scottish Provident Institution, was working on forming two businesses: a life assurance company and an actuarial and accountancy consultancy.[44] He was to be the manager (chief executive) of the former and a partner of the latter, although he was qualified in neither profession. Born in 1847 and educated at Irvine Academy where his father was rector, he left school at 15 and joined the Clydesdale Bank. It was said that his mother's family were the first holders of a private account with the Bank. Paulin, active in the YMCA and a strong supporter of temperance reform, gradually became aware of the needs of the bank's customers for both life and general assurance. He joined the Scottish Provident in 1873 but had become restless as a result of what he regarded as a frustrating atmosphere of nepotism in high places. He was an energetic participator in the affairs of the Actuarial Society of Edinburgh to which he read a number of papers that demonstrated both a capacity for work and a "mature and well stocked mind, not only in the fields of sociology and political economy but in many other areas".[45]

It would have come as no surprise to many in Edinburgh who knew (or knew of) this able and ambitious young man to learn that he was planning to launch a new venture or two. He seemed to have no difficulty in persuading prominent men of business to be sponsors and later directors of the life company or to attract investors. The 50,000 shares of £5 each (of which only £1 was paid-up) in The Scottish Life Assurance Company Limited were oversubscribed.[46] Earlier in 1881 Paulin had written:

> A firm of Accountants and Actuaries consisting of three members with good connections, is about to be formed. Two of the partners are about to assume the respective duties of Manager and of Actuary of a new Life Assurance Company about to be started with an influential directorate and an exceptionally good connection throughout Scotland. The third member of the firm is already in business as a Chartered Accountant and has many influential friends in Edinburgh.[47]

The actuary was James Sorley who did indeed become Scottish Life's first actuary and secretary. The partnership of Paulin, Sorley & Brown (later Paulin, Sorley & Martin) flourished. It operated initially from Scottish Life's office at 26 George Street and, when the company moved to 19 St Andrew Square, it took offices at No. 18.

In 1893 Paulin was admitted to the fellowship of the Faculty of Actuaries without examination but two years later he and Sorley had a difference of opinion and went their separate ways. It happened as a result of a plan to amalgamate Scottish Life with the long-established Pelican Life Insurance Company of Lombard Street in the City of London. In fact the deal was more acquisition than amalgamation – Scottish Life would have ceased to exist and the role of the board in Edinburgh would be limited to supervising Pelican's expanded business in Scotland. At first, the Scottish Life directors supported the proposal, and (to their subsequent great embarrassment) intimated as much to Pelican, but at the last moment changed their minds and withdrew from the transaction. Their problem was that the company's two officers fundamentally disagreed: Sorley, who may already have had aspirations to move south at some stage in his career, was in favour while Paulin was against. When the deal collapsed, Sorley left Scottish Life, joining Pelican in London as general manager and actuary, and the partnership was dissolved.[48]

Scottish Life provided ordinary life assurance. Premiums, generally due annually, were paid to the company and were not collected by an agent calling on a weekly basis, although initially Paulin had been keen for the company to provide a modified form of industrial assurance. When Scottish Life was launched it contained a National Thrift Assurance Department for wage earning classes that was offering: "Non-forfeitable Assurances for small sums. Monthly payment of Premiums. Participation in Profits, and other advantages attaching to larger Policies". It was not a success. By the end of the second year, more than 550 agents had been appointed, but only five of them were in the thrift department that was unable to operate at a profit and was closed in 1890.[49] There was also a Personal Injury and Accident Department, prompted in part by the Employers' Liability Act 1880, that flourished for a while but in due course it too was abandoned.

It was as a life assurance and later pensions company that Scottish Life prospered. Sir David Paulin – he was knighted in 1909, "the first occasion in Scotland on which the approval of His Majesty in this manner has been given to an insurance manager"[50] – remained manager until 1917 and was a director until his death in December 1930, aged 83, just a few months before the company celebrated its jubilee. By 1930 the company that he had founded had a premium income of £530,914 and funds of £6.4 million (today: £25.0 million and £300.4 million). In 1955, the premium income was £2.2 million and the funds £16.7 million (today: £43.3 million and £328.0 million).

The growing financial strength of Scottish Life was, strange as it may seem, increasingly a matter of concern for the board because it was becoming "apparent that the small capital of 50,000 shares... not only provided very little protection to the policyholders but, in fact, represented a potential threat to the security of their assets since control of these assets could be acquired by the simple expedient of purchasing the share capital at relatively modest cost".[51] The first serious attempt had been in 1922 when the board, relying on a provision in the articles of association that gave them power to reject any proposed transferee without giving any reason for so doing, responded by simply refusing to register transfers that they believed came from the speculators. Understandably they were put under huge pressure by the Edinburgh Stock Exchange that threatened to withdraw Scottish Life's quotation, on the basis that no exchange can function if purchasers of shares do not know if they will be able to register the transfer. But the directors held their nerve and the speculators lost interest and went away.[52]

By 1966 the assets had risen to £60 million and the board was convinced that the threat was such that proactive steps were needed. They decided that the "obvious method of protecting the policyholders' interests completely was to mutualise the Company by the purchase of the shares by the policyholders".[53] This would involve the policyholders buying out the interests of the shareholders, and Scottish Life converting from a proprietary to a mutual company. Undaunted by technical and logistical problems that would have overwhelmed lesser men, they set out to implement their bold strategy. An independent actuary was required to value the shareholders' interests so that a share price could be determined, then an extraordinary general meeting would be convened at which the members would be asked to vote on the proposed sale. Finally, a Bill would be presented to Parliament that set out the constitution of the new mutual company. This process would inevitably take a while, and by late 1966 the threat was felt to be so imminent that some form of immediate protection was required. Again the directors and their advisers turned to the articles and, on the basis of a provision that (it was admitted afterwards) was probably intended to do no more that to 'dot the i's and cross the t's' came up with a creative solution. They established a policyholders committee, segregated the funds and placed all the assets of the life assurance and annuity fund under the control of the committee. The reaction from some shareholders and media was so adverse that the board was convinced that a hostile bid was about to be made for Scottish Life.[54] These were nervous times with a law suit being commenced in the Court of Session. But once again, the directors were not intimidated. The litigation came to nothing, the mutualisation proposals were accepted almost unanimously at an extraordinary general meeting in June 1967 and the Bill passed through Parliament and received the Royal Assent in May 1968.[55] Scottish Life was now a mutual company.

In the next three decades, Scottish Life's two main product lines were mortgage-related life policies and group pensions but it also built up businesses in unit-linked investment plans and individual pensions. By the late 1990s the mortgage-related business had faded and the principal products were individual and group pensions. The company also offered administration services for defined contribution pension schemes and investment products via Scottish Life International, an Isle of Man-based subsidiary established in 1996. Despite recording record new business premiums of £780 million in 1998, the board, through Brian Duffin, the new group chief executive, was conducting a detailed review of the future of the company. There had been significant changes and increasing competition within the UK pensions market and the question, quite simply, was whether Scottish Life should stay on its own or combine with another company. Remaining independent was seen as offering reasonable business prospects but the board ultimately concluded that a partnership with a large financial services group which could provide enhanced financial strength and capital for accelerated growth would be in the best interests of Scottish Life's members and policyholders.

Scottish Life was not the only Edinburgh-based mutual seeking or being sought by a suitor in 2000. Scottish Widows had demutualised and become part of the Lloyds Bank Group in March, and on 7 September Abbey National (which had acquired Scottish Mutual in 1997) confirmed the purchase of Scottish Provident for £1.8 billion. The talk of windfalls was in the air when reports appeared suggesting that Scottish Life could be the next to go, as they were thought to be in discussions with GE Capital, the financial services arm of General Electric. 'One source familiar with the situation' suggested that the deal "could still fall apart, but they are heading towards an announcement".[56] The latter seemed more than likely when on 12 September, Scottish Life introduced measures to prevent carpet-bagging by providing that anybody who became a member after 11 September would not be entitled to a windfall if (which was not admitted) any windfall was to be payable.[57] But by 16 September the talks with GE Capital seemed to have collapsed, Scottish Life apparently being encouraged to adopt a robust position by the belief that other bidders who missed out on Scottish Provident would now enter the fray. It is no secret that Royal London had been one of those interested in Scottish Provident.

There was no doubt now that Scottish Life was up for sale. Mike Yardley called Ruaridh Budge, their deputy chief executive, who Yardley knew as a fellow member of the asset management fraternity, suggesting that Royal London might have something of interest to say to the Scottish Life board. A meeting was set up almost at once. The senior management and advisers of a number of potential bidders were hurrying to Edinburgh to meet Scottish Life executives and to view the information about the company which was available in the data room, and then hurrying back to discuss the results with their boards and to seek approval to take the matter further. Those still standing – four in number – were invited to submit formal offers by 5 pm on Wednesday 27 September and all did so.

On 2 October 2000, it was announced that an agreement had been reached by which Scottish Life would transfer its business to Royal London. The Scottish Life board believed that the Royal London proposal represented the best overall value for members and policyholders, given Royal London's financial strength and complementary business mix. The transfer, which would involve each Scottish Life member receiving £500 for loss of membership and Royal London making a further payment to strengthen the Scottish Life fund, would create a combined group with a premium income of £1.9 billion and funds under management of nearly £30 billion. The deal still had to be approved by the members of Scottish Life and the Court of Session, and was also subject to the satisfactory conclusion of discussions with regulatory and tax authorities. Mike Yardley was enthusiastic:

> We are creating a leading UK life and pensions group with nearly £30 billion of funds under management. This transaction diversifies Royal London's distribution capability by adding an established position in the IFA market and significantly increases our new business volumes. As a result, it strengthens our business and creates enhanced value for our members.[58]

There was still much work to be done. The discussions with the regulators and tax authorities were satisfactorily concluded, 93.3 per cent of the Scottish Life members who voted at the extraordinary general meeting on 31 May 2001 were in favour of the transfer and on 28 June approval was given by Lord Johnston in the Court of Session. At 00.01 am on 1 July 2001 the transfer of the business of Scottish Life to Royal London was completed. Tom Ross and Brian Duffin, the chairman and chief executive of Scottish Life, joined the Royal London main Board, and Duffin and three of his colleagues became members of the executive Board. Royal London paid £823 million for Scottish Life: £114 million to the members and £709 million to strengthen the fund relating to the policies that were transferred to Royal London. The value of the assets received was some £350 million less than the amount paid but, as Stephen Shone explained, the "financials around this acquisition were different to the United Assurance deal". The acquisition of Scottish Life was about additional distribution, not reducing costs although there would be some savings. "The main difference was that Royal London was paying for Scottish Life's distribution infrastructure and brand, and in particular, the value that can be generated through future new business through this channel.[59] In essence Royal London was investing the 'profit' from the United Assurance deal in acquiring the Scottish Life infrastructure and a brand known and respected by independent financial advisers that would serve as a platform to access the IFA market and to diversify its products in the future.

The strategy identified by the Board in late 1999 had been implemented: the traditional business had been expanded, facilitating economies of scale, the over-reliance on the direct sales force as the only means of distribution had been addressed and the activities of the asset management company widened… and all of this had been achieved in less than two years. The visual identity of Royal London had changed too. The hand around the family had been replaced by a new logo. The hand was retained – although it was a left hand with only three visible fingers – but now it was beneath a squirl that was, in fact, the bud of a fern unfolding, representing growth. The new logo reflected the Group's values: "we aim to be professional, and focused on performance. In all our dealings, we are fair, open and honest, and straightforward and direct with each other and with our customers".

CHAPTER 15

Traditions Change

In 1998, the Group had a large door-to-door home service sales staff. The burden of regulation and the lack of scale and diversity within the Group resulted in a loss-making business model, which required major change to continue adding value for members. Royal London has tackled these challenges through a major transformation of its business model over the last few years.

Royal London Business Review (2007)[1]

There was much to fault the 'industrial branch' home service delivery of insurance products, not least their failure to comply with some of the regulations under the Financial Services Act (1986) and which resulted in some high profile fines and the recall of field staff for lengthy periods of retraining. However, they provided a necessary financial discipline for the less well-off consumers that currently has no clear substitute.

Social Policy & Society, Cambridge University Press (2004)[2]

By the end of 2001 The Royal London Group had three operating businesses – the traditional home service, expanded by the addition of the customers of Refuge and United Friendly, Scottish Life, primarily selling pensions through independent financial advisers, and RLAM, managing the assets of both external clients and the Group. The term 'Royal London Group' was one of convenience rather than law – the parent company remains The Royal London Mutual Insurance Society Limited created at those stormy meetings in the summer of 1908.

The decision was made in May 2000 to stop selling industrial branch policies. With fewer and fewer people being paid in cash, industrial assurance was past its sell-by date and it was uneconomic for the offices to take on more commitments to call regularly on homes to collect small cash payments from the decreasing number of customers who still required this service. The hope following the United Assurance acquisition was that a 'best of both' direct sales force could be created. By 2001 Royal London had 700 financial consultants (as the agents were now called) operating from 40 area offices, although during 2002 it became clear that a full advice service to all customers was no longer viable, and the financial consultants were now focusing "on those customers who are more likely to require a full advice service, usually because they have higher levels of income and existing savings".[3] A separate sales force was established for the majority of customers who needed to protect their home and family with straightforward solutions.

The traditional home service offices were finding it difficult to comply with regulation, while the additional cost of compliance – training, accreditation, completion of the documents needed to support each sale, sales monitoring – was making it difficult to operate profitably what was already a high cost business. The Prudential closed its sales force in 2001 with the loss of 2,000 jobs[4] and many other home service offices were doing the same. The Board was reluctant to accept that a profitable business could not be created serving both Royal London policyholders and other traditional home service customers now without a product provider, or at least those of them with 'higher levels of income'. Sadly this did not prove possible, despite all the hard work within Royal London Retail to reduce operating costs and increase productivity, and in 2004 the Board came to the view that there was no alternative but to close the face-to-face sales operation. By then numbers had reduced considerably but there were still nearly 400 employees who were directly affected by the decision. Tradition, however, was no justification for an annual subsidy out of the reserves to fund the business. Once again strategic decisions that prompted a loss of jobs in the insurance industry were not limited to the former home service companies. On the same day that Royal London closed its direct sales force, Norwich Union announced that it would be cutting 700 jobs and 250 contract posts in an overhaul of its business services division. In his annual review, Mike Yardley reported that in mid-2004:

> *... the Board decided to close the face-to-face sales force following an in-depth review of its viability. The Group has for some years been working to reposition its retail business model in the light of regulatory changes so as to achieve a profitable position, but we reached the conclusion that this could not be achieved in the current market conditions.*

The Group's strategy now was to focus on the successful growth of the "product manufacturing businesses which distribute through intermediaries".[5] So Royal London would no longer have a sales force and, apart from a few simple products that could be purchased over the telephone, its policies would be available only from independent financial advisers. What had for so long been Royal London's only business was at an end. This has to be one of the most significant events in Royal London's history although, at the time, the impact of the decision was lessened by what many saw as its inevitability, and by the gradual reductions in the size of the operation that had taken place during the previous few years.

There were now no, or very few, insurance men or women out and about, reminding families of the risks inherent in life, encouraging them to take out insurance, and then to keep up the premiums. Some of those households who had traditionally looked to home service were well aware of the need for insurance and ready, willing and able to turn to the telephone, the internet or independent financial advisers as the means of providing it. Some, however, were not. Many families lacked cover – a survey in 2000 had revealed that a third of households had no savings or investment products, 27 per cent of employees had no occupational or private pension, up to a quarter of households had no home contents insurance and 45 per cent of households had no life cover.[6] The dangers of financial exclusion were increasingly being recognised, and it was to become government policy to ensure that everyone had access to appropriate financial services.[7]

That some form of regulation was required cannot be denied, but when a definitive history of financial services regulation is written, its author will need to opine with the benefit of hindsight on two questions that were much debated at the time. The first was whether it would have been in the public interest to introduce a lighter touch regulatory regime, enabling a service to be maintained to those households who were not ready to convert to other methods of distribution. Such a regime, applying to a limited range of products, would have had to provide adequate protection for consumers, a reasonable living for agents and a profit, at least for those companies that were

Royal London House, Finsbury Square: "*From the basement to the top of this tower the height is two hundred and fifty feet, the loftiest commercial building in the City of London. Crowning the tower is a figure representing Mercury, the God of Prudence...*"

Sir William Waterlow, the Lord Mayor of London, opens the central section of Royal London House on 5 February 1930. Alfred Skeggs looks on from behind his top hat.

The Lord Mayor's procession leaves the building with Alfred Skeggs in the rear.

Alfred Skeggs
Managing Director 1920–1936
Chairman 1932–1936
(The portrait by Richard Jack)

The executive suite was panelled
in Cuban mahogany, decorated in
gold leaf, with walnut borders to
the parquet floors.

The accommodation for staff at Royal London House was rather less grand – the agency department at work in the 1930s.

The coat of arms granted to Royal London in January 1934 by the College of Arms with the motto *Sustentet Nos Deus* – God Sustain Us.

John Wiseman
Joint Managing Director 1937–1951, Chairman 1945–1951

Some head office staff and documents were evacuated in 1939 to Peverel Court, near Aylesbury, in Buckinghamshire.

SOME DISTRICT OFFICES

Torquay

Bath

Preston

Monmouth

Hackney

Exeter

Forest Hill

Swansea

The Right Reverend Bertram Simpson
Bishop of Southwark 1942–1959

John Wiseman – the portrait by
Maurice Codner (1951)

Royal London House, showing the 1958 extension. The stonework of the existing
buildings displays the covering of soot and grime that was so much a feature of urban life
before smokeless zones.

Ernest Haynes
Joint Managing Director 1955-1969
Chairman 1956–1973

Jim Bailey, Samuel Swetnam, Ernest Haynes, H Webb, Stanley Goodall and Len Wiseman (secretary). The event, that must have taken place before April 1961, and the identity of Mr Webb, are not disclosed on the original of this photograph in the archives.

Christopher Shuttleworth
Chairman 1951–1956

Stanley Goodall
Joint Managing Director
1956-1959

Jim Bailey
Chairman 1973–1976

Tom Cowman
Chairman 1976–1978

Billy Skinner
Chairman 1978–1983

Bill Forsey
Chairman 1983–1987
(and behind him, Mercury)

ROYAL LONDON
INSURANCE

The 'hand around the family' logo, introduced in 1978, gradually replaced the coat of arms.

Royal London House, Colchester.

The four actuaries: Michael Pickard, Jimmy Duffell, Peter Taylor and Brian Jones in 1982.

Michael Pickard
Chairman 1988–1999

The Board in the early 1990s. Standing: Sven Farmer (secretary), Tom Slee, Brian Jones, Bob Erith, Mike Yardley. Sitting: Cyril Brill, Norman Wooding, Michael Pickard, Brian Knights.

The Board in the late 1990s. Standing: Barry Fitzgerald, Tom Slee, Barry Skipper.
Sitting: Brian Jones, Mike Yardley, Michael Pickard, Hubert Reid, Murray Ross.

The Board in 2004. Mike Yardley, Tom Ross, Fields Wicker-Miurin, Hubert Reid.

Royal London makes £1.5bn bid for United

MARTIN FLANAGAN
City Editor

ROYAL London Mutual Insurance Society made an agreed £1.5 billion bid for United Assurance yesterday, as takeover fever gripped the sector for the second consecutive day.

The bid, the largest yet by a mutual for a publicly quoted company, came just 24 hours after CGU and Norwich Union confirmed their own planned £19 billion merger.

But early speculation that Britannic Assurance, the owner of the Glasgow-based Britannic Asset Management, might mount a counter offer for United appeared to be fading last night.

Britannic held unsuccessful talks with the group last November, and it put out a statement late on Monday saying it continued to monitor events with interest.

However, it is believed that Britannic, which owns 6.38 per cent of United, has been sharply surprised by the high price that Royal has been prepared to pay. It is thought its executives feel its top this bid would risk destroying shareholder value at Britannic, which owns 75 per cent of Glasgow-based Britannic Asset Management.

The current offer values United at 445p a share, but also allows shareholders to keep a 20p dividend declared with United's annual results also announced yesterday.

United's shares closed up 45p, or 10 per cent, at 465p

yesterday, as Royal upped the ante by buying 12.3 per cent of United in the market.

Royal said the combined group would achieve substantial economies of scale as part of cost savings across the combined group. However, following the controversy over the 4,000 UK jobs that will go as a result of the CGU/Norwich merger, Royal said it was too early to say how many redundancies the latest merger would cause.

Including staff "in the field",

> **'We welcome
> Royal's offer ... the
> group will compete
> more effectively'**

Royal employs 3,100 and United 3,000. Mike Yardley, Royal's chief executive, said job losses were inevitable, but would not specify levels before a review.

Analysts said some cost savings could come from combining the groups' field workforces and removing the headquarters functions from United's head office in Wilmslow, Cheshire.

The headquarters of the proposed group will be Royal's base in Colchester, Essex, although it is planned that the Wilmslow offices will remain a key operational centre.

There could be other job losses in the plan to merge the two groups' life funds and to combine investment management

at a single site in London. Roger Lyons, the general secretary of the Manufacturing Science and Finance union, said yesterday: "We welcome Royal London's commitment to consult with us on behalf of the staff, and we will do everything possible to avoid compulsory redundancies."

Hubert Reid, Royal's chairman, said: "The combined group will be better placed to take advantage of the opportunities that exist to distribute life, pension and other investment products through new distribution channels."

The merged company would have combined premiums of £3 billion, total assets of £16 billion and three million customers.

The chairman of United, Andrew Longhurst, said that the decision to accept Royal's offer was made easier because the quoted insurer had found it "difficult to make substantial progress against a tough regulatory and market background".

He added: "We therefore welcome Royal's London's offer, believing that the combined group will have the scale to compete more effectively in its chosen markets."

The fall in United's profits was largely due to £109.4 million of one-off charges, the biggest one being a further £49 million to cover compensation following the pensions mis-selling review.

mflanagan@scotsman.com

Business View, Page 25

The Scotsman
23 February 2000

Scottish Life
a division of Royal London

Tim Melville-Ross, Stephen Shone, Robert Jeens, Brian Duffin.

Scottish Life to join the Royal London fold

Royal London beat off some fierce competition to acquire Scottish Life recently. "Royal seals £1.1bn Scottish Life deal" explained the Daily Telegraph; "London Calling" roared The Mirror. Following on from the acquisition of United Assurance many were surprised at the pace at which Royal London moved again within the market. So who are Scottish Life and why the deal with Royal London?

- Scottish Life was founded in 1881, it is a mutual company with over 500,000 policyholders.
- It has 1450 employees, around 1000 are based at the Edinburgh Head Office.
- It is known as the 'PENSION company' because its principal focus is in the pensions market, both personal and corporate.
- Other significant markets are in mortgages, investment and third party administration.
- Scottish Life leads the way in the provision of technological support for IFAs especially through its award-winning website - diylplus.
- It is fully committed to the IFA marketplace, with no appointed representatives or direct salesforce.
- Total new business in 1999 was £808 million.
- It has associated companies: Scottish Life International and Premier Capital.
- Scottish Life sponsors the coverage of the European Golf Tour on Sky Sports.

Brian Duffin, group chief executive of Scottish Life, summed up the agreement to transfer Scottish Life's business to Royal London like this: "Scottish Life has been, and is, a very successful company. With the resources of Royal London to give us extra financial muscle, we're looking forward to being even more successful in future. Put simply, it's a winning combination."

Mike Yardley stated, "We're creating a leading UK life and pension group with nearly £30 billion of funds under management. This transaction will give us an established position in the IFA market and significantly increase our new business volumes. It strengthens Royal London's business and is really good news for our members."

The transfer is subject to approval by Scottish Life members, who will receive a windfall if the deal goes ahead, satisfactory discussions with the regulatory and tax authorities and the sanction of the Court of Session in Edinburgh. The transfer is expected to be completed by the summer of 2001.

Brian Duffin and Mike Yardley

Connections
July 2001

Robert Jeens
Director 2003–

Andy Carter
Director 2007–

John Deane
Director 2007–

Duncan Ferguson
Director 2010–

David Williams
Director 2006–

Hubert Reid
Chairman 1999–2005

Tim Melville-Ross
Chairman 2006–

Stephen Shone
Group Finance Director 1999–

Mike Yardley
Group Chief Executive 1998–

John Deane, the chief executive of Royal London's intermediary division, supported by Royal London staff on one of the stages of his bike ride from Land's End to John O'Groats raising money for Macmillan Cancer Support and a children's hospice.

Royal London House, Alderley Road, Wilmslow.

efficiently and economically managed. The second question, assuming the first was answered in the affirmative, was whether it would have been possible to achieve all these objectives. In a consultative paper published in January 2002, the Financial Services Authority put forward for discussion a two-tiered system for advisers, with the lower-tier of less qualified advisers advising on only a limited range of lower risk products.[8] A report to HM Treasury later in the year proposed a set of safer, good-value, easy to understand 'stakeholder' investment products that could be sold through a lighter touch regime.[9] There was extensive consultation over a very long period, but in the end the price-cap imposed on the stakeholder products was such that selling them through a direct sales force would not have been viable. That decision represented the death knell of home service.

Those who were engaged in, or who benefited from, home service (or its predecessor industrial assurance) will hope that a balanced view is presented in the history of regulation.[10] Its author would do well to consider statements made by two chief general managers of Royal London that remain valid even if today, as their authors would have readily acknowledged, they have to be read in the context of the regulatory failings that occurred or came to light later. Bill Forsey was "quite sure that without the home service agent, there would be less thrift in many families and greater destitution in times of need if insurance cover had not been taken out".[11] Michael Pickard felt that criticism of the industry:

> ... *fails to recognise the outstanding returns that companies such as Royal London are providing to long-term savers. It fails to recognise the financial protection that is granted and for which many a widow or widower has been very grateful. And it fails to recognise the unique and invaluable contribution to the United Kingdom economy via long-term savings channelled through our industry*".[12]

Many of those involved – both at the head office and in the field – were proud to be working for a company that was making insurance available to those who otherwise would not have access to it.

When most companies shut down a business, all activity soon stops. After a brief period of run-off, during which the company continues to perform its contracts until they are terminated or assigned, staff are made redundant or re-employed elsewhere in the group, assets are sold and properties disposed of, there will generally be little ongoing evidence of the business. Life assurance and pensions are very different, however, because of the long-term nature of the contracts. For so long as any of the current policies exist, premiums have to be collected, a service provided to policyholders to deal with claims and others administrative matters and the assets in the fund supporting the policies managed.

There were now more than two million industrial branch policies within the Group where collection involved calling on policyholders' homes. United Assurance had separated collecting from selling, and this was extended after the acquisition to Royal London policies. By January 2001 there were more than 1,320 collectors calling on 900,000 customers – at the time, this was the largest collections force of any home service life company. Inevitably, for most of its history, collection of industrial assurance premiums has been a paper-based operation, involving significant reconciliation and controls in branch offices. The gradual roll-out to Premium Operations staff of hand-held electronic devices revolutionised their work. Now when a payment was recorded by the representative, the central records were updated automatically. Collections staff no longer needed an office and the Group's branch office network was gradually closed down. For so long as policies remained governed by the Industrial Assurance Act 1923, premiums had to be collected from the policyholders at not less than two-monthly intervals. Regulations were introduced in 2001, however, that permitted the policyholder and the company to agree other methods of payment at less frequent intervals.[13]

The collection staff now had the additional role of encouraging their customers to move away from regular cash payments, and they were hugely successful. By 2010, there were just 90,000 customers still receiving a home collection and Premium Operations had been reduced to 67 field staff. The stage had been reached when there were no further reorganisations that could make the service cost-effective, and consultation began in August 2010 with the trade union and employee committee with a view to withdrawing home collections and closing Premium Operations during the first quarter of 2011. In future, policyholders will be able to pay their premiums by direct debit, at PayPoint outlets or at Post Offices. The role of the Premium Operations field staff was unusual because, the more effective they were in doing their job and achieving conversions, the sooner their role would cease to exist and they would be made redundant. The loyalty they showed to both their employer and their customers was much appreciated.

The customer service operation at the Wilmslow office became known as Royal London Administration Services and has recently been re-named Royal London Plus. It administers four million policies originally issued by Royal London, Refuge, United Friendly and Canterbury Life (a company acquired by Refuge and long-since closed to new business)[14] for more than two million customers. The administration and customer services for Scottish Life's individual pensions and life policies was moved to Wilmslow where various staff functions of the Group such as finance, actuarial and human resources are also located.[15] In all, nearly 800 people now work on the Wilmslow site.

The word 'administration' conveys a rather inward-looking role, with long hours spent working with records on the screen, and sometimes having to refer back to dusty files and original documents. There is an element of this, but Royal London Plus is the customer-facing part of the Group – every day, the Wilmslow office receives 1,000 telephone calls and 2,000 items of mail. It is irrelevant to the customer service representatives that the potential for new business is limited – they are keen to provide a good service and are constantly at, or near to, the objective of turning round 95 per cent of enquiries within five days, 100 per cent within ten days. Most maturities of with-profits policies are received by the policyholder just before the maturity date as a result of a largely automated process. There are six direct service teams to whom all inquiries are initially referred (a seventh team constitutes a replacements bench, ready to fill gaps that arise in the other teams), and six technical support teams to whom points that cannot be addressed in the front line are referred, with ten or so in each team. The teams have their assigned tasks, and the telephone sorting system assists in directing enquiries to the appropriate team. The range of topics that routinely arise is considerable: change of name (for example, on marriage) change of address, communications to policyholders that arrive back marked 'return to sender', assignments and re-assignments of policies, loans made on the basis that they would be repaid out of maturities, points that arise from the bankruptcy of the policyholder or death of the proposer (and payer of premiums) under a life-of-another policy, lost policies, surrenders including providing quotations, issues relating to payment (or lack of payment) of premiums, death claims and maturities.

Royal London Plus is also responsible for some impressive mailings. Bonus statements have to be sent to with-profits policyholders every year, the voting pack has to be mailed to all members of Royal London before the annual general meeting and from time to time legislation or regulation demands that circulars are sent to certain categories of policyholders. A mailing of more than a million is not unusual. External mailing-houses are responsible for the printing and posting but this is on the basis of data created by Royal London Plus.

Within Royal London Plus is the customer contact centre that has on offer a basic portfolio of products likely to be of interest to former home service customers. Some of the products come from Royal London (a life policy, a savings plan and a with-profits bond) and the others are provided by third parties, following the tradition of Royal London for most of its history to outsource general insurance and thus avoid the need for the costly infrastructure that would be required if it was manufacturing, selling and administering the policies.[16] Most of the business of the centre comes from contact with customers over an existing policy where they are asked if they have any future needs. Some comes from letters sent out prior to a customer receiving a maturity and the remainder comes from leaflets inserted in mailings. The products are sold over the telephone and no advice is given – if customers are interested, they are sent an information pack and those who want to proceed complete and post back an application form. There are currently seven consultants within the centre.

There were other consequences of the acquisitions. Tidying-up the pensions is a piece of housekeeping that has to be done from time-to-time. Traditionally there had been the four pension schemes – for agents with book interest/nominating rights (closed to new members), salaried agents, staff and executives – and in the 1970s these were merged into the Royal London Staff Pension Scheme. Now more work was needed because the acquisitions had brought into the enlarged Group a number of pension schemes for employees. In 2003 these were merged into the Royal London Group Pension Scheme. This was a complex exercise, with the trustees of each scheme having to satisfy themselves that all the requirements had been met, and then agreements being entered into by which the assets and liabilities of the schemes were transferred into the RLGPS. On the merger of the schemes, the RLGPS had assets of £1.46 billion, putting it amongst the top 100 private sector occupational pension schemes in the UK.[17] The chairman of the trustees is Richard Balding – REB of Chapter 14 – and, in addition to the group finance and HR directors, there are two member-nominated trustees and an independent corporate trustee.[18] RLGPS was closed to new members on 1 September 2005 when a defined contribution arrangement was put in place for employees joining after that date.

As part of one of the several reformulations of the sales force, those members of the management of Royal London Retail based at Colchester were transferred to Wilmslow to achieve cost savings and greater operational effectiveness. This prompted an investigation into the viability of maintaining the Colchester office that often had a deserted air about it as executives' duties increasingly took them to other offices within the Group. It came as no surprise to the 50 or so survivors when in August 2003 the decision was made to close Royal London House (as Royal London Court was now known) Colchester and to transfer the activities and roles based there to London or Wilmslow. Extra space was acquired at 55 Gracechurch Street so that the head office of the Royal London Group could cohabit there with RLAM. By early 2004 the registered office, the boardroom and the offices of the chief executive, the finance director, the company secretary and legal director and the human resource, compliance and risk directors were all in the City of London. 'Royal London House' was proving a portable name – from Finsbury Square to two buildings in Colchester and then northwards to Wilmslow. What had been opened as Refuge House, between Wilmslow and Alderley Edge, Cheshire, was now Royal London House.

Leaving Colchester may have disrupted the lives of many Royal Londoners but the policyholders need not have worried – The Octagon (the former Royal London House), Royal London House (the former Royal London Court) and the sports centre were all sold between 2004 and 2006 for good prices.[19] Triton Court had been sold in 2002. The original leases had only a few years to run, and another comprehensive redevelopment would soon be required. The floor plates were felt to be on the small size for modern use, and the expert investment view was that the better course this time would be to sell rather than to undertake the development. The Board decided that the history of a particular asset was irrelevant and that it had to act in the interests of the members and policyholders. Triton Court remains a memorial to Royal London regardless of who owns the building.

By now the governance of mutuals was coming under scrutiny and a criticism put to Royal London management in 1872 was finally remedied in 2004. Responding to the questions of the Royal Commission, Joseph Degge admitted that few members attended the general meetings of the Royal London Friendly Society or had any means of knowing when and where they were taking place. The rules then provided for a general meeting to be held in October every year of which notice had to be given "either by advertisement in one or more of the London papers, or by circular, forwarded to each member by post" at least 14 days before the meeting. No written notice was given to members and so the only members who would know about the meeting were those alerted by their agent, and any Londoners who happened to see the press advertisement,[20] although Degge suggested, no doubt correctly, that few members in the provinces would go to the expense of coming up to them.[21] He had to concede that as only 5,000 copies of the balance sheet were printed for distribution by the agents, there would be many of the 25,000 members who would be ignorant of the finances of the Society.[22] Members were if anything worse off after the conversion – the articles of association provided that a general meeting would be held on the last Tuesday in April every year at the registered office and there was now no requirement for any newspaper advertisement. Proxies were not permitted under the rules or the articles, only those members who attended the meeting being permitted to vote.

In practice, very few members who had no other connection with the Society were prepared to devote time on a Tuesday in April to discharging their function as owners of the business. Not even the splendid buffet that was available after the meetings in Colchester attracted them. Most of those who attended general meetings were current or former staff, including some retired agents and their immediate managers taking the opportunity to do something that had been denied to them by legislation while they were employed.[23] This unsatisfactory situation in which the Board was essentially accountable to this small group, while most members had no say at all, was tolerated for so long for three reasons: the concern proved to be theoretical rather than real – at times this was a difficult constituency but one that caused no major problems in practice,[24] the directors were far from convinced that the cost of mailing several hundred thousand members every year was justified and a centralised mailing to members would not have been possible for much of the life of the Society because most of the information that would have been required (such as industrial branch policyholders' current addresses) was available only in the district offices.

Gradually, however, attitudes changed although the first attempt at reform ended in failure. With hindsight the Board made two errors. Firstly December 2000 was the wrong time to seek significant changes in governance – this was the year in which Royal London had seen the biggest shake-up in its history with the acquisition of United Assurance and the mass redundancies at Colchester. Many attending the extraordinary general meeting were not favourably disposed towards the Board and were attracted by the prospect of a protest vote. Secondly the proposal was too limited. The thinking had been to change the articles of association as little as possible in the hope that this would encourage support: all that was being suggested was the abolition of the fixed-date annual meeting, a requirement to advertise meetings in the national press and the introduction of proxy voting. The problem was that this opened up another source of opposition – speakers from the floor were either opposed to any change or felt that the changes on offer did not go far enough. In the end, this alliance of opposites succeeded in defeating the resolution.

The prospect of one day having to mail the entire membership highlighted a significant omission – there was no list of members. One had never been needed as admission to general meetings was fairly relaxed, with those attending merely producing some evidence of an existing policy, and it seemed unlikely that requirement in the Companies Acts to maintain a list of members would ever be enforced against a mutual company. The list of members was not the same as the list of policyholders. Whether a person who takes out a policy with a mutual company will become a member, and when that membership will terminate, depends upon the relevant provisions of the constitution of that company – in the case of Royal London, the articles of association. It was soon clear that producing a list of members would not be easy. The original 1908 membership article was straightforward – any person "who effects an insurance on his own life with the Society shall… become a member thereof" and "on ceasing to be insured shall also cease to be a member". This, however, had been amended in 1937 and 1995. The minute books indicated the reasons that had prompted the changes but in both cases the wording that had been adopted produced some uncertainties.[25] Lawyers were needed to construe the articles and apply them to the policies issued over the years. Then computer experts had to develop a programme that could be applied to the data base of all the in-force policies to identify those that gave membership. They conceived a computerised membership list known as MERLIN (Membership of Royal London Insurance). MERLIN operated as a filter, allowing through only membership-conferring policies where no event had occurred, such as an assignment, that had caused membership to be lost. Then duplicates had to be eliminated – there was only one membership regardless of the number of policies – and various anomalies addressed.

The Board returned to the task in 2003. By now the view was increasingly held that good governance of mutuals required members to be treated in the same way as shareholders.[26] They had to be told in advance about meetings, sent at least a summarised form of the report and accounts and given the opportunity to vote regardless of whether they could attend the meeting. Royal London had mailed 70,000 of its members in a consultation exercise in late 2003 and the 7,000 who responded overwhelmingly supported this view. An extraordinary general meeting was called in London for 19 November 2004, at which the result of the consultation was presented. Again, the ardent opponents were there – the old way worked, they claimed, so why change? Some of those who rejected this simplistic approach were still uneasy about the cost of what was being requested in the interests of good governance. Hubert Reid's chairmanship of the meeting, at which robust views were expressed on both sides, won the respect even of the Board's most ardent opponents. Although the contributions from the floor tended to be more in favour than against, it was clear as he put the resolution to the vote that the views of those who had not spoken would determine the outcome. To the relief of those on the platform, the resolution was passed by an overwhelming majority.

The 2005 annual general meeting at the Waldorf Hotel in central London was the first one to operate under the new regime. Several weeks in advance, thanks to MERLIN, the 600,000 members received notice of when and where the meeting would take place, together with an agenda, a copy of the 2004 report and accounts and a form and reply envelope to enable them to vote by proxy even if they could not attend. More than 35,000 members did just that. The votes for and against each resolution, combining the proxy votes received in advance with the votes cast at the meeting, appeared on a screen behind the platform as soon as each vote was taken. Voting at the meeting was by hand-held devices and the whole voting process was under the control of independent scrutineers. All the resolutions were passed with healthy majorities. A number of changes had been made to the articles of associations at various times, all of which had been implemented using a 'cut and a paste' approach, but there had been no thorough overhaul of the articles for more than 60 years. By now, they were showing signs of wear and tear. Over and above the ordinary business, a resolution was passed at the meeting approving a completely new, coherent set of articles, drafted in modern English that adopted current best practice and had been prepared following a consultation exercise involving more than 1,000 members.

In the early years of the twenty-first century, Royal London was doing very much more, however, than modifying and tidying-up what already existed and improving its governance – exciting new businesses were being acquired or created.

CHAPTER 16

A Dramatic Metamorphosis

2001–2011

Royal London Group has a clear vision to focus on its core business – namely distributing our pensions, protection and investment products via our intermediary partners – underpinned by a strong asset management and service proposition.

Mike Yardley, Group Chief Executive, Royal London Group (June 2004)[1]

Against a generally dismal economic backdrop, I am very pleased to report that Royal London had a successful year [in 2009] *with new business at record levels and EEV profits after tax of £404m, increasing the Group's embedded value to £1,840m. Our results evidence the fundamental good sense in Royal London's strategy of concentrating on specialist market segments and providing superior products and services.*

Tim Melville-Ross, Chairman, Royal London Group (2010)[2]

As a result [of the successful execution of its strategy to revitalise its business operations], *the business has been transferred from a home service sales operation into an intermediary office. Royal London has also undertaken initiatives in relation to information technology, service, and product innovation within the U.K. pensions market. These actions are intended to differentiate Royal London by providing a higher level of customized service and products to clients and intermediaries (independent financial advisers and employee-benefit consultants). During this period, management has delivered significant efficiencies, cutting the cost base in half while significantly improving service quality.*

Standard & Poor's, Research Update (July 2010)[3]

In the 21st century, Royal London continued to expand, acquiring Union Fund Management from Union plc for £6.2 million in 2001. The companies, which had funds under management of £1.4 billion, were renamed Royal London Cash Management and Royal London Asset Management (Channel Islands). They provide specialist cash management services for many different types of clients including charities, insurance companies, universities and plcs and gave the Group a significant additional asset management capability. Tom Meade and Chris Chudley both became involved with the business in the late 1970s with Union. By 2010 their team had £5.6 billion under management, making RLCM the UK's largest segregated cash manager. They invest in money market instruments with a range of banks, seeking out the most attractive interest rates relative to their risk rating. Their skill is knowing where to get the best rate of interest for that amount, for that period and at that time. Their traditional 'safety first' approach to cash management has become a key component of many treasurers' and bursars' liquidity solutions.

The acquisition of companies is not the only means of expanding. The 2001 report and accounts referred to the Group's intention to set up a new business to focus on protection products, including term assurance and critical illness cover.[4] It told of a team of senior executives with considerable knowledge and experience of the protection market that had been recruited, and of the huge amount of preparatory work that was under way, ranging from systems development to market research and testing, from product design and procuring to employee recruitment and training. That team was headed by David Robinson, the former head of marketing and business development at Scottish Provident, who had left after its acquisition by Abbey National. The idea was conceived on a flight back from San Francisco with Tracey Ashworth-Davies, then Scottish Provident's HR director. Robinson later told *Connections*: "I was thinking about what to do next in my career and wondered if it was possible to build a protection business from scratch. And not only that, but to be able to do so differently".[5]

Robinson and Ashworth-Davies joined Royal London in September 2001. They had hoped to be able to launch the new business in the summer of 2002 but the requirements of putting together the business were such that it did not roll out until March 2003. Its name – Bright Grey – was intended to reflect the contrast the new business would present in a market perceived as grey, complex and confusing: "The Bright Grey customer-first philosophy will bring clarity and bright new thinking as well as assurance and support during the difficult 'grey' periods in consumers' lives".[6]

Bright Grey's objective is to make life insurance flexible and accessible, with jargon-free documents written in clear and simple language, and to provide an outstanding customer service. The time in establishing the complex framework of systems, procedures and skilled staff was soon vindicated – in

2004 Bright Grey was writing business with an annual premium of £18.5 million and winning plaudits from customers and intermediaries. The products are available through intermediaries – initially only independent financial advisers, but latterly via internet intermediaries selling through comparison websites – and include life and critical illness cover and income and payments sickness protection. The *Helping Hand* service, available to policyholders and their families, provides access to 24-hour helplines and a wide range of practical, medical and personal support, including specialist physiotherapy, speech therapy, a cancer nurse and bereavement counselling.

Robinson talked to *Connections* about hierarchy and bureaucracy killing innovation, interaction and creativity and how a key theme around the setting-up of Bright Grey had been that people were valued for their contribution rather than their status. In April 2010 Bright Grey was awarded the *Investors in People* gold standard. This is a national standard which aims to increase the productivity of the UK economy by helping organisations achieve success by engaging their people. IIP, as it spokesperson put it, is not about a badge or a logo, but "rather about ensuring that the organisation was performing as well as possible both for its people and its customers". By the end of 2009, Bright Grey had an intermediary market share of around 8 per cent, despite fierce competition, with new business during the year of £167 million.

Observers may have felt that after several acquisitions and creating a new business from scratch, the Royal London transformation was complete, at least for a while. It was not. A report in 2007 pointed out:

> The retail life fund market has changed rapidly and dramatically over the past decade during which time many funds closed to new business. In the first quarter of 2007, more than 11 million policyholders had assets in 70 formally closed life office funds worth in aggregate about £190bn. Of this figure, the consolidators – companies set up specifically to buy and aggregate closed insurance company funds – have bought closed funds valued at approximately £80bn.[7]

The direct sales force was generally the only source of a company's new business and so no new policies would be issued after it had been shut down. For so long as any of the company's existing policies remained in force, however, premiums would have to be collected and a service provided for the policyholders to deal with the day-to-day administration and claims under perhaps several hundred thousand (or even millions) of policies, while the investments in the fund supporting the policies had to be managed. The attraction of disposing of a closed fund to a consolidator was that the company could make a clean break, and did not have to continue administering policies long after it had withdrawn from the market. Often economies of scale could be achieved by a third party administering many closed funds that had the systems and processes in place to do so.

Resolution Life was formed in 2004 to acquire closed funds. It purchased the life assurance business of Royal & Sun Alliance and Swiss Life in the UK and then merged with Britannic, which had closed to new business in 2003. In 2006 Resolution acquired from Abbey (by now part of Santander, a Spanish banking group) Scottish Mutual, Scottish Provident and Abbey National Life. Corporate strategies soon change, especially after an acquisition: Abbey had only acquired Scottish Provident in 2001.

In July 2007 a merger between Resolution and Friends Provident was announced, subject to shareholder approval. By September, however, other proposals were being discussed – Standard Life and Swiss Re were in the running – but in January 2008 Resolution's shareholders voted to accept an offer from Pearl Group, another consolidator headed by entrepreneur Hugh Osmond who had made his name creating Pizza Express.[8] The offer was supported by Royal London who agreed to pay Pearl some £1.27 billion – and to provide a loan of £0.3 billion – on the basis that, on completion of the deal, the active businesses that Resolution had acquired along the way would be transferred to Royal London. These were:

- the protection business of Scottish Provident and Scottish Mutual, including the in-force policies
- Phoenix Life Assurance Limited, formerly Abbey National Life, the products of which were distributed through Abbey's national branch network
- Scottish Provident International Life Assurance, based in the Isle of Man.

The acquisition included the new business operations of these companies and the investment management of the underlying funds. More than 1.25 million policies were ultimately transferred to Royal London. The purchase was in part funded by the £400 million of subordinated debt that had been raised in December 2005 when Royal London completed a major transaction in the capital markets via a subsidiary, RL Finance Bonds plc. The bonds were offered to institutional investors and were almost three times oversubscribed. As Stephen Shone explained at the time, "The new capital raised will add to our financial strength and make greater financial resources available for the further development and growth of the Group".[9]

The agreement with Pearl was completed on 1 May 2008. Mike Yardley saw the acquisition of the businesses from Resolution Life as a means of driving forward the Group's strategy and anticipated major benefits:

Scottish Provident is a well-known and well-respected brand, which together with Bright Grey [will] consolidate our position as the leading provider in the UK protection sector. Phoenix Life Assurance will add further new business capability and provide us with a new channel to market through the Abbey branches. Internationally, Scottish Provident International will add significant scale to our existing offshore operations through Scottish Life International.[10]

The protection business of Scottish Provident signified an acceleration in Royal London's ambitions in the protection market. Scottish Provident offers a wide range of protection plans for either a set term or for whole of life, their products being distributed via financial advisers. Scottish Provident's 200 employees in Glasgow are now part of Royal London, although the customer services operation and some support functions continue to be outsourced. There were those who expected a merger with Bright Grey but Royal London remains committed to a dual brand strategy. Scottish Provident was a pioneer in the protection industry and is the provider of market-leading, award-winning products. Bright Grey is seen as having a larger presence in the middle market with a younger clientele whereas Scottish Provident is stronger in the older, high net worth market. In 2009 Scottish Provident achieved £203 million of new business.

Another element of the Resolution-Pearl transaction for Royal London was an exclusive agreement to distribute protection products through the retail branch network and telephone distribution team of Abbey, formerly Abbey National, now owned by Santander. The agreement covered the right to sell, under the Phoenix Life brand, life, critical illness, stakeholder pension and life investment products. After the agreement had been transferred (technically 'novated') to Royal London, the branding was changed and the products are now sold under the Royal London name. Royal London's involvement was soon extended to include the branches of Alliance & Leicester and Bradford & Bingley following their acquisition by Santander. From mid-2011, this business will be written by Aviva.

Royal London 360° is the international business of the Royal London Group launched at the beginning of 2009, following the coming together of Scottish Provident International Life Assurance (acquired as part of the Resolution and Pearl transaction) and Scottish Life International. Royal London 360° is based in the offshore financial centre of the Isle of Man and does business in the Far East, Africa, Germany, the Middle East and the United Kingdom, with offices in Hong Kong, South Africa, Lebanon and Dubai. The acquisition of SPILA was indicative of the Group's intention to increase its presence in international markets – Royal London now had a 360° approach to international business, hence the name of the new business that aims to provide offshore investors, generally high net worth individuals, with a combination of investment choice, security and quality service. It offers a broad range of offshore investment and savings plans, protection policies, and tax and estate planning products via financial advisers. In its first year, Royal London 360° achieved new business of £237 million. Such are the challenges of an international business that, more than 60 years after an enemy invasion disrupted Royal London's operations in the Channel Islands, SLI's regional sales manager for the Middle East had to be evacuated from Beirut by a Royal Navy destroyer during the 2006 Lebanon War.

If closed life books demand ways of dealing efficiently and profitably with legacies from the past, 'wrap platforms' are very much of the present and future. They enable financial advisers to view and manage online a client's savings and investments portfolio. Clients generally spread their investments around – they may have a couple of ISAs, several private pensions and a number of investments in funds, all from different providers and asset managers. Traditionally financial advisers had to deal with each investment individually. The reports of performance that they received may have covered different periods, and been in various formats, and the adviser had to aggregate all of this for the client. The report could only be a snapshot at that moment – if during the year clients wanted to review their investments, the adviser had to update the position in relation to each investment. A wrap puts all of this together, and provides a living report online that allows the adviser (and increasingly the client) access at any time to see the value of each investment and assess the performance of the portfolio as a whole. A wrap platform is, however, more than a means of reporting. The investments are made and held in the name of the wrap-provider, as the client's nominee. The wrap provider is, in effect, a non-discretionary asset manager that invests and disinvests only on the client's instructions, received via the adviser. As a result, because the asset managers are not having to deal with individual customers, investments will be free of any initial charge that would normally be payable, and may well benefit from reduced annual charges.

As financial advisers were by now the key new business channel for Royal London, it came as no surprise that "the Group continually seeks further business opportunities to strengthen its offerings through IFAs". The corporate development team had identified the growth potential of wrap services and, in November 2007, Royal London acquired the Investment Funds Direct Group and its systems provider, Investment Sciences. Funds Direct was at the forefront of this fast-growing market through its 'Ascentric' wrap platform and had already established a good market presence with a strong and well respected management team and robust systems. The history of Funds Direct began in a firm of stockbrokers in Bath and the company was briefly owned by Prudential. Back in private hands, its entrepreneurial owners realised that they needed financial support beyond what could be provided by private individuals. Hugo Thorman and his team were attracted to Royal London because they liked the people and because Royal London was keen for them to continue as an 'independent' service to IFAs, and not to create a 'Royal London wrap' as a means of promoting its own products.

Ascentric charges an agreed annual fee (a percentage of the value of the portfolio) and a fee for each transaction, and the process is totally transparent with the client seeing every transaction on the report – there are no hidden deductions by way of commission. It is then a matter for the client to agree a fee for his adviser. This approach is very much in line with Royal London's, and now the FSA's, thinking and a wrap platform will provide valuable support to the adviser charging regime.[11] For Ascentric, 2008 was a transitional year of systems improvements and only a limited increase in new business. During 2009, however, 182 adviser firms signed-up, and by the end of the year, Ascentric had assets of £1.15 billion under administration – a 94 per cent increase in 12 months.

RLAM (Royal London Asset Management), the very first diversification from home service, has gone from strength to strength. The fund management arm of the Royal London Group employs more than 130 people at 55 Gracechurch Street, near to the Monument in the City of London, and has a range of external clients including institutions (pension schemes, charities, local authorities and universities), wealth managers, fund-of-fund managers and private investors. RLAM manages a number of segregated funds – funds that comprise the investments of one client. They may extend over the asset classes, and require RLAM to maintain specified percentages of the fund in equities (stocks and shares), bonds, property and cash. This is the basis upon which RLAM manages the Royal London life fund and other funds within the Group. External institutional clients, however, often split their assets between several managers so the RLAM mandate may be limited to one asset class. In either case RLAM will have discretion over the individual assets purchased and sold and there will be an investment objective – generally to outperform a published index by a specified percentage. Where less than £50 million is involved, it is generally not practical to set up a segregated fund but RLAM can offer pension schemes a number of pooled pension funds in which they can invest.[12]

RLAM's wholesale distribution channel is made up of various types of intermediaries looking to invest on behalf of their clients. An asset manager with the discretion to invest without the client's approval may choose one of RLAM's open-ended investment companies,[13] or a 'multi manager' may include a RLAM fund in a packaged investment product that it is creating to offer externally, typically to high net worth individuals. Some of RLAM's funds are also available to private individuals via their financial advisers. This type of business is increasingly being transacted through fund supermarkets or wrap platforms that help financial advisers and their clients organise investments from a number of different providers, and limits the number of client accounts that asset managers have to maintain.

RLAM offers a number of equity funds – some are confined to a region (for example the Far East or Europe) or to a country (such as the UK) or a particular type of company (such as mid-cap companies). In 2010, 50 per cent of RLAM's actively managed equity funds performed in the top two quartiles, earning prestigious *Citywire* ratings for a number of its fund managers. RLAM's fixed income team is led by Jonathan Platt, a well respected UK bond manager, who joined RLAM in 1985 and became Head of Fixed Income in 1992. He and his team regularly win industry awards. The assets, that range from government bonds to corporate debt, managed by the team have grown by over 60 per cent over the past five years to £18.7 billion at the end of 2010. *The Royal London Pooled Corporate Bond Fund*, the flagship corporate bond fund, outperformed its benchmark in 2010 by 2.4 per cent. RLAM is a major property investor, managing a number of broadly diversified UK commercial property funds for internal and external clients. The property team has won awards, in particular for management of the property assets in the Royal London life funds and 2010 was a good year for the investment operations of the Group. The asset management businesses added £2.3 billion in new assets during the year, including fixed income, equities, property and cash.

Scottish Life was a business new to Royal London that had been acquired in 2001 to address the over-reliance on the direct sales force as the only method of distribution. It was wanted for what it was, not for what it could be converted into. As a result there was little of the trauma often experienced after an acquisition and it was almost business as usual for Scottish Life. Steady progress was made – new business increased by 14 per cent in 2002 and by 2003, 68 per cent of the Group's business was being sold via intermediaries.

Scottish Life provides (what used to be called private) pensions to individuals, or to companies for their employees. Nowadays the latter are mainly 'group personal pensions', where a number of individual pension plans are set up by an employer who deducts an agreed amount from the employees' salaries, adds the employer's own contribution, and pays the total amount for each employee to the pensions company.[14] A pension plan traditionally involved building up a fund with a pensions provider to be used on the retirement date to purchase an annuity – a financial product that pays a regular income for at least the rest of the policyholder's life in exchange for the lump sum.[15] Policyholders can generally take up to 25 per cent of the value of their fund as a tax-free lump sum on retirement. Now, however, early payment options are permitted – for example, in certain circumstances, policyholders may receive a tax-free lump sum from their pension plan after the age of 55 while still building up the fund. Scottish Life is a market leader in this field and its *Income Release* product won the 2009 *Innovators Awards* from Scotland Financial Enterprise for the best new innovation.[16] Scottish Life was successful not only in its category – innovation in customer focus – but was also the overall winner.

There needs to be flexibility to meet the changing needs of the customer. Single or regular payments, or payments transferred from an existing pension plan, are all accepted and 'premium holidays' can be accommodated. Scottish Life offers a choice of investment options. The company will invest policyholders' pension funds in accordance with their risk profiles in a selection of investment funds, managed by a number of leading investment managers, that provide access to a range of assets from company shares (equities) to cash and property. Alternatively policyholders can make their own investment choices or request that their funds are invested in a way that will enable them to track an index. Here too Scottish Life has received recognition, winning the 2010 *Ultimate Default Fund* award at the annual Corporate Adviser Awards.

All Scottish Life's sales are via independent financial advisers who give advice to their clients, and recommend products and providers. There is no direct selling. This differs from the traditional Royal London model of an employed sales force but, in another respect, nothing has changed. The industrial assurance offices long made the point that they gained nothing from lapses – policies that quickly went off the books because the policyholder, for whatever reason, stopped paying the premiums. The same is true in relation to pensions in the twenty-first century:

> *Persistency and loyalty of our customers is critical to profitability. This is why* [Scottish Life has]*... invested in delivering a high standard of customer experience. However, we also believe that the levels of persistency needed to deliver adequate profitability require fundamental change in the charging structure of pension products and in particular how IFA remuneration is recovered through the charging structure. In 2005 we extended the use of our Financial Adviser's Fee (FAF) commission option... FAF is an explicit and transparent charge to the customer's pension fund to remunerate the IFA for the service provided to the pension scheme. The transparency of the charge is critical as it allows customers to understand the value of the services provided by the IFA.*[17]

The point is simple – IFAs should be remunerated like any other professional adviser by a fee disclosed to and agreed with their client rather than by a commission set by the product provider. Scottish Life is not prepared to 'buy' business by offering high commission, and in 2009 the disappointing sales of group pensions "reflected our decision not to compete in the initial commission sector. There are still serious issues with unsustainable commission rates being paid by some companies which distort the current market".[18] These views on remuneration are now shared by the FSA and from January 2013 advisers will no longer be able to receive commissions set by product providers in return for recommending pensions or investment products. Instead they will have to operate their own charging tariffs based on level of service and agree these with their clients.[19] Scottish Life maintains a team of 110 sales consultants around the country and an account management unit to support financial advisers. There are now more than 1,100 Scottish Life and other Royal London Group employees based in Edinburgh. Scottish Life's new business is hitting record levels. In 2009 it was £1,578m, 4 per cent up on 2008, and a significant increase is anticipated for 2010.[20]

The performance of any company will be influenced by the environment in which it is operating and the enlarging Royal London Group was not greeted by a period of economic stability. 2001 was "one of the worst in recent history for total investment returns; following on from the previous poor year we have now seen a classic bear market in world stock markets".[21] The FTSE All-share fell 15.4 per cent over the year with the Dow Jones falling 14.3 per cent in a week following the attacks of 9/11. Far from improving, the situation worsened the following year:

> The board paid close attention throughout 2002 to the financial strength of the Group. The falls in equity markets seen in 2000 and 2001 continued and accelerated in 2002, with further deterioration at the start of 2003. The extent of the falls required a careful response and we have actively managed our asset mix during the year. We have been steadily reducing the proportion of equities which we hold in the Royal London with profits funds since the summer of 2001. By switching into bonds we limited the reduction in the value of our funds and also ensured that the Group's liabilities were matched against less volatile assets.[22]

In fact more benign times were imminent. Equity markets fell to new lows at the time of the invasion of Iraq in 2003 but the situation improved in the second half of the year. By the year-end all major markets were delivering returns in excess of 15 per cent and they continued to produce good returns between 2004 and 2006, despite a slight deterioration in 2006. By autumn 2007 the FTSE 100 had almost recovered to where it had been at the start of the new millennium, but then Northern Rock admitted that it was being supported by the Bank of England, triggering the first run on a British bank for over a century. The impact of 'the credit crunch' soon began to be felt and while Royal London had not been direct investors in 'sub-prime', it was not immune to the wider impact on asset values and to achieve a positive return of 3.9 per cent was a pleasing result. 2008 was the year of banking collapses and staggering losses made by those who invested in complex, property-backed investments, and when 'collateralised debt obligations' became a term of everyday speech. Royal London had no significant exposure to either but could hardly escape the effect of a fall of over 30 per cent of the FTSE 100 during the year, and comparable falls in other world markets. The with-profits fund made a negative return of 15.2 per cent in 2008, with the Group's embedded value dropping from £2,198 million to £1,436 million during the course of year. There was no shortage of grounds for pessimism at the beginning of 2009 – global economies were in free-fall, the financial crisis looked set to continue and the UK was in a recession. To the surprise of many, the year ended with some signs of economic stabilisation and rising equity markets. The with-profits fund was back into the positive, posting a 12 per cent return, and the Group's embedded value had increased to £1,840 million. The noughties were a lost decade for the FTSE 100 – on 31 December 1999 it closed at 6930.20. Ten years later it was at 5412.88.

All of this was of particular interest to Royal London policyholders with maturing policies. Bonuses continued to compare well with those of other companies, and to provide good long-term returns, although they were falling in absolute terms. For example, the payout on a 25-year Royal London policy maturing in 2006 (taken out by a male aged 29 paying £50 a month) was £55,096, representing a return of 9.2 per cent per year. Payouts from some companies under comparable policies were less than £40,000. Prudence demands today that pay-outs on maturity are in line with the policy's underlying value or 'asset share', after allowing for smoothing that reduces the impact of any extreme variations on returns in particular years.[23] Royal London had at times in the past paid maturities in excess of asset share, and its bonuses are reducing partly because of the need to bring them down over time to asset share. But it is not all bad news – asset shares can be enhanced. The Board was very keen to highlight the benefits of Royal London's mutual status and in 2007 committed itself to the principle of allocating a proportion of the profits earned on the businesses as a form of 'mutual dividend'. In 2007 this amounted to £39 million which was allocated by means of enhancement to asset shares of relevant policies. Because of the poor market conditions, no mutual dividend was declared in 2008 but in 2009 a dividend of £25 million was used to enhance asset shares of the relevant policies.[24]

Since the days of Wooding, Erith and Slee, a number of non-executive directors have passed through the boardroom – Barry Skipper, a former director of Booker and a director of Norwich City Football Club, Tony

Percival, a chartered accountant and former partner of Coopers & Lybrand and finance director of Kingfisher, Fields Wicker-Miurin, who had been chief financial officer and director of strategy at the London Stock Exchange and was co-founder of Leaders' Quest (an international non-profit leadership development organisation), Tom Ross, the chairman of Scottish Life at the time of the acquisition and a past president of the Faculty of Actuaries, and Trevor Bish-Jones, who after holding senior retail, buying and marketing roles at Boots and Dixons was chief executive of Woolworths.

Hubert Reid retired at the end of 2005 after nine years as a director, six of them as chairman. He had been responsible for driving forward the huge changes that had occurred during that period, not least in the area of corporate governance. He was supportive of, and challenging to, the executive team who benefited from his wise counsel and wholehearted encouragement. He was succeeded by Tim Melville-Ross, a non-executive director since 1999 and deputy chairman since 2002, whose business career had begun with BP and included a posting to Libya, just after the Gaddafi revolution. He had been chief executive of the Nationwide Building Society and director-general of the Institute of Directors, and was chairman of several companies and the Council of the University of Essex.

The current non-executive directors are Robert Jeens, a chartered accountant, formerly a partner of Touche Ross and finance director of Kleinwort Benson and the Woolwich, David Williams who was an executive at Diageo, PepsiCo and Whitbread and is a non-executive director of Mothercare, and Duncan Ferguson, who has had 40 years' experience in senior management of insurance companies and as a consulting actuary, and is a past president of the Institute of Actuaries. Tim Melville-Ross was awarded the CBE in 2005 and is now chairman of the Higher Education Funding Council for England.

There are four executive directors – Mike Yardley, Stephen Shone, Andy Carter and John Deane. Carter joined RLAM in 2001 as chief investment officer after an investment management career with Provident Life and Gartmore, where he was head of UK equities, and became chief executive of RLAM in 2003. Deane, who is chief executive of Royal London's intermediary division, is an actuary with many years' senior management experience in IT, administration, compliance, risk, distribution and corporate development. He joined in 2007 from Old Mutual where he had been corporate development director. He was amongst a group of senior financial services executives who, in 2009, cycled 977 miles from Land's End to John O'Groats in ten days to raise money for Macmillan Cancer Support and Naomi House, a children's hospice.

Royal London provides an example of the way in which boards have developed over 50 years. In 1961 there were seven regional managers, a former regional manager (Stanley Goodall, joint managing director) and one member of a profession (Ernest Haynes, joint managing director and chairman) around the board table. All but the professional had joined straight from school. All were executive directors with no outside business interests. In 2010 there were three actuaries, two accountants and six members of the Board who had held senior executive office elsewhere, five of them in financial services. Three of the four executive directors joined Royal London after successful careers elsewhere. Only Yardley has a length of service anything like comparable with the archetypal Royal London director of years gone by. Non-executives comprise the majority of the Board (or at least will do again when a replacement for Bish-Jones has been appointed) and all serve as directors or trustees of other organisations.

The Board is relatively low-key and modest in describing this latest phase of Royal London's history, referring to the evolutionary journey over the past 12 years as being one of successful adaptation to a changing financial services market:

> *Driven by the core objective of delivering good returns for the benefit of our members and policyholders, our strategy has been one of improving profitability and capital strength. We have achieved this through improving growth prospects and lowering the risk profile of the Group, making acquisitions that make financial sense, improving the economics of the business and re-shaping the Group to meet future challenges.*[25]

The points are well made, suggesting as they do that measuring success is not just a question of reviewing figures, although the figures taken from the 2009 report and accounts are certainly impressive.

Table No. 6

Performance of the Royal London Group: 1998–2009

	1998 £m	2009 £m
Gross Premium income (including general insurance)	515	2,916
Investment income	841	3,071
Total assets at year-end	7,105	31,377
Funds-under-management at year-end	7,600	37,529

During that journey, the presentation and language of the annual accounts of life assurance companies have changed as a result of legislation (much of it originating from the European Union), international reporting standards and regulatory requirements. By 2009 measures as crude as 'premium income' and 'assets' are things of the past – the accounts now refer to profitability, rather than premium income, and capital strength (using such terms as 'available working capital', 'regulatory capital' and 'unallocated divisible surplus') rather than assets. A fundamental bottom-line indicator has emerged. 'Expense ratio' is no more – the latest accounts reveal that in 2009 Royal London made a profit (after tax) of £404 million.[26]

In 1861 Royal London was founded as an assurance company that employed agents to call on customers in their homes. The nature of that business evolved, and competent chief executives coped with a multitude of problems and drove through significant changes, without some of which the Society's future might have been in doubt. A recurring concern was the cost of providing the service. At the end of the twentieth century, Royal London was still an assurance company that employed agents to call on customers in their homes. The only diversification was that those in the company responsible for investing its assets could now pitch for external funds. Expenses remained high relative to the premium income. The Royal London that Degge, Ridge and Hambridge had created by the 1880s was still in place more than a century later.

Few, if any, organisations are ready to embrace change but Royal London, given the consistency of its business model, probably found it more difficult than most. The serene progress of the previous 140 years, coupled with assets of more than £7 billion, inspired an air of confidence, verging on 'we know best'. Any modifications to the daily practice were regarded by some with suspicion and new business initiatives were often seen as threats. Those striving for change at an operational level sometimes struggled to make their voices heard. There had long been a recognition that expenses were high and needed to be reduced, and attempts were constantly being made to do so, but there was little focus on the profit and loss account, and the profitability or otherwise of the business. The favoured financial measure remained the expense ratio, with much emphasis on the balance sheet and the Society's very healthy reserves. On top of all of this, the direct sales force – apart from RLAM, the only source of new business in 1999 – was finding it hard to meet the ever more demanding requirements of the regulators. This was the Royal London that confronted Mike Yardley and Stephen Shone. As Yardley said, looking back on this time: "The first question was 'is Royal London a survivor?' The answer was 'unlikely'. We had to get bigger and change the footprint of the company in the market".[27]

In the first decade of the twenty-first century, that footprint certainly changed. The traditional business was closed and replaced by a portfolio of financial services businesses whose products were available via independent financial advisers. While all of this was happening, the annual premium income was increasing from £515 million to £2.9 billion and the assets from £7.1 billion to £31.3 billion. In 2009 the Group's profit after tax was £404 million. Performance during 2010 was impressive – by December, the forecast for the full year suggested that all parts of the Group will have performed well. In 2009 the Group's embedded value increased 28 per cent to £1.84 billion – it is predicted to have increased to more than £2 billion during 2010.

The Group's success did not go un-noticed. Standard & Poor's, the rating agency, revised its outlook on Royal London from 'stable' to 'positive' in July 2010,[28] referring to the successful execution of its strategy to revitalise its business operations. The word 'transformation' is often used but this seems somehow inadequate to describe the change to Royal London since the turn of the century, and 're-engineer' or 'recreate' are no better. It was surely Hubert Reid who best captured what was taking place when he referred to "a dramatic metamorphosis".[29] And yet, it is wrong to suggest that there is no connection between the old and the new. It is as true now as it was then that the best way to attract new business is to impress customers and potential customers with the way in which you deal with existing business. Margaret Jones and Naomi Lovett (see Chapter 3) were just two of the many who wrote to William Hambridge in the 1870s expressing their satisfaction with the service they had received and commitment to recommend Royal London to their friends. Matilda Priss de Austein, for example, wrote from St David's Place, Swansea, in December 1876 to thank the Society for the prompt payment on the death of her husband. It was clear to her "that great attention is paid by your Office to such matters". The success of Royal London has been due in no small measure to the fact that great attention has always been paid to such matters. This remains so in the metamorphosed business. The *Financial Adviser Awards* have established themselves as the benchmark for service levels in the industry, with around 10,000 advisers voting. In 2010 Scottish Life was voted 'Best for Service' in the life and pensions category and retained the 5 Star Award gained for 'Excellent Service' in 2008. We can only conclude from this that, 134 years after the death of Richard William de Austein, the Royal London Group is still paying great attention to the service that it provides, and that this must have been a major contributor to its outstanding success.

At the end of August 2010 Mike Yardley, after 32 years with Royal London, 12 of them as group chief executive, decided that this was the appropriate time for the search to begin for the person who would lead the company in its next phase of development. He announced that he would leave the company as soon as a successor had been appointed. There were good grounds for his confidence that Royal London was in an excellent position to continue to grow profitably for the benefit of its members.

The fact that few of Royal London's traditional competitors have survived illustrates the extent of the challenges when he took over. In responding to Yardley's decision, Tim Melville-Ross said:

> When Mike was appointed chief executive officer in 1998, Royal London was a home service provider with a high cost base and a diminishing franchise. Mike built a strong executive team and, through a series of transactions and a robust approach to cost control and business development, Royal London has now become a strongly capitalised, diversified group offering quality products and services to its members and customers. Royal London, its customers and members have every reason to be grateful for what he has achieved.
>
> Mike is an outstanding CEO who has transformed Royal London into the successful and well-regarded organisation it is today. He has also played a leading role in bringing about some of the changes in the financial services market place which will lead to higher quality and better value products and services for customers everywhere.[30]

From time to time, all chief executives find themselves featured in the financial press. Soon after his appointment, *Money Marketing* referred to Yardley's modesty but suggested that there was "absolutely nothing casual about his plans for Royal London. Just scientific analysis".[31] The *Daily Mail* has described him as a shy six footer, short of bull and bluster.[32] Those who reported to him refer to his calmness, whether the news they brought was good or bad. Almost inevitably, interviewers ask about the relevance of his previous role as a fund manager in view of the portfolio of businesses into which Royal London has been converted. His response to *Money Marketing* was that:

> It might seem a little haphazard and opportunistic but it is like running a fund, looking at your portfolio all the time and seeing where you can add to it. It also means looking at process and having the ability to say no... You must be prepared to pit your skills against everyone in the market. There is a huge intellectual and competitive challenge. You know there is a minefield in front of you but you have to have the attitude to walk through it and it gives you a great buzz.[33]

Yardley's role in changing the financial services marketplace included his chairing of one of the five working groups as part of the Retail Distribution Review. The work of his group contributed to the FSA's decision to prohibit independent financial advisers from receiving commissions from product providers, and requiring them to agree their charges with their clients.[34] He is on the board of the Association of British Insurers, chairman of the Association of Financial Mutuals (the trade body representing mutual insurers, friendly societies, and other financial mutuals in the UK) and a director of the Juvenile Diabetes Research Foundation.

Mike Yardley has proved to be a clear thinker, prepared to take brave decisions, and with that same determination to succeed that his illustrious predecessors must have possessed. He has a relaxed, engaging manner that has probably attracted people to do business with or work for Royal London who before talking to him had no thoughts of so doing. He is the first to acknowledge the contribution made by Stephen Shone. Both were determined to put Royal London on the twenty-first century financial services map and neither saw its mutual status as an impediment to achieving their objectives. The metamorphosis would not have been achieved without Stephen's energy, drive, financial acumen, commitment to getting the deal (or whatever other task he is working on) done and sense of humour.

Just as Joseph Degge, Henry Ridge and William Hambridge founded the original Royal London, Mike Yardley and Stephen Shone are the founders of the Royal London of 2011. The only obvious similarity between the two sets of leaders is the combination of northerners and southerners – maybe this created a vital dynamic at the top of Royal London during these two crucial periods. What is certain is that they would not have accomplished what they did without trusting and respecting each other, or without the support of directors who were prepared to back them, and to take bold decisions in the interests of members and policyholders.

Appendix 1

Industrial Assurance and its Critics

Industrial assurance is defined by the Industrial Assurance Act, 1923, as the business of effecting assurance upon human life, premiums in respect of which are payable at intervals of less than two months and are received by collectors; these collectors make house to house visits for that purpose; in the main the premiums are collected weekly. The business can be carried on only by friendly societies registered under the Friendly Societies Act, 1896, or by assurance companies within the meaning of the Assurance Companies Act, 1909, which are either registered under the Companies Acts, or the Industrial and Provident Societies Acts, or incorporated by special Act of Parliament.

Report of the Committee on Industrial Assurance and assurance on the lives of children under ten years of age, chaired by Sir Benjamin Cohen KC (July 1933)[1]

A household to which wages are brought home weekly frames its budget accordingly; it seldom has a reserve of income from which to make large payments at infrequent intervals [such as insurance premiums payable yearly, half yearly or quarterly], and still more seldom a bank account on which cheques can be drawn. If systematic contributions to assurance are to be kept up in these conditions, they must be related to the weekly or monthly pay envelope and collected when the money is in hand. Failing this, the odds are that the money will be used in other ways.

Dermot Morrah, industrial life assurance historian (1955)[2]

Industrial assurance was subjected to regular critical analysis – there was a Royal Commission in the 1870s,[3] an examination by a distinguished economist during World War I[4] and two government committees between the wars.[5] A comprehensive book was published, inspired by the report of the second of the two committees, followed by a potted version that was rather more palatable to the general reader,[6] while William Beveridge expressed unfavourable views in his report that was instrumental in creating the welfare state.[7]

One early concern was gradually addressed, but six criticisms were made and repeated in these reports, and an eighth was added in the 1940s as part of the debate on the welfare state and nationalisation. No history of Royal London could be complete without referring to them, but they hardly benefit from an investigation-by-investigation approach. Instead they are gathered together here with the responses advanced by the offices at the time and a few observations of the author.

The appendix refers essentially to industrial assurance in the narrow sense of the regular cash collection of premiums for life policies, although some of the criticisms were still being made in the days of "home service" when industrial assurance was available from the agent alongside general insurance, such as building and contents cover, and ordinary life assurance, where premiums were paid over longer periods – quarterly, half yearly and annually – and increasingly by monthly standing order and then direct debit.

Table No. 7

Criticisms of Industrial Assurance

	Criticisms	Response of the offices at the time
1	The insurance company might well become insolvent before the benefits were due so that premiums would have been paid in vain.	The complaint was valid in the mid-nineteenth century but not subsequently. As the years progressed the solvency of the offices ceased to be an issue.
	Comments of the author	
	The great financial strength built up by the offices came to be one of their great attractions.	
2	Insuring the lives of young children could lead to premature deaths at the hands of parent or guardians.	There will always be isolated cases where a killing is prompted wholly or in part by the fact that the victim is insured, and this applies to adults as well as children, but no credible evidence has been produced that supports the view that children whose lives were insured are at any more risk than those who are not. Legislation limits the sums for which children can be insured, and provides that payment can be made only to the parent or guardian of the child.
	Comments of the author	
	There were clearly those who genuinely believed that this was a serious risk but there was a lack of any general evidence. As the 1889 Select Committee of the House of Commons robustly put it, anybody who is in a position to profit pecuniarily by the death of another may be said to be exposed to temptation.	

	Criticisms	Response of the offices at the time
3	Too high a proportion of premiums were used to pay agents and other expenses of the offices.	Policies would not have been taken out and payments made without canvassing and collecting. The ill-fated Post Office scheme (under which only 6,500 policies were issued between 1865 and 1882) provides evidence that home visits were essential for working-class assurance. Many reviews of the Post Office scheme were undertaken and the lack of success was blamed on the absence of canvassers and collectors, and the fact that post offices were not open at times that suited the working man.

Canvassing and collecting inevitably involve a cost and the small premiums mean that expenses will always represent a material proportion of the total premiums collected. |

Comments of the author

Of course canvassing and collecting was expensive, and the proportion of expenses to premiums would always be significant, but the question was whether the proportions achieved by the offices were appropriate. The Cohen Committee suggested in 1933 that 30% should be the maximum permitted expense ratio.[8] It was not until after the World War II that Royal London consistently achieved an expense ratio below 40% and this was not maintained. The Prudential had already reduced its expense ratio to 25% by assigning specific territories to agents.[9] Other offices should have quickly followed their example, although for many this would have involved abolishing the agents' right to sell their books (see 7 below), and given the level of trade union and agent opposition, this was easier said than done.

The annual expense ratio may have been the traditional indicator but this was a crude measure that ignored inflation, the profitability of the new business and investment income.

	Criticisms	Response of the offices at the time
4	Persistency was poor – too many policies were forfeited when the payment of premiums lapsed.	Discontinuance is inherent in any system involving frequent regular payments. The policyholder may have over-estimated his/her ability to pay, suffered a change in circumstances such as illness or loss of employment, or simply changed his/her mind and decided that the protection provided by the policy was no longer a priority. Legislation requiring the service of a forfeiture notice and the grant of a free policy provides a measure of protection. Many of the policies that are not eligible for a free policy lapse after only one or two payments and so the loss to the policyholder is minimal. Policies that almost immediately lapse are of no benefit to the offices whose time setting them up is wasted, nor (at least latterly) to agents who have their commission for such sales 'clawed-back'. There are many cases where a customer discontinues a policy for whatever reason, and then later takes out a similar policy with the same or a different office.

Comments of the author

The various committees were quick to criticise on the basis that so high an overall proportion of lapses suggested that there must have been over-persuasion by agents, but the lack of case reviews and statistical analysis makes it difficult to identify the extent. Industrial assurance could not have existed without persuasion by the agents – people sometimes need to be persuaded to do the right thing. Given the millions of policies sold, there probably were many cases of over-persuasion and, by modern standards, the offices should have done more sooner to establish exactly what was happening and taken more strenuous action to improve persistency.

Switching the provider might not have been prudent – a reduced sum may have been payable if death occurred within the first year of the new policy and a change may have had an adverse impact on bonuses, where these were payable – but the point does illustrate that not every 'lapser' suffered from long-term lack of cover.

	Criticisms	Response of the offices at the time
5	Industrial assurance was wrongly focused. There was over assurance of funeral expenses and under insurance on the life of the breadwinner to make provision for dependents.	Our customers remain as anxious as ever to provide their relatives with a decent funeral and this involves an expense that they would not be able to meet without taking out insurance.

Comments of the author

The view had been expressed from the very beginning that 'the poor' spent too much on funerals: they were grander than anything they enjoyed in life.[10] But even allowing for the right of a person to insure what he/she likes, there was over assurance of funeral expenses. Sometimes, many family members took out policies on the same relative's life, so that the funeral expenses were covered many times over, and some of the insurance money represented 'a windfall' for the proposers.[11]

The Cohen Committee believed that the "average husband and father of the British industrial class is certainly much under-insured" but, in suggesting that persuading customers to switch the insurance money into policies on the lives of husbands and fathers could transform "industrial assurance into a real provision for the family of the breadwinner", was overlooking how small the sums payable under these policies would have been, unless premiums could also have been increased.[12] But any provision would probably have been better than nothing.

	Criticisms	Response of the offices at the time
6	Many life-of-another policies were illegal and should never have been issued because the proposer did not have the required relationship with the life assured.	Agents are instructed to comply with the law, but given the number of policies, there probably are some illegal ones.

Comments of the author

The law provided that a person can only insure the life of another where the life assured has a defined relationship with the proposer.[13] The offices tended to ignore the law and were bailed out by the government in 1909 with legislation that extended the number of permitted relationships but restricted the cover to funeral expenses.[14] Compliance thereafter was better but still patchy.[15] The policy that provided the windfall in 5 above would be illegal.

	Criticisms	Response of the offices at the time
7	The friendly societies and mutual companies were run by former agents for the benefit of agents rather than for the members – accountability to members was illusory.	All commercial organisations benefit the staff. The collecting societies and the mutual offices exist for the benefit of the staff no more or less than a well-conducted proprietary life office.

Comments of the author

The accountability to the members was certainly illusory. Most members would not have known when and where general meetings were being held, or the business being discussed, and would have had no interest in attending even if they did. Proxy voting was a long way off. The 1908 conversion debate, for example, was conspicuous for the lack of involvement of members. The former agents who made it to the boardroom seemed to have been reasonably successful in detaching themselves from their agency roots although, as most of them had known no other life and no other company, they were unlikely to devise radical changes. Each of the offices had its own dedicated trade union and this made it very difficult to implement reforms that could be prejudicial to the agents. An agent's right to sell his collecting book to a successor should have been abolished much earlier so that consolidation could take place, and the minimum sum for new industrial branch polices ought to have been maintained at a higher level. Both were resisted by and on behalf of the agents.

8	Offices had the unrestricted power to invest huge sums.	These funds, large as they are, represent only a fraction of the country's capital, are spread over many offices and, as a matter of law, have to be invested in the interests of the policyholders. No evidence has been produced of abuse of financial power by the life offices and it seems that no specific complaint of misuse was ever made.

Comments of the author

This was a 1940s concern, often expressed in rather intemperate terms.[16] No justification was ever produced.

The views of two writers, expressed over a period of more than half a century, help to put these criticisms in context. The creation of industrial assurance was seen by many at the time as a significant force for good. The editor of *Post Magazine* wrote on 19 January 1901:

> *The century which has just closed has been so crowded with great movements and important events, and we are at present separated from it by so short an interval of time, that it is as difficult to single out those things which will be seen by the future historian to have been the events of vital importance as it is to form an adequate idea of a great painting when standing close to it. A fairly safe prophecy is, however, that when the social and economic history of the period comes to be written, the rise and progress of Industrial Assurance will be regarded, and justly so, as one of the most remarkable and influential among the many movements, for the amelioration of the lot of the working classes, to which the Nineteenth Century gave birth.*[17]

Harris Prochansky, an American academic, provided an independent and robust response to the critics when he wrote in *The Business History Review* in 1958:

> *Affecting as they have a sizable portion of the population with low incomes, the failings of industrial insurance have loomed large in the public eye. The accomplishments, tremendous as they have been in a field of insurance beset with inherent difficulties, have been accepted as a matter of course by the generality of Britons. In the wonderland of politics, where, like Alice, political issues can be magically enlarged or diminished with amazing ease, it is too much to expect that the vital institution of industrial insurance will be objectively studied and analyzed.*[18]

Many millions of people benefited from industrial assurance – decent funerals were provided, cash was available in times of need and, after some mid-nineteenth century failures, policyholders could rely upon the financial stability of the offices. Industrial assurance was not perfect but it is difficult to believe that so much hard-earned money would have been entrusted to industrial life offices by so many wage-earners over so many years, and that successive governments would have refrained from passing draconian legislation, if it had been fundamentally flawed.

Appendix 2

Legal Background

Many areas of law will be relevant in the operations of any organisation. Rarely is their impact such that they warrant attention in the history of the company. Industrial assurance, however, constantly brought into play the concept that taking out an insurance policy on somebody else's life is a practice open to abuse. The first part of this note expands upon the problems experienced by the industrial assurance offices in this area. The second part explores in a little more detail than would be appropriate in Chapter 7 legal advice given to the directors at the time of The Royal London Auxiliary Insurance Company, Limited.

Life-of-another funeral policies

There were two ways of insuring against funeral expenses. A person could insure his or her own life with the specific intention that the proceeds would be available for the funeral. Relations were often told 'you won't have to pay to bury me – it's all taken care of'. The other involved somebody who might have to pay for the funeral of a family member taking out a life-of-another policy. So, for example, a son would insure the life of a parent. The son (the proposer – 'P') paid the premiums and, on the death of the life assured (the parent – 'LA'), received the insurance money.

Insuring somebody else's life had always been severely restricted by law. Friendly societies legislation permitted societies to issue policies for funeral expenses but only where the LA was the husband, wife or child of P.[19] The Life Assurance Act 1774 to which the companies were subject, was less definitive but required P to have an "insurable interest" in the life of LA – essentially the P had to show that he or she would suffer loss on LA's death. The 1774 Act was often referred to as the Gambling Act, the preamble making the point that it had "been found by experience that the making [of] insurances on lives or other events wherein the assured shall have no interest hath introduced a mischievous kind of gaming".

Throughout the nineteenth century, both collecting societies and companies issued millions of policies with scant regard to the law. Some parents were insured many times over, so a sum far in excess of funeral expenses was covered. Policies were sometimes taken out by those who would not have had to pay for the funeral. These were little more than bets on elderly persons' lives. Then there were cases where the required relationship between P and LA had been ignored altogether. In 1909 the Government generously expressed its willingness to assist and section 36 of the Assurance Companies

Act 1909 was intended to legalise existing policies, set out clear rules for the future and impose a sanction on the policy providers who issued policies in breach of the new rules.

Sub-section (2) declared that no existing life-of-another policy would be deemed to be void provided "the policy was effected by... a person who had at the time a bona fide expectation that he would incur expenses in connection with the death or funeral of the assured, and if the sum assured is not unreasonable for the purpose of covering those expenses." This was hardly an absolute declaration of legality, imposing as it did two conditions that had to be fulfilled, but this was probably all that the industry could reasonably have expected.

Sub-section (1) permitted the collecting societies and industrial assurance companies to issue policies "insuring money to be paid for funeral expenses of a parent, grandparent, grandchild, brother or sister". The omission of wife and husband from the list was understandable because the courts had held that a husband has an insurable interest in his wife's life and a wife in her husband's.[20] The fact that child was not included was either an error or based on an assumption that it was obvious that parents had an insurable interest in the life of their child or (and this was certainly not the case) that the courts had already so decided. When the provision was re-enacted as section 3 of the Industrial Assurance Act 1923, 'child' was included. There was no clarification, however, on the meaning of 'funeral expenses' – it was uncertain if this was to be narrowly construed, to cover only the payments made to the undertakers and the cemetery, or could include the related costs such as mourning clothes, the 'funeral tea', fares travelling to, and earnings lost by attending, the funeral.

Breach of the sub-section exposed the assurance company or friendly society, and any individual director, manager or other officer or agent who was "knowingly a party to the default" to a penalty not exceeding £100 or £50 per day while the default continued.

After the introduction of the death grant in 1946, the offices promoted the view that this was a minimum only and that insurance could be used as a supplement. It soon became clear, however, that widespread selling of life-of-another policies to augment the death grant would not be permitted. The Industrial Assurance and Friendly Societies Act 1948 brought to an end all the existing statutory powers that offices had to effect life-of-another policies, along with all the uncertainties and abuses that went with them, and replaced them with one simple and restrictive provision. Proposers could now insure only their parents or grandparents for a sum not exceeding £20. This was an aggregate maximum – once a person was insured for £20 (increased to £30 in 1958[21]), no future policies could be issued.

The 1948 Act was repealed by the Financial Services and Markets Act 2000.

The Royal London Auxiliary Insurance Company, Limited

Two important pieces of legal advice were given to the directors. They were advised in 1910 that the court would be unlikely to approve an extension of the Society's powers beyond those referred to in the 1910 Act, although there were deficiencies with the instructions sent to counsel. They were advised in 1914 that there would be great difficulties in merging the Society and the Auxiliary Company, but counsel was not told about the allegations that had been made nor that litigation was imminent.

1910 advice

The directors could claim with some justification that they had been advised that a court would be unlikely to approve an extension of powers in August 1910. The instructions sent to counsel, however, were misleading and he was never asked the crucial question.

In July 1910, just before the Companies (Converted Societies) Act 1910 became law, a Case to Advise was sent to John Roskill KC. He was told that the Society was "now transacting a considerable amount of business in excess of and outside its previous scope" as a friendly society. This was something of an exaggeration – the only business outside the scope was the 41,000 fire policies. It was suggested to counsel that, when the Act became law, there were three options: "(a) to apply to the Court for further powers (b) to register an Auxiliary Company to transact the extended business (c) abandon the present business altogether."

Roskill advised that it was most improbable that "the Court would before a reasonable period had elapsed sanction any alteration or enlargement of the Company's objects so as to include those which have been held to be invalid." In his opinion, "the only safe course to adopt is to register a new Company immediately the Act is passed which will carry on that portion of the business which it is then no longer within the power of the converted society to undertake."

Roskill's advice was criticised during the subsequent litigation, and certainly in coming to his view he seems to have attached great (perhaps too much) weight to some comments made almost in passing by one of the judges in *Blythe v Birtley* and to have paid little regard to the special circumstances of the Royal London conversion, where wider powers had been 'de-authorised' after two years, and the specific statement in the Act (that need not have been included) that nothing in it prejudiced the right of any company to apply to the court to change its objects.

In fairness to counsel, however, his instructions were drafted on the basis that the new company would only undertake business that could not be undertaken by the Society, and there was, of course, a fourth option to which he was not referred. He should have been asked the question:

*If Counsel comes to the view that the Court would be unlikely to enlarge the Society's objects to restore **all** the powers included on the conversion, would Counsel advise on the likely outcome of an immediate application to the Court to authorise only fire insurance on the basis that (a) this business has satisfactorily been undertaken by the Society for two years and (b) it is the **only** part of the Society's business being carried on the date upon which the Act became law that is no longer permitted.*

1914 advice

The directors were advised in 1914 that there would be great difficulties in merging the Society and the Auxiliary Company but counsel was not told about the allegations that had been made or that litigation was being commenced.

In May 1914, when the litigation was being commenced, the Board sought the advice of W H Upjohn KC. The instructions contained a brief overview of the events of the last six years and continued: "It is now a question of determining whether it is advisable for the Society and the [Auxiliary Company] to be more intimately associated, and which is the best method of adopting this course." Those instructing him believed that there were three ways in which this could be achieved – the Society acquiring the shares of the Auxiliary Company, the amalgamation of the Auxiliary Company and the Society, or Special Act of Parliament. Counsel was asked to advise on the best course.

Upjohn recited the significant hurdles that would have to be overcome to achieve an acquisition or amalgamation. These included amending the Society's memorandum and articles of association, obtaining the court's authority to a significant widening of its insurance powers, giving notices to policyholders and persuading the shareholders of the Auxiliary Company to sell their shares. Counsel did not regard it as his role to advise as to the attitude of Parliament to a Special Act contenting himself with a comment that he believed "that many members of radical and labour parties are opposed to legislation of such character and sometimes block it". Clearly there was no easy way of bringing the two Royal London companies together.

The instructions to counsel referred to the provision in the agreement of 11 August 1910 that prohibited the Auxiliary Company from competing with the Society but said nothing about the actual competing or the composition of the boards of the two companies. Nor did they mention that litigation was known to be imminent.

Appendix 3

Directors and Officers:
The Royal London Friendly Society 1861–1908

Secretary

> *A secretary shall be appointed at the first meeting of the members of the society... The secretary shall give his daily attendance at the office of the society, unless his absence be occasioned by illness or other unavoidable causes, and he shall attend all meetings of the members of the society and of the committee of management thereof... he shall record the names of the committee of management present at any meetings, and take minutes of their proceedings... keep, or cause to be kept, the accounts, documents, deeds, instruments, and papers of the society... receive all monies payable to the society, and give the necessary receipts for the same, and cause them to be entered in the account books of the society. He shall, under the committee of management's direction, carry on all correspondence with the agents, collectors and canvassers, medical officers, members, or any other person that may have business or correspondence with the society. He shall on all occasions, in the execution of his office, act under the superintendence, control, and directions of the committee of management.*

Rule 8 (extract) of the Royal London Friendly Society

Joseph Degge	1861–1874
Henry Ridge	1874–1875
William Hambridge	1875–1899
William Bowrey	1899–1908
Edward Smith	1908
Alfred Skeggs	1908

Ridge and Smith were both interim appointments made to ensure that there was a secretary "giving daily attendance at the office of the society" at all times.

Treasurer

> *A treasurer shall be appointed at any general or special meeting of members of the society... He shall be responsible for all sums of money from time to time paid into his hands by any person on*

account of the society, and for the investment or application of the same under the authority of the trustees, in such manner as they and the committee of management shall direct.

Rule 4 (extract)

Robert Hilton	1861–1862
Joseph Degge	1862
Thomas Holland Forster	1862–1877
Henry Ridge	1877–1890
William Coombes	1890–1908

Trustees

All property belonging to a registered society... shall vest in the trustees for the time being of the society, for the use and benefit of the society and the members thereof, and of all persons claiming through the members according to the rules of the society.

Friendly Societies Act 1896, section 49(1)
re-enacted from earlier friendly societies acts

There shall be two trustees elected at any general or special meeting of the members of the society...They shall do and execute all the several duties delegated to them by the Act of Parliament relating to Friendly Societies.

Rule 3 (extract)

William Head	1861–1862
Edgar Cheesman	1861
Charles Sheffield	1862
Laurence Barrett	1862–1893
Thomas Forster	1862–1877
Henry Ridge	1877
Augustus Beane	1877–1888
Frederick de la Bertauche	1888–1908
Thomas Byrne	1894–1908

Members of the Committee of Management (Directors)

The business and affairs of this society shall be conducted by a committee of management, consisting of seven members, who shall be elected at a general meeting of the members of the society [and] such committee of management shall meet at the society's office once every week.

Rule 2 (extract)

A friendly society had members of the committee of management (or 'committee-men' as they are referred to in the rules) and not directors. They tended, however, to be referred to as directors. The Royal London minute books consistently referred to the committee as the 'Board of Management'.

George Atherton	1890–1908
Laurence Barrett	1862–1893
Augustus Beane	1875–1888
Frederick de la Bertauche	1875–1908
Benjamin Bexfield	1862–1863
James Birnie	1862–1884
Thomas Bowen	1861
William Bowrey	1885–1899
Thomas Byrne	1877–1908
Edgar Cheesman	1861
William Davies	1868–1874
Joseph Barnes Degge	1863–1893
Horace Duffell	1893–1908
Thomas Forster	1862–1877
Thomas Fyans	1890
Henry Green	1861–1862
Edward Hambridge	1899–1908
William Hambridge	1861–1875
John Head	1861–1862
William Head	1861–1862
Robert Hilton	1861–1862
John Monk	1865–1868
John Price	1889–1908
Henry Ridge	1862–1890
Thomas Robinson	1862–1865
Edward Smith	1894–1908

Monk's initial appointment in 1864 was invalid – there were already seven members of the Committee (see Chapter 3).

Fyans was appointed by the Committee to fill a vacancy, but his appointment was not confirmed at the next general meeting

Appendix 4

Directors and Officers:
The Royal London Mutual Insurance Society Limited 1908–

Chairman

Edward Smith	1908–1920
No appointment	1921–1932
Alfred Skeggs	1932–1936
No appointment	1937–1945
John Wiseman	1945–1951
Christopher Shuttleworth	1951–1956
Ernest Haynes	1956–1973
James (Jim) Bailey	1973–1976
Thomas (Tom) Cowman	1976–1978
Billy Skinner	1978–1983
William (Bill) Forsey	1983–1987
Michael Pickard	1988–1999
Hubert Reid	1999–2005
Tim Melville-Ross	2006–

Chief Executive

John Price & Horace Duffell	1908–1920
Alfred Skeggs	1920–1936
John Skinner & John Wiseman	1937–1944
Wiseman & Ernest Thomlinson	1945–1948
Wiseman & Christopher Shuttleworth	1948–1951
Shuttleworth & Robert Lundie	1951–1955
Shuttleworth & Ernest Haynes	1955–1956
Haynes & Stanley Goodall	1956–1969
James (Jim) Bailey	1969–1972
J A S (Tony) Lamb	1972–1973
Thomas (Tom) Cowman	1973–1975
Leslie Poll	1976–1977
Billy Skinner	1977–1979
William (Bill) Forsey	1979–1983
Michael Pickard	1983–1998
Michael (Mike) Yardley	1998–

The chief executive(s) were referred to between 1908 and 1969 as managing director or joint managing directors and between 1969 and 1988 as chief general manager. (Michael Pickard was known only as "Chairman" after 1988.) The term group chief executive is now used.

Actuary

F G P Neison	1908–1921
James (Jimmy) Duffell	1921–1947
Ernest Haynes	1947–1955
J A S (Tony) Lamb	1955–1970
Peter Taylor	1970–1974
Michael Pickard	1974–1982
Brian Jones	1983–1998
John Tovey	1998–2005
Colin Pountney (AFH) & Stephen Wilson (WPA)	2005–

In 1974 the Insurance Companies Act created the role of appointed actuary with specific statutory responsibilities. In 2005 the FSA decided to split the appointed actuary's role between the actuarial function holder, whose responsibilities relate to the financial management of the company, including both non-profit and with-profits business, and the with-profits actuary, whose responsibility it is to ensure that the with-profits policyholders are treated fairly.

Secretary

Alfred Skeggs	1908–1920
John Skinner	1920–1932
John Pipe	1932–1943
Thomas Haswell	1943–1946
James (Jimmy) Duffell	1946–1949
Leonard (Len) Wiseman	1950–1976
Colin Wigmore	1976
John Gann	1976–1980
Norman Wood	1980–1984
Sven Farmer	1984–1996
Murray Ross	1996–2007
Chris Aujard	2007–

Solicitor

Evan Hayward	1931–1941
Arthur Russell Firth	1941–1967
Billy Skinner	1967–1977

David Bailey	1977–1981
Colin Cannings	1981–1989
David Parker	1989–1993
Murray Ross	1994–2007
Chris Aujard	2007–

Evan Hayward was the first in-house solicitor (see Chapter 8) although the Society's external solicitor was referred to in the pre-1931 annual reports and accounts, sometimes by name (James Cornford, H Kingsley Wood) and sometimes by reference to his firm (H Kingsley Wood & Co, Chas G Bradshaw & Waterson, and Smith & Hudson). The title changed to legal director in 1996 and to group legal director in 2002.

Directors

Henry Anderton	1940–1946
Charles Ashling	1949–1962
George Atherton	1908
James (Jim) Bailey	1956–1976
Frederick Baker	1920–1936
Jack Baker	1946–1953
Frederick de la Bertauche	1908–1919
Trevor Bish-Jones	2005–2010
Walter Boness	1909–1920
Benjamin Braham	1909–1917
Cyril Brill	1978–1993
James Butler	1909–1920
Thomas Byrne	1908–1911
George Cannell	1967–1973
Colin Cannings	1987–1989
Andrew (Andy) Carter	2007–
George Conyer	1939–1949
Lewis Cooke	1980–1985
William Coombes	1908–1920
Thomas (Tom) Cowman	1961–1978
Gerard (Gerry) Coyle	1995–1997
John Deane	2007–
Horace Duffell	1908–1920
Brian Duffin	2001–2007
Robert (Bob) Erith	1987–1996
George Fennell	1933–1945
Arthur Russell Firth	1961–1972
Barry Fitzgerald	1997–2003

William (Bill) Forsey	1973–1987
Alan Frost	2000–2001
Duncan Ferguson	2010–
John Gann	1978–1980
Ernest Henry (Harry) Goodall	1939–1951
Stanley Goodall	1951–1980
George Gray	1935–1945
Ernest Haynes	1952–1973
Henry Helliwell	1946–1961
Edward Hambridge	1908–1920
Arthur Houlding	1937–1945
Robert Jeens	2003–
Brian Jones	1985–1998
Harlow Irwin	1935–1947
Brian Knights	1980–1995
Andrew Longhurst	2000–2002
J A S (Tony) Lamb	1965–1973
William Lowe	1921–1934
Robert Lundie	1945–1955
William C Martin	1909–1920
William R D (Roly) Martin	1963–1967
Hubert Massey	1948–1966
Tim Melville-Ross	1999–
William Missett	1920–1939
Donald Overy	1968–1978
Henry Parr	1921–1938
Michael Pearce	1973–1977
Anthony (Tony) Percival	1999–2001
Christopher Phillips	2001–2003
Michael Pickard	1977–1999
Leslie Poll	1968–1977
John Price	1908–1920
Hubert Reid	1996–2005
Murray Ross	1997–2001
Thomas (Tom) Ross	2001–2010
David Rowland	1985–1986
John (Jack) Saward	1954–1968
Stephen Shone	1999–
Christopher Shuttleworth	1946–1956
Alfred Skeggs	1920–1936
John Skinner	1932–1944
Billy Skinner	1972–1983

Barry Skipper	1995–2000
Thomas (Tom) Slee	1989–1999
Edward Smith	1908–1920
George Sorrell	1920–1935
Charles Spencer	1937–1946
William Stanbury	1921–1931
Samuel Swetnam	1946–1961
Peter Taylor	1973–1987
Ernest Thomlinson	1921–1948
James Wall	1945–1955
Sydney Webb	1951–1965
John White	1920–1933
Fields Wicker-Miurin	2003–2006
Colin Wigmore	1976–1989
David Williams	2006–
Thomas Williams	1920–1938
John Wiseman	1920–1951
Norman Wooding	1987–1996
Michael (Mike) Yardley	1989–

The Royal London comma

As the resolution to convert from friendly society to company indicates (see page 103), the company was incorporated in 1908 with a comma in its name: The Royal London Mutual Insurance Society, Limited. The comma was much in evidence for many years – for example, until 1932 it was included every time the company's name appeared in the annual report and accounts. Then it was dropped from the front cover but retained on the inside pages. A similarly inconsistent approach was adopted with other documents. The use of the comma gradually declined over the years and it has rarely been included since the late 1960s.

Appendix 5

Directors and Officers:
The Royal London Auxiliary Insurance Company, Limited 1910–1922

Chairman

Edward Smith	1910–1922

Managing Director

John Price	1910–1921
Horace Duffell	1910–1922
Alfred Skeggs	1921–1922

Secretary

Alfred Skeggs	1910–1920
William Coombes	1920–1921
Walter Boness	1921–1922

Directors

Frederick de la Bertauche	1910–1919
Walter Boness	1910–1922
Benjamin Braham	1910–1913
James Butler	1910–1922
Thomas Byrne	1910–1911
William Coombes	1910–1922
Horace Duffell	1910–1922
Edward Hambridge	1910–1922
William Martin	1910–1922
John Price	1910–1922
Edward Smith	1910–1922
Samuel Derbyshire	1921–1922
Frederick Thoresby	1921–1922
Harry Wheelock	1921–1922
Alfred Skeggs	1921–1922

Appendix 6

Royal London: Premium income, reserves and new business: 1913–1998

	1913	1924	1936	1948
The Royal London Mutual Insurance Society Limited				
Total premium income (Today)	£1.3m (£97.1m)	£3.5m (£151.0m)	£6.6m (£336.0m)	£11.2m (£305.0m)
Funds at year-end (Today)	£3.3m (£267.0m)	£12.6m (£536.0m)	£38.0m (£1.93bn)	£82.3m (£2.24bn)
Industrial Branch				
New policies issued during year	907,377	860,375	947,580	556,454
Sum assured by new policies	£8.1m	£13.4m	£15.5m	£16.98m
Average sum assured (Today)	£9 (£660)	£16 (£680)	£16 (£810)	£31 (£843)
Ordinary Branch				
New policies issued during year	Nil	21,678	41,919	20,698
Sum assured by new policies		£2.9m	£6.3m	£8.4m
Average sum assured (Today)		£132 (£5,610)	£151 (£7,650)	£408 (£11,100)
Price of an average house (Table 502, Housing Market: Dept of Communities and Local Government)			£550	£1,751
The Royal London Auxiliary Insurance Company, Limited				
Total life premiums (all OB)	£0.059m			
New policies issued during year	7,389			
Sum assured by new policies	£0.507m			
Average sum assured (Today)	£69 (£5,060)			
General insurance premiums (net of re-insurance)	£0.033m			

	1960	1972	1985	1998
The Royal London Mutual Insurance Society Limited				
Total premium income (Today)	£16.3m (£282.0m)	£26.0m (£257.0m)	£123.9m (£281.0m)	£514.7m (£679.0m)
Funds at year-end (Today)	£161.8m (£2.79bn)	£296.0m (£2.93bn)	£1.75bn (£3.97bn)	£6.84bn (£9.02bn)
Industrial Branch				
New policies issued during year	326,399	187,582	113,196	80,875
Sum assured by new policies	£26.5m	£43.3m	£151.4m	£271.1m
Average sum assured (Today)	£81 (£1,400)	£231 (£2,280)	£1,338 (£3,040)	£3,352 (£4,420)
Ordinary Branch				
New policies issued during year	23,091	29,468	38,752	40,159
Sum assured by new policies	£22.9m	£69.5m	£326.0m	£708.7m
Average sum assured (Today)	£994 (£17,100)	£2,357 (£23,300)	£8,412 (£19,100)	£17,647 (£23,300)
Price of an average house (Table 502, Housing Market: Dept of Communities and Local Government)	£2,530	£7,374	£31,103	£81,774

Notes

Chapter 1 – The Beginning

1   Extract from *The Pauper's Drive*, aka *The Pauper's Funeral* (1845), attributed to Thomas Noel (1799–1861), Wilson and Levy, *Burial Reform and Funeral Costs*, p. 56, www.geocities.com/unclesamsfarm/songs/paupersfuneral.htm. See also The Pauper's Funeral (1797), Robert Southey (1774–1843, Poet Laureate 1813–1843), www.readbookonline.net/readOnLine/20165/.

2   Extract from *Pop Goes the Weasel*, W R Mandale (1853), also attributed to Charlie Twiggs, Iona and Peter Opie (eds), *The Oxford Nursery Rhyme Book*, p. 71, www.rhymes.org.uk/a116a-pop-goes-the-weasel.htm.

3   The document dated 2 February 1861 that Ridge and Degge signed can be validated (see Note 78 below). In *We the Undersigned...*, referred to in the Introduction, Gore Allen placed the meeting at a coffee shop in City Road, and a photograph is included with the caption "It all started here: the coffee shop in the City Road where the Royal London was born in 1861." I have adopted Gore Allen's finding, on the basis that he was an experienced author (he had written biographies of Derick Heathcoat Amory and King William IV and a corporate history of John Heathcoat and Co, a Tiverton textile firm), and I am sure that he would have had good grounds for making this statement. I have, however, discovered nothing in the archives that reveals anything about the venue of the meeting. Royal London were in touch with Ridge's grandson at the time of the centenary (see Note 60 below) and the City Road coffee shop may have been passed down within the Ridge family. Gore Allen was wrong, however, in suggesting that the day of the meeting was cold and snowy. The Meteorological Office has confirmed that 2 February 1861, although preceded by a couple of months' severe weather, was a mild winter's day.

4   Charles Dickens, *Oliver Twist*, Chapter V.

5   Ibid.

6   Ibid.

7   The Helen Fawcett Professor of History, University of California, Berkeley. Winner of a Mellon Foundation Distinguished Achievement Award for his study of unconventional topics such as the history of sexuality, death and dying.

8   Thomas Laqueur, 'Bodies, Death and Pauper Funerals', *Representations* (University of California Press) No. 1 (1983) p. 109.

9   Laqueur, pp. 109 and 117.

10 Geoffrey Crossick, *An Artisan Elite in Victorian Society*, p. 134. For a discussion of the 'slippery concept' of respectability, see Strange, *Death, Grief, and Poverty*, p. 6.

11 To be "put away by the parish" in late nineteenth-century Salford was for the survivor's family to bear a "life-long stigma"; Robert Roberts, *The Classic Slum*, p. 87 (Manchester University Press); pp. 84–88 (Penguin). Another consequence of death in the workhouse was that any body not claimed could be made available for dissection under the Anatomy

Act 1832, passed to 'regulate' the activities of the resurrection men.

12 Quoted in Strange, p. 2.

13 *Report of Sir George Young*, Assistant Commissioner to the Royal Commission appointed to inquire into Friendly and Benefit Building Societies, Parliamentary Papers, 1874, Vol. XXIII, Part II, p. 25. As to the extent of mourning items that were available, see James Steven Curl, *Victorian Celebration of Death*, Chapter 7.

14 Wilson and Levy, p. 71; Strange, p. 132.

15 Charles Lamb, 'On Burial Societies and the Character of an Undertaker', *The Reflector*, No. III, Art. Xi, 1811. The poor would "sell their beds out from under them sooner than have parish funerals": evidence of a witness to the Select Committee of the House of Commons on the Improvement of the Health of Towns 1842. Both quoted by Laqueur, pp. 109 and 125.

16 See P Gosden, *The Friendly Societies in England*, 1815–1875 and S Cordery, *British Friendly Societies*, 1750–1914.

17 F M Eden, *Observations on Friendly Societies for the Maintenance of the Industrious Classes during Sickness, Infirmity, Old Age and other Exigencies* (London, 1801).

18 Gosden p. 14, Fourth Report of the Friendly and Benefit Building Societies Commission, Parliamentary Papers, 1874, Vol. XXIII, Appendix IV.

19 33 Geo. III, c. 54 (1793): *An Act for the Relief and Encouragement of Friendly Societies*, commonly called Rose's Act after its parliamentary sponsor, Secretary of the Treasury George Rose, who had taken a keen interest in friendly societies and savings banks.

20 59 Geo. III, c. 128 (1819): *An Act for the further Protection and Encouragement of Friendly Societies and for preventing Frauds and Abuses therein.*

21 4 & 5 Wm. IV, c. 40 (1834): *An Act to consolidate and amend the Laws relating to Friendly Societies.*

22 9 & 10 Vict, c. 27 (1846): *An Act to amend the Laws relating to Friendly Societies.*

23 10 Geo. IV, c. 56 (1829): *An Act to consolidate and amend the Laws relating to Friendly Societies.*

24 See Gosden, *Friendly Societies,* Chapter IV.

25 Dermot Morrah, *A History of Industrial Life Assurance,* p. 16.

26 The general societies did business over the counter and their members "transmit their contributions by post-office order, and receive sick pay and other benefits in the same manner." (Young p. 5) The members of the Royal Standard and Hearts of Oak were "mostly of a higher degree of respectability, artisans, tradesmen, domestic servants and others who... dislike the nonsense and mixed company of the club nights and who look for an investment of their savings on purely business principles" (Young, p. 7).

27 The most basic of funerals could cost £3 but the expense depended upon the area and in 1843 a parliamentary report suggested that, in London, the cost of a funeral for "the lowest tradesman" would exceed £10 (*A Supplementary Report on... the Practice of Interment in Towns,* (1843) (509) xii, pp. 50–51 and 69–71). Cassell's *Household Guide* in its 1870 edition listed various funerals costing between £3 5s to £53: quoted by Laqueur, p. 115. See also Wilkie Collins, *The Diary of Anne Rodway* in which Anne (possibly the first fictional

female detective), a poor "plain needlewoman", has to raise £2 8s 4d (today: £163) to avoid a pauper's burial for Mary, her dear friend and fellow lodger. Assisted by her fiancé, newly returned from America, she later brings Mary's murderer to justice.

28 Victorian burial clubs were not the first organisations to provide a payment on death. A collegium was an association of people formed for a particular purpose with its own regulations and often its own meeting place. Collegia were organised among the Greeks, by the first century BC they were common in Egypt and reached their prime in Rome where many collegia – known as *collegia tenuiorum* – were organised solely for the purpose of guaranteeing members a decent burial. It was believed that only those properly buried could hope for repose and happiness after death and many working-class Romans, including freedmen and slaves, joined a *collegium tenuiorum* to ensure protection for their souls. An inscription dating back to AD 136 refers to members paying an entrance fee of 100 sestertii, providing an amphora of good wine and contributing five asses monthly with 300 sestertii being paid out on the death of a member to meet the funeral expenses. The medieval guilds encompassed a wide range of associations. Some had religious and charitable objectives; others were formed to protect the interests of local merchants or craftsmen. Many made a payment so that a guildsman who had fallen on hard times could have a decent burial. Academics debate whether an unbroken continuity can be said to exist between collegia, guilds and friendly societies although, as few guilds for the working man survived Henry VIII's dislike of any organisation of self-government that he regarded as a challenge to his sovereignty, it is difficult to see any continuity between guilds and friendly societies in Britain. Nevertheless, there were those who wanted that continuity to exist – the secretary to the Royal Commission on Friendly Societies, J M Ludlow, wrote in 1873, "I feel convinced that there is no historical gap between the guild of old times and the modern friendly society; that if we knew all, we could trace the actual passage from one to the other": *The Contemporary Review,* April 1873, p. 748. The greater similarity would seem to be between the collegia and the Victorian burial societies. See Jack, *Introduction to the History of Life Assurance.*

29 Young, p. 27.

30 Of those "general collecting or burial societies" that were listed in the early 1870s as being "the more important bodies of [that] class", only United Assurance (formerly St Patrick's), founded in 1832, and United Legal Friendly (also known as Royal Oak), founded in 1840, both with their headquarters in Liverpool, were older that Liverpool Victoria: Fourth Report of the Friendly and Benefit Building Societies Commission, Parliamentary Papers, 1874, Vol. XXIII, Part I, p. civ, para. 470.

31 See Ian Saddler, *A Mission in Life* and *Liverpool Victoria Friendly Society: Centenary Celebration 1843–1943* (Liverpool Victoria, 1943). The statement of the objects appears in the first half-yearly report for the period 3 March to 3 September 1843. It is an extract from a 'Declaration' credited with the date June 1842. There is no record of the incorporation of the society, or its original rules, and the earliest meeting for which records have survived is that of a sub-committee on 8 March 1843.

32 Nigel Watson, *A Lifetime of Care: 150 years of Royal Liver Assurance* (Royal Liver, 2000);

Centenary of the Delegation System 1886–1986 (Royal Liver, 1986); *Royal Liver Friendly Society: Centenary 1950* (Royal Liver, 1950); *Historical Sketch of the Royal Liver Friendly Society* (Royal Liver, 1900).

33 J Frome Wilkinson, *Mutual Thrift*, p. 134.

34 Cordery, p. 83.

35 Laurie Dennett, *A Sense of Security: 150 years of Prudential*, p. 37.

36 Select Committee of Assurance Associations: Report and Evidence, Parliamentary Papers, 1853, Vol. XXI.

37 "According to Mr Harben, secretary to the Prudential, the first insurance company that undertook 'industrial business', ie. the insurance of the working classes, was Industrial and General, which insured only adults. The next, an offshoot from the former, was British Industry, which took lives between 10 and 55, but after a few years was absorbed by the Prudential." (Fourth Report of the Friendly and Benefit Building Societies Commission, Parliamentary Papers, 1874, Vol. XXIII, Part I, p. cxxix, para. 549). So Industrial and General that had operated from Waterloo Place since 1849 (Dennett, p. 39) may have been the source of the term 'industrial assurance'.

38 A local inhabitant reported that: "The country around [Rugeley] is most beautiful for miles. There are nothing else but noblemen's mansions and grounds; and do you think they would come down and live here if it wasn't a pretty spot? There is the Marquis of Anglesey's within four miles – the beautiful desert, as they call it – Beau Desert, with the most lovely scenery, all along the road leading to it, you can imagine. There, in the other direction, is Lord Hatherton's park and woods, from which half the navy dock-yards are supplied. Oaks, sir, as big round as cart-wheels. Then there is Lord Bagot's; the finest woods in Europe Lord Bagot's got. Then there is the Earl Talbot's estate, and Weston Hall, and a hundred such." (*The Illustrated Times*, 2 February 1856 and repeated in the *Illustrated Life and Career of William Palmer of Rugeley* (Ward and Locke, 1856) p. 35).

39 Robert Graves, *They Hanged My Saintly Billy*, p. 19.

40 Rugeley was to achieve notoriety when William Palmer, a local doctor, was convicted of murder in 1856 and hanged in public. The case attracted huge interest in the national press that provided readers with widely conflicting descriptions of Rugeley, that varied from "a long straggling town of small houses, kept very clean, and occupied by persons extremely well to do in the world", said by "Commercial travellers [to be] a good place for business", (*The Illustrated Times*, 2 February 1856 and repeated in the *Illustrated Life and Career of William Palmer of Rugeley* (Ward and Locke, 1856) p. 35) to a place where "the old village street... is built of sad, sullen-looking dirty-brown stone, miserable without the once-adjoining fields, and most disheartening to the passenger from the utterly unprosperous look of the place." (*The Illustrated London News*, 19 January 1856).

41 Six children were baptised although others may have been born who did not survive to be baptised. The year is the one in which they were baptised. Joseph was given his mother's surname as a second forename and he is referred to throughout as Joseph Barnes Degge to distinguish him from Joseph Degge, his nephew.

42 The members of the Degge family were inconsistent in recording their birthplace in census

returns: John, William and Joseph Barnes alternated between Blithfield and Newton and Joseph, between Newton and Abbots Bromley. The *International Genealogical Index* states that all of Mary and William's six children were baptised at Blithfield. Newton is a hamlet within the parish of Blithfield and, so far as a place of birth is concerned, Newton and Blithfield were virtually synonymous.

43 Abbots Bromley was: "a decayed market town, consisting of one long street of irregularly built houses... seven miles S of Uttoxeter, six miles NNE of Rugeley and twelve miles E by N of Stafford. Its parish is watered by the Blithe and several smaller streams, and contains 8360 acres of land, divided into three liberties and constablewicks of Abbot's Bromley, Bagot's Bromley and Bromley Hurst, which have only 1508 inhabitants. Lord Bagot is impropriator of the great tithes, principal owner of the soil, and lord of the manors of Bagot's Bromley and Bromley Hurst, but the Marquis of Anglesey has the advowson of the vicarage, and is lord of the manor of Abbots Bromley... About a mile to the NE is Bagot's Park, which contains many oaks of ancient growth and numerous herds of deer. It belongs also to Lord Bagot, but Bromley Park, which lies a little to the south, is now enclosed, and contains about 1,000 acres, all belonging to the Earl of Dartmouth." (White, *History, Gazetteer and Directory of Staffordshire*).

44 A baptism certificate ("a true copy of the entry of the Baptism of Joseph Degg in the Register of Baptisms for the said Parish") was obtained by Royal London in 1959. The Register of Baptisms 1812–49, in which the name is spelt Degg, states that his parents were John, a labourer, and Sarah, and that their 'abode' was Bromley Park, but is silent on the date of birth. Joseph was their eldest child in the sense of being the first to be baptised. There could have been previous children who did not survive to be baptised.

45 The census returns show Degge born in Newton (1861) and Abbots Bromley (1871).

46 Some 790 acres of the area between Newton and Abbots Bromley have since been flooded to create the Blithfield Reservoir, opened in 1953. Much of the land was acquired from the Bagot family.

47 The 1841 census return for Blithfield that included Newton did not include William and Mary Degge and a search for them under all place-names in Staffordshire known to be associated with the Degge family failed to find them. There was, however, a Mary Dey, living alone in Newton, whose age corresponds with that of Mary Degge. Early census enumerators were not always entirely accurate and the Degges were inconsistent with the spelling of their name – Degg could well have been recorded as Dey. It seems reasonable to assume that William had died and that this was Mary Degge. *We the Undersigned...* (see the Introduction) includes a photograph (apparently recently taken), captioned: "The farm at Newton, Staffordshire, where Joseph Degge was born in 1836". Nothing has been discovered either in the Royal London or public archives that enables the birthplace of Degge to be determined with absolute certainty, nor to identify the farm in the photograph. The *In Memoriam* booklet produced by Royal London shortly after Degge's death states that he was born at Newton.

48 In attending the village school in Abbots Bromley, young Joseph was benefiting from the generosity of Richard Clarke, a local man who had prospered as "a dyer and citizen of

London", who in 1606 had left £300 in his will so that the people of Abbots Bromley could buy land which could be leased at a rent of £20 per annum and which would then enable them to build and maintain a free school within the village where children could be educated "in grammar and good literature". By 1860 Clarke's Grammar School was doomed, the buildings eventually passing to the Charity Commissioners in 1875. The school has changed many times over the years and is now the Richard Clarke First School. The present schoolhouse at the top of Schoolhouse Lane is the original school building, www.richardclarkeonline.co.uk.

49 William's birth was registered in the September quarter 1843 in Liverpool and he was baptised in St Peter's on 28 September 1843. Three other children followed before the 1851 census but of the four children, only Louisa (baptised in November 1845) survived infancy, although the couple subsequently had two more children after 1851. In later documents, Bishop is referred to as a licensed victualler.

50 In May 1851 she transferred the license to a Walter Ridgway. William was shown in the census return as a publican at 1 Longville Street and in trades directories as a victualler of 79 Park Street.

51 That John and Sarah had six children is based on the 1851 census return. There may have been others who did not survive until 1851.

52 The 1851 census shows William (32) and Elizabeth Degge (27) living with their son, William (1) and Joseph Degge (15), William's nephew, at 1 Longville Street. There is little to suggest when each member of the family left for Liverpool and nothing on whether they went collectively or individually. William Degge did not appear in the directories until 1851 (when he was listed as a victualler at 79 Park Street) but had married Elizabeth Hill in the Church of St John the Baptist, Toxteth Park, in the summer of 1848. Early in 1851, Joseph Barnes Degge married Catherine Bevans at the same church. This suggests that William and Joseph Barnes moved to Liverpool in the late 1840s. Their mother Mary may have travelled with, or soon after, them. The fact that they were all in the pub trade suggests that Joseph Bishop, their brother-in-law, may have found jobs for them. Joseph Degge may have left Abbots Bromley only when his grandmother and uncles had established themselves in Liverpool. Robert, the youngest son of William and Mary, stayed in Newton working there as a shoemaker.

53 Derek Whale, *Lost Villages of Liverpool*, p. 54: The Mersey Forge "built the monstrous Horsfall Gun in 1856. Then the largest gun in existence, at 21 tons 17 cwt, it was tested on the North Shore before big crowds and proved that a 300 lb ball could be shot for five miles."

54 *In Memoriam* booklet produced by Royal London shortly after Degge's death in 1874. No author is shown.

55 The first mention of Hughes and Bishop in the trades directories was in 1853 when both "John Hughes (Hughes and Bishop)" and "Joseph Bishop (Hughes and Bishop)" were listed individually in the alphabetical section as living at Grassendale Park, Aigburth. The firm itself was first mentioned in the 1855 directory when its address was 25 Stanhope Street. The *Liverpool Mercury*, however, had reported in December 1852 that Hughes and Bishop had given £50 to the licensed victuallers' orphanage fund and mentioned in October 1853

that Hughes and Bishop's spirit vaults were on the corner of Stanhope Street. The firm was mentioned in *The Theory and Practice of Brewing Illustrated* by W L Tizard (p.10) where there was a testimony from Messrs Hughes and Bishop, Liverpool, to the great efficiency of "your patent Mashing Machine which we consider to be the greatest improvement ever introduced to the brewery. The benefits of the Attemperator are beyond all conception." (10 June 1852).

56 Notice of the dissolution of the partnership appeared in the *Liverpool Mercury* on 11 April 1856.

57 Aigburth was then a village on the outskirts of Liverpool but only a couple of miles away from Toxteth where the Degge families were living. The Aigburth Hotel, opposite the Liverpool Cricket Club, was demolished when Aigburth Road was made dual carriageway.

58 A letter from Degge appeared in the next issue of *Lloyd's Weekly Newspaper* (17 April 1859). He was anxious to confirm that the confusion on the part of some Royal Liver members over the dismissal of an agent following a case in the Lambeth police court had been resolved.

59 Degge's address appears as 77 Westminster Place, Lambeth, in his 1861 census return. The Post Office Directory of London 1861 shows the "Royal Liver Friendly Society (Joseph Degge, Manager)" at 77 Bridge Road. The street index, however, for Westminster Road states "See Bridge Road" suggesting that Bridge Road and Westminster Road are one and the same. The present name – Westminster Bridge Road – combines the two. "Place" may have been an error by the census enumerator.

60 Dudley Ridge, *A Sussex Family*. It was at the suggestion of Ernest Haynes, the chairman of Royal London, that Dr Ridge undertook the task of searching for information that would throw light on the ancestors of Henry Ridge and in the preface he thanked the directors of the Royal London for their continued interest, encouragement and generous assistance with the costs of publication.

61 Dr Ridge explains (p. 9) that originally "a husbandman was anyone who cultivated the land, but with the evolution of the freeholder, the name in Elizabethan times had become restricted to those who were copyholders, whilst those who held free land to the value of 40s. per annum were classed as yeomen."

62 Grosvenor Row was renamed Pimlico Road in the early 1900s.

63 Thomas Cubitt (1788–1855) the first, and probably most influential, speculative builder who built large areas of London. His company provided a one-stop-shop – it employed a wide range of tradesmen and professionals and was able to design, lay out and build streets, squares and whole districts.

64 Eccleston Square was laid out in 1835; and St George's Square in 1839, initially as two roads and only later as a square. Chelsea Bridge was opened in 1858 and Grosvenor Railway Bridge and Victoria Station in 1860.

65 *Post Office London Directory*:
   1847: Geo. Hen. Ridge, Cheesemonger, 12 Grosvenor Row, Pimlico (p. 942).
   1848: Directory missing from the National Archives.
   1849: Neither George Henry Ridge nor 12 Grosvenor Row listed.

66 *In Memoriam* booklet produced by Royal London after Ridge's death. No author is shown.

67 There is no York Street in Haggerston today. There were several York Streets in the locality at the time but the one at the centre of Haggerston is now known as How's Street. Weymouth Terrace virtually runs into York Street/How's Street. I am indebted for this information to Bruce Hunt and his monumental project on the renaming of London streets, www.maps. thehunthouse.net/Streets/Street_Name_Changes.htm.

68 The *In Memoriam* booklet states: "In the year of 1859, the year of the great lock out in the Building trade, he was appointed district manager for the Royal Liver Friendly Society at Hammersmith." This conflicts with the marriage certificate that shows him living in Haggerston, East London, in August 1860. It is also surprising that a 21-year-old carpenter would be appointed as a manager in a business of which he had no experience.

69 See Note 3 above. *A Sussex Family,* written after *We the Undersigned...*, states that the meeting was in a coffee shop in City Road.

70 Data supplied by the National Meteorological Archive at the Meteorological Office.

71 *Post Magazine* 9 April 1887, p. 217.

72 In 1862, several Royal Liver agents in Glasgow left to found the City of Glasgow Friendly Society. There is no suggestion, however, that Messrs Sinclair and Robertson were active defectors: nobody of either name was a member of the initial committee of management. (Jack House, *The Friendly Adventure*).

73 Laqueur, p. 109.

74 Anthony Ashley-Cooper (Lord Ashley), 7th Earl of Shaftesbury (1801–1885), a Tory MP, was active in promoting the Factory Acts 1847 & 1845, the Coal Mines Act 1842 and the Lunacy Act 1845. The statue of Eros at Piccadilly Circus (more correctly the Shaftesbury Memorial Fountain) was erected to commemorate his philanthropic works – the figure was intended to be the Angel of Christian Charity rather than the God of Love.

75 Laqueur, p. 110. Hodder, *The Life and Work of the Seventh Earl of Shaftesbury* (London, 1887) p. 25.

76 Royal London Centenary Banquet, 2 February 1961, Transcript of Speeches, p. 13.

77 In his evidence to the Royal Commission in 1872 (See Chapter 2) Degge said, "I have never been a collector myself". Although he was giving evidence in relation to Royal London, "never" suggests that this reply covered his time at Royal Liver as well: Joseph Degge, Minutes of Evidence relating to Friendly Societies, Parliamentary Papers, 1873, Vol. XXII, p. 39, q. 25,096.

78 The original of the document is now in the possession of Royal London. The first reference to it in the archives is a letter from Charles Ridge dated 24 November 1924. Charles was Henry's son and worked as a clerk in the chief office and then as an agent of the Society for many years. The letter was addressed to his former superintendent, Walter Thomas (Tom) Challis, who was a founder member, treasurer and president of the Royal London Staff Association, the in-house trade union. Challis had joined the Society as an agent in 1888 and was superintendent at Huddersfield, Brighton, Camden Town and Stoke Newington, retiring in 1934 and dying aged 94 in 1962. He held Sunday social evenings for his agents and, while at Brighton, Charles Ridge was a regular attender. Charles had obviously been

asked to set down all he knew about the founding of the Society and included with his letter a copy of the document in his own handwriting. The minutes of the Society's Board meeting of 3 April 1947 refer to a document dated 2 February 1861 being "received on loan from Charles Ridge, the son of Henry Ridge, one of the Founders of the Society, which document signed by the said Henry Ridge and J Degge set out an agreement between them to promote the Royal London Life Insurance and Benefit Society." Copies were made, one of which was pasted into the minute book. It would appear that the document was returned to Charles Ridge, who died in 1948, aged 86. In the late 1950s, when interest in the history of the Society was growing with the approach of its centenary, the original document was apparently acquired from Dudley Ridge, Charles' son.

Chapter 2 – Early Years: 1861–1874

1   Henry Liversage, Minutes of Evidence relating to Friendly Societies, Parliamentary Papers, 1873, Vol. XXII, q. 1251.

2   Joseph Degge, Minutes of Evidence relating to Friendly Societies, Parliamentary Papers, 1873, Vol. XXII, p. 44, q. 25,112.

3   *Post Magazine* 9 April 1887, p. 127.

4   Degge, p. 39, q. 24,958.

5   Degge, p. 40, q. 24,971.

6   Called to the bar in 1824, John Tidd Pratt (1797–1870) was a prolific legal author who wrote or edited more than twenty works, including an early edition of one of the current landlord and tenant textbooks. His *The Law relating to Friendly Societies* was a bestseller and ran to several editions. In 1828 he was appointed counsel to approve the rules of friendly societies and then in 1834 became the first registrar, a position he held until his death. He did much to expose the financial frailty of many of the traditional societies and frequently refused to approve rules that referred to socialising and conviviality. State intervention was generally unwelcome at the time and his critics complained that, instead of contenting himself with the administration of the law, Tidd Pratt continually tried to make it. See *Dictionary of National Biography*, Compact Edition (1975) p. 1703; Cordery, *British Friendly Societies*, pp. 88–91, 92–93, 106, 145 and 178–179.

7   Research has failed to identify a Phoenix House, Shepherd's Bush. It may be no more than a coincidence that in 1861 Phoenix House, Hammersmith was the address of James Bird, a solicitor whose practice was such that he might have been consulted in drafting the rules for a new friendly society and who may have allowed his office address to be used for a new venture with which he was involved professionally and that had not yet acquired a trading address.

8   Charles Ridge in the 1924 letter referred to in Note 78 to Chapter 1 stated that the offices "were first in Bridge Rd Hammersmith also Uxbridge Rd finally at 5 Aldermanbury Postern… and was transferred from there to Finsbury Pavement" but his omission of 51 Moorgate Street may perhaps cast some doubt on his reliability as a witness. A report of the opening of the central section of Royal London House that appeared in *Post Magazine*

of 8 February 1930 stated that in "its earliest days, the Royal London was invested with a savour of romance. Two very earnest young men with high principles and no capital launched out in Hammersmith to insure folk on the mutual principle". The Lord Mayor had been briefed accordingly and in his speech referred to the Society commencing business in two rooms in Hammersmith. In the Royal London archives is a letter dated 5 August 1958 from F W Evans, a pensioner, who comments that "this year is the 60th anniversary of my connection with the 'Royal London'". He wrote that he would always remember Frederick de la Bertauche, one of the early directors, "particularly as he never failed at any function we had to tell the origin of the Society, how it started in a room over a Coffee Shop in Hammersmith [and] how when the first claim arose, they hadn't sufficient funds to meet the claim and had to turn out their pockets on the Board Room Table – a deal [pine] kitchen table – to meet the claim". James Wall, who had joined the Society as an agent in 1908 and was a director from 1945 to 1955, suggested in an interview in the late 1950s that the "Society started in old rooms over a coffee house. The furniture was removed from one office to another by handcart". The notes of the interview do not indicate if Wall opined on the location of the old rooms. On the other hand, there is a photograph in *We the Undersigned...* (See Note 3 to Chapter 1) of a building with shops on the ground floor that purports to be the Society's first head office, captioned "Shepherd's Bush 1861".

9 A typed note to this effect is in the Royal London archives, apparently prepared as part of the pre-centenary work in the late 1950s. No contemporary document exists, although some limited corroboration is provided by the fact that, as Mr Hepden was 57, the premium and sum assured are in accordance with the Table No. 1 attached to the original rules of the Society.

10 Fourth Report of the Friendly and Benefit Building Societies Commission, Parliamentary Papers, 1874, Vol. XXIII, Part I, p. cxxiv, para. 534.

11 Degge, p. 45, q. 25,130.

12 Fourth Report, p. cix, para. 489.

13 Queen Victoria, letter to King Leopold of Belgium (her uncle), 3 May 1851: *The Letters of Queen Victoria: A Selection From Her Majesty's Correspondence between the years 1837 and 1861* (London, John Murray, 1907).

14 George Sala, *Twice Round the Clock*, published in 1859, includes this description of the New Cut market between Waterloo Road and Blackfriars Road: "The howling of beaten children and kicked dogs, the yells of ballad-singers... ; the bawling recitations of professional denunciators... ; the monotonous jodels of the itinerant hucksters; the fumes of the vilest tobacco, of stale corduroy suits, of oilskin caps, of mildewed umbrellas, of decaying vegetables, of escaping (and frequently surreptitiously tapped) gas, of deceased cats, of ancient fish, of cagmag meat, of dubious mutton pies, and of unwashed, saddened, unkempt, reckless humanity; all these make the night hideous and the heart sick".

15 Hansard, House of Commons, 15 July 1858, Col. 1508.

16 Michael Paterson, *Voices from Dickens' London*, Introduction, p. 10.

17 See Note 78 to Chapter 1.

18 The minutes for the meetings held between 23 April and 17 September 1862 have not

survived and so it is possible that Hambridge went missing during that period. Charles Ridge was not always the most reliable of witnesses (see Note 8 above). However, he could have had no first-hand knowledge.

19 "If any committee-man shall die, or be desirous of resigning, or shall become incapable to act, or shall become bankrupt or insolvent, or compound with his creditors, or shall be removed from his office by a resolution of a special general meeting of the members of the society, he shall thereupon cease to be a member of the committee of management, and the secretary shall forthwith convene a special meeting of the committee of management, and at such special meeting another member of the society shall be appointed a member of the committee of management in his place." (Royal London Friendly Society, Rule 2.)

20 Degge, p. 46, q. 25,176.

21 Degge, p. 45, q. 25,121, Fourth Report p. cxxiii, para. 530.

22 "The earliest recorded appointment of an agent in the Manchester district is that of Mr. Thomas W Pile, dated March 29, 1865 – approximately four years after the formation of the Society. This was followed six months later by the appointment of Mr. Edward Powell, and during the succeeding twelve months other agents were appointed – Messrs. Littlewood, Booth and Tracey – whilst Messrs. Blundell and Shannon were appointed canvassers on October 3, 1866". *The Policy-Holder*, 27 June 1923.

23 A photograph suggests that the building had shops at street level and three floors above them – hardly lofty, except perhaps to somebody who had just climbed the stairs up to the office.

24 There was not to be another run on a British bank until Northern Rock in 2007.

25 An industrial assurance collector with a debit (weekly collection) of £10 and thus (commission was at the rate of 25 per cent) an income of £2 10s 0d a week (today: £162 a week) might sell for £200–£300 (£250 today: £16,200) although it would be a while before any Royal London book would sell for more than £100.

26 Degge, p. 41, q. 25,008.

27 Degge p. 46, qq. 25,174; 25,175.

28 Degge, p. 43, q. 25,093.

29 *Report of Sir George Young*, Assistant Commissioner to the Royal Commission appointed to inquire into Friendly and Benefit Building Societies, Parliamentary Papers, 1874, Vol. XXIII, Part II, p. 25 and Fourth Report, p. ciii, para. 467.

30 Degge, pp. 45,46 qq. 25,140–25,160; 25,178; 25,179.

31 Degge, p. 45, q. 25,142.

32 Degge, p. 46, qq. 25,159; 25,160.

33 Degge, pp. 39, 42, qq. 24,935, 25,060; 25,061.

34 It seems as though the Society did not strictly operate the rule even while in force. As drafted, it applied to *any* person seeking to become a member. Degge, however, suggested to the Royal Commission that it applied to any person "proposing to insure for more than £12" (Degge, p. 40, q. 24,974). Perhaps this was how Rule 13 was applied in practice. In its revised form, the committee of management could require the proposer "to appear before a medical officer acting for the society to be examined by him in reference to his past and

present state of health".

35 "Whereas" the policy began, before setting out the name and address of the member: "the person hereby assured hath signed a proposal, dated the... day of... in the year of our Lord One thousand Eight hundred and... proposing to become a Member of the ROYAL LONDON FRIENDLY SOCIETY, by effecting an Assurance with the said Society upon his [her] life aged... years, for the whole continuance thereof, (and hath [not] been examined by a Medical Officer acting for the said Society,) and hath made the declaration required by the Rules of the said Society.

NOW THIS POLICY WITNESSETH that in consideration of the payment of the Sum of... Shillings and... Penny [Pence] this day made to the said Society, the Receipt whereof is hereby acknowledged, and also in consideration of the future payments of the like sum to be made at the office of the said Society; or to a duly authorised Agent thereof, on each and every subsequent Monday to the date hereof, in this and every succeeding year during the life of the said Assured, the Funds and other Property of the said Society shall, and they are hereby declared to be subject and liable upon the death of the said Assured to pay to the Widower, Widow, or any particular child or children of the said Assured, (as the case may be), if nominated to receive the sum by the said Assured, or in default of nomination then to the Executors, Administrators or Assigns of the said Assured the sum of... Pounds... Shillings and... Pence.

IT IS HEREBY DECLARED that the said Assured shall be a paying member of the said Society six calendar months before becoming entitled to any benefit in the event of death, (after the expiration of the said period, the said Assured shall become entitled to half the sum assured, and in twelve calendar months to the whole of the sum assured in the event of death). AND IT IS FURTHER DECLARED if the assured shall die by the hand of justice, dueling, suicide or by violence of parents or any interested party, that this policy shall become absolutely forfeited and at an end, and all engagements and contracts concerning the same shall cease and become absolutely void, and all sums of money and premiums paid on account of same, and all benefits and advantages arising therefrom, shall become absolutely forfeited for the use of the said Society and that the said Assurance is effected under and in pursuance of the Rules and Regulations of the said Society, and the same is and shall be subject and liable to the several conditions, restrictions and stipulations therein contained, (so far as the same may be applicable thereto,) And to the Conditions and Rules of the said Society hereupon endorsed.

GIVEN UNDER OUR HANDS etc."

36 See Appendix 1.

37 Degge, pp. 40,42, qq. 24,987; 25,067–25,070.

38 Degge, p. 40, q. 24,988.

39 Sir Stafford Northcote, later Earl of Iddesleigh (1818–87). MP (1855–85), Financial Secretary to the Treasury (1859), President of the Board of Trade (1866), Secretary of State for India (1867), Chancellor of the Exchequer (1874), Leader of the Conservative Party in the House of Commons (1876), First Lord of the Treasury (1885) and Foreign Secretary (1886).

40 Committee on Industrial Assurance and Assurance on the lives of Children under ten years of age (Cohen Committee), Report, Cmd 4376, London 1933, p. 4.

41 Sir Michael Hicks Beach, later Earl St Aldwyn (1837–1916). MP (1864–1906), Parliamentary Secretary to the Poor Law Board and Undersecretary of State for Home Affairs (1868), Chief Secretary for Ireland (1874), Secretary of State for the Colonies (1878), Chancellor of the Exchequer and Leader of the House of Commons (1885), Chief Secretary for Ireland (1886), President of the Board of Trade (1888), Chancellor of the Exchequer (1895).

42 Sir Sydney Waterlow (1822–1906). Born in Finsbury and brought up in Mile End and Hoxton, Waterlow, was apprenticed to a printer and joined the stationers business started by his father, enabling it to expand into printing. In 1857 he was elected a common councilman and advanced through the City corporation to alderman, sheriff and (in 1872/73) to Lord Mayor. He was managing director of Waterlow and Son Limited, a Liberal MP, chairman of the Union Bank and a generous philanthropist who laboured hard to secure decent housing for the poor in London.

43 In the transcript of the evidence, each question is numbered. Degge's first question is 24,931 and his last 25,198.

44 Degge, pp. 40, 42, qq. 24,982–24,984; 24,986; 25,038.

45 Degge, p. 40, q. 24,984.

46 Degge, p. 46, q. 25,175.

47 Degge, p. 47, q. 25,186.

48 Degge, p. 47, q. 25,191.

49 Degge, p. 40, q. 24,990.

50 Degge, p. 41, qq. 25,024–25,029.

51 Degge, p. 44. q. 25,115.

52 The Hon. Edward Lyulph Stanley, later Lord Sheffield, later Lord Stanley of Alderley (1839–1925), a barrister, who after his role as assistant commissioner, was MP for Oldham (1880–85), a member of royal commissions on housing the poor and elementary education, and actively involved over many years in the development and administration of education in London. In 1886, he was appointed by the registrar of friendly societies to undertake an inquiry into the affairs of the Royal Liver Friendly Society. His report prompted radical changes in the constitution of Royal Liver and the introduction of the delegate system that remains in place today. Later he served as a trustee of Royal Liver for nearly 40 years and in 1908 laid the foundation stone of the Royal Liver Building. He lived at Alderley Park, Cheshire.

53 Degge, p. 42, qq. 25,040–25,058; *Report of the Hon. E L Stanley*, Assistant Commissioner to the Royal Commission appointed to inquire into Friendly and Benefit Building Societies, Parliamentary Papers, 1874, Vol. XXIII, Part II, p. 136.

54 It seems likely that this sum included the superintendent's travelling expenses.

55 The items listed by Stanley add up to £8,187. Both in his report, and in evidence, the total expenditure is expressed to be £8,647. This miscellaneous item has been included by the author to reconcile the two.

56 Degge, p. 40, q. 24,991.

57 Degge, p. 39, qq. 24,957–24,963.

58 Degge, p. 46, qq. 25,183–25,185.

59 Degge, p. 46, qq. 25,180–25,182.

60 Degge, p. 46, qq. 25,167–25,173.

61 See Chapter 15.

62 Degge, p. 43, qq. 25,090–25,091.

63 Degge, p. 40, qq. 24,987; 24,987.

64 Degge, p. 42, qq. 25,065; 25,066.

65 Fourth Report, p. cxv, paras. 504, 506.

66 Report, p. cx, para. 489 and James Atherton, Minutes of Evidence relating to Friendly Societies, Parliamentary Papers, 1873, Vol. XXII, q. 22,385.

67 Report, p. cx, para. 489.

68 Fourth Report of the Friendly and Benefit Building Societies Commission, Parliamentary Papers, 1874, Vol. XXIII, Part I, p. cxxv, para. 539. Industrial assurance was analysed and criticised by the Royal Commission in the 1870s, by a distinguished economist in a detailed report commissioned during World War I, by two government committees between the wars and in two books inspired by the second committee's report. Similar complaints tended to be made each time. To avoid repetition, I have set out in Appendix 1 the criticisms, the responses of the offices at the time and some comments of my own.

69 De Beauvoir Town lies to the west of Kingsland Road (now the A10, heading north from the City, past Liverpool Street) between the Regent's Canal and the Balls Pond Road. The 1840s development, only two miles from the City, with its tree-lined streets and air of spaciousness, attracted successful City workers. De Beauvoir Square (Enfield Street where Degge lived linked the square with Kingsland Road) "with its neo-Jacobean villas, with ornately shaped 'Flemish' gables, is a unique architectural set-piece, a pioneering piece of town planning". (Tony Aldous, *The Illustrated London News Book of London's Villages* (Secker & Warburg, 1980) p. 46.

70 Fourth Report, pp. civ–cvi, paras. 470–473. In addition, the Prudential had around 900,000 policyholders: *Report of the Hon. E L Stanley*, Assistant Commissioner to the Royal Commission appointed to inquire into Friendly and Benefit Building Societies, Parliamentary Papers, 1874, Vol. XXIII, Part II, p. 210.

Chapter 3 – Expansion: 1875–1899

1 *Post Magazine*, 27 February 1879, p. 144.

2 *Post Magazine*, 3 March 1900, p. 155.

3 These and other favourable reports in the press and appreciative letters from the recipients of claims appeared with the list of London claims in what appears to be the 1877 prospectus in use at the district office at 31 Knapp Road, Bow, where the superintendent was Edward Hambridge, the secretary's younger brother. It refers to just two products – the basic life policy and an endowment policy.

4 *Post Magazine*, 13 June 1885, p. 321.

5 Sadly, no plan could be devised a century later to save Barings from the damage inflicted by a single employee. Those striving to save Barings in 1890 would have been horrified had they known that in 2009 their successors would be working simultaneously on plans to save not one but several banks, all of which had got themselves into difficulties at the same time.

6 Dyos and Wolfe, *The Victorian City*, p. 4.

7 *Post Magazine*, 15 March 1879, p. 100, derived from the report of the Chief Registrar of Friendly Societies 1877, Parliamentary Papers, 1878, Vol. LXIX. Only the Canterbury Friendly Society (founded in 1737) had more than 500 members. The oldest surviving society was the Defoe Friendly Benefit Society (founded in 1687).

8 Report of the Chief Registrar of Friendly Societies 1877, Parliamentary Papers, 1878, Vol. LXIX, Table 1, p. 71. The reports speak of "members" – every policyholder would be a member but some members would have many policies and so the number of in-force policies should exceed the number of members. Pre-computerisation, however, one wonders how effective the offices were in de-duplicating multi-policy members – these returns could well relate more to policies than to members.

9 Report of the Chief Registrar of Friendly Societies 1900, Parliamentary Papers, 1901, Vol. LXXI, Appendix K, p. 179.

10 See the two previous notes.

11 Dennett, *Sense of Security*, p. 147.

12 An expense ratio below 30 per cent was never achieved again, and the impressive 29.9 per cent probably appeared in the 1876 accounts only because "other incidental expenses" were included within claims. This suggests that in reality the expenses (and expense ratio) were higher and claims lower but, because the other incidental expenses were not quantified, we cannot determine by how much. The expense ratio was 48.1 per cent in 1877 and for the next five years exceeded 50 per cent although, by the end of the period, had stabilised in the mid–forties.

13 *Post Magazine*, 3 March 1900, p. 148: Horace Duffell seconding the resolution to adopt the annual report and accounts.

14 In these pre-computer days, it clearly took a while to get new policies onto the books and so the annual analysis ignored those sold in the previous year. On 1 January 1899, there were 766,271 Royal London policies in force (excluding those sold in 1898). Over 250,000 of these had been sold in 1896 and 1897. During 1899, 55,595 policies lapsed, 34,413 of which had come into force during 1896 and 1897. So although it was certainly true that little would have been paid by way of premiums in 60 per cent of the cases, it was equally true that in some of the other 40 per cent, the policyholder would have been paying premiums for some time.

15 *Post Magazine*, 1 June 1895, p. 398, quoting from the report of the Chief Registrar of Friendly Societies for the quinquennium ending 31 December 1891.

16 *Post Magazine*, 1 March 1902, p. 155.

17 *Report of the Hon. E L Stanley*, Assistant Commissioner to the Royal Commission appointed to inquire into Friendly and Benefit Building Societies, Parliamentary Papers,

1874, Vol. XXIII, Part II, p. 27.

18 William Sutton, Minutes of Evidence taken before the Select Committee on Friendly Societies Parliamentary Papers, 1888, Vol. XII, Part I, p. 69, qq. 1200, 1201.

19 Report of the Select Committee (HC) to inquire into the operation of section 30 of the Friendly Societies Act 1875 (as amended), Parliamentary Papers, 1889, Vol. X, p. xiii.

20 Minutes of Evidence taken before the Select Committee on Children's Life Assurance Bill, Parliamentary Papers, 1890–91, Vol. XI, p. 180, evidence of W H Hambridge.

21 *Post Magazine*, 2 June 1884, p. 385.

22 So, for 1d-a-week (today: 35p), a 20-year-old could be insured under Table 1 for £8 10s (today: £704). If he was 40, then the benefit reduced to £4 12s and at 60 it dropped to £2. Under Table 2, a 20-year-old who could afford 2d a week would receive £18 17s 8d (today: £1,560) at the age of 50, while his dependents would have received the same amount if he died before then. This was at a time when a manual labourer would be earning less than 4s a week, a housemaid 5s, a skilled tradesman (carpenter or mason) 6s and a junior clerk 7s.

23 A 20-year-old who could afford 1s 6d (today: £6.30) every four weeks would be covered for £50 (today: £4,200). As was only fair, paying the premiums every four weeks was beneficial – the 20-year-old would have had to pay 6d a week under Table 1 to receive £51.

24 The superintendent at Mexborough in 1899 was Elisha Gibbs. 'Elisha' is a name given to boys and girls and the evidence is conflicting as to the gender of the superintendent. A printed letter that included 'Mr' was sent every week from the chief office acknowledging the account and none of those that survive were amended to 'Mrs'. On the other hand, the superintendent is often referred to in the account book as "Gibbs (late Davis), E" suggesting marriage or reverting to a former name on the death of or separation from a husband.

25 From the beginning of 1900 an expense of 5s was included each week for office rental.

26 *Post Magazine*, 1875, p. 403.

27 *Post Magazine*, 13 June 1885, p. 326.

28 *Post Magazine*, 18 September 1886, p. 581.

29 *Post Magazine*, 25 September 1886, p. 595.

30 *Post Magazine*, 11 November 1887, p. 717.

31 *Post Magazine*, 1 June 1889, p. 371.

32 *Post Magazine*, 31 May 1890, p. 394.

33 *Post Magazine*, 3 June 1893, p. 394.

34 *Post Magazine*, 2 June 1894, p. 392.

35 *Post Magazine*, February 1897, p. 144.

36 *Post Magazine*, 9 April 1887, p. 217.

37 Steve Else – see Note 1 to Chapter 5.

38 Rule 4 (extract), Royal London Friendly Society.

39 *Post Magazine*, 2 June 1894, p. 386.

40 *Post Magazine*, 1 June 1895, p. 393.

41 *Agents Chronicle*, 30 October 1897.

42 *Post Magazine*, 5 May 1888, p. 307.

43 There are reputable sources in which Fulton's forename is spelt "Forest".

44 www.oldbaileyonline.org ref. t18950520-459.

45 *Post Magazine*, 1 November 1894, p. 423.

46 *Dictionary of National Biography*, Compact Edition (1975) p. 2594.

47 Sir Charles Biron, *Without Prejudice*, p. 240.

48 *The Policy-Holder*, 11 November 1896, p. 832.

49 Arthur Harding talking about his childhood in the East End of London: Raphael Samuel, *East End Underworld*, p. 24.

50 Minutes of Evidence taken before the Select Committee on Children's Life Assurance Bill, Parliamentary Papers, 1890–91, Vol. XI, p. 180, evidence of W H Hambridge.

51 The obituary in *Post Magazine* (18 January 1890, p. 43) went into rather more detail: "On Thursday, 9th inst., Mr Henry Ridge, the treasurer and a director of the Royal London F.S. while sitting at a Board meeting of the society, and just at the moment that he had expressed his opinion on the business before the Board, was seized with a fit of apoplexy. He was removed to the library adjoining, and Drs. Turner and Long were in immediate attendance. The attack, however, was of so serious a character that death took place about 3 hours afterwards. Deceased was 51 years of age, and leaves a widow and seven children".

52 Within the archives is a small slip of paper cut from a journal that contains an anonymous letter signed 'Trotter' that reads: "I see by the Chronicle that the old soldier from Wigan is a candidate for the vacancy on the Board of the Royal London. As his policy has been reduction of commissions, non-interest in books, and opposition to the Agents' Union, I think the London agent will see what sort of committee man he would make! I hear he did a lot of work in Manchester, before coming to Wigan, in the shape of getting old agents discharged and their books collected on salary. If this be so, I don't wish him success". Mr Fyans seems to have been ahead of his time in seeking cost-efficiencies and if only more of the members voting at the general meetings had been aware of this, he may have stood a better chance of being elected.

53 Harvie and Matthews: *Nineteenth Century Britain*, p. 100.

54 Elizabeth Blackwell, on the basis of her US qualification, was the first woman entered on the medical register, in 1859. Elizabeth Garrett Anderson was the second, in 1865, and the first women to have qualified in Britain. Carrie Morrison, admitted in 1922, was the first woman solicitor.

55 See Chapter 10, Note 40.

56 *Post Magazine*, 30 May 1891, p. 379.

57 *Post Magazine*, 2 June 1894, p. 384: "The Chairman [William Bowrey] read a doctor's certificate to the effect that Mr Hambridge was suffering from nervous debility and required rest and change of air at a seaside place".

58 *Post Magazine*, 3 March 1900, p. 148: Edward Smith, chairing the 1900 annual general meeting.

59 Reported in the *In Memoriam* booklet produced by Royal London after his death.

60 *Post Magazine*, 15 April 1899, p. 251.

61 *Post Magazine*, 1900, 3 March 1900, p. 148.

Chapter 4 – The Founders

1   *Post Magazine*, 18 January 1890, p. 43.

2   See the letter referred to in Chapter 2.

3   At the time of the meeting in the coffee shop, Joseph Bishop, the husband of Joseph Degge's aunt, might have been seen as a likely benefactor. It had probably been their prosperity that brought the Degge family to Liverpool. After the break-up of Hughes and Bishop, he continued brewing for a while as "Joseph Bishop and Company", and was later a wine merchant and spirit dealer, but the businesses did not prosper, and in 1862 Joseph Bishop was declared bankrupt. He died in 1870. Soon afterwards, his widow, Joseph's Aunt Mary, was working as a confectioner. Joseph Degge had three uncles: William remained in the pub trade in Liverpool; Joseph Barnes joined his nephew at Royal London; and Robert, the only sibling to remain in Staffordshire, was a shoemaker in Newton. It seems unlikely that William or Robert would have been able to provide financial assistance, but perhaps Joseph Barnes agreed to defer the commission due to him in those weeks when cash was short. Degge's father, John, a farm labourer during much of Joseph's childhood, might have been able to help – his parents had followed the rest of the family to Liverpool, where John set up a successful business as a hay and straw dealer.

4   The Ridge family history refers to Henry's father, George Henry, the cheesemonger, as not "being obsessed with perpetual chasing of money", retiring in his 60s and dying at the age of 69 in Hackney in 1883: "He was a true Dickensian character and his grandson [Charles Ridge] remembered him as something larger than life, carrying a gold-headed cane and wearing his top hat at a rakish angle. He was a happy and contented man full of boisterous good humour". (Ridge, *A Sussex Family*, p. 56) In fact, the 1861 census returns suggest that George Henry had given up cheesemongering and was now a debt collector, and that he and Martha were living in Lambeth in a property shared with two other families, with Kate, said to be their daughter, aged seven. At the time of her birth, George would have been 41 and Martha 40. There is no mention of Kate in *A Sussex Family* – she features in neither the text nor the Ridge family tree. The records of the Abney Park Cemetery indicate that George Henry was buried in a common grave, but that Martha, who died in 1893 aged 79, was buried beside Henry, her name being added to the monument to her son erected by subscription within Royal London.

5   See Appendix 1.

6   For more detail on the history of Royal Liver and Liverpool Victoria, see the publications referred to in Chapter 1, Notes 31 and 32.

7   See Chapter 2, Note 52.

8   The cause of death on Elizabeth's death certificate is almost illegible but it appears to be 'Phthisis' a term formerly applied to many wasting diseases but later restricted to pulmonary tuberculosis, then known as consumption.

9   See Chapter 2, Note 69.

10 According to the *In Memoriam* booklet produced by Royal London after Degge's death. No author is shown.

11 *In Memoriam*: Degge.

12 See Chapter 2.

13 Ridge, p. 57.

14 *Post Magazine*, 18 January 1890, p. 43.

15 Ridge, p. 59.

16 Ridge, p. 57.

17 *In Memoriam* booklet produced by Royal London after Hambridge's death. No author is shown.

18 *In Memoriam*: Hambridge.

19 A former director speaking at the same time remembered Edward Hambridge, William's brother, as one of the best-dressed men that he had ever met. The few photographs suggest that William too, took care over his appearance.

20 Gore Allen, *We the Undersigned...*, p. 22.

21 Minutes of Evidence taken before the Select Committee on Children's Life Assurance Bill, Parliamentary Papers, 1890–91, Vol. XI, p. 180, evidence of W H Hambridge.

22 *Post Magazine*, 9 April 1887, p. 217. See Chapters 2 and 3.

23 *In Memoriam*: Hambridge.

24 *Post Magazine*, 3 March 1900, p. 148.

25 The 1861 census return shows William aged 24 and Edward aged 6. A difference of 18 years between the ages of the brothers may suggest an error but it is probably correct. According to the 1851 census return, Martha, their mother, was born about 1820 and so would have been 18 when William was born and 36 at the time of Edward's birth. Edward joined Royal London about 1873 initially working for Henry Ridge and then as sub-collector to his brother William whose collecting book he, in due course, acquired.

26 The average family size in mid-Victorian Britain was six and that had reduced to three by 1914 (R Soloway, *Birth Control and the Population Question in England, 1877–1930*). Ann Ridge gave birth eight times in fourteen years, seven of which were within a period of nine years.

27 Clearly coincidences are possible but there is confirmation in the 1871 census return that this is the Jane who married Hambridge in 1857. Living with her in 1871 was Walter Hepden, her brother, who was born in Tonbridge. The 1852 census return of the Hepden family confirms that Jane had a brother called Walter, born in Tonbridge, whose ages on the two returns match. Confirmation in the other census returns is less specific but the place of birth of Jane Hambridge is consistently shown as Tonbridge and the ages more or less match. The lack of a precise age match is of no concern as the returns require not the date of birth but the age on the day on which the census is taken.

28 The Occupation section of Jane's death certificate reads "Widow of William Henry Hambridge An Accountant's Clerk" although it is not clear if the occupation was intended to refer to the late husband or the deceased herself. The informant was "R. Vowles Daughter" probably Rosina (aka Rosa), Jane's first post-1863 child.

29 All three certificates refer to the mother as "Jane Hambridge formerly Hepden", leaving no doubt that this is the same Jane who married Hambridge in 1857.

30 Ginger Frost, 'Bigamy and Cohabitation in Victorian England', *Journal of Family History*,

(1997) 22(3):286.

31 Jane seems to have had a nomadic existence with no two documents showing her living in the same place: Deptford (1861, with Hambridge), Rotherhithe (1865), Hackney (1866), Stoke Poges (1868), Battersea (1871), Bromley (1881), Newington (1891), Herne Hill (1901) and Tooting (1908). But for the various identifying features (see Notes 27–29 above) – and the fact that Hambridge acknowledged in his will that his (first) wife was still alive in 1895 – one might question whether this was the same person.

32 Frost, p. 294. Bigamists pose difficult sentencing questions even today. On 14 April 2010 in Stirling Sheriff Court, Alexander Roy admitted going through a marriage ceremony at Dunblane Hydro in 2007 despite the lack of any divorce from his wife. His solicitor suggested that the separation from his wife in 2001 had left him depressed and suffering from adjustment disorder so that he recalled very little from the period. It emerged that while living with his second 'wife' he set up home in different parts of the country with two other women, both of whom became pregnant. His wife and current employers had written to the court pleading that he should not be imprisoned. The sheriff ordered Roy to carry out 240 hours community service. One of the 'other women' was devastated that he had not been jailed: "The maximum sentence he could have got was six years. I thought that would be a bit much, but he needs to be stopped before he ruins anyone else's life". ("Mercy plea from bigamist's wife", BBC News, 14 April 2010).

33 Gore Allen, *We the Undersigned...*, p. 22.

34 *Post Magazine*, 15 April 1899, p. 251.

35 Royal London Centenary Banquet, 2 February 1961, Transcript of Speeches, p. 13.

36 *Post Magazine*, 3 March 1900, p. 148.

Chapter 5 – Conversion: 1900–1908

1 In the late 1950s there was an increasing awareness of the impending centenary of the Society and efforts were made to collect material for the museum that was being established and for a history of the Society that had been commissioned. Steve Else had retired as chief clerk of the General Department on 31 December 1948. He may have had a reputation as a raconteur because it appears that he was approached specifically. On 24 August 1959 he sent four (single-spaced) pages of recollections with a covering letter beginning "Dear Len" – presumably Leonard Wiseman, the secretary. None of this material was used in *We the Undersigned...*

2 In due course, Royal London's telephone number became Monarch 3044.

3 John Belcher (1841–1913) spent two years in France studying architecture. He was articled to, and later in partnership, with his father, was the winner in 1907 of the Royal Gold Medal of the Royal Institute of British Architects and wrote *Essentials in Architecture: An Analysis of the Principles and Qualities to be Looked for in Architecture*.

4 The Ashton Memorial in Williamson Park (the site of a former quarry) was built in memory of his wife between 1907 and 1909 by Lord Ashton, a local industrialist (who, as James Williamson, was Liberal MP for Lancaster 1886–1895).

5 See Chapter 2.

6 The Friendly Societies Act 1896, section 8, essentially restricted friendly societies to whole life and endowment policies, and funeral expense policies on the lives of the husband, wife or child of a member, where the sum assured did not exceed £200. General insurance such as fire policies were not permitted with the exception that a member could insure the tools of his trade for a sum not exceeding £15.

7 The 1896 Act, section 41(1).

8 The 1896 Act, section 71(1) provided that a society may "by special resolution, determine to convert itself into a company under the Companies Acts 1862 to 1890". By section 74(a) a special resolution had to be "passed by a majority of not less than three fourths of such members... entitled under the rules to vote as may be present" at the meeting, providing due notice had been given of the intention to propose the resolution at the meeting.

9 Most of the major industrial assurance offices had their own self-contained trade union that was, in due course, to become affiliated to either (in the case of the Royal London Staff Association) the National Federation of Insurance Workers or the National Amalgamated Union of Life Assurance Workers. These were essentially federations of the unions from the various offices, with each section retaining a degree of independence. The RLSA was one of the few sections of the NFIW to produce a badge for its members. In 1964 the NFIW and NAULAW merged to form the National Union of Insurance Workers that, by virtue of several subsequent mergers, is now part of Unite.

10 Arbitration, *Lovett v Smith*, Transcript, main hearing, Day 1, 27 July 1920, p. 60.

11 Transcript, Day 1, p. 61.

12 Transcript, Day 1, p. 77.

13 Transcript, Day 1, p. 80.

14 Saddler, *A Mission in Life*, p. 51.

15 The circular was dated 18 December 1907: Transcript, Day 1, p. 89.

16 This is taken from an undated template of a letter that begins: "We understand that certain Trade Councils and other bodies have communicated with you regarding the proposed registration of this Society as a Mutual Insurance Society, and we think it probable that, at least in some instances, these organisations have not been correctly informed. We desire to submit a plain unvarnished statement of fact and shall esteem it a favour if you will oblige us by carefully perusing same."

17 The memorandum was sent in advance of the meeting on 29 June 1910 (see Chapter 6).

18 In the matter of the Royal London Mutual Insurance Society Ltd, Memorandum [to the President of the Board of Trade] relating to the Conversion of the Royal London Friendly Society into the above Mutual Company, 1910, National Archives.

19 During the 1920 arbitration (Chapter 7), the plaintiffs' counsel produced a cash book that he claimed proved that the directors were personally making contributions to Royal London Collectors' Watch Committee. The directors' counsel had never seen the book and so could not respond and the proceedings were settled before any evidence was given: Transcript, Day 2, 28 July 1920, p. 36.

20 Saddler, *A Mission in Life* p. 53.

21 *The Eastern Post and Chronicle*, 29 February 1908.

22 *The Anti-Conversionist*, No. 18, 2 March 1908, Edward Wright had advocated introducing a delegate system that was already in place at Royal Liver (see Chapter 2, Note 52) and City of Glasgow: "I am in favour of the Delegate system of representation as it would be a health check on the management of the Society". (*The Anti-Conversionist*, No. 7, 2 December 1907. A delegate was elected for every 1,000 members of City of Glasgow and a triennial meeting was held in every district where there were more than 1,000 members to elect the delegate(s). Glasgow was divided into four electoral districts. The delegates, rather than the membership at large, attended the annual general meeting.

23 A member of the Independent Labour Party and supported by the Labour Representation Committee, O'Grady (1866–1934) had been elected at the 1906 general election. He was active in the amalgamated Union of Cabinet Makers and, while still an MP, was appointed general secretary of the National Federation of General Workers in 1918. He became governor of Tasmania (1924–30) and of the Falkland Islands (1931–34).

24 Hansard, 6 April 1908, pp. 949, 950.

25 Hansard, 23 June 1908, p. 1519.

26 Edward Wright wrote in *The Anti-Conversionist* (No 7, December 2 1907) that he had before him a prospectus from both Scottish Legal and the Ideal Benefit Society and an advertisement for the Aberdeen and Northern Friendly Society. The former referred to policies being issued that gave deferred bonuses and the latter referred to a "Reversionary Bonus of 30s per £100 per annum".

27 Minutes of Evidence, Board of Trade Departmental Committee on the business of industrial assurance companies and collecting societies, Day 9, 28 October 1919, q. 6356.

28 When Smith gave evidence to the Parmoor Committee in 1919 (see Chapter 8) one of the members of the Committee (possibly Lord Parmoor) commented: "What always strikes me as very curious in these conversions is, it is really equivalent to asking the member to consent to a small reduction in the sum assured by his policy, because instead of having to pay 1 shilling for a death certificate, his representatives have to pay 3 shillings and 7 pence." Smith responded that this disadvantage might be offset by other advantages such as the larger volume of business reducing expenses but the Committee seemed unconvinced. Minutes of Evidence, qq. 6353–6357.

29 *The Anti-Conversionist*, No. 22, 3 June 1908.

30 *The Policy-Holder*, 1908, 24 June 1908, p. 496.

31 *The Policy-Holder*, 1 July 1908, p. 515.

32 *Insurance Mail*, 20 June, 1908.

33 Transcript, Day 2, p. 45.

34 *Post Magazine*, 27 June 1908, p. 518.

35 Hansard, 10 July 1908, p. 215.

36 Hansard, 15 July 1908, p 861.

37 Kingsley Wood (1881–1943). His personal ambitions were (or became) political – after membership of the London County Council, he was elected to Parliament, and was to

become Postmaster-General, Minister of Health, Secretary of State for Air and Chancellor of the Exchequer (see Chapter 7).

38 Hansard, 30 July 1908, p. 1763, 1764. A partially completed draft of the agreement is in the National Archives. The agreement provided that (a) the agents would use their utmost endeavours to make their agencies successful, and would not compete with the Society, nor employ sub-collectors without the consent of the Society (b) the trade union and the agents would not interfere with the Society nor induce policyholders to discontinue payments to the Society nor induce persons not to become members, and (c) any agent who was dismissed other than for wilful dishonesty would be guaranteed by the Society the local market value of his collecting book. The agreement was to run for five years and any disputes would be resolved by the chief registrar.

39 Although the directors may have done so personally – see Note 19 above.

40 15 August 1908.

41 See Chapter 1.

42 See Chapter 1, Note 78.

43 The figures that follow are taken from a table that appeared in the *Memorandum relating to the Conversion of the Royal London Friendly Society*.

44 Assurances Companies Act 1909, section 36 (see Appendix 2).

45 *Memorandum relating to the Conversion of the Royal London Friendly Society*, p. 4.

46 The emphasis is added by the present author.

Chapter 6 – Threats to Conversion: 1910

1 [1910] 1 Ch 228, at p. 235.

2 Arbitration, *Lovett v Smith*, Transcript, main hearing, Day 3, 29 July 1920, p. 46.

3 Mr Justice Joyce at p. 232.

4 Few made a greater contribution to company law than Henry Burton Buckley (1845–1935) as barrister, author and judge. Called to the bar in 1869, he wrote a text book on company law in 1873 that quickly became a standard work – 11 editions were published in his lifetime. He was appointed a judge in 1900 and promoted to the Court of Appeal in 1906. Soon after his appointment to the bench, he was regarded as a "cold, able, hard-working Judge" whose manner was "somewhat repellent" (Thomas Bowles aka Jehu Junior, *Vanity Fair*, 5 April 1900) but as his judicial career developed "a lucid and well ordered mind, a solemn presence, great learning and rigid impartiality, coupled with a strong will" combined to make Buckley "an almost ideal Chancery Judge". If he had a failing, it was perhaps "an excessive leaning towards technicality, due largely, no doubt, to his temperament and training". He was said to have "a keen appreciation for a good point, and unalloyed contempt for a bad one." (Leslie Ward, *The Book of the Bench*, (James MacKenzie Limited, 1909)) On his retirement from the Court of Appeal in 1915 he was created Lord Wrenbury and sat as a judge in the House of Lords. Well into his 80s he was still working on the latest edition of his book.

5 [1910] 1 Ch 228 at p. 238.

6   In the Public Archives is a letter dated 1 July 1910 from J H Hall of the Central Office of the Registry of Friendly Societies to G S Barnes of the Companies Department of the Board of Trade. Enclosed with the letter was a list showing all the friendly societies that had converted to companies since 1879. The Central Office's records for the seven conversions between 1879 and 1889 seem to have been incomplete but the 18 conversions since 1896 (apparently there were none between 1890 and 1895) can be divided into one of three categories (see Table 8 overleaf). Most had remained as mutual organisations – only those marked with an asterisk had a share capital.

7   See the previous Note.

8   John Rutherford was the junior counsel for the cases brought by Blythe, McGlade and McCormick. The fact that he was led by a different KC in each case suggests that Rutherford identified the lack of any specific provision in the Act permitting an extension of objects on a "section 71 resolution" and that leading counsel was retained to add weight to the presentation of the argument in court. Rutherford was one of several sons of William Rutherford, a Liverpool timber merchant, to go into the law. His elder brother, William Watson Rutherford, a solicitor and partner in the firm of Miller, Peel Hughes and Co, was Lord Mayor of Liverpool and later MP for Edge Hill. John Rutherford died in April 1918 on his way to court, aged 57.

9   *McGlade v Royal London Mutual Insurance Society Limited* [1910] 2 Ch 169.

10   *McCormick v Byrne, In re The Royal London Friendly Society* (1910) TLR 11 June.

11   *Wilkinson v The City of Glasgow Friendly Society* 1911 SC 476 (1911) 48 SLR 504. The decision was affirmed on 18 January 1911 by the Inner House of the Court of Session, the Scottish appeal court. The case also illustrated an uncertainty created by a delegate system of management – the judge held that a resolution to convert could validly be passed by the delegates, but he was overruled on this point, the Inner House deciding that a full meeting of members was required. This would have invalidated the resolution to convert, regardless of the *Blythe v Birtley* point.

12   House, *The Friendly Adventure*, p. 11.

13   The law reports did not give Mr Wilkinson's address but it appeared in *The Scotsman*, 23 April 1910.

14   *The Assurance Agents Chronicle*, 28 January 1911, printed in full the judgment in the appeal court and (unlike the law report) referred to Edinburgh solicitors acting as agents for Carruthers & Gedye who, in their correspondence with the Board of Trade referred to in the next chapter, confirmed that they acted for Wilkinson.

15   A transcript of the meeting at Sir Edward Grey's room in the House of Commons is in the National Archives (Transcript, *Deputation to the Right Hon. Sydney Buxton MP, President of the Board of Trade, from The Royal London Mutual Insurance Society, Limited*, 29 June 1910).

16   The directors had set out their case in advance of the meeting in a note, a copy of which is in the National Archives: *In the matter of the Royal London Mutual Insurance Society Ltd, Memorandum relating to the Conversion of the Royal London Friendly Society* into the above Mutual Company, 1910.

Table No. 8

Conversions from friendly society to company: 1879–1910

Date	Objects not or hardly extended	Objects extended	Objects widely extended
1896	Dusty Miller Sick & Burial Society (Rochdale)		
1898		Clapham Victoria Club*	
1899	Rochdale Equitable Provident Society	Annitsford & District Working Mens' Club	
1901			Worcester Permanent Money Society
1903			Carters Green Permanent Money Society
1904		St John's Hospital for Diseases of the Skin (Benevolent Society)	Birmingham Excelsior Permanent Society
1905		South Birmingham Permanent Money Society Hanham & District Permanent Money Society West Birmingham Permanent Money Society	West Bromwich Permanent Money Society
1906		National Accident Compensation and Epidemic Permanent Society *	Winson Green Permanent Money Society
1908		Wulfruna Permanent Money Society	Royal London Friendly Society
1909	Abertillery Silver Band Working Mens' Club		
1910			Llanarth Mutual Investment & Loan Society *
Total	3	8	7

17 I had hoped that it might be possible to learn something about Carruthers & Gedye that would reveal – or at least give a clue as to – the identity of their clients. Robert Carruthers was admitted in 1881 and in 1910 was in partnership with Reginald Gedye, who had been admitted in 1903. The firm had offices at 20 Castle Street, Liverpool and at Grange-over-Sands. In or about 1912, the partnership was dissolved and Gedye, a private client lawyer, took over the office at Grange. The firm he set up continues today and I am indebted to Richard Roberts, the senior partner of Gedye & Sons, for his assistance. Gedye's granddaughter was consulted but could add only that the family had known very little about the Liverpool connection. Carruthers & Gedye's correspondence with the Board of Trade says nothing about their underlying clients. Other enquiries in Liverpool failed to reveal anything about the firm or its clients.

18 *Evening Citizen*, 23 June 1910.

19 *Labour Leader*, 22 June 1910.

20 Transcript of meeting, p. 5.

21 Transcript of meeting, p.10.

Chapter 7 – The Royal London Auxiliary Insurance Company, Limited: 1910–1921

1 High Court of Justice (Chancery Division), *The Royal London Auxiliary Insurance Company, Limited v Lovett*, February 1921, Day 2, 23 February, Transcript, p. 10.

2 Royal London Staff Association, Executive Council's Report & Balance Sheet, 30 June 1930, p. 2.

3 Work must have been proceeding on the Auxiliary Company for some time – the use of 'Royal' in its name was authorised in a letter from the Secretary of State, Home Department dated 18 July 1910 that referred back to a meeting on 12 July: Arbitration, *Lovett v Smith*, Transcript, main hearing, Day 3, 29 July 1920, p. 94.

4 "Now, Sir, what are the certificates: are they shares or are they debentures? It is a question of some difficulty to decide. They are a kind of hermaphrodite, because there is a charge and at the same time there is a right to take practically the whole of the profits of the undertaking." Sir Malcolm Macnaghten KC, Transcript, Day 3, p. 27.

5 See Chapter 5.

6 *The Policy-Holder*, 24 August 1910, p. 669. See also 31 August, p. 688.

7 *Post Magazine*, 20 August 1910, p. 674.

8 Macnaghten, Arbitration, Transcript, third hearing, 19 December 1921, p. 54.

9 "Now if there had been present an intelligent and inquisitive member of the Society one would have thought that he might have asked Sir Edward Smith this: 'If this business has been so successful in the past, the fire and accident, and so forth, and if it is likely to be so profitable in the future, and if we can apply to the Court now for liberty to carry on that business, why do we not do so?' It seems to be a very natural question which would arise in the mind of anybody who really heard and understood what Sir Edward Smith was saying. I cannot imagine what Sir Edward Smith's answer would have been." Macnaghten, Transcript, main hearing, Day 4, 30 July 1920, p. 54.

10 "I do say any scheme whereby you created a proprietary share capital would have been a breach of their duty to the members of the Mutual Society... You must bear in mind there are... these two great classes of the institutions, the proprietary [company] and the mutual societies, and [the directors] had no right to twist any part of [the Society's] business into a proprietary [company] without the assent of the members." Macnaghten in response to a question from the arbitrator: Transcript, Day 3, pp. 37, 38.

11 It is not possible to give precise figures for the directors' shareholdings. There were two classes of shares: 100,000 shares of 10s, all of which were issued to the certificate holders, and 450,000 shares of £1 of which 80,000 were issued with only 10s being paid per share. The share register for the £1 shares has survived, although it says nothing of nominees or connected persons. No list of certificate holders or register for the 10s shares exists but there is a Board minute (14 June 1922) setting out the number of both classes of shares held in 1910 by those directors and their nominees who were still on the Board in 1920. A comparison of the holdings of the £1 shares set out in the minute with those shown in the share register indicates that the use of nominees was extensive.

12 Saddler, *A Mission in Life*, pp. 51–54, 59, 62. A Liverpool Victoria agency was established with Commercial Union, the commissions from which compensated the Corporation's shareholders (most of whom were staff) for the loss that they had suffered, although it took six years to complete the process.

13 In a letter to Smith dated 28 June 1910, Braham wrote, "For the time being I wish you to take my name out of the memo and arts of the proposed new company and oblige." Transcript, Day 3, p. 65.

14 (1876–1958). Major in the Worcester Regiment, solicitor, Liberal MP for South East Durham 1910–18 and Seaham, County Durham 1918–22, author of *Guide to the Industrial Assurance Act, 1923 for the use of Agents and Policy-holders*.

15 The original letter is in the Royal London Archives.

16 *The Policy-Holder*, 24 December 1913, p. 1032.

17 Transcript, Day 5, 2 August 1920, p. 37.

18 It was on this basis that members had brought *Blythe v Birtley* and the other anti-conversion actions and that had been referred to by Mr Justice Joyce (see the previous chapter): [1910] 1 Ch 228 at p. 232.

19 *The Policy-Holder*, 1 July 1914, p. 515.

20 See Chapter 8; Appendix 1.

21 Minutes of Evidence, Board of Trade Departmental Committee on the business of industrial assurance companies and collecting societies, Day 9, 28 October 1919, qq. 6342–6376.

22 George Talbot KC (1861–1938) Winchester and Christ Church, Oxford. Called to the Bar 1887, KC 1906, Judge (King's Bench Division) 1923–37. According to Lord Justice MacKinnon, Talbot "had a cold bath every morning, and was never known to wear an overcoat in town or country". *Dictionary of National Biography*, Compact Edition, 1975, p. 2918.

23 Malcolm Macnaghten KC (1869–1955) The son of Lord Macnaghten of Runkerry, Co. Antrim who in 1887 had been appointed straight to the House of Lords (a Lord of Appeal in Ordinary) without serving as a judge in the High Court. Educated at Eton and Trinity

College Cambridge, President of the Union 1890. Called to the Bar 1894, Director of Foreign Claims Office 1915–19, KC 1919, KBE 1920, MP (Unionist) 1922–29 and Recorder of Colchester 1924. Judge (King's Bench Division) 1928–47, Privy Council 1948. He married Antonia, eldest daughter of Charles Booth, the statistician and social reformer, and their three daughters all became socialists and married communists: Margaret Campbell, Obituary of Anne Macnaghten, the *Independent*, 8 January 2001.

24 Macnaghten had been an unpaid civil servant for much of the war with an office in Downing Street – at 45 he would have been too old for active service. The Foreign Claims Office was established by the Foreign Office in 1915 to deal with claims from British subjects and businesses in respect of losses of foreign assets through enemy action, with a view to seeking compensation in due course.

25 (1871–1943) Jones, the youngest of six sons of a Denbigh stonemason, left school early and before he was 16 became a reporter on a local paper. His career spanned journalism, politics, historical research and the law. He had been the successful plaintiff in a libel action where a newspaper referred to an imaginary "Mr Artemus Jones, a church warden at Peckham" enjoying the social scene at the French seaside resort of Dieppe. The writer said that he had picked the name on the basis that no real person could be called Artemus Jones. The jury awarded Jones damages although he was neither a church warden nor a resident of Peckham. He became a County Court Judge in North Wales and was knighted.

26 (1876–1944) King's School Canterbury and Jesus College, Cambridge. Called to the Bar 1899, KC 1919, Judge (Chancery Division) 1929, Court of Appeal 1938.

27 Ronald F Roxburgh, *DNB*, p. 2762.

28 Sir Paul Ogden Lawrence (1861–1952). Son of a solicitor, educated at Malvern, called to the Bar 1882, QC 1896, Judge (Chancery Division) 1918, Court of Appeal 1926. Initials are not generally included in judicial titles but were required to distinguish the two Mr Justice Lawrences – A T and P O.

29 High Court of Justice (Chancery Division), *The Royal London Auxiliary Insurance Company, Limited v Lovett*, Day 2, 23 February 1921, Transcript, p. 17.

30 "He brought to the judicial office the qualities of an eminently practical man of the world and scholarly lawyer, shrewd, cautious and strong." F H Cowper, *DNB*, p. 2744.

31 Mark Romer KC, Day 2, High Court Transcript, p. 34.

32 *The Policy-Holder*, 2 March 1921, p. 179.

33 The 10/15s per share applied to both classes of share – the £1 shares for which only 10s had been paid, and the 10s shares issued free of charge to the certificate holders, who had previously paid 4s for each certificate.

34 Charles Bretherton, Minutes of Evidence relating to Friendly Societies, Parliamentary Papers, 1873, Vol. XXII, qq. 23,380–23,393.

35 Fourth Report of the Friendly and Benefit Building Societies Commission, Parliamentary Papers, 1874, Vol. XXIII, Part I, p. cxxii, para. 526.

36 The nearest to a statement came during the final exchanges of the main hearing before the arbitrator when Owen Thompson KC, the directors' counsel, said: "The whole of the matters have been carefully gone into by us [Thomson, his junior counsel and the Auxiliary

Company's counsel], and I desire to say this, that if the arbitration had proceeded, I should have, of course, put into the box all the Directors whom I represent, and I think they would have assured you that throughout they have desired the interest of the two Companies, and have exerted all their powers in order, so far as possible, to serve the interests of those two Companies; but that they now recognise the difficulty of the position in which the Directors of two Companies of this nature must be placed, and with that in view, they have assented to these terms which they believe and hope will effect the best interests of these Companies which they have, in the case of the Mutual, served in many capacities for many years, and in the case of the Auxiliary, have served since its formation." Transcript, Day 6, 3 August 1920, p. 15.

37 Two of the most respected counsel specialising in company matters – Sir Francis Gore-Browne KC and Sir Francis Palmer – advised that the scheme was lawful in a technical legal sense, although it seemed doubtful if either counsel had approved the final form of the trust deed. But as Macnaghten put it: "These questions do not concern me because whether the Deed was in fact lawful under the Companies Act or not I do not care; whether lawful or unlawful it was wholly contrary to the promises that has been made specifically, clearly and repeatedly to the members of the Society in the provisions made, and the triumvirate [Smith, Duffell and Price] must have known it." Transcript, Day 3, 29 July 1920, p. 31.

38 See Appendix 2.

39 See Appendix 2.

40 He passed his law finals with honours, winning the John Mackrell prize. He was admitted in 1903.

41 See Chapter 6.

42 Helen M Palmer, *DNB*, p. 2972.

43 H Kingsley Wood, *The Industrial Assurance Agent's Legal Handbook* (London, The Insurance Publishing Company Limited, 1909).

44 Hansard, HC Debates, 22 September 1943, vol. 392, cc. 211–9.

45 Sir Percy Harris (Bethnal Green, South-West).

46 Palmer.

47 He may have held more shares. If Wood or any of his family had acquired certificates in 1908, these would have been converted in 10s shares in the Auxiliary Company in 1910. Neither the list of certificate holders nor the share register for the 10s shares has survived.

48 See Chapter 8.

49 Macdonald Critchley (editor), *Notable British Trials: The Trial of August Sangret* (William Hodge, 1959) Introduction, p. xi.

50 Transcript, Day 5, p. 40.

Chapter 8 – The Mutual Company: 1908–1936

1 From an article reporting the opening of the central section of Royal London House, Finsbury Square.

2 Minutes of Evidence taken before Committee on Industrial Assurance and Assurance on the

lives of children under ten years of age (1931), Appendix 1, p. 9.

3   The Interdepartmental Committee on Physical Deterioration.

4   B S Rowntree, *Poverty: a study of town life*, pp viii – x, 297, 298, *Poverty: the York enquiry*, *The Times*, 1 January 1902 p. 13.

5   See Dennett, *A Sense of Security*, p. 186.

6   See Chapter 5, Note 1.

7   Royal London, Report and Accounts 1915.

8   The London Regiment, a territorial force created in 1908 by bringing together various existing battalions, was the largest peace-time infantry formation within the British army. Each of the 26 battalions constituted an independent regiment and in 1922 'battalion' was to be replaced by 'regiment'. Battalions 1–8 were administered by the City of London Territorial Force Association and 9–28 by the County of London Territorial Force Association. The 15th Battalion was based at Somerset House in the Strand and the 12th at 14 Chenies Street, near Bedford Square, Holborn. During the war, many of the existing battalions raised second and third battalions, extending the London Regiment to 88 battalions. The battalion was the basic unit of the infantry during the war, consisting, at full establishment, of 1,007 men, of whom 30 were officers.

9   Simon Rae, *W G Grace* (Faber and Faber, 1998), p. 488.

10 I am indebted to Tom Ford, a former senior official of the Society, who undertook extensive research during the late 1990s into the 147 members of staff whose deaths are commemorated on the Society's World War I memorial. Of the missing 22, five could not be traced in any of the sources and 17 could not be identified because of identical names and initials. For example, 71 members of the Royal Field Artillery with the name "A Brown" were killed during the war. Unfortunately, the staff records no longer existed and so it was not possible to include in the report where they worked in the Society. I will ensure that the additional material that I have identified about the three cricketers is filed with Tom's report in the archives.

11 The memorial was later moved to Colchester and is now at Royal London House, Wilmslow.

12 See Chapter 5, Note 1.

13 The name was referred to in the recollections of a pensioner in the *Royal Londoner*, August 1973.

14 Today: £333.

15 *Royal Londoner*, August 1973.

16 Sidney Webb, later Lord Passfield (1859–1947). Early member of Fabian Society, founder of London School of Economics where he was Professor of Public Administration, member of the LCC, MP for Seaham (1922, defeating Evan Hayward), chairman of the Labour Party (1922), President of the Board of Trade (1924), Secretary of State for Dominion Affairs and Colonies (1929).

17 Charles Cripps, later Lord Parmoor (1852–1941). Barrister, politician and judge. A Conservative MP who, after his peerage, sat as a judge in the House of Lords (although he had held no previous judicial office) and then served as a minister in the Labour Government, as Lord President of the Council and leader of the Labour peers.

18 Minutes of Evidence, Board of Trade Departmental Committee on the business of industrial

assurance companies and collecting societies, Day 9, 28 October 1919, qq. 6301, 6303.

19 Report of the Board of Trade Departmental Committee on the business of industrial assurance companies and collecting societies (Parmoor Committee), Cmd 614, London, 1920, p. 2.

20 Parmoor Committee Report, p. 3.

21 Report of the Board of Trade Departmental Committee on the business of industrial assurance companies and collecting societies (Parmoor Committee), Cmd 614, London, 1920.

22 A more draconian Bill introduced into the House of Lords by Lord Onslow in August 1921 met with a hostile reception from the industrial assurance offices and was withdrawn by the Government on the basis that it had served its purpose as the focus of debate, although Lord Parmoor was satisfied that the new Bill, that had the support of the offices, would implement all the reforms suggested by his committee.

23 The criticism of free policies was that the sums were often insignificant, and the policies tended to be lost or overlooked by the time the life assured died so no claim was made under them: see Cohen Report, p. 35. Industrial assurance was analysed and criticised by a Royal Commission in the 1870s, by Sidney Webb during World War I, by the Parmoor and Cohen Committees between the wars, and in two books inspired by the report of the Cohen Committee. Similar complaints tended to be made each time. To avoid repetition, I have set out in Appendix 1 the criticisms, the responses of the offices at the time and some comments of my own.

24 *The Policy-Holder*, 2 March 1921, p. 179.

25 Sir Harold Elverston (1866–1941). In Parliament he had represented insurance interests, according to Oliver Westall, *The Provincial Insurance Company 1903–38: family, markets and competitive growth*, p. 118. Elverston was on the executive committee of the National Liberal Federation (1906–10 and 1921–35) and a member of Manchester City and Cheshire County Councils. He lived for a time at Fulshaw Hall, Wilmslow, now owned by Royal London.

26 See Chapter 7.

27 Sir Alfred Brumwell Thomas (1868–1948). His style was similar to that of John Belcher – he may even have been one of the unsuccessful candidates for the design of the first phase of Royal London House. His views on the work of Belcher and Joass at Finsbury Square are not recorded.

28 See Chapter 12.

29 J K Wiseman, Speech at the Royal London AGM, 26 April 1949, p. 3.

30 Every friendly society had to have one or more trustees (Friendly Societies Act 1896, s. 25). The investments of the society were held in the name of the trustees (s. 44). A company, however, held its investments in its own name and so there was no requirement for trustees.

31 Sir Edwin, later Lord, Cornwall (1863–1953) was a coal merchant, mayor of Fulham, and a founder member (later chairman) of the London County Council where he sat with Edward Smith as a Progressive. He was Liberal MP for Bethnal Green North East (1906–22) and served as a minister and deputy speaker.

32 Sir Henry Dalziel, later Lord Dalziel of Kirkcaldy (1868–1935), the son of a shoemaker,

was a journalist, Liberal MP for Kirkcaldy (1892–1921) and a newspaperman. He owned *Reynolds' Weekly Newspaper* (later *Reynolds' Illustrated News* and then *Reynolds' News*) and the *Pall Mall Gazette* and was chairman and political director of the *Daily Chronicle*. A bachelor until he was 60, he married in 1928 and died 19 days after the sudden death of his wife in 1935.

33 Some reference works show Mitchell's date of birth as 5 January 1898 but it was in fact 16 November 1895… or at least that is what Royal London believed it to be as he retired in November 1955, aged 60.

34 Royal London, *HO News* (Issue 9, July 1979) p. 2.

35 *The Policy-Holder*, 12 July 1939 contained a lengthy feature on the insurance industry sports clubs and leisure organisations from which this and the following paragraph are derived, augmented by the *Souvenir Handbook* of the London Insurance Offices Football Association produced in 1928 to mark the 21st season.

36 Jimmy Jewell, Webb's successor as general secretary, who worked for a motor insurer, refereed the 1938 FA Cup Final between Preston North End and Huddersfield – the only goal was a penalty he awarded to Preston in the last minute of extra time. He left insurance in 1939 to become secretary-manager of Norwich City.

37 According to *The Policy-Holder*, 12 July 1939.

38 Peter Sanders, *The Simple Annals*, p. 127.

39 *Royal London News*, No 24, May 1980.

40 *Royal Londoner*, August 1970, p. 8.

41 See Appendix 6.

42 Committee on Industrial Assurance and Assurance on the lives of Children under ten years of age (Cohen Committee), Report, Cmd 4376, London 1933, p. 5.

43 Evidence to the Cohen Committee of J H Hurry, General Secretary of the British Undertakers' Association, Minutes of Evidence, Day 13, p. 526, q. 4334.

44 Benjamin Cohen (1862–1942) was a barrister with chambers in the Temple. The committee included Sir Alfred Watson, the first Government Actuary, Steuart Macnaghten (1873–1952), President of the Faculty of Actuaries and manager (in effect, chief executive) of Standard Life (and a distant relation of Sir Malcolm Macnaghten KC – see Chapter 7) and Sir John Fischer Williams KC (1870–1947) who, after practising at the Bar, had been the British legal representative on the Repatriation Commission under the Treaty of Versailles and was to become a member of the Permanent Court of Arbitration at The Hague.

45 Committee on Industrial Assurance and Assurance on the lives of Children under ten years of age (Cohen Committee), Report, Cmd 4376, London 1933. See Appendix 1.

46 Minutes of Evidence, Cohen Committee, Appendix 1, p. 11, quoted in the Report, p. 6

47 See Appendix 2.

48 John James Joass (1868–1952) was born in Dingwall, the son of an architect. He served his articles in Glasgow, joined Belcher's practice in 1986 and became a partner in 1905.

49 The "loftiest… building in London" was achieved only by including the tower, the top part of which could not, in view of a condition imposed by the LCC, be used as offices.

50 James Alexander Stevenson (1881–1937) was a fellow of the Royal Society of British

Sculptors who studied at the Chester School of Art and the Royal College of Art. He was a Landseer Scholar and exhibited at the Royal Academy. His work included war memorials in Mauritius, Nairobi, Mombassa and Dar-es-Salaam, a bronze eagle on the monument to French prisoners of war at Norman Cross, Cambridgeshire and sculptures for the hall of the Institute of Chartered Accountants in the City.

51 According to J J Joass in his speech at the lunch following the opening of the building: *The Policy-Holder*, 12 February 1930.

52 Sir Walter Lawrence, a passionate cricket follower, created his own ground at Hyde Hall, near Sawbridgeworth in Hertfordshire and in 1934 presented a trophy to be awarded for the fastest hundred scored in a first class season in England. Frank Woolley of Kent was the first winner. Lawrence died in 1939 and the award of the Walter Lawrence Trophy lapsed. It was revived in 1966 as a result of the efforts of the son-in-law of Lawrence's son who had inherited the trophy. It has been awarded every year since then – winners include Gary Sobers, Alan Knott, Ian Botham, Viv Richards and Andrew Flintoff. www.walterlawrencetrophy.com.

53 Bridget Cherry and Nikolaus Pevsner, *London 4: North*, p. 640.

54 *The Policy-Holder*, 12 February 1930.

55 See Note 32 above.

56 The new coat of arms was to be used on all notepaper and formal documents until replaced in the late 1970s by the *Hands around the Family* logo.

Chapter 9 – Smith, Skeggs and the Royal London of 1936

1 *The Insurance Mail* p. 638.

2 *Royal London Head Office Staff Magazine*, No. 1, July 1920.

3 The London County Council, established by the Local Government Act 1888, was the first metropolitan authority to be elected directly by the people of London. The Progressive Party, founded in 1888 by liberals, trade unionists, Fabians and socialists, had a majority from 1889 to 1895 and again from 1898 to 1907. The Municipal Reform Party (the Conservatives) controlled the council from 1907 until 1934 when the Labour Party achieved a majority that was to be retained until the council was abolished in 1965. Smith did not stand or was not re-elected in 1919.

4 He and his wife applied for shares in 1910, but in 1911 they sold all the shares they had been allotted. Then Skeggs acquired 316 shares in 1917 and 1919 but disposed of 200 of them in 1919. He retained the balance of 116 shares until the end.

5 H S Cautley KC, Arbitration, *Lovett v Smith*, Transcript, main hearing, Day 5, 2 August 1920, p. 87.

6 Sir William Llewellyn (1858–1941). Painter of portraits and landscapes. Born at Cirencester, exhibited at the Royal Academy from 1884, Royal Academician 1920, KCVO 1918, GCVO 1931, trustee of the National Gallery.

7 Richard Jack (1866–1952). Painter of portraits, interiors, landscapes and Word War I battle scenes. Born in Sunderland, exhibited at the Royal Academy from 1893, Royal Academician

1920, settled in Canada in the 1930s.

8 Henry Liversage, Minutes of Evidence relating to Friendly Societies, Parliamentary Papers, 1873, Vol. XXII, q. 1251.

9 *The Policy-Holder*, 30 December 1936, p. 2124.

10 See Appendix 6.

11 J K Wiseman, Speech at the Royal London AGM, 27 April 1937, p. 6.

12 Wiseman, p. 7.

13 Wiseman, p. 9.

14 Wilson and Levy, *Industrial Assurance – An Historical and Critical Study*, pp. 134, 135.

15 Table 502, Housing Market, house prices from 1930, Department of Communities and Local Government.

16 Royal London Prospectus, 1936:

Table No.	Industrial Branch	Premiums payable weekly
1	Whole life infantile	Age next birthday 1–10. Maximum premium 1d.
1	Whole life adult	The basic life policy.
21	Endowment	Young person's policy, age next birthday 11–25. Term 15 or 20 years. Payment in full on prior death.
2	Endowment	Payable at 50, 55 or 60. Payment in full on prior death.
17	Endowment	Payable at 65. Payment in full on prior death.
16	Double Endowment	Full amount payable at end of term, ½ payable on prior death. 15, 20, 25 or 30 year terms.
5B	Pure Endowment	Full amount payable at end of term, premiums refunded on prior death. Any term from 10–25 years.
14	Juvenile Endowment	Under 10 yrs. Weekly premium of 6d. Any term from 14 to 21 years. Payable in full on prior death but reduced payment when death within first six months.
15	Children's Endowments	For "making provision for apprenticeship, educational or similar expenses". Parent's life insured for terms between 14 and 21 years. Payable on expiry of term even if parent previously died.
6	Joint Whole Life	Payment on the first death of two lives.
	Industrial Branch	Premiums payable every 4 weeks
3	Whole life	As 1.
18	Endowment	Payable after 15, 20, 25 or 30 years. Premium of 2s every 4 weeks. Payable in full on prior death.
19	Double Endowment	As 16 but premium of 2s every 4 weeks.
20	Pure Endowment	As 5B but premium of 2s every 4 weeks.

	Ordinary Branch	Premiums payable yearly, half yearly or quarterly
1 2 3 4	Whole Life	The basic life policy £1,000 with profits £1,000 without profits £100 with profits £100 without profits
5	Whole Life: Limited payments, with profits	Premiums ceased after 10, 15, 20 or 25 years but life cover remained in force.
6	As 5 but without profits	
7	Endowment, with profits	10, 15, 20, 25 or 30 years.
8	As 7 but without profits	
9	Double Endowment, with profits	Full amount payable at end of term, proportionate payable on prior death where half the term has expired. 15, 20, 25 or 30 year terms.
10	As 9 but without profits	
11	Pure Endowment, with profits	Full amount payable at end of term, premiums (and accrued bonus) refunded on prior death. Any term from 10–30 years.
12	As 11 but without profits	
61	Whole life guaranteed bonus, with medical	2% bonus added on payment of each annual premium.
62	As 61 but without medical	
63	Endowment, guaranteed bonus	2% bonus added on payment of each annual premium. 15, 20, 25 and 30 year terms.
Table No.	Industrial Branch	Premiums payable weekly
23	Short term assurance	Yearly premiums to assure death within 1–10 years.
24	Convertible Term	Life policy that could be converted to an endowment.
15	Joint Life: Whole Life, with profits	Payment of first death of two lives.
16	As 15 but without profits	
19	Joint Life: Endowment, with profits	Payment after 10, 15, 20, 25 or 30 years or on prior first death of two lives.
20	As 19 but without profits	
50	Annuities	Purchase of a payment for life for the over-50s.

17 Report of the Industrial Assurance Commissioner for the year ended 31 December 1937, p. 2.

18 Wiseman, p. 11.

19 *The Policy-Holder*, 5 May 1937, p. 671.

20 *The Policy-Holder*, 6 May 1936, p. 705.

21 Wiseman, p. 11.

22 The arrangement lasted until 1970 when a new reinsurance agreement was entered into with Norwich Union that ran until the end of 1985: see Chapter 12.

23 *Post Magazine*, 24 September 1927, p. 1757

24 Wiseman, p. 4.

25 Derived from the Industrial Assurance Commissioner's report for 1937, Abstract of Accounts (1936) p. 34–39.

26 These figures relate to 1932 and are included in the Cohen Committee's Report, Appendix B. They include full-time and part-time agents.

27 Committee on Industrial Assurance and Assurance on the lives of Children under ten years of age (Cohen Committee), Report, Cmd 4376, London 1933, p. 21.

28 Industrial Assurance Commissioner's report for 1937, p. 35.

29 Cohen Committee's report, pp. 108,109. In 1929 Royal London issued 1,038,380 new policies and paid out claims on 156,279 policies. 34,529 policies were surrendered for cash and 606,036 policies were forfeited.

30 *Post Magazine*, 8 February 1930.

31 *The Policy-Holder*, 12 February 1930.

32 *Financial Times*, 6 February 1930.

33 By 1936 *The Policy-Holder* (6 May 1936, p. 705) was prepared to go even further and to regard Royal London as "the life office with the largest mutual membership in the British Empire".

34 See Appendix 1.

Chapter 10 – The Middle Phase: 1937–1960

1 Harry Henry, *The Insurance Man and his Trade*, p. 8.

2 C H Shuttleworth, Speech at the Royal London AGM, 27 April 1954, p. 6.

3 Wilson and Levy, *Industrial Assurance – An Historical and Critical Study*, 1937.

4 Arnold Wilson (1884–1940) was a man of many parts – soldier, explorer, civil administrator, oil company executive, author and MP. Aged 55, he volunteered for service in the RAF in 1940, serving as an air gunner, and was killed when his plane was shot down near Dunkirk. Dr Hermann Levy (1881–1949) was, according to Morrah (*History of Industrial Life Assurance*, p.123) a scholar of international reputation who had been writing on British social history for 20 years.

5 Committee on Industrial Assurance and Assurance on the lives of Children under ten years of age (Cohen Committee), Report, Cmd 4376, London 1933.

6 Dennett, *A Sense of Security*, p. 181.

7 Report of the Board of Trade Departmental Committee on the business of industrial assurance companies and collecting societies (Parmoor Committee), Cmd 614, London, 1920, p. 7.

8 Committee on Industrial Assurance and Assurance on the lives of Children under ten years of age (Cohen Committee), Report, Cmd 4376, London 1933, p. 2.

9 Morrah, p. 122.

10 G D H Cole, *The Economic Journal*, Vol. 48, No. 189 (March 1938), p. 110.

11 Cole, p. 111.

12 Harry Henry (1916–2008) was to become "the father of the market research industry in Britain". He was the founder of Marplan and while on the board of Thomson Newspapers was closely involved in the launch of *The Sunday Times* colour magazine, the first of its kind, and was responsible for the introduction to Britain of *Yellow Pages* directories: Mike Waterson, Obituary: Harry Henry, *Guardian*, 5 December 2008. William Beveridge – referred to later in this chapter – was director of the London School of Economics when Henry was a student there.

13 Mike Waterson, *Guardian*, 5 December 2008.

14 Harry Henry, *The Insurance Man and his Trade* (London, *Fact*, June 1938), p. 5. It was the 15th monthly monograph published by *Fact*, a socialist periodical edited by Raymond Postgate, one of the founder members of the British Communist Party, who subsequently edited *Tribune*.

15 Industrial assurance was analysed and criticised by a Royal Commission in the 1870s, by a distinguished economist in a detailed report commissioned during World War I, by the Parmoor and Cohen committees between the wars and in these two books. Similar complaints tended to be made each time. To avoid repetition, I have set out in Appendix 1 the criticisms, the responses of the offices at the time and some comments of my own.

16 J K Wiseman, Speech at the Royal London AGM, 25 April 1939, p. 4.

17 *Royal London News*, No. 4, 17 March 1978, *The Royal Londoner*, No. 13, Summer 1985 and No. 14, Autumn 1985.

18 Report of the Committee of Management, Associated Life Offices Central Fund (Jersey) to the associated offices for period of occupation of Jersey by German Forces (1945), p. 3. Just as the committee kept meticulous records of payments into and out of the fund, they produced a detailed report recording their actions and the reasons behind them. It was apparently maintained on an ongoing basis ("As will be obvious to the reader this report has been prepared in stages, and often in conditions of crises." (p. 52)) so that it could be available as soon as hostilities ended.

19 The offices participating in the Associated Life Offices Central Fund (Jersey) were Britannic, Eagle Star, General Accident, Liverpool Victoria, London Guarantee and Accident, Pearl, Phoenix, Prudential, Refuge, Royal Liver, Royal London, Salvation Army, United Friendly and United Kingdom Temperance and General Provident.

20 Peter Sanders, *The Simple Annals*, p. 191.

21 The Bugle Horn Hotel today is apparently a popular 'gastro pub'.

22 See Chapter 5, Note 1.

23 The allowance was increased in line with disability pensions and continued until her death in 1999.

24 J K Wiseman, Speech at the Royal London AGM, 30 April 1946, p. 3: "The war claims actually paid have numbered 55,306, totalling £1,124,000, including 21,452 for £399,000 on the lives of civilians killed by enemy action."

25 Wiseman, p. 3.

26 *Social Insurance and Allied Services*, Report by Sir William Beveridge, Cmd 6404, London, 1942.

27 J K Wiseman, Speech at the Royal London AGM, 27 April 1943, p. 2.

28 W A Robson, *The Modern Law Review*, Vol. 10, No. 2 (April 1947), p. 177.

29 J K Wiseman, Speech at the Royal London AGM, 30 April 1946, p. 2.

30 Wiseman, p. 3.

31 See Appendix 2.

32 The general death grant was to survive only until 6 April 1987 when it was abolished: Social Security Act 1986, section 41, Social Security Act (Commencement Order No.4) 1987. Now those on a low income can apply for a funeral payment out of the social fund operated within the benefits system. It covers only the essential costs and applies only where it is reasonable for the applicant to pay for the funeral and where the estate is insolvent. Life policies continue to be promoted to the over 50s to help towards funeral expenses (and any outstanding bills) and funeral plans are available, that provide for a sum that is guaranteed to cover the cost of the funeral, to be paid into a trust fund, the funeral being organised and paid for (essentially) by the trustees, so that the money never passes to the family.

33 J K Wiseman, Speech at the Royal London AGM, 26 April 1949, p. 9.

34 See Appendix 1.

35 Maurice Codner (1888–1958).

36 Ernest Blaikley, *Dictionary of National Biography*, Compact Edition, 1975, p. 2572.

37 The official line seems to have been that Shuttleworth's death came as a surprise although the previous October, when recording his appointment as chairman of the Industrial Life Offices Association, the Royal London Board had expressed "their earnest desire that he will be blessed with health and strength to continue to carry out his duties in that capacity with the dignity and competence that he had already shown". This is hardly standard wording for minuting such events, suggesting that perhaps he was known to have a health problem.

38 E H Haynes, Speech at the Royal London AGM, 24 April 1956, p. 3.

39 Thomas William Haynes, who was three years older than Ernest, was to become director and general manager of the Northern Insurance Group.

40 "Given that Alleyn's School in this period was recognised overtly as a school for 'preparation for business or commercial life' [quoted from Board Meeting, Governors' Minutes, Dulwich College, March 1888, p. 57]... it enjoyed great success under J H Smith, the Headmaster from 1888, and under his successors, and bestowed an education well beyond this aim. As time went by, and Alleyn's became filled with London County Council scholars, and accordingly benefited from Board of Education grants, it became less of a financial worry to the Governors; their books balanced better than the College's; moreover the Annual Reports by the headmasters gave great satisfaction." (Jan Piggott, *Dulwich College: A History, 1616–2008*, (Dulwich College, 2008) p. 188).

41 "No regrets after 55 years – Stanley Goodall Retires", *Royal London News*, No. 24, May 1980, p. 3.

42 Industrial Assurance Commissioner's report 1952, p. 2.

43 See Appendix 6.

44 Industrial Assurance Commissioner's Reports: 1953, pp. 9, 11; 1960, pp. 13, 15.

45 The Industrial Assurance Commissioner defined 'lapse ratio' as the number of policies forfeited without the grant of a free policy or payment of a surrender value during the year expressed as a percentage of the number of policies issued during the year. The significance of the absence of a free policy or payment on surrender was that it indicated that payment of premiums had ceased early in the life of these policies, generally within the first two years.

46 Calculated (retrospectively for the purpose of comparisons) in accordance with the definition established by the Industrial Assurance Commissioner: see previous Note.

47 E H Haynes, Speech at the Royal London AGM, 30 April 1957, p. 5.

Chapter 11 – Centenary and the Haynes Reforms: 1961–1972

1   Dominic Sandbrook, *White Heat*, p. xvii.

2   See Introduction.

3   The *Royal Londoner*, 1961 Centenary Souvenir issue, p. 3.

4   E H Haynes, Speech at the Royal London AGM, 24 April 1962, p. 3.

5   It is interesting that 2 February (when the "We the undersigned" statement was signed) was regarded as the anniversary date. It would seem that 10 April has a better claim – the date when the registrar of friendly societies certified that the Royal London Friendly Society was duly established.

6   Maudling's father was an actuary, and a founder member in 1923 of the Denarius Club, a dining club for actuaries working on industrial assurance business. The club, which was well supported by Royal London actuaries over the years, held its winding-up dinner in November 2009.

7   The grandsons were Dudley Ridge and Norman Hambridge. Ridge, the son of Charles, was to write a history of the Ridge family (*A Sussex Family*) – see Chapters 1 and 4 – and Hambridge had worked for the Society since 1924 (see Chapter 4). Degge's great-grandson was George Greasby. His mother, Hilda, was the daughter of Herbert Peter Degge who was the youngest of Joseph and Elizabeth Degge's five children. Herbert was born in 1868 and his mother died the following year. Greasby became an agent in 1960, attached to the Sale district office, and was later assistant superintendent and district inspector at Urmston and superintendent at Kendal. It was, according to Haynes' speech at the centenary banquet, only when Greasby went home and told his mother that he had taken a job with Royal London that he learnt that his great-grandfather was one of the founders of the company.

8   Tottenham went on to become the first club to win the League and Cup double since 1897 but South Africa lost to the Barbarians by two tries to nil on the Saturday following the banquet.

9   E H Haynes, Speech at the Royal London AGM, 25 April 1962, p. 4.

10 Haynes, AGM, 1962, p. 4.

11 The Truck Act 1881 provided that employees engaged in manual labour had to be paid

their wages in cash. The Payment of Wages Act 1960 introduced other permissible methods of payment (for example by cheque or direct to a bank account in the employee's name) although this was hedged around with detailed requirements. The employee had to request the employer to pay him in one of the permitted ways.

12 Royal London Centenary Banquet, 2 February 1961, Transcript of Speeches, p. 3.

13 Banquet, 961, Transcript, p. 4.

14 *Opportunity Knocks Now* (Royal London, undated, c. 1959), p. 2.

15 Joseph Degge, Minutes of Evidence relating to Friendly Societies, Parliamentary Papers, 1873, Vol. XXII, p. 44, q. 25,008.

16 Henry, *The Insurance Man and his Trade*, p. 48.

17 A pension scheme was set up for head office staff and Field officials in 1908. With the advent of salaried agents in 1965 a third pension scheme had to be created for them.

18 Saddler, *A Mission in Life*, p. 93.

19 Watson, *A Lifetime of Care*, p. 31.

20 For a while, 'Staff Association' was retained. The notepaper at the time of the book interest negotiations was headed 'The Royal London Staff Association/Section of National Union of Insurance Workers'. It also included the Society's original coat of arms, that closely resembled the coat of arms of the Corporation of the City of London, that the Society itself had not used since 1934 (see Chapter 8). Later 'Staff Association' was dropped and the union became 'The Royal London Section of the National Union of Insurance Workers'.

21 Sanders, *The Simple Annals*, p. 192.

22 E H Haynes, Speech at the Royal London AGM, 26 April 1966, p. 4.

23 This was to continue until the late 1970s.

24 Brian Knights, General Manager, letter to all members of the sales staff, 14 July 1980, referring to the Cavendish Hotel, Eastbourne, the regular venue at the time.

25 *Triton* (the magazine of the Royal London Club), No. 113, September 1962, p. 19.

26 *Triton*, No. 123, July 1963, p. 38.

27 *Triton*, June 1961, p. 19.

28 The *Royal Londoner*, Vol. II, No. 3, May 1969, p. 8.

29 W D Scattergood, 'Office Methods for Dealing with Ordinary Life New Business', *The Actuary*, SIAS, 9 February 1962, p. 18 identified the following sets of records: brief sheet (paper summary of policy for filing with the file), accounting details card, two valuation cards, life index card, embossed address plate, filing index, two reassurance cards (where applicable), two fatal accident cards (an additional benefit), branch office record and premium collection and commission payment cards. It was the practice of industrial assurance offices to deal with renewals of ordinary branch policies by means of a visit from the agent. So the system would have been modified so that the renewals papers were sent to the district office.

30 Scattergood, p. 23.

31 Scattergood, p. 16.

32 Industrial Assurance Act 1923, section 22. If required for the purpose of legal proceedings against the agent, the premium receipt book could be retained for longer but a copy had to

be issued to the policyholder.

33 E H Haynes, Speech at the Royal London AGM, 25 April 1972, p. 6.

34 See Chapter 12.

35 See Appendix 6.

36 Royal London, Directors' Report and Statement of Accounts for 1965, p.4.

37 Royal London, Directors' Report and Statement of Accounts for 1968, p.4.

38 Industrial Assurance Commissioner's Report for 1968, p. 12.

39 IAC's 1968 report, p. 15.

40 *The Times*, 19 July 1971. He was Bishop of Kensington (1932–42) and Southwark (1942–59).

41 Len Murray (1922–2004) was assistant general secretary, and later general secretary, of the Trades Union Congress.

42 Sanders, p. 193.

43 *Daily Telegraph*, 24 July 2008.

44 *Triton*, March 1961, p. 3.

45 The *Royal Londoner*, No. 23, Winter 1987, p. 6.

Chapter 12 – Colchester: 1972–1999

1   The article appeared in the December edition – after the building had been completed and opened. Clearly it was written for, but not included in, the previous edition.

2   Susan Allen Toth, *The New York Times*, 10 July 1994.

3   See Appendix 3.

4   William Forsey, the *Royal Londoner*, No 23, Winter 1987, p. 3.

5   The *Royal Londoner*, May 1973, p. 12.

6   Lamb had been actuary from 1955–70 and a director since 1965. He was on the council of the Institute of Actuaries, deputy chairman of the Life Offices Association and a member of the Industrial Assurance Council and the executive committee of Industrial Life Offices Association.

7   The line, which was little more than a shuttle service between Drayton Park and Moorgate, calling at Highbury & Islington, Essex Road, Old Street and Moorgate, is no longer part of London Underground and is now the final stage of First Capital Connect services to London from Luton and Bedford.

8   Leslie Poll, Dear *Royal Londoner* letter, 20 April 1976.

9   Leslie Poll, Dear *Royal Londoner* letter, 18 June 1976.

10 Leslie Poll, Dear *Royal Londoner* letter, 6 September 1976.

11 In 1999, following a conversation at a lunch about work then being carried out on the Royal London archives, Billy Skinner sent to Mike Yardley, the chief executive of Royal London, a copy of a document dated January 1997 that he had written for his family entitled *A Few Lifetime Reminiscences: 1914–1997*. It was placed in the archives and extracts from it appear in these paragraphs.

12 In the document Skinner makes light of his wartime experiences – suffice to say that he saw action in the front line – but was clearly proud of his defence at a court martial of "one of

our men" charged with striking an officer. Although not entirely convinced of his client's innocence, "he was a very good soldier and we could ill afford to lose him". Skinner's cross-examination of the witnesses created sufficient doubt in the minds of the court for the soldier to be acquitted.

13 See Chapter 10.

14 A fact reported by Michael Pickard in his speech at a dinner on 28 April 1983 to mark Bill Forsey's retirement as chief general manager. Pickard had spoken to Whiston and received a letter from him about Forsey's early days in Bristol. Whiston was clearly very proud of his protégé.

15 The *Royal London News*, No 23, February 1980, p. 3.

16 Billy Skinner, Dear *Royal Londoner* letter, 2 June 1978.

17 The *Royal London News*, No 29, June 1981, p. 5.

18 The *Royal Londoner*, Winter 1982, p. 17. Duffell died on 7 April 1983; he appears in the photograph of the 1912 cricket team to the extreme left of the middle row.

19 The *Royal Londoner*, No. 10, Autumn 1984, p. 9.

20 Richard Ellis, letting particulars, June 1984.

21 The sculptor of Mercury and the two Tritons was James Alexander Stevenson: see Chapter 8.

22 Cannings, who was appointed a director of the Society in 1987, left in 1989 to become a full-time property lawyer, and later was one of the founders of a firm of solicitors in the City specialising in property work.

23 Then, as now (according to the school's website) "an 11–18 charitable boarding school for children from all backgrounds near Horsham, West Sussex".

24 Michael Pickard made the point to the author that he had no option but to attend in uniform because the interview was in term time and boys were not permitted any other clothes at school – at least none suitable for a job interview.

25 *Triton*, February 1961, p. 6. The game against Twickenham RFC on 22 January 1961 was lost 11–6. A try then counted three points.

26 *Triton*, September 1963, p. 22. London Midland Athletic had declared at 190 for 9 and Pickard was the only Royal Londoner to offer any serious resistance.

27 *1969 Divisions*: North London, South London, Southern, Eastern, Birmingham, South Wales & Western, Sheffield, Liverpool, Manchester, Northern and Scottish. *1973 Divisions*: North London (later North & West London), South London & Southern (later South East), Eastern, Midlands, South Wales & Western, Yorkshire & North Midlands, Lancashire and Scottish & Northern. *1980 Regions*: South East, North Thames & Eastern, South West & South Midlands, Yorkshire & North Midlands, Lancashire, and Scottish & North.

28 A separate company was needed because there would have been tax concerns if the investments of the Society and those of the unit trusts could not have been separated.

29 In 1941 an agreement was entered into with London & Lancashire that became part of Royal Insurance. In 1971 the reinsurance of the Society's general insurance was transferred to Norwich Union.

30 The *Royal Londoner*, Summer 1986, p. 8.

31 Chairman's Statement, 1985 Report & Accounts, p.4. In 1988 Baker Rooke and Howard

Tilly merged becoming Baker Tilly. BPT had also been auditors to the Auxiliary Company – see Chapter 7.

32 The *Royal Londoner*, Souvenir Issue, 125th Anniversary Celebration, 1986, p. 3.

33 The Society reverted to outsourcing its "general insurance business to Norwich Union with effect from 1 December 1999... The business continues with the Royal London brand, and Norwich Union provide the administration and also take the insurance risk. Royal London's sales force provides leads to Norwich Union and we receive remuneration on new business and renewals." Royal London, Annual Report and Accounts, 1999, pp. 4, 6.

34 The *Royal Londoner*, May 1972, p. 21.

35 See Appendix 6.

36 E H Haynes, Speech at the Royal London AGM, 30 April 1957, p. 6.

37 B G Skinner, Speech at the Royal London AGM, 24 April 1979, p. 7.

38 See previous Note.

39 *Money Management*, October 1997.

40 Determining separate expense ratios for industrial and ordinary branch involved apportioning all the Society's expenses to one or the other. This was a difficult exercise – many expenses applied across both and apportionments could be somewhat arbitrary although the final outcome had to be certified by the auditors – and accordingly expense ratios were indicative rather than precise.

41 The Prudential had stopped selling industrial branch policies in 1995.

42 FSA/PN/097/2001.

43 Acronyms prevailed in view of the unwieldy names of the organisations. The overall regulator was the Securities and Investment Board (SIB). The Investment Management Regulatory Organisation (IMRO) dealt with those managing investments on behalf of others. Life assurance and unit trust business was regulated by The Life Assurance and Unit Trust Regulatory Organisation (LAUTRO) that dealt with those involved in marketing or selling 'packaged products' and by the Financial Intermediaries Managers and Brokers Regulatory Authority (FIMBRA) that covered those selling products of others. In due course LAUTRO and FIMBRA merged to form the Personal Investment Authority (PIA).

44 The Government had announced its intention to create a single regulator in May 1997 and the FSA was set up later that year to prepare itself for the powers it would be given under future legislation.

45 The *Royal London News*, No. 1, November 1977, p. 5.

46 Speech to the National Association of Pension Funds, 20 November 1997: www.fsa.gov.uk/Pages/Library/Communication/Speeches/1997/sp03.shtml. The FSA retains the copyright.

47 See, for example, Office of National Statistics, *Pension Trends*, Chapter 1, July 2008, p. 1.4. http://www.statistics.gov.uk/pensiontrends/.

48 In order to determine the suitability of the product for the customer, the agent was required to gather and record in a 'factfind' document all relevant information about the customer – for example his/her personal situation, income & expenditure, existing insurance and pension arrangements, attitude to risk, financial objectives etc.

49 The purpose of the 'reason-why letter' was to remind the customer why a product was

recommended, summarise the discussions, provide a record of any advice given and demonstrate that the agent 'knew the customer'. The requirement for documentary evidence to prove the suitability of the sale was much seen in relation to the sale of endowment policies and in particular whether customers had been warned the policy might not pay off the mortgage on maturity. United Friendly and Refuge (see Chapter 14), for example, were each fined £350,000 and required to compensate 30,000 policyholders because during 1997 and 1998 they had failed "in some instances to have regard to the suitability of advice... failed to keep sufficient customer records to show that the recommendations made were suitable [and] failed to ensure that customers received a clear written explanation as to why their recommendation was appropriate". (FSA/PN/008/2001).

50 See Chapter 13.

Chapter 13 – Today's Fundamentals Begin to Appear

1 p. 11.

2 *Post Magazine*, 9 April 1981, p. 944.

3 *Royal London News*, No. 29, June 1981, p. 4.

4 In 1979 the 18 members of the Industrial Life Offices Association (that transacted more than 99 per cent of the industrial branch business) sold 3.87 million policies, with a total sum assured of £2.76 billion and an annual premium value of £176 million, as well as a significant amount of ordinary branch business. Total industrial branch funds exceeded £4 billion, there were 57.5 million policies in force and 22.9 million free policies, with 35.8 per cent of the adult population paying premiums to a calling agent. (Quoted by Forsey in his paper: see previous Notes).

5 When a normal business is trading at a loss this becomes obvious all too quickly – there is no money to pay the bills. The policyholders' funds in a life company mean that this does not arise – cash is available, but the current trading operations of the industrial life offices were increasingly being subsidised out of the reserves. In times of good investment returns, it could be argued with some justification that a small trading subsidy from the reserves was of little or no significance. Forsey touched upon this pointing out that over the last five years "the very high level of interest rates, together with the expansion of dividends and property income, has, to a very large extent, offset the sharp escalation of expenses...". He went on to remind his readers that a continuation of good returns could not be guaranteed. Where returns were poor, there was rather less justification for the new business subsidy.

6 Michael Pickard, The *Royal Londoner*, 1994.

7 Norman Wood, Dear *Royal Londoner* letter, 7 May 1980.

8 Cooke retired after five years and was replaced briefly by David Rowland, the chairman of insurance brokers Stewart Wrightson, who resigned after little more than a year when he was appointed to the Council of Lloyd's. Later, as its first full-time chairman, he led Lloyd's from the brink of financial disaster into one of the largest financial reconstruction programmes ever put in place.

9 Norman Wooding (1927–2005). He was appointed a non-executive director in April 1987

and deputy chairman in January 1988 when Michael Pickard became executive chairman on Bill Forsey's retirement. The son of an estate worker in Warwickshire, he obtained his degree by day-release (later earning "a PhD in just over half the usual time"), was appointed to the main board of Courtaulds, then one of the world's leading textile companies, at the age of 46 and developed considerable experience in trade with Russia and Eastern Europe. He "had a deep, and increasing, interest in things charitable, and particularly in projects directed to helping Russians as they struggled to come to terms with a new, postcommunist world." (Obituary, *The Times*, 10 August 2005) He was appointed CBE in 1986 and knighted in 1992.

10 Erith's ancestors were yeoman farmers in East Anglia and since retirement from the City he has farmed the family's 270 acres at Lamarsh, near Bures, a few miles from Colchester. In 1997 he was High Sheriff of Essex.

11 Slee was later a director of Pittencrieff Resources plc, an oil and gas company based in Edinburgh, and a member of the Coal Authority.

12 That last non-executive (former executive) director was Colin Wigmore. Appointed to the Board in 1976 after a brief spell as secretary, he had been responsible for the installation of the first computer, the transfer of the Society's general insurance from the Royal Insurance to Norwich Union and a decade later for the early development of Royal London General. He chaired the building committee that oversaw the new head office at Colchester, retiring as an executive in February 1985 and remaining on the Board until December 1989.

13 Wooding: *Recollections*, pp. 153–155.

14 On his retirement in 1993: *The Royal Londoner*, Spring 1993, p. 3.

15 *Money Marketing*, 3 December 1998.

16 *Money Marketing*, 3.December 1998.

17 *Money Marketing*, 3 December 1998.

Chapter 14 – The Transformation: 1999–2001

1 Royal London, Annual Report and Accounts 1999, chief executive's review, 29 February 2000, p. 4.

2 Royal London, Annual Report and Accounts 2001, chairman's statement, 19 March 2002, p. 3.

3 With the score at 1–1 after extra time and 5–5 on penalties, Gareth Southgate's penalty was saved. Steven Redgrave and Matthew Pinsent won Gold in the coxless pairs.

4 Listing Particulars, p. 3.

5 Nic Cicutti, *Independent*, 9 August 1996.

6 Listing Particulars, p. 3. There were suggestions in the press (Cicutti and Curphey) that around 100 offices would close. Curphey referred to the 650 workforce at the United Friendly head office. There was initially some shareholder opposition – see Nic Cicutti, *Independent*, 30 August 1996.

7 John Waples, *Sunday Times*, 11 August 1996.

8 The following paragraphs are based on Cyril Clegg, *Friend In Deed: the history of a Life*

Assurance Office (Stone and Cox Limited, 1958), commissioned by Refuge to mark its centenary. Clegg joined Refuge in 1909, aged 16, and immediately began his actuarial studies. He became actuary in 1930 and joint general manager in 1946. On his retirement from executive office, he was appointed a director in 1953.

9   Clegg, p. 6.

10 Alfred Waterhouse (1830–1905) was born in Liverpool and practised in Manchester and then London. "At the height of his career, Waterhouse was regarded as the chief figure in the profession by a large majority of his fellow architects and his eminence was recognised at home and abroad" (*Dictionary of National Biography*, Compact Edition, 1975, p. 2950).

11 "For the Refuge Chief Office, Waterhouse produced some of his most ornately gothic work giving it an elegance and symmetry that for almost a hundred years has continued to draw admiring looks from passers-by. Inside he enhanced the spacious working areas with richly-glazed decorative tiles and produced a truly magnificent boardroom with its fine timber and plasterwork" (*Refuge* magazine, Summer 1987, p. 8) http://www.heritagegateway.org.uk/Gateway/Results_Single.aspx?uid=454854&resourceID=5.

12 Clegg, p. 134. The Stock Exchange quotation was not achieved until 1955.

13 Clegg, Appendix A, pp. 143–148.

14 In games against UK opposition, New Zealand had then been beaten only by Wales (in 1905 and 1935), Swansea (1935) and the British Lions (1930). England won by a dropped goal (then 4 points) and three tries (then 3 points) to nil. Alexander Obolensky, a Russian prince, scored two of the tries and Harry (Hal) Sever the other. One of the leading critics rated Sever as the most impressive wing of the 1930s. He scored ten tries and a dropped goal for England and was selected for the British Lions tour of South Africa in 1938 but withdrew because of business and family commitments. But for the war, he may well have won more caps. He played cricket for Cheshire.

15 Federated was sold and later became Independent Insurance which collapsed in 2001 with three of its directors subsequently being imprisoned for fraud.

16 The building was voted 'Office of the Year 1989' by the Institute of Administrative Management. Fulshaw Hall, a Grade 2 listed building, said to be haunted by the ghosts of a woman in white and a child, was refurbished and used as a staff training centre.

17 The following paragraphs are based on K Kirkaldie, K B Parkerson, G A Quantrill and G A Smith, *The First 75 years – Service: An honour and a privilege* (United Friendly Insurance, 1983) commissioned by United Friendly to mark its 75th anniversary. All the authors were former employees: Kirkaldie and Quantrill were divisional managers, Parkerson was manager of the house purchase department and Smith had been a pensions administrator and editor of *The Bridge*, the staff journal.

18 Its early products included:
    • Table 3 – for 1d a week, the policyholder was entitled to a fatal accident benefit of £13 and fire and lightning cover of £100 on the contents of his home (Table 1, a monthly version of Table 3, failed to catch on and was soon withdrawn)
    • Table 2 – 2d a week provided weekly compensation of 5s 4d for any sickness or disease

- Table 8 – for 4d a week, Table 2 could be extended to include a weekly benefit for incapacity due to an accident, a fatal accident benefit and a 'confinement payment' of 14s
- Table 9 – 2d (or 3½d for husband and wife) provided a combination of Tables 3 and 8 – fire cover, fatal accident and weekly accident benefits and an indemnity for major accidents – loss of limb, loss of sight etc.

19 The letter is reproduced in Kirkaldie, p. 4.

20 Kirkaldie, p. 4.

21 The words appear in quotes in Kirkaldie p. 14 but no source is shown.

22 Quoted in Kirkaldie, p. 20.

23 *Connections*, No. 18, February 1999, p. 4.

24 *Connections*, No. 20, June 1999, p. 3.

25 See Chapter 12.

26 Royal London, Annual Report and Accounts 2000, 15 March 2001, chairman's statement, p. 2.

27 Stephen Shone, *Connections*, December 2000, p. 8. By the 1990s a methodology had been developed that enabled life companies to determine the value of the policies that they were issuing: this in turn enabled them to determine extent of profit or loss being made by the operating business so that clear targets (break even, x per cent profit etc.) could now be set. This replaced the traditional measure of the expense ratio (the proportion that expenses represented of total premium income during the same period), which was flawed because (a) it was relating apples to oranges (income was the result of business built up over many years whereas the expenses related to that year's activity) (b) it failed to recognise that high expenses in any type of business can be justified if they will create good future income and (c) clearly a high expense ratio was bad and a low one was good but nobody could say with any authority what was the acceptable ratio. In 1933, the Cohen Committee had suggested a target of 30 per cent.

28 Recommended Offers on behalf of RLM Finance plc, a wholly owned subsidiary of The Royal London Mutual Insurance Society Limited for the whole of the issued share capital of United Assurance Group plc, 7 March 2000, p. 4.

29 Vanessa Fuhrmans, *Wall Street Journal* (Europe edition), 23 February 2000.

30 Royal London, letter to staff, 20 April 2000. Strange to say, the directors of 2000 were not the first Royal Londoners to manage the business of Refuge and United Friendly. Following the deportations to Germany from Jersey in September 1942, several offices were left without adequate supervision and as a result "the Secretary, Mr B C Whiston, took over direct responsibility for both the Refuge Assurance Co. Ltd. and the United Friendly Assurance Co. Ltd." (Report of the Committee of Management, Associated Life Offices Central Fund (Jersey) to the associated offices for period of occupation of Jersey by German Forces (1945), p. 51) See Chapter 10.

31 Recommended Offers, p. 9.

32 Royal London, Annual Report and Accounts 2000, p. 11.

33 James Doran, *The Times*, 23 February 2000.

34 Royal London, Annual Report and Accounts 2000, p. 8.

35 Royal London, script for presentation by managers at briefing meetings, 25 May 2000.

36 Sarah Oxley, *Evening Gazette*, 25 May 2000.

37 Julia Gregory, *Essex County Standard*, 26 May 2000.

38 Juliette Maxim, *East Anglian Daily Times*, 26 March 2000.

39 See previous Note.

40 Laurence Cawley, *Evening Gazette*, 1 June 2000.

41 Louise Fuller, *Evening Gazette*, 26 May 2000.

42 *Link* 6 July showed 410 people in the proposed new structure at Colchester, of which 270 were the pension review team and 20 were the team working on new ways of distributing products.

43 *Evening Gazette*, 7 July 2000.

44 The following paragraphs are based on James Denholm, *One Hundred Years of Scottish Life* (W & R Chambers Limited, 1981), commissioned by Scottish Life to mark its centenary. Denholm joined Scottish Life from university in 1934 and retired as deputy general manager in 1974. He was vice-president of the Faculty of Actuaries in 1973.

45 Denholm, p. 12: In December 1878 Paulin presented a paper on "The Increase and Distribution of Population in the United Kingdom since 1801" in which he "vigorously challenged the Malthusian doctrines of the inter-relation of population and the means of subsistence".

46 Denholm, p. 10.

47 Denholm, p. 2: Letter from Paulin to the Secretary of the Sun Fire Office in London, 31 January 1881.

48 When in 1908 Pelican was itself taken over by Phoenix Assurance, Sorley became a director of Phoenix and remained on the board until he retired in 1924.

49 Denholm, pp. 4, 5. When he was forming the company, Paulin was convinced that "the great body of better class workmen throughout the country were thoroughly dissatisfied with the collecting and burial companies at present getting so much of their savings... [and]... were anxious to see a wise and well matured scheme uniting provision for families in the event of death and provision for advanced age". (Letter to Mrs Traynor, 25 February 1881, quoted in Denholm.) Later he wrote that the "upper and middle classes are well provided for in the way of good economically managed Life Offices and they take advantage of them fairly well, but there is at present no good office managed at a moderate rate of expenditure which adapts itself to the requirements of the wage earning classes. The ratio of expense of the Prudential and other offices is nearly 50% of the premium income!! I feel certain an Agency system could be devised to gather in a large premium income to a new office at 15%". (Letter to Rev W L Blackley, quoted in Denholm.) In this instance, Paulin's optimism was misplaced. Thrift agents were issued with perforated sheets of receipts for 12 months, each one personally signed by James Sorley. As premiums were paid, the appropriate slip was detached and handed over to the payer.

50 Denholm, p. 53 quoting *Scottish Life Notes*.

51 In Chapter 20, p. 120–127, Denholm sets out in full a note (apparently written in 1968) by George Waugh, Scottish Life's assistant general manager, on the mutualisation.

52 Denholm, p. 79. There were stock exchanges in a number of cities, including Birmingham, Bristol, Leicester, Liverpool, Manchester, Newcastle, Northampton and Oldham with a further seven in Yorkshire, five in Scotland and three in Wales. The Edinburgh exchange

was set-up following a meeting of local brokers in 1844. It began its operations in the front room of a flat in Princes Street and later moved to South St David Street. All these exchanges had closed by the early 1970s. See W A Thomas, *The Provincial Stock Exchanges* (London, Frank Cass, 1973).

53 Denholm (Waugh), p. 124.

54 "It is no secret that our suitors were Slater Walker Securities. The registration of a growing number of transfers into the names of individuals who could readily be identified with Slater Walker was accompanied by transfers of shares into nominee names which our Director Mr Murray Prain recognised as having been used in their bid for Tayside Floorcloths Ltd. (of which he was also a Director)". (Denholm, p.122). Slater Walker were in the business of acquiring control of public companies, often by corporate raids of the type apparently being attempted here, and then maximising the return on the assets of the acquired company. After considerable success, Slater Walker failed in 1975. See Michael Hope, "On being taken over by Slater Walker", *The Journal of Industrial Economics*, Vol. XXIV, March 1973, No. 3, p. 163.

55 The Scottish Life Assurance Company Act 1968.

56 Simon English, *Daily Telegraph*, 12 September 2000.

57 During this period when many building societies and mutual life and pensions companies were demutalising, the practice grew of 'carpet-baggers' (as they came to be called) acquiring membership of mutuals by investing small sums or taking out small policies with them in the hope that the organisation would soon demutualise and they would receive a windfall payment as compensation for loss of membership.

58 Joint Press Release, 2 October 2000.

59 *Connections*, December 2000, p. 9.

Chapter 15 – Traditions Change

1 Royal London, Annual Report and Accounts 2007, Business Review: Recent history, p. 2.

2 C Alferoff, D Knights, A Leyshon and P Signoretta, "The 'Let them eat cake' strategy for 'industrial branch'", *Social Policy & Society* (Cambridge University Press, 2004) 3:4, pp. 353–363.

3 Royal London, Annual Report and Accounts, 2002, group chief executive's review, p. 9.

4 "Prudential announces restructuring of direct sales force and customer service channels in the UK", Prudential Group News Releases, 13 February 2001.

5 Royal London, Annual Report and Accounts, 2004, group chief executive's review, pp. 5, 16

6 FSA/PN/093/2000, 12 July 2000.

7 HM Treasury, press release 95/09, 20 October 2009. The HM Treasury Financial Inclusion Taskforce established in 2005 was re-appointed for another three-year term in 2008.

8 FSA/CP121: *Reforming Polarisation: Making the market work for Consumers*, Chapter 5.

9 Ron Sandler's *Review of Medium and Long-term Retail Investment*, HM Treasury, press release 67/02, 9 July 2002.

10 For criticisms of industrial assurance, and comments that put these criticisms in context,

see Appendix 1.

11 *Post Magazine*, 9 April 1981, p. 944.

12 Royal London Insurance, Group Accounts 1992, p. 5.

13 The Financial Services and Markets Act 2000 (Consequential Amendments and Savings) (Industrial Assurance) Order 2001.

14 And Phoenix Life, formerly Abbey National Life plc, that became part of the Group in 2008 as a result of the Resolution Life-Pearl transaction.

15 The administration of the Phoenix Life policies is outsourced, Royal London inheriting the arrangement in place at the time of the acquisition.

16 The other products are the Scottish Bond and Child Bond (from Scottish Friendly Assurance), a guaranteed funeral plan (a Dignity Funeral Services product), a guaranteed over-50 life assurance plan (provided by Axa Sun Life), home insurance (by Aviva) motor insurance (Churchill), and identity theft insurance (from CPP). Scottish Friendly, originally the City of Glasgow Friendly Society (see Chapter 6), changed its name in 1992 on its purchase of Scottish Friendly Assurance.

17 Royal London, Annual Report and Accounts, 2003, group finance director's review, p. 17

18 The single corporate trustee is, in fact, RLGPS Trustee Limited and the individual 'trustees' are directors of the company.

19 The Colchester sports centre was to go the same way as the Mill Hill sports field. By the time Royal London came to leave Colchester, the whole area had been zoned for housing and it was sold for residential development. It too, is now covered with houses.

20 Degge, p. 46, qq. 25,183–25,185.

21 Degge, p. 46, qq. 25,167–25,173.

22 Degge, p. 46, qq. 25,180–25,182.

23 The Industrial Assurance Act 1923, section 33(2) provided that a "collector or superintendent shall not be present at any meeting of the society or company". Section 33(1) prohibited a collector from being on the board (or committee of management of a friendly society) or from holding any office other than superintending collectors within a specified area. This re-enacted (and slightly expanded) legislation first seen in the Friendly Societies Act 1875 and repeated, for example, in the Collecting Societies and Industrial Assurance Companies Act 1896, section 8 that prohibited a collector from "voting at or taking part in the proceedings of any meeting of the society or company". This wording apparently permitted a collector to attend provided he took no part in the meeting and did not vote.

24 The Board had failed to obtain the required majority at the 1994 annual general meeting to make some tidying-up amendments to the memorandum and articles of association – they were approved in slightly different form the following year. The problem in 1994 was that a number of those attending the meeting were convinced that the Board had a 'hidden agenda' and were not prepared to take at face value the explanations for the changes. This uncertainty as to the real reason for the changes being proposed may well have contributed to the failure in 2000.

25 The amendment in 1937 was to address what was seen as the anomalous position that a policyholder who was more than 13 weeks in arrears could not attend and vote at general

385

meetings while the policy remained in force but, if and when the policy was forfeited and a free policy was issued, full rights of membership were restored. In 1995 the aim was to limit membership to with-profits policies and to include single-premium policies. It would have been preferable if specific wording had been used to cover these points. As it was, the more general drafting that was adopted caused uncertainties that were not anticipated at the time. The changes were not retrospective and applied only to policies issued after they had been made.

26 The position envisaged in Royal London's articles would have been difficult to sustain in the light of the *Report of the Equitable Life Inquiry* by Lord Penrose (dated 23 December 2003 and published by HM Treasury on 9 March 2004) and Paul Myners' review of the corporate governance of mutual life companies requested by the Government in the light of the Penrose report. A consultation paper was circulated in July 2004 and Myners' report published in December 2004. (HM Treasury, press release, 111/04, 20 December 2004).

Chapter 16 – A Dramatic Metamorphosis: 2001–2011

1 Royal London, Group Internal Announcement, 9 June 2004.

2 Royal London, Annual Report and Accounts 2009, Business Review, chairman's statement, p. 6.

3 Standard & Poor's, Research Update, "Royal London Mutual Insurance Society Ltd, Outlook to Positive on Track Record Of Strong Strategic Execution", 9 July 2010.

4 The expression 'protection insurance' tends to be used to include basic life cover (as opposed to with-profits policies, savings plans etc.), critical illness (payment to insured if diagnosed with a specified critical illness), income protection (payment to insured – generally until retirement – if unable to work due to accident or sickness), payment protection (covers inability of insured to meet debt repayments because of accident, sickness or unemployment) and accident insurance (lump sum or weekly benefits in the event of insured's accidental death or specified injury). It can also include private medical insurance and insurance against the cost of long-term care for the elderly.

5 *Connections*, Summer 2004, p. 7.

6 Bright Grey, press release, August 2003.

7 "Are customers in closed life funds being treated fairly?", Financial Services Consumer Panel, September 2007.

8 Pearl had traditionally been one of Royal London's industrial assurance competitors. The Pearl Life Assurance Loan and Investment Company Limited was formed in 1864 by the merger of the Pearl Loan Company (which had started business from a pub in Whitechapel in 1862) and the Pearl Life Assurance and Sick Benefit Society, set up nearby a couple of years later. Pearl was to become a major force in life assurance and financial services. In March 1990 it was taken over by the Australian group AMP. In 2003 Pearl, NPI and London Life were de-merged from AMP to become part of HHG. In 2004 HHG accepted an offer for the three companies and in 2005 they became part of the newly formed Pearl Group Limited which was backed by two large investment organisations, Sun Capital Partners and

TDR Capital. In 2010, following the acquisition of the Resolution Life companies, Pearl Group Limited changed its name to Phoenix Group Holdings Limited.

9   Royal London, Annual Report and Accounts, 2005, group finance director's review, p. 30.

10 Royal London, Annual Report and Accounts, 2007, Business Review, Group chief executive's statement, p. 7.

11 See below in relation to Scottish Life.

12 These include the Royal London UK Aggregate Bond Pension Fund, the Royal London UK Gilt Pension Fund and the Royal London Overseas Bond Pension Fund.

13 RLAM is in the process of converting its unit trusts into open-ended investment companies (OEICs) that are grouped under two investment companies with variable capital (ICVC) structures: Royal London Fixed Income Funds ICVC and Royal London Equity Funds ICVC.

14 Another form of group pension, although less common today, is a company pension scheme administered by trustees. Again the payments are deducted from employees' earnings and paid to and invested by Scottish Life at the direction of the trustees. The pension may depend upon the contributions made and the investment returns (defined contributions) or may be a fixed proportion of the employee's final salary (defined benefits).

15 Sometimes payment of pension for a defined period (perhaps five years) is guaranteed or the plan provides that the policyholder's surviving spouse will receive a pension.

16 *Innovators Awards* are a Scottish Financial Enterprise initiative in association with Ernst & Young.

17 Royal London, Annual Report and Accounts, 2005, Business Review, p. 10.

18 Royal London, Annual Report and Accounts, 2009, Business Review, group chief executive's statement, p. 10.

19 FSA, PS10/6, Distribution of retail investments: Delivering the RDR – feedback to CP09/18, March 2010.

20 Royal London, Annual Report and Accounts, 2009, Business Overview p. 32.

21 Royal London, Annual Report and Accounts 2001, group chief executive's review, group overview, p. 12.

22 Royal London, Annual Report and Accounts 2002, chairman's review, p. 22.

23 Asset share is defined as "the accumulation of premiums paid into a policy after taking off amounts to cover expenses, charges and tax [for life policies] and after crediting or debiting amounts to reflect the investment returns achieved by the fund." (Royal London, A guide to how we manage our with-profits fund, January 2010). At the most basic level, it is as if each policy had its own notional 'sub-fund' and every year:
- the premiums are paid into the sub-fund
- the expenses incurred in relation to the policy are paid out of the sub-fund
- the investment return earned by investing the contents of the sub-fund is paid into the sub-fund, although this may be adjusted to smooth out any wide variations in particular years
- when the policy matures, the amount in the sub-fund is paid to the policyholder. Royal London has at times in the past paid in excess of asset share – that is, more than was in the sub-fund.

24 So in these two years a dividend was paid into the notional sub-funds.
25 Royal London, Annual Report and Accounts 2009, Business Review, Group strategy in action, p. 12.
26 Total EEV (European Embedded Value) operating profit, after tax.
27 *Money Marketing*, 2 October 2003.
28 Standard & Poor's, July 2010.
29 Royal London, Annual Report and Accounts 2000, chairman's statement, p. 3.
30 Royal London press release, 27 August 2010.
31 *Money Marketing*, 3 December 1998.
32 *Daily Mail*, 13 May 2007.
33 *Money Marketing*, 2 October 2003.
34 See Note 19 above.

Appendices: 1 (Industrial Assurance and its Critics) and 2 (Legal Background)

1   Committee on Industrial Assurance and Assurance on the lives of Children under ten years of age (Cohen Committee), Report, Cmd 4376, London 1933, p. 4.
2   Morrah, *A History of Industrial Life Assurance*, 1955, p. 25.
3   Fourth Report of the Friendly and Benefit Building Societies Commission, Parliamentary Papers, 1874, Vol. XXIII, Part I. See Chapter 2.
4   By Sidney Webb, later Lord Passfield, *New Statesman* Special Supplement, 13 March 1915.
5   The Parmoor Committee (Report of the Board of Trade Departmental Committee on the business of industrial assurance companies and collecting societies, Cmd 614, London, 1920) and the Cohen Committee (Note 1 above). See Chapter 8.
6   Wilson and Levy, *Industrial Assurance – An Historical and Critical Study*, 1937; Henry, *The Insurance Man and his Trade*, 1938. See Chapter 10.
7   *Social Insurance and Allied Services*, Report by Sir William Beveridge, Cmd 6404, London, 1942. See Chapter 10.
8   Cohen Report, p. 82.
9   Cohen Report, p. 19.
10 See Chapter 1.
11 Cohen Report, p. 10.
12 Cohen Report, p. 9.
13 See Appendix 2.
14 See Appendix 2.
15 Cohen Report, p. 13.
16 In proposing nationalisation of industrial assurance, the Labour Party in their manifesto for the 1950 election stated that "in the past, the hard-won savings of working people have been invested as the industrial assurance companies thought fit. The companies have often made extremely high profits for their shareholders. Private profit has come before public interest. In future, public interest will come first." Sir Arnold Wilson (quoted by Morrah, p. 186) alerted his readership to "the vast aggregations of capital in a very few hands [the

committees of management and the boards of the offices] with unlimited power, exercised in secrecy, and uncontrolled by any external agency, to give or withhold financial assistance in any country, at home or abroad, to any industry or trade".

17 Morrah, p. 45.

18 *The Business History Review*, Vol. 32, No. 1 (Spring, 1958), pp. 135–136.

19 Friendly Societies Act 1896, ss. 8(1)(b).

20 *Griffiths v Fleming* [1909] 1 KB 805, *Reed v Royal Exchange Assurance Co* (1795) Peake Add Cas 70.

21 By the Industrial Assurance and Friendly Societies Act 1948 (Amendment) Act 1958.

Acknowledgements

There have been many people involved in this book. Without their help, understanding and encouragement, it would not have happened. The acknowledgements that follow may be brief but my appreciation is huge. I give my very sincere thanks to: Myra, my wife, for reading and commenting on every draft of every chapter, for allowing our home to be invaded by boxes of archives, for travelling with me to Wilmslow to refresh our supply of archives, for proofreading and for her support throughout; Susan Nickalls, an Edinburgh-based journalist, for reviewing all that I had written at various stages and making corrections and valuable suggestions; Kate Blackadder, for editing what was meant to be (but proved not quite to be) the final version and Jennie Renton for proof-reading the final version; Laura Berry of Sticks Research Agency and *Your Family History* for alerting me to what is hidden away in registers of births, deaths and marriages, census returns and the like, and for revealing so much about the early Royal Londoners; Sarah Newbery, Amber Strang and Nick Barratt, the chief executive of Sticks, for augmenting Laura's work; Dr Christine Barnes for her local research, which took Joseph Degge from rural Staffordshire, via the pub trade in Liverpool, to Royal Liver and then to London; everyone at the National Library of Scotland who helped me (a novice in such matters) identify the volumes that I required and then produced them for me in the reading room; Adam Parkinson and Hannah West in the library of the Chartered Insurance Institute for maintaining a constant supply of the bound volumes of *Post Magazine* and *The Policy-Holder*; Kevin Field of Royal London's Wilmslow office for providing so much practical assistance with the archives there; Katherine Gale of the Prudential for giving me access to their archives and answering my questions; Kevin Dobson and his team at Royal Liver for providing me with a number of publications on their history and for investigating several lines of enquiry; Fiona McBain, the chief executive of Scottish Friendly (formerly the City of Glasgow Friendly Society) for making available two histories of the society and a scrapbook of press cuttings from between 1907 and 1911; Richard Roberts, the senior partner of Gedye & Sons, for attempting to throw some light on the clients of Carruthers & Gedye; Michael Pickard, for correcting many of my errors and misunderstandings and for responding to many questions; Cyril Brill, Sven Farmer, Hubert Reid, Barry Fitzgerald and Mike Mead for their recollections and input; many of my former colleagues at Royal London for their help with the recent history (including Andy Carter, Alasdair Buchanan, Carol Bamford, David Bird, Richard Harrison, Colin Pountney, Stephen Shone, Hugo Thorman, Graham Trill, Helen Wiles, Mark Worboyes, Mike Yardley and many more); Tom Booth, Richard Balding and

Brian Duffin for augmenting and updating the histories of their companies, professors Lawrence H Officer and Samuel H Williamson for creating their website www.measuringworth.com and for the assistance that it provided in calculating what sums in the past might be worth today; Susan Sneddon for managing in such a hands-on way the process by which my typescript was converted into a book; Piet Johnson for creating illustrations from dusty old photographs many of which had been hidden away in the archives for years; Helen Hart of SilverWood Books for guiding me through the intricacies of publishing; and many others far too numerous to mention. We have made reasonable efforts to trace the current holders of the copyright of material that I have quoted. If any copyright holder believes that their material has been used without due credit, Royal London will make reasonable efforts to correct omissions in any future re-printing. We gratefully acknowledge the permissions from Taylor & Francis Books (UK) to quote from *East End Underworld*, the Financial Services Authority to quote from Howard Davies' speech and Richard Wooding to quote from his father's autobiography.

The Author

Murray Ross was legal director and company secretary of Royal London until his retirement in 2007. He qualified as a solicitor in 1971 and before joining Royal London in 1994 had worked for a US multinational and an asset management and banking group, and been a partner of a London law firm. He wrote the early editions of what has become a standard work on the leasing of commercial property. He now lives in Edinburgh and enjoys the city's festivals, watching sport and time spent with his granddaughters.

Bibliography

Allen, W Gore: *We the Undersigned...* (Newman Neame, 1961)

Biron, Sir Charles: *Without Prejudice: Impressions of Life and Law* (Faber and Faber, 1936)

Cherry, Bridget and Pevsner, Nikolaus: *Architectural Guides, London 4: North* (Yale University Press, 1998)

Collins, Wilkie: *The Diary of Anne Rodway* (*Household Words* (instalments) 19–26 July 1856)

Cordery, Simon: *British Friendly Societies, 1750–1914* (Palgrave Macmillan, 2003)

Crossick, Geoffrey: *An Artisan Elite in Victorian Society* (Croom Helm, 1978)

Curl, James Steven: *The Victorian Celebration of Death* (Sutton Publishing, 2000)

Dennett, Laurie: *A Sense of Security: 150 years of Prudential* (Granta, 1998)

Dickens, Charles: *Oliver Twist* (*Bentley's Miscellany* (instalments) 1837–1839; Richard Bentley, book form, 1838)

Dyos, H J and Wolfe, Michael: *The Victorian City: Images and reality* (Routledge & Kegan Paul, 1973)

Gosden, P H J H: *The Friendly Societies in England, 1815–1875* (Manchester University Press, 1961)

Graves, Robert: *They Hanged My Saintly Billy* (Cassell, 1957)

Harvie, Christopher and Matthew, H C G: *Nineteenth Century Britain: A very short introduction* (Oxford University Press, 2000)

Henry, Harry: *The Insurance Man and his Trade* (Fact No. 15, June 1938)

House, Jack: *The Friendly Adventure: the story of the City of Glasgow Friendly Society's first hundred years* (Maclehose, 1962)

Hodder, Edwin: *The Life and Work of the Seventh Earl of Shaftesbury* (Cassell, 1886)

Jack, A Fingland: *An Introduction to the History of Life Assurance* (King & Son, 1912)

Morrah, Dermot: *A History of Industrial Life Assurance* (George Allen and Unwin, 1955)

Paterson, Michael: *Voices from Dickens' London* (David & Charles, 2006)

Ridge, Dudley: *A Sussex Family: the family of Ridge from 1500 to the present day* (Phillimore & Co. Limited, 1975)

Roberts, Robert: *The Classic Slum: Salford Life in the First Quarter of the Century* (Manchester University Press, 1971; Penguin, 1973)

Rowntree, B S: *Poverty: a study of town life* (Macmillan 1902)

Saddler, Ian: *A Mission in Life (The History of Liverpool Victoria Friendly Society)*, (Liverpool Victoria Group, 1997)

Sala, George: *Twice Round the Clock* (Maxwell, 1859)

Samuel, Raphael: *East End Underworld* (Routledge & Kegan Paul, 1981)

Sandbrook, Dominic: *White Heat: a history of Britain in the swinging sixties* (Little, Brown, 2006)

Sanders, Peter: *The Simple Annals: the history of an Essex and East End family* (London, Alan Sutton Publishing, 1989)

Thomas, W A: *The Provincial Stock Exchanges* (Frank Cass, 1973)

Strange, Julie-Marie: *Death, Grief, and Poverty in Britain, 1870–1914* (Cambridge University Press, 2005)

Watson, Nigel: *A Lifetime of Care: 150 years of Royal Liver Assurance* (Royal Liver, 2000)

Westlake, Ray: *The British Army of August 1914: an illustrated directory* (Spellmount, 2005)

Whale, Derek M: *Lost Villages of Liverpool*, Part 1 (printed for the author, 1984)

White, William: *History, Gazetteer and Directory of Staffordshire* (Robert Leader, 1851)

Wilkinson, J Frome: *Mutual Thrift* (Methuen, 1891)

Wilson, Arnold and Levy, Hermann: *Industrial Assurance: an historical and critical study* (Oxford University Press, 1937)

Wilson, Arnold and Levy, Hermann: *Burial Reform and Funeral Costs* (Oxford University Press, 1938)

Wooding, Norman: *Recollections* (The Memoir Club, 2005)

Index

Note: The index includes the appendices, but not the notes or illustrations. Page numbers followed by *t* indicate a table. References to 'the Auxiliary Company' mean The Royal London Auxiliary Insurance Company, Limited.